CONTEMPORARY WOMEN PLAYWRIGHTS: INTO THE TWENTY-FIRST CENTURY

Breaking new ground in this century, this wide-ranging collection of essays is the first of its kind to address the work of contemporary international women playwrights. The book considers the work of established playwrights such as Caryl Churchill, Marie Clements, Lara Foot-Newton, Maria Irene Fornes, Sarah Kane, Lisa Kron, Young Jean Lee, Lynn Nottage, Suzan-Lori Parks, Djanet Sears, Caridad Svich, and Judith Thompson, but it also foregrounds important plays by many emerging writers. Divided into three sections—Histories, Conflicts, and Genres—the book explores such topics as the feminist history play, solo perform-ance, transcultural dramaturgies, the identity play, the gendered terrain of war, and eco-drama, and encompasses work from the United States, Canada, Latin America, Oceania, South Africa, Egypt, and the United Kingdom. With contri-butions from leading international scholars and an introductory overview of the concerns and challenges facing women playwrights in this new century, *Contemporary Women Playwrights* explores the diversity and power of women's playwriting since 1990, highlighting key voices and examining crucial critical and theoretical developments within the field.

Contemporary Women Playwrights

Into the Twenty-First Century

Edited by

Penny Farfan

and

Lesley Ferris

palgrave
macmillan

Contents

Acknowledgements

We are grateful to the participants in the working session on Contemporary Women Playwrights at the American Society for Theatre Research Conference in San Juan, Puerto Rico in November 2009 for introducing us to many new plays and for their insightful contributions to the pre-conference wiki-discussions and the lively three-hour conversation at our meeting in San Juan. Anna Birch convened the session with us, and participants included James Al-Shamma, Ryan Claycomb, J. K. Curry, Sharon Friedman, Anne García-Romero, Katherine E. Kelly, Melissa Lee, Karen O'Brien, Juliana Omoifo Okoh, Chris Olsen, Susan Russell, and Jenny Spencer. Thanks also to Mina Choi for her research and technical assistance in preparation for the working session and to the College of Arts and Humanities at The Ohio State University for the Faculty Research Grant that funded her work.

We have also benefited greatly from the encouragement, advice, and support of Palgrave's commissioning editors Kate Haines, Jenna Steventon, and Jenni Burnell, as well as from the invaluable feedback provided by the three anonymous readers who provided reports for Palgrave. Thanks also to the University of Calgary's Centre for Research in the Fine Arts; to Amany Seleem and Assem Nagaty for their editorial assistance while at The Ohio State University; and to Amie Ferris-Rotman, who assisted with her knowledge of women and human rights.

Lastly, we would like to express our appreciation of the contributions of feminist theatre historian Helen Krich Chinoy (1922–2010) and playwrights Pam Gems (1925–2011) and Franca Rame (1928–2013), and also our thanks to Maria Irene Fornes, who continues to inspire us with her work.

Earlier versions of the chapters by Elaine Aston, Soyica Diggs Colbert, Sharon Friedman, Katherine E. Kelly, Amelia Howe Kritzer, and Nehad Selaiha with Sarah Enany are republished here with permission as follows:

Aston, Elaine. "Feeling the Loss of Feminism: Sarah Kane's Blasted and an Experiential Genealogy of Contemporary Women's Playwriting." *Theatre Journal* 62:4 (2010), 575–591. © 2010 by The Johns Hopkins University Press. Reprinted with permission of The Johns Hopkins University Press.

Colbert, Soyica Diggs. "Black Leadership at the Crossroads: Unfixing Martin Luther King Jr. in Katori Hall's 'The Mountaintop'." *South Atlantic Quarterly* 112:2 (2013), 261–283. Copyright: Duke University Press. All rights reserved. Republished by permission of the copyright holder, Duke University Press (www.dukeupress.edu).

Friedman, Sharon. "The Gendered Terrain in Contemporary Theatre of War by Women." *Theatre Journal* 62:4 (2010), 593–610. © 2010 by The Johns

Hopkins University Press. Reprinted with permission of The Johns Hopkins University Press.

Kelly, Katherine E. "Making the Bones Sing: The Feminist History Play, 1976–2010." *Theatre Journal* 62:4 (2010), 645–660. © 2010 by The Johns Hopkins University Press. Reprinted with permission of The Johns Hopkins University Press.

Kritzer, Amelia Howe. "Enough! Women Playwrights Confront the Israeli-Palestinian Conflict." *Theatre Journal* 62:4 (2010), 611–626. © 2010 by The Johns Hopkins University Press. Reprinted with permission of The Johns Hopkins University Press.

Selaiha, Nehad, with Sarah Enany. "Women Playwrights in Egypt." *Theatre Journal* 62:4 (2010), 627–643. © 2010 by The Johns Hopkins University Press. Reprinted with permission of The Johns Hopkins University Press.

One section of Penny Farfan's chapter is abridged and adapted from her essay "Monstrous History: Judith Thompson's *Sled*," which was originally published in *Canadian Theatre Review* 120 (Fall 2004): 46–49.

Contributors

Natalie Alvarez is an associate professor in the Department of Dramatic Arts at Brock University, where she teaches in the Theatre Praxis concentration. She has two edited books on Latina/o Canadian theatre and performance forthcoming with Playwrights Canada Press (2013). In 2010, she received a Social Sciences and Humanities Research Council of Canada Standard Research Grant for her book project on simulations, interculturalism, and performance in military training and dark tourism. Her work has appeared in a number of periodicals, as well as in national and international essay collections. She also serves as co-editor of *Canadian Theatre Review*'s Views and Reviews.

Wendy Arons is associate professor in the School of Drama at Carnegie Mellon University. She is the author of *Performance and Femininity in Eighteenth-Century German Women's Writing: The Impossible Act* (2006) and has published articles in *Theatre Topics, The German Quarterly, Communications from the International Brecht Society, 1650–1850, Text and Presentation,* and *Theatre Journal,* as well as chapters in a number of anthologies. She guest-edited a special issue of *Theatre Topics* on "Performance and Ecology," co-edited (with Theresa J. May) the anthology *Readings in Performance and Ecology* (2012), and was Festival Director of the Earth Matters on Stage Festival and Symposium at Carnegie Mellon University in 2012. She is also co-translator (with Sara Figal) of the first complete English edition of Lessing's *Hamburg Dramaturgy,* which is appearing serially online, and is the author of an arts and culture blog, *The Pittsburgh Tatler.*

Elaine Aston is professor of contemporary performance at Lancaster University. Her monographs include *Theatre As Sign-System* (1991, with George Savona), *Caryl Churchill* (1997/2001/2010), *An Introduction to Feminism and Theatre* (1995), *Feminist Theatre Practice* (1999), *Feminist Views on the English Stage* (2003), and *Performance Practice and Process: Contemporary [Women] Practitioners* (2008, with Geraldine Harris). She is the co-editor of *The Cambridge Companion to Modern British Women Playwrights* (2000, with Janelle Reinelt); *Feminist Futures: Theatre, Performance, Theory* (2006, with Geraldine Harris), *Staging International Feminisms* (2007, with Sue-Ellen Case), and *The Cambridge Companion to Caryl Churchill* (2009, with Elin Diamond). She has served as Senior Editor of *Theatre Research International* (2010–2012).

Soyica Diggs Colbert is an assistant professor of English at Dartmouth College. She is the author of *The African American Theatrical Body: Reception, Performance, and the Stage* (2011) and is currently working on a book project titled *Black Movements: Performance, Politics, and Migration.* She has published articles and reviews in *African American Review, Theatre Journal, Boundary 2, South Atlantic Quarterly,* and *Theatre*

Melissa Lee is completing her PhD at The Ohio State University, where her research focuses on dramatic representations of the actress, linking aesthetics and characterization to larger issues of gender in performance. Her research has been funded by a Coca-Cola Critical Difference for Women Research Grant, as well as a Presidential Fellowship from the Graduate School at Ohio State, and she has presented papers at the Mid-America Theatre Conference, the American Society for Theatre Research, the Comparative Drama Conference, and the International Federation for Theatre Research.

Diana Looser is a lecturer in drama at the University of Queensland. Her primary research interests are postcolonial, intercultural, and transnational theatre and performance, with a particular focus on the Pacific Islands. She has recently published essays in *Theatre Journal, Theatre Research International, The Contemporary Pacific*, and *Contemporary Theatre Review*, and her monograph, *Remaking Pacific Pasts: History, Memory, and Identity in Contemporary Theatre from Oceania*, is forthcoming from the University of Hawai'i Press.

Theresa J. May is associate professor of theatre arts at the University of Oregon, where she is co-founder and served as artistic director of the Earth Matters on Stage Ecodrama Festival and Symposium (EMOS). She is co-editor (with Wendy Arons) of *Readings in Performance and Ecology* (2012) and has published widely about the intersections of ecology, cultural studies, and performance studies, including "Grotowski's Deep Ecology" in *Performing Nature* and "Beyond Bambi: Towards a Dangerous Ecocriticism in Theatre Studies" in *Theatre Topics*. She developed and directed *Salmon is Everything*, a play about the role of salmon in Native culture in the Klamath watershed, and her book on this project is forthcoming from Oregon State University Press. She is also co-author of *Greening Up Our Houses*, the first book on sustainable theatre management, and was founding artistic director of Theatre in the Wild in Seattle.

Ana Elena Puga is an associate professor at The Ohio State University, where she holds a joint appointment in the Departments of Theatre and Spanish and Portuguese. She is the author of *Memory, Allegory, and Testimony in South American Theater: Upstaging Dictatorship* and is now working on *Spectacles of Suffering and Migrant Melodrama*, about the relationship among migrant suffering, performance, and human rights. She has published two books of translations of Latin American plays: *Spectacular Bodies, Dangerous Borders: Three New Latin American Plays* and *Finished from the Start and Other Plays*, an anthology of plays by the Chilean dramatist Juan Radrigán. Her articles on Latin American and US Latina/o performance have appeared in *Latino Studies, Theatre Journal, Theatre Survey*, and *Latin American Theatre Review*, and in 2010–2011 she was an external faculty fellow at Stanford University's Center for Comparative Studies in Race and Ethnicity.

Nehad Selaiha is professor of drama and criticism at the Academy of Arts in Cairo and resident drama critic of the English-language national newspaper *Al-Ahram Weekly*. She has published many books in Arabic and English on theatre in both the Arab and Western worlds, as well as several translations of literary texts and critical studies.

Sara Warner is associate professor in the Department of Performing and Media Arts at Cornell University. The author of *Acts of Gaiety: LGBT Performance and the Politics of Pleasure* (2012), she has published widely on feminist and queer studies, prison theatre, affect theory, and academic labor. She is currently at work on two books: *Suzan-Lori Parks on Stage and Screen* (Methuen 2014) and *SCUM: Valerie Solanas and the Art of the Chronic*. Sara is a past president of the Women and Theatre Program, a former Secretary of the Association for Theatre in Higher Education, and has served on the Board of Directors of the Center for Lesbian and Gay Studies.

Introduction

Penny Farfan and Lesley Ferris

> The 21st Century will be the century of girls and women.
>
> –Michelle Bachelet, First Under-Secretary General and
> Executive Director of UN Women, 2010[1]

In July 2010, the United Nations (UN) General Assembly voted unanimously "to create a new entity to accelerate progress in meeting the needs of women and girls worldwide." The new UN Entity for Gender Equality and the Empowerment of Women, or UN Women, was the "result of years of negotiations between UN Member States and advocacy by the global women's movement."[2] Although the UN, founded in 1945, has a remit to serve the world at large in terms of human rights, it took until 2010 for member nations to vote unanimously for the creation of a sub-group to focus exclusively on gender equality and the empowerment of women. That same year, Michelle Bachelet became the first Under-Secretary General and Executive Director of UN Women, supporting initiatives on gender equality and the empowerment of women throughout the world. A centerpiece of her work was leading the UN's Commission on the Status of Women (CSW), established in 1946 with fifteen member states attending the first annual meeting. In March 2013, at the fifty-seventh session of the CSW, 131 member states attended the session.

In her closing address to the commission at the 2013 meeting, Bachelet stated:

> We have all the evidence to know that progress for peace that is lasting, and for development that is sustainable, depends on progress, the long overdue progress, for the women and girls of this world. They are half the world's population. If we are to make real progress for peace, equality and development, then we must make real progress for and with girls and women.[3]

Bachelet also spoke clearly and concisely about the significant number of high-profile cases of violence against women that had been the continuous backdrop to the two-week meeting. Each CSW annual meeting designates a theme with plans to develop an agreement signed by the member states. In 2003 and again in 2012, the commission had pursued the issue of violence and human rights, but members were unable to reach an agreement either time. This issue was at the heart of Bachelet's position in the UN – to keep pressure on world leaders to take action in relation to the continuous aggression against women. "We all know," she stated, "how pervasive violence against women is. Violence knows no borders. Violence does not discriminate according to nationality, ethnicity, social class, culture, or religion. And it takes a heavy cost on individuals, families and societies."[4] It was thus a significant achievement when, at the 2013 session, the CSW passed an agreement entitled "The Elimination and Prevention of All Forms of Violence against Women and Girls."[5]

While addressing the issue of violence was of crucial importance to Bachelet in her work with the UN, her more general sense of the need to "make real progress for and with girls and women" points toward how other primary issues interface with disquieting acts of brutality and aggression against women: lack of health-care (more women die from complications giving birth than from war or cancer), lack of education, and justice systems geared through a history of male domi-nance to deny women their human rights. A 2011 article in *The Wall Street Journal* reported that "[w]omen represent 40% of the world's labor force but hold just 1% of its wealth."[6]

Against this backdrop of international relations and affairs of state, with world leaders such as Bachelet setting an agenda that demands action for women within and beyond the borders of nation states, women playwrights are engaged and grappling with similar concerns. An event in 2013 that crossed borders and took a global perspective on women's issues was the fifteenth anniversary of V-Day, created by Eve Ensler. Since its founding in 1998, V-Day, with its performances worldwide of Ensler's play *The Vagina Monologues*,[7] has raised more than $90 million for grassroots anti-violence groups. In 2012 alone, there were 5,800 performances around the world and the V-Day nonprofit established "spotlight" campaigns that "contributed directly to groups in particular danger zones, including Afghanistan, New Orleans, Haiti, Juarez, and the Democratic Republic of Congo."[8] In an effort to acknowledge this work for its anniversary on 14 February 2013, Ensler and her team decided to organize a single event – "The Biggest Mass Global Action to End Violence Against Women & Girls in The History of Humankind" – entitled "One Billion Rising," which was "an appreciation, amplification and an escalation" of its previous work.[9] Ensler explains the event's rationale: "Fifteen years ago, we started V-Day to end violence against women. Fifteen years on, we've had a lot of achievements, but the violence is still going on.... We can either keep picking up the shattered body parts of women all over the world, or we can escalate."[10] Ensler's remarks recognizing tremendous achievement but also ongoing struggle against a deeply entrenched culture of devaluing women and their work resonate with the analogous situation of contemporary women playwrights, whose artistic and political interventions, like Ensler's own work, are so often linked to the larger conditions and experiences of women's lives.

In 1989, Lynda Hart published a ground-breaking edited volume, *Making a Spectacle: Feminist Essays on Contemporary Women's Theatre*, in which she remarked, "The latter half of the twentieth century has seen an emergence of women play-wrights in numbers equal to the entire history of their dramatic foremothers."[11] Hart's volume included essays on now-canonical playwrights like Maria Irene Fornes, Ntozake Shange, and Caryl Churchill, as well as Peggy Shaw and Lois Weaver of the celebrated performance company Split Britches, among many other important women writers for the stage during this key period in the history of feminist theatre. Clearly, the book captured a ground-swell of women's writing for the theatre that seemed to augur well for the years to come, and indeed the intervening near-quarter-century has seen some truly remarkable work by women playwrights. The present book of essays foregrounds some of the extraordinary diversity and power of women's playwriting since 1990, encompassing works by continuing yet still innovative playwrights who first came to prominence in the 1960s, 1970s, and 1980s, but also many striking new voices that have emerged since the 1990s and into the twenty-first century.

The plays that constituted the creative ground-swell that Hart's book both captured and fostered corresponded with the development of feminist theatre scholarship and the resulting promotion and circulation of the work of women playwrights within the academy, in undergraduate and graduate classrooms and the production seasons of university theatre departments, and as a field of research. Beyond Hart's *Making a Spectacle*, a number of other key texts of the late 1980s and early 1990s included analyses of contemporary women's playwriting, among them now-classic works of feminist theatre studies like Sue-Ellen Case's *Feminism and Theatre* (1988, 2008) and Jill Dolan's *The Feminist Spectator as Critic* (1988, 2012).[12] These key years generated a rich archive of women's playwriting and of feminist theatre history, theory, and criticism that promoted and illuminated it. The following years also saw the increasing visibility of women's stories in popular culture, ranging from the television sitcom *Ellen*, in which lesbian performer Ellen DeGeneres's eponymous character came out in 1997, through to more recent series like *The L Word* (2004–2009), *Nurse Jackie* (2009–), and *Girls* (2012–), on which Jill Dolan has posted commentaries on her blog *The Feminist Spectator*.[13]

Despite such advances, in 2008, nearly twenty years after Hart's volume signaled a kind of golden age of women's theatre writing, US playwrights Julia Jordan and Sarah Schulman convened a town hall meeting in New York City, attended by more than 150 playwrights, to discuss the fact that the 2008–2009 Off-Broadway season included four times more plays by men than women.[14] Subsequent US-based research has provided further and more specific details on women playwrights' status within mainstream theatre. Sandra Richards and Kathy Perkins, for example, have noted that while there has been a "surge" in African American playwriting since the 1990s, regional theatre productions of works by African American women playwrights tend to be of a limited number of proven plays by a small number of "stars" that are produced in multiple theatres in a given season.[15] As well, Brandi Wilkins Catanese has observed in an analysis of the 2010–2011 season announcements for the League of Resident Theatres that LORT productions of leading African American women playwrights like Lynn Nottage do not necessarily eventuate in Broadway productions. Catanese rightly notes that productions in LORT theatres or on Broadway are "not the only – or, in some cases, even the desirable terms by which to evaluate success," and that "[f]or some playwrights, a true feminist politics is incompatible with the social, economic, and aesthetic arrangements according to which mainstream theatre operates."[16] Still, she suggests, such absences have inestimable consequences in

terms of emerging genealogies of African American playwrights inspired by exposure to precursors in the field;[17] in Lynn Nottage's words, "A lack of access perpet-
uates a lack of access."[18] Clearly, despite the ground-swell in women's writing for
and about theatre that Hart both captured and prompted in 1989, what she called
"the last bastion of male hegemony in the literary arts" has, in the early twenty-
first century, not yet been dismantled.[19]

The lack of parity for women playwrights has not been confined to the United
States. In Canada, for example, a 2006 report by Rebecca Burton, updating a 1982
report by Rina Fraticelli, found that women still remain significantly behind men in
terms of their status in the theatre,[20] while in the UK a 2009 report for Arts Council
England noted that "the increased prominence of women playwrights in the 1980s
has not been sustained. Women receive fewer commissions than men; of those
commissions fewer are delivered; and of those delivered fewer are put on."[21] Janelle
Reinelt, one of the authors of the Arts Council England report, has further stated of
the UK context that while "the presence of significant women's writing, supported
by a number of well-placed artistic directors or other institutional benefactors," is
grounds for optimism, as is the "striking diversity of fresh and strong voices," "there
is still a gender gap in full participation by women as playwrights."[22] In Australia,
leading theatre companies have come under intense scrutiny and critique for the
minimal presence of women directors and playwrights in their recent seasons.[23]

In still other contexts, the issue of parity for women playwrights is so far from
the realm of possibility that it seems not yet thinkable. In their essay in this
book, for example, Nehad Selaiha and Sarah Enany note that "[t]he number of
women playwrights and theatre-makers in Egypt is still very modest,"[24] while a
recent article by Elif Batuman in *The New Yorker* reports on a remarkable women's
theatre company in rural Turkey that was founded in 2000 by Ümmiye Koçak, a
farmworker who saw her first play at the local school when she was in her forties
and decided that theatre was an appropriate form for considering the situation of
the women in her village

> – the many roles they had to play. In the fields, they worked like men; in
> villas, they became housekeepers; at home, they were wives and mothers. "I
> kept turning it over in my head, how it is that I do all these things," she later
> recalled. "Then I saw [the school principal] Hüseyin's theatre. That's when I
> decided that the thing I'd been turning over in my head was theatre."[25]

Far from "feeling the loss of feminism," as Elaine Aston describes the affect underlying the work of 1990s UK playwright Sarah Kane and others in her essay in this
book, Koçak had not heard the word *feminism* when she founded her company
with seven village women and began staging original plays based on the women's
experiences, as well as works by other authors, including Shakespeare, in an all-
female production of *Hamlet*.[26]

A range of solutions have been implemented or proposed to remedy what Sara
Warner refers to in her essay in this book as the "chronic" under-representation
of women playwrights. During the 1998–99 season, for example, the feminist

arts activist group the Guerilla Girls targeted major New York theatres that had not produced a play by a woman by posting stickers in the women's washrooms that read: "In this theater the taking of photographs, the use of recording devices, and the production of plays by women are strictly prohibited."[27] Other solutions have ranged from the creation of awards to recognize the contribution of women playwrights and theatre artists[28] to the inauguration of the New York City-based parity campaign known as "50/50 in 2020," which seeks "to acknowledge the contribution of women to theatre and to achieve employment parity for women theatre artists by the 100th anniversary of American suffrage in 2020," and which has posted a list of the "Top Ten Things To Do" to help achieve this objective.[29] Reinelt underscores the necessity of institutional support for women playwrights,[30] and the value of such support is evident in the achievements of organizations like Toronto's Nightwood Theatre, which was founded in 1979 and has fostered the development of new work by many important Canadian women playwrights, including, for example, African Canadian playwright Djanet Sears, whose work is discussed in Penny Farfan's chapter in this book. Institutional support for women playwrights might also take the form of particular events like the "Women, Power and Politics" festival held at London's Tricycle Theatre in 2010, for which ten women were commissioned to write plays that responded to the issue of women and political power through history up to the present day.[31]

In this book, we aim to support, promote, and advance the work of women playwrights by providing a resource for researching, teaching, producing, and appreciating it, asserting its artistic and political worth through rigorous scholarly attention to a large number and wide range of highly significant and engaging plays. In arguing for the need to trace out a history of women's writing, Virginia Woolf wrote in *A Room of One's Own* that women writers "think back" through their mothers.[32] Knowing that women have written is certainly, as Woolf suggests, a fundamental condition for women's writing, but whereas the "think" of Woolf's phrasing signals the ability to imagine one's self into a lineage of women writers, such "thinking" is also crucial to the development of spectators, producers, directors, performers, critics, and scholars of the work of women playwrights. This book of essays contributes to this generative project, creating awareness of, disseminating knowledge about, modeling critical methods for understanding, and, we hope, giving rise to further research on women's playwriting.

In assembling the essays that comprise the book, we wanted first to foreground key voices in women's playwriting as it has developed since 1990, including some playwrights that are very well-known and others that may be new to many readers. We also wanted to articulate some of the concerns and techniques that distinguish the work of these playwrights and to set forth contextual research, theoretical frameworks, and critical methods that seem particularly useful in articulating their political and aesthetic affiliations and interventions. Cognizant of the dominance of US and UK perspectives in much of the existing research on women playwrights and on feminist theatre more generally, we have sought in this book to engage a broader field of work, with contributions relating to women's playwriting in Egypt, South Africa, Latin America, the Pacific Islands, and Canada, as well as the United Kingdom and the United States, and with attention to the broad diversity among women's playwrights not only across but also within national boundaries. While we cannot presume by any stretch of the imagination to have the global reach or political clout of UN Women, we aspire to begin to move toward the possibility of global inclusion for women playwrights, acknowledging their work and realizing their promise.

Any collection is, however, inevitably partial and necessarily incomplete: it is simply not possible to include everything. In our case, our commissioning editor Jenna Steventon advised us that she was "keen for the volume to not become too much a door-stopper in order to keep the price at an accessible point, and to not become uninviting for students in terms of sheer size."[33] Loving the material, we would have loved to include more of it, but we were, with the present contents, at our maximum assigned word limit and so could not. We hope, though, that the necessary and inevitable incompleteness of our book will serve as a spur to further research, which we very much look forward to reading.

As part of the book's inevitable incompleteness, we acknowledge too that the plays on which the essays focus were primarily, though not exclusively, written in English or are available in English translation. We recognize the politics and limitations of this focus on works in English, but at the same time, we see great value in providing a resource relating to plays that will be widely available to a broad readership of students, researchers, and theatre artists.

In taking as its focus dramatic texts by women playwrights since 1990, the book updates and extends the pioneering feminist studies of playwriting by women that appeared in the late 1980s and early 1990s, but it also complements the performance-oriented studies of the 1990s and 2000s and enhances the recent move toward the internationalization of feminist theatre studies. In this way, it adds to the existing critical literature on particular national contexts, for example, Aston's *Feminist views on the English stage: Women playwrights, 1990–2000* (2003), Lynette Goddard's UK-focused *Staging black feminisms: identity, politics, perform-ance* (2007), and Philip C. Kolin's edited volume *Contemporary African American Women Playwrights: A Casebook* (2007), as well as less period-specific works such as *The Cambridge Companion to American Women Playwrights* (1999), edited by Brenda Murphy, *The Cambridge Companion to Modern British Women Playwrights* (2000), edited by Aston and Reinelt, and *Women in Irish Drama* (2007), edited by Melissa Sihra, all of which include essays dealing with contemporary women play-wrights. As well, it accords with the broader geopolitical scope of such works as Julie Holledge and Joanne Tompkins's *Women's Intercultural Performance* (2000) and Case and Aston's edited volume *Staging International Feminisms* (2007), while focusing closely on scripted plays.[34]

In the 2012 edition of *The Feminist Spectator as Critic*, Dolan surveys develop-ments in the history and status of feminist theatre studies and of feminism within the larger culture in the past two and a half decades, as do critics like Reinelt in her essay "Navigating Postfeminism: Writing Out of the Box," Aston in *Feminist views on the English stage: Women playwrights, 1990–2000* and in her foreword to the reissue of Case's *Feminism and Theatre,* and Aston and Geraldine Harris in *Feminist*

Futures: Theatre, Performance, Theory.[35] These developments include the shift from women's studies to gender studies, from gay and lesbian studies to queer theory; the emergence of a third wave of feminism more attuned to issues of sexuality, race, and class, as well as to popular culture, than second-wave feminism had been; the myth of "girl power" and the backlash against feminism in conjunction with a seeming post-feminist era, despite what Reinelt has described as "feminist residue from the Second Wave – serious issues [that] have been identified and are still present, but...are ignored, pushed aside or simply denied";[36] and the increased attention to international, transnational, and intercultural feminisms and their articulations in and through performance. Beyond these developments within feminism and the academy, the years covered in the book have been marked by momentous world events: the end of apartheid in South Africa; the Gulf Wars; continuing violence between Israelis and Palestinians; brutal conflicts in the former Yugoslavia and in African countries such as Rwanda, Liberia, and the Democratic Republic of Congo; the HIV/AIDS epidemic in Africa; the 9/11 terrorist attacks in the United States and the subsequent invasion of Iraq; the NATO-led war in Afghanistan; the events of the Arab Spring; technological and scientific developments ranging from the internet to cloning; and climate change and ecological catastrophes like the 2010 BP oil spill in the Gulf of Mexico. The chapters in this book capture some of the ways that such historical developments and events have been addressed and engaged in and through contemporary women's playwriting.

The book is organized into three parts: "Histories," "Conflicts," and "Genres." These divisions are artificial insofar as there are overlaps among essays located within different sections. For example, Soyica Diggs Colbert's essay on Katori Hall's *The Mountaintop* appears in the "Histories" section because of its concern with reconceiving the historiography of the civil rights movement to more effectively represent the contributions of women, but it might also have appeared in the "Genres" section, given Hall's revision of preceding models of African American history plays, most notably those of August Wilson and Suzan-Lori Parks. Similarly, Diana Looser's essay appears in the "Conflicts" section because it foregrounds the contributions of women playwrights in Oceania to postcolonial struggles for Indigenous political and cultural self-determination, but it might also have been included in the "Histories" section as a survey of the historical development of women's playwriting in the Pacific Islands over the past two decades. Despite such overlaps among the three parts of the book, the broad headings of "Histories," Conflicts," and "Genres" usefully identify overarching approaches to the field of contemporary women's playwriting that the essays in the book exemplify, and suggest both direct and tangled threads of conversation across and among chapters.

Within the broad approaches suggested by the three-part structure of the book, individual contributors model different methodologies, ranging from overviews that begin the work of mapping out women playwrights' contributions within particular cultural contexts, to synoptic surveys around particular themes, to densely theorized interventions into theatre historiography. Thus, Aston's essay deploying affect theory to rewrite conventional accounts of "in-yer-face" theatre and articulate how 1990s UK women playwrights, most notably Sarah Kane, responded in their work to what was supposedly a post-feminist moment is grouped in the "Histories" section along with Nehad Selaiha and Sarah Enany's important introductory overview of the history of women playwrights in Egypt, from the rare pioneers of the early twentieth century to the larger numbers of playwrights and playwright-directors who have come increasingly to the fore since the 1990s. The former essay offers a re-reading of an already canonical recent text, while the latter brings to attention an insufficiently known body of work by women playwrights from a particular context. We hope that the juxtaposition of different methodologies and types of essays will combine to create a picture of the field of contemporary women's play-writing that is at once wide and deep, but also that the different approaches will be complementary, serving a defamiliarizing function in the Brechtian sense of enabling fresh perspectives on familiar phenomena, reminding us of the different conditions under which women have come to playwriting and the different relations to "feminism" of playwrights across national contexts.

Part I, "Histories," considers the recent history of feminism as it has informed women's playwriting, but also new and continuing histories of women's play-writing, as well as playwriting as a means of writing women into and reimag-ining history. Aston's "Feeling the Loss of Feminism: Sarah Kane's *Blasted* and an Experiential Genealogy of Contemporary Women's Playwriting" situates Kane's epochal 1995 play within the supposedly post-feminist context of 1990s England, "disinterring" Kane from her usual position within the canon of "in-yer-face" theatre, establishing her cross-generational connection to feminist precursors such as Caryl Churchill, considering how her harrowing experiential drama-turgy elicits a feeling of the loss of feminism, and tracing her legacy through subsequent works by millennial UK women playwrights, most notably debbie tucker green. In "Female Alliances and Women's Histories in Contemporary Mexican and Argentine Drama," Ana Elena Puga analyzes the challenges that historically situated female characters in plays by Estela Leñero Franco, Sabina Berman, Patricia Suárez, and Patricia Zangaro face in forging alliances in the face of poverty and exploitation and across class, religious, and generational divides; Puga suggests that in writing plays that stage such challenges, the playwrights themselves enact feminist alliances, despite the difficulty and questionable efficacy of alliances among women in the particular historical circumstances in which the plays transpire. Drawing on queer theories of temporality, Sara Warner notes in "Chronic Desires: Theatre's Aching Lesbian Bodies" that the chronic under-representation of women playwrights in US theatre is matched by an equally chronic attachment to writing for the theatre on the part of lesbian playwrights Lisa Kron, Lenelle Moïse, and Madeleine George, displaying what Warner, referencing Lauren Berlant, describes as "cruel optimism" in their commitment to the feminist politics and poetics of an earlier time. Selaiha and Enany's essay "Women Playwrights in Egypt" traces the contours of women's dramatic writing in Egypt from its beginnings in the early twentieth century through the particularly rich period of the 1980s and '90s and into the twenty-first century, analyzing how the traditional position of women in Arab culture and society has been challenged in and through the work of women playwrights;

in the process, Selaiha and Enany establish a canon that helps to fill one of the gaps in the existing research on the global history of women's playwriting. In "Transcultural Dramaturgies: Latina Theatre's Third Wave," Natalie Alvarez charts the most recent stage in the history of Latina theatre, considering how a new generation of playwrights, including Caridad Svich, Tanya Saracho, and Carmen Aguirre, whose work is responsive to experiences of migrations across borders, stage Latina subjectivity as transcultural – multiple rather than dual, situated within and contingent upon context, processual and performative, in generative formation rather than fixed in advance through bicultural structuration. Soyica Diggs Colbert turns, in "Black Women Playwrights Making History: Katori Hall's *The Mountaintop*," to how Hall's play rewrites the historiography of the US civil rights movement, shifting focus away from the great man who typically dominates historical accounts to recuperate the contributions of less visible women, and using innovative techniques – particularly the incorporation of spoken-word poetry – to reimagine history, leadership, and legacy and, correspondingly, to democratize theatre and engage new audiences.

Part II, "Conflicts," foregrounds some of the ways that women playwrights have used the power of theatre and drama to respond to, and engage audiences in, some of the most pressing concerns of our time. Sharon Friedman's "The Gendered Terrain in Contemporary Theatre of War by Women" surveys a range of recent works that center on the experience of women in war and the gender dynamics of the military, particularly Judith Thompson's *Palace of the End*, which represents the war in Iraq from the perspectives of a US soldier inspired by Lynndie England, notorious for her involvement in the torture of Iraqi prisoners at Abu Ghraib prison; UK-based Iraq weapons inspector David Kelly; and Nehrjas Al Saffarh, an Iraqi communist party member and torture victim under Saddam Hussein's regime. Amelia Howe Kritzer's "Enough! Women Playwrights Confront the Israeli-Palestinian Conflict" takes Caryl Churchill's controversial 2009 work *Seven Jewish Children: A Play for Gaza* as a starting point for a consideration of a series of dramatic responses to the conflict – and, in some instances, to Churchill's play. In "Women Playwrights in Post-Apartheid South Africa: Yael Farber, Lara Foot-Newton, and the Call for *Ubuntu*," Yvette Hutchison considers how South African women playwrights have extended but also addressed the limitations of the work begun by the Truth and Reconciliation Commission; these playwrights use the power of theatre to represent the legacies of apartheid beyond its official dismantlement, including a culture of extreme sexual violence against women and children, and to reimagine the nation through the human connections – among characters, and between performers and spectators – that their plays both stage and facilitate. Diana Looser's "Writing Across Our Sea of Islands: Contemporary Women Playwrights from Oceania" traces out the broad participation of Pacific Islands women playwrights in the representation of postcolonial history, contemporary indigeneity, and Pacific Islands diasporic experience, and the relation of their work to transnational movements for Indigenous political and cultural self-determination. In "Ecodramaturgy in/and Contemporary Women's Playwriting," Wendy Arons and Theresa May survey how women playwrights have used drama to respond to the ecological crisis and how an ecodramaturgical approach combining elements of literary ecocriticism, ecofeminism, and queer ecology can illuminate their work.

Finally, Part III, "Genres," considers how women playwrights have used dramatic genre as a mode of critical intervention, articulating integral linkages between form and content. Katherine Kelly's "Making the Bones Sing: The Feminist History Play, 1976–2010" charts the development of the feminist history play by playwrights Caryl Churchill, Suzan-Lori Parks, and Anna Deavere Smith, linking their dramaturgical innovations to contemporaneous developments in the broader field of feminist historiography and concluding with a survey of recent history plays by women set in the late nineteenth and early twentieth centuries as a key period in the history of feminism and the formation of modern (gender/sexual/race/class) identities. In "Performing (Our)Selves: The Role of the Actress in Theatre-History Plays by Women," Lesley Ferris and Melissa Lee consider how playwrights April De Angelis and Maria Irene Fornes interrogate the role of women and the tension between past possibilities and present realities through their metatheatrical staging of the figure of the actress at key moments in theatre history – the Restoration, when actresses first began to appear on the British stage, and the emergence of modern drama, with its many powerful central female roles, including Hedda Gabler. Penny Farfan's "Historical Landscapes in Contemporary Plays by Canadian Women" considers how plays centering on landscape by Judith Thompson, Djanet Sears, and Marie Clements represent the national, local, and transnational histories that are embedded in place, dramatizing racial and ethnic divisions that have marked Canada's past and reimagining "national" identity through alternative relations across cultures and generations. Esther Kim Lee's chapter, "Asian American Women Playwrights and the Dilemma of the Identity Play: Staging Heterotopic Subjectivities," looks at how playwrights Julia Cho, Diana Son, and Young Jean Lee have navigated expectations that they write in what has come to seem like an obligatory genre, the identity play, at once complying with and resisting the conventions of the genre in order to stage the complex interplay of gender, race, and class in shaping the subjectivities of contemporary Asian American women. Lastly, Elin Diamond, in "Deb Margolin, Robbie McCauley, Peggy Shaw: Affect and Performance," looks at representations of illness and aging in recent works by three enduring solo performance artists, considering how their risking of shame through the performance of illness articulates the intersection of affect, feminism, and performance.

Taken together, the sixteen chapters of the book engage a wide range of works by women playwrights, offering original analyses of key plays and exemplifying how some of the critical and theoretical developments of the past two decades have infused the way "feminist" criticism is understood and practiced. The book thus models methods for research while surveying key features of and developments within the field of recent women's playwriting. And, as we said earlier, the book is a generative project, one that, like One Billion Rising with its escalation of purpose or Michelle Bachelet's vision of calling for "inclusion, equality and for women's full and equal rights, opportunities and participation," expands the possibilities of change on numerous fronts. We are, in Bachelet's words, "at a tipping point in history,"[37] and it is called the twenty-first century.

Notes

1   Michelle Bachelet, "The 21st Century Will Be the Century of Girls and Women," UN Women, 23 September 2011, available at *http://www.unwomen.org/2011/09/keynote-address-at-39th-commencement-of-laguardia-community-college/* (accessed 30 March 2013).

2   "UN Creates New Structure for Empowerment of Women," Press Release from UN Women, 2 July 2010, available at *http://www.unwomen.org/2010/07/un-creates-new-structure-for-empowerment-of-women/* (accessed 1 May 2013).

3   Michelle Bachelet, "Closing Statement at the 57th Session of the Commission on the Status of Women," UN Women, 13 March 2013, available at *http://www.unwomen.org/2013/03/closing-statement-michelle-bachelet-csw57/* (accessed 30 April 2013).

4   Ibid.

5   "UN Women welcomes Agreed Conclusions at the Commission on the Status of Women," available at *http://www.unwomen.org/2013/03/un-women-welcomes-agreed-conclusions-at-the-commission-on-status-of-women/* (accessed 24 May 2013).

6   Sudeep Reddy, "New Facts on the Gender Gap from the World Bank," *Wall Street Journal*, 18 September 2011, available at *http://blogs.wsj.com/economics/2011/09/18/new-facts-on-the-gender-gap-from-the-world-bank/?mod=WSJBlog* (accessed 10 May 2013).

7   *The Vagina Monologues* is based on Ensler's interviews with women about their vaginas, was first performed by Ensler as a solo piece in 1996, and was published by Random House/Villard in 1998 with a foreword by Gloria Steinem. As Elaine Aston notes in *Feminist views on the English stage: Women playwrights, 1990–2000* (Cambridge: Cambridge University Press, 2003), the play, like Judy Chicago's equally famous 1979 installation *The Dinner Party*, "risks an essentialist reduction of women to Woman/vagina," yet has had an enormous impact, "regenerating a grass roots feminist movement" in the 1990s and providing, through its many celebrity performances featuring high-profile actresses and other public figures, "a modern echo" of work of the Actresses' Franchise League, which was formed in the early twentieth century in the UK in service of the campaign for votes for women (2–3).

8   Laura Flanders, "Eve Ensler Rising," *The Nation*, 26 November 2012, 11.

9   See "One Billion Rising," available at *http://onebillionrising.org/* (accessed 19 May 2013).

10 Flanders, "Eve Ensler Rising," 12.

11 Lynda Hart, "Introduction: Performing Feminism," *Making a Spectacle: Feminist Essays on Contemporary Women's Theatre*, ed. Hart (Ann Arbor: University of Michigan Press, 1989), 2.

12 Sue-Ellen Case, *Feminism and Theatre*, reissued ed., foreword by Elaine Aston (Basingstoke, UK: Palgrave Macmillan, 2008); Jill Dolan, *The Feminist Spectator as Critic*, 2nd ed. (Ann Arbor: University of Michigan Press, 2012). Enoch Brater's edited volume *Feminine Focus: The New Women Playwrights* (New York: Oxford University Press, 1989) included important contributions from key feminist theatre scholars like Case and Elin Diamond, but the book as a whole did not have the same commitment to articulating the intersection of feminist theory and criticism and contemporary women's playwriting that distinguished Hart's 1989 volume and the 1988 Case and Dolan books. Other key works of feminist theatre and performance theory and criticism during this period include Sue-Ellen Case, ed., *Performing Feminisms: Feminist Critical Theory and Theatre* (Baltimore: Johns Hopkins University Press, 1990) and Lynda Hart and Peggy Phelan, eds., *Acting Out: Feminist Performances* (Ann Arbor: University of Michigan Press, 1993), both of which included essential readings on works by contemporary women playwrights, although neither volume was concerned solely with dramatic criticism.

13 See *www.thefeministspectator.com*. Dolan's blog was started in 2005; a book based on the blog, *The Feminist Spectator in Action: Feminist Criticism for the Stage and Screen*, was published by Palgrave Macmillan in 2013.

14 Patricia Cohen, "Charging Bias by Theaters, Female Playwrights to Hold Meeting," *New York Times*, 25 October 2008, available at *http://www.nytimes.com/2008/10/25/theater/25women.html?scp=1&sq=%E2%80%9CCharging%20Bias%20by%20Theaters,%20Female%20Playwrights%20to%20Hold%20Meeting,%E2%80%9D%20&st=cse* (accessed 12 May 2013). See also Patricia Cohen, "Rethinking Gender Bias in Theater," *New York Times*, 24 June 2009, which reports on a 2009 study by Emily Glassberg Sands that confirmed gender bias against women playwrights, including on the part of female artistic directors and literary directors; available at *http://theater.nytimes.com/2009/06/24/theater/24play.html?_r=0* (accessed 12 May 2013).

15 Kathy A. Perkins and Sandra L. Richards, "Black Women Playwrights in American Theatre," special issue: *Contemporary Women Playwrights*, ed. Penny Farfan and Lesley Ferris, *Theatre Journal* 62, no. 4 (December 2010): 542–43.

16 Brandi Wilkins Catanese, "Taking the Long View," special issue: *Contemporary Women Playwrights*, ed. Penny Farfan and Lesley Ferris, *Theatre Journal* 62, no. 4 (December 2010): 551.

17 Ibid.

18 Lynn Nottage, quoted in Susan Jonas and Suzanne Bennett, "Report on the Status of Women: A Limited Engagement," New York State Council on the Arts Theatre Program, January 2002, available at *http://www.womenarts.org/nysca-report-2002/* (accessed 26 May 2013).

19 Hart, *Making a Spectacle*, 1.

20 Rebecca Burton, "Adding It Up: The Status of Women in Canadian Theatre; A Report of the Phase One Findings of Equity in Canadian Theatre: The Women's Initiative," Canada Council for the Arts, October 2006, 2, available at *http://www.playwrights-guild.ca/sites/default/files/AddingItUp.pdf* (accessed 12 May 2013). Burton's report was modeled on and updated Rina Fraticelli's 1982 report, "The Status of Women in Canadian Theatre," which "revealed that women comprised only 10% of the total number of produced playwrights, a mere 13% of the productions' directors, and a paltry 11% of the companies' artistic directors" (Burton, "Adding It Up," 2). Part of Fraticelli's report was published as "The Invisibility Factor: The Status of Women in Canadian Theatre," *Fuse* 6, no. 3 (September 1982): 112–124. Burton's 2006 report was summarized in her article "Dispelling the Myth of Equality: A Report on the Status of Women in Canadian Theatre," special issue: *Canadian Women Playwrights: Triumphs and Tribulations,* ed. Ann Wilson and Hope McIntyre, *Canadian Theatre Review* 132 (Winter 2007): 3–8. For a dissenting (some might say post-feminist) view on Burton's research, conclusions, and recommendations, see Krista Dalby, "*Adding It Up* Takes More Than Just Numbers," special issue: *Canadian Women Playwrights: Triumphs and Tribulations,* ed. Ann Wilson and Hope McIntyre, *Canadian Theatre Review* 132 (Winter 2007): 14–17. Bruce Barton offers another perspective on the report, noting the presence of Canadian women "playmakers" within alternative structures that do not fit easily within the quantitative measures of Burton's report and the need for further research to "complement and complicate" Burton's findings; see "Tributes of Another Order," special issue: *Canadian Women Playwrights: Triumphs and Tribulations,* ed. Ann Wilson and Hope McIntyre, *Canadian Theatre Review* 132 (Winter 2007): 23.

21 British Theatre Consortium, "Writ Large: New Writing on the English Stage 2003–2009," Arts Council England, July 2009, 12, quoted in Janelle Reinelt, "Creative Ambivalence

and Precarious Futures: Women in British Theatre," special issue: *Contemporary Women Playwrights*, ed. Penny Farfan and Lesley Ferris, *Theatre Journal* 62, no. 4 (December 2010): 555. The report is available in its entirety at *www.artscouncil.org.uk/media/uploads/publications/writ_large_report.doc* (accessed 12 May 2013).

22 Reinelt, "Creative Ambivalence and Precarious Futures," 553, 556. Lucy Powell discusses some of the diverse new voices to which Reinelt refers in "Shakespeare's sisters," *Times* (1 August 2009): 40, 41, available at *Newspaper Source, EBSCO host* (accessed 23 May 2013).

23 For a summary of the controversy over the imbalance between male and female playwrights and directors in the 2010 season at Australia's major theatre companies, and particularly at Company B Belvoir in Sydney, see Richard Watts, "Breaking Down the Boy's Club," *ArtsHub*, 7 October 2009, available at *http://www.artshub.com.au/au/newsPrint.asp?sId=179399* (accessed 23 May 2013). The controversy resulted in a 2012 government-sponsored report by Elaine Lally in consultation with Sarah Miller, entitled "Women in theatre: A research report and action plan for the Australia Council for the Arts," which focuses on "women in creative leadership" and notes that "there has at best been no progress over the decade since 2001, and there is evidence that the situation for women in creative leadership deteriorated over that time" (4–5); available at *http://www.australiacouncil.gov.au/__data/assets/pdf_file/0008/127196/Women-in-Theatre-April-2012.pdf* (accessed 12 May 2013). An article by Rosemary Neill, "The sound and fury of Australia's women playwrights and theatre directors," notes marked improvements for women directors in the 2013 season and more modest ones for women playwrights, but cautions that "whether these newly minted gains for theatre's female creatives herald a permanent shift or are a temporary response to negative publicity about the under-representation of female directors and playwrights is an open question"; available at *http://www.theaustralian.com.au/arts/review/the-sound-and-the-fury-of-australias-women-playwrights/story-fn9n8gph-1226508371732* (accessed 12 May 2013).

24 Nehad Selaiha with Sarah Enany, "Women Playwrights in Egypt," 79 (in this volume).

25 Elif Batuman, "Stage Mothers: A women's theatre in rural Turkey," *The New Yorker* (24 and 31 December 2012): 72.

26 Ibid., 80.

27 The Guerilla Girls, "Parody and Parity," interview by Alisa Solomon, *Theater* 29, no. 2 (1999): 45.

28 Maya E. Roth has documented the history, mandate, and impact of the Jane Chambers Contest for Women Playwrights, which has been sponsored since 1984 by the Women and Theatre Program of the US-based Association for Theatre in Higher Education; "Revealing and Renewing Feminist Theatrical Engagement: The Jane Chambers Contest for Women Playwrights," *Theatre Topics* 20, no. 2 (2010): 157–69. In another example, the Committee for Recognizing Women in Theater, formed in 2010, initiated the Lilly Awards, named in honor of playwright Lillian Hellman and intended "to honor the work of women" in all aspects of American theatre; see *http://www.thelillyawards.org/about/* (accessed 14 May 2013). For an account of the formation of this committee and the launch of these awards, see Melissa Silverstein, "The Lilly Awards Honor Women in Theatre," *Women's Media Center*, 3 June 2010, available at *http://www.womensmediacenter.com/feature/entry/the-lilly-awards-honor-women-in-theatre* (accessed 14 May 2013).

29 "50/50 in 2020: About" and "Top Ten Things To Do: 50/50 in 2020 Action List," available at *http://5050in2020.org/about/* and *http://5050in2020.org/2010/12/13/top-ten-things-to-do/* (accessed 14 May 2013). See also Marsha Norman's essay "Not There Yet," *American Theatre*, 26, no. 9 (November 2009): 28–30, 79, in which she offers further suggestions

to literary departments, artistic directors, funders, donors, and patrons, as well as to the writers themselves, regarding how to achieve parity for US women playwrights.

30 Reinelt, "Creative Ambivalence and Precarious Futures," 553–556.

31 For information on Nightwood, see the company's website at *http://www.nightwood-theatre.net/,* as well as Shelley Scott's article "Nightwood Theatre: A Woman's Work Is Always Done," special issue: *Canadian Women Playwrights: Triumphs and Tribulations,* ed. Ann Wilson and Hope McIntyre, *Canadian Theatre Review* 132 (Winter 2007): 24–29. Tricycle's "Women, Power and Politics" festival was in two parts: "Then" and "Now." The "Then" section featured works that looked at history from the reign of Elizabeth I, to the suffrage era, to the protests at Greenham Common, whereas the "Now" section explored a variety of perspectives on voting, from student elections to national elections. See *http://www.tricycle.co.uk/about-the-tricycle-pages/about-us-tab-menu/archive/archived-theatre-production/women-power-politics-then/* and *http://www.tricycle.co.uk/about-the-tricycle-pages/about-us-tab-menu/archive/archived-theatre-production/women-power-politics-now/* (both accessed 21 May 2013).

32 Virginia Woolf, *A Room of One's Own* (1929; San Diego: Harvest, 1989), 76.

33 Jenna Steventon, email to the authors, 30 January 2012.

34 See Lynette Goddard, *Staging black feminisms: identity, politics, performance* (Basingstoke, UK: Palgrave Macmillan, 2007); Philip C. Kolin, ed., *Contemporary African American Women Playwrights: A Casebook* (London: Routledge, 2007); Brenda Murphy, ed., *The Cambridge Companion to American Women Playwrights* (Cambridge: Cambridge University Press, 1999); Elaine Aston and Janelle Reinelt, eds., *The Cambridge Companion to Modern British Women Playwrights* (Cambridge: Cambridge University Press, 2000); Melissa Sihra, ed., *Women in Irish Drama: A Century of Authorship and Representations* (Basingstoke, UK: Palgrave Macmillan, 2007); Sue-Ellen Case and Elaine Aston, eds., *Staging International Feminisms* (Basingstoke, UK: Palgrave Macmillan, 2007); and Julie Holledge and Joanne Tompkins, *Women's Intercultural Performance* (London: Routledge, 2000). Other recent works on contemporary women's playwriting include, for example, Gabrielle Griffin, *Contemporary Black and Asian Women Playwrights in Britain* (Cambridge: Cambridge University Press, 2003); Sharon Friedman, ed., *Feminist Theatrical Revisions of Classic Works: Critical Essays* (Jefferson, NC: McFarland, 2009); and Barbara Ozieblo and Noelia Hernando-Real, eds., *Performing Gender Violence: Plays by Contemporary American Women Dramatists* (Basingstoke, UK: Palgrave Macmillan, 2012).

35 See Dolan, "Introduction to the Second Edition," *The Feminist Spectator as Critic,* xiii–xliv; Janelle Reinelt, "Navigating Postfeminism: Writing Out of the Box," in *Feminist Futures: Theatre, Performance, Theory,* ed. Elaine Aston and Geraldine Harris (Basingstoke, UK: Palgrave Macmillan, 2006), 17–33; Aston, "A feminist view of the 1990s," *Feminist views on the English stage,* 1–17; Elaine Aston, foreword, *Feminism and Theatre,* by Case, ix–xxiii; Elaine Aston and Geraldine (Gerry) Harris, "Feminist Futures and the Possibilities of 'We,'" in *Feminist Futures: Theatre, Performance, Theory,* ed. Aston and Harris, 1–16.

36 Reinelt, "Navigating Postfeminism," 20; quoted in Elaine Aston, "Feeling the Loss of Feminism: Sarah Kane's *Blasted* and an Experiential Genealogy of Contemporary Women's Playwriting," 20 (in this volume).

37 Bachelet, "Closing Statement."

Part I
Histories

1 Feeling the Loss of Feminism: Sarah Kane's *Blasted* and an Experiential Genealogy of Contemporary Women's Playwriting

Elaine Aston

Introduction: feminist impressions/impressions of feminism

In 1977, Ann McFerran, theatre editor for *Time Out* magazine, published interviews with nine UK-based women playwrights under the heading "The Theatre's (Somewhat) Angry Young Women."[1] The "somewhat" signaled the possibility that the future was beginning to look a little brighter for women playwrights, as their work benefited from the "fashionable" moment of feminism and gained in cultural visibility. However, the expectation that this somewhat better future for women playwrights in the late 1970s and 1980s would herald the 1990s as *the* decade for women playwrights in British theatre was overturned by the emergence of a new wave of "angry young men," Jez Butterworth, David Eldridge, Martin McDonagh, Antony Neilson, and Mark Ravenhill significant among them.

In 1997, exactly twenty years after McFerran's interviews and reacting to the outcrop of young male angries in British theatre, Heidi Stephenson and Natasha Langridge published *Rage and Reason,* a series of interviews with twenty women playwrights.[2] The title of the collection gestured to the "rage" of women playwrights over the continuing gender inequalities of the theatre industry, making this one compelling "reason" for the collection. Designed to celebrate the "titanic achievements" of women playwrights in "broaden[ing] the agenda of British drama" despite the continuing gender inequalities of the profession,[3] *Rage and Reason* demonstrates that without paying particular attention to gender, women playwrights risk, yet again, becoming invisible. The achievements may be "titanic," but they can so easily sink almost without a trace.

In the introduction to the interview collection, male directors are called to account for the 1990s gender gap. In response, Royal Court Theatre director Stephen Daldry suggested that women dramatists were not "capturing the zeitgeist of fashion," and that "work within the context of feminism is unfashionable."[4] Equally, Mike Bradwell of the Bush Theatre pointed to how women playwrights

government under the Iron Lady meant that Thatcherism had done its utmost to discredit socialism; internationally, the 1989 overthrow of communist rule in Eastern Europe and the dissolution of the Soviet Union in 1991 undermined the credibility and viability of socialist ideologies and regimes. At the same time, feminism, as deftly illustrated in Caryl Churchill's *Top Girls* (1982), was a casualty of Thatcher's right-wing "superwoman" – the individual, materially successful woman privileged above any altruistic concern for women's collective welfare – and of the international, transatlantic backlash against its women-centered ideologies.[14] Heralding cultures of postmodernity and heavily invested in global capitalism, the 1990s, in brief, witnessed the dismantling of the "grand [political] narrative" that previously had woven together different sets of socially progressive interests – feminist interests included.

While there are any number of studies one might reference to evidence the 1990s disintegration of (feminist) political identities, I turn instead to a dramatic work that captures the 1990s zeitgeist of political disidentifications: Churchill's poignant twenty-minute play *This is a Chair*, directed by Daldry and performed at the Duke of York Theatre in London shortly after New Labour's 1997 victory. *This is a Chair* gestures to a political ideal – to an idea of society principled by freedom and equality[15] – as a casualty of both the Conservative past and New Labour's designs on selling socialism short by rebranding left-wing politics into a "Cool Britannia" future. The play is a series of eight scenes: snapshots of personal moments that have no obvious, explicit connection to one another. Equally, each of the scenes has its own Brechtian-styled political title, such as "The Labour Party's Slide to the Right" or "The Northern Ireland Peace Process," but none of the titles bears any relation to the personal moments that accompanied them. The directorial decision to have the action played in the auditorium, and to dislodge the audience from its traditional comfort zone of viewing by positioning it onstage, *gestically* figured the spectators as looking back at "themselves" as a politically disconnected "body." At once a gesturing to the Brechtian landscape that had long informed Churchill's socialist dramaturgy, *This is a Chair* also positions that political perspective as vanishing from view. Brecht's critical distancing technique of "disillusioning"[16] is turned on the spectator as a politically disinterested or disillusioned subject.

As Churchill reveals the divorce between the personal and the political and the dissolve of a Brechtian-inflected dramaturgy, she opens up the question of how to *form* attachments to political identities. Coming from the dramatist whose reputation for politicizing strategies of theatrical inventiveness is unsurpassed in modern British theatre, the question Churchill rehearses in *This is a Chair* is one that resonates for all playwrights concerned with what forms of theatre might serve to disillusion audiences of dehumanizing, self-serving interests that conspire against the possibility of making sociopolitical connections to "others." Moreover, coming from the playwright who pioneered a feminist theatre culture in British theatre, Churchill's question has a particular resonance for women's playwriting that remains committed to what Janelle Reinelt has termed a "feminist residue from the Second Wave – serious issues [that] have been identified and are still present but…are ignored, pushed aside or simply denied."[17]

In respect of a "feminist residue," one scene in *This is a Chair* is particularly significant. It appears twice in the play and features a mother and father pressuring their daughter to eat. "Yes, eat up, Muriel" is the mother's refrain that endorses the threatening, patriarchal insistence that the girl eat.[18] The doubling of this tiny scene suggests a patriarchal haunting of the contemporary landscape. By showing the masculine "remains" as a threat to the girl reluctant to be nourished by "a special bite" from "daddy's" plate,[19] Churchill disillusions the spectator of a healthy feminine by gesturing to a disempowered feminine at the patriarchal table. McRobbie's analysis of "post-feminist disorders" and of the "illegible rage" of young women still confined to the patriarchal table though without recourse to a feminist politics now lost to the postfeminist "illusion of positivity and progress"[20] affords a persuasive diagnosis of Muriel's trouble. How are young women to cope with the patriarchal "leftovers," given the loss of feminism? Churchill's question is one that arguably underpins women's playwriting by younger generations of women dramatists whose response, I maintain, is to offer an experiential, viscerally and emotionally charged articulation of *feeling* the loss of feminism.

Enter the experiential: feeling the loss of feminism and *Blasted*

All theatre, whatever form it takes, has designs on the experiential. Ideally, playwrights want audiences to feel involved in or a part of their plays. In British theatre during the 1990s, however, the experiential became a byword for "in-yer-face" theatre: the "shock fest" of violent, taboo-breaking drama by a new wave of angry young men, and just a handful of angry young women – most significantly Sarah Kane. Early feminist interest in Kane's theatre was delayed arguably because of the way in which, as the "bad girl" of the British stage, she was grouped with the young male "angries," and because of how, as I argued earlier, her position on the "woman writer" label was (mis)interpreted. Subsequent assessments and re-assessments of her theatre, my own included,[21] have, however, paid more attention to the ways in which gender concerns are very much a concern of her plays, most particularly her representations of masculinities in crisis.

Moreover, to disinter Kane from the laddish culture of in-yer-face theatre helps us to see *Blasted* and other of Kane's oeuvre as a titanic legacy for women's playwriting. Her theatre figures the generational feminist shift from Churchill's second-wave understanding of *"what I feel is quite strongly a feminist position"* to what one might rephrase as "what I feel is quite strongly the *loss* of a feminist position." With plays that resonate with Churchill's dystopian view of a *personal* divorced from the *political*, as illustrated in *This is a Chair*, Kane is representative of the 1990s "woman" playwright who is genealogically connected to feminist theatre histories, but is generationally divorced from an "old" style of feminist attachment. Her debut play, *Blasted,* figures the fault line between a "personal as political feminist past" and a "personal without a feminist political present/future."

As one of the most talked-about plays of the 1990s, *Blasted* requires very little introduction. Briefly, the play begins as a domestic rape story. A hotel bedroom in Leeds is where the terminally ill journalist Ian and the young, vulnerable Cate rendezvous. They have a history: they were lovers, but are lovers no longer. They catch up on personal news, quarrel, and fight. Ian rapes Cate, and the intimate gender wars of the bedroom turn into an epic war-zone as a Soldier armed with a sniper's rifle forces his way into the room. After torturing and raping Ian, the Soldier blows his brains out, leaving Ian as the unwilling survivor, the living-dead "nightmare" to whom Cate returns in the final moments of the play.

As I revisit *Blasted* for the purposes of this discussion, it is the matter of how the play experientially "blasts" a *feeling* for the loss of feminism that interests me. In stating this, I am arguing for a political purpose to Kane's experiential style, though this goes somewhat against the grain of the classic accounts of in-yer-face theatre. For instance, Aleks Sierz characterizes in-yer-face theatre as an intense, confrontational, emotional roller-coaster ride of extreme experiences; as an aesthetic experience that favors more visceral, immediate ways of "waking up the audience,"[22] rather than rehearsing a politically explicit wake-up call for less oppressive, more democratically organized futures. Gone are the "wordy, worthy and woolly" types of "political theatre and the issue plays of the seventies and eighties," Sierz argues, replaced by a "nineties theatre" that is "[u]nencumbered by ideology."[23] However, being unencumbered by ideology forecloses on the political and fails to ask how the emotional overload might be politically affective and effective. Moreover, the move away from the political-theatre "isms" of the 1970s and '80s (theatres of socialism and feminism) is generally offered as the reason for the turn to an emotional, visceral, experiential style of theatre. While this is a highly plausible explanation, at the same time, it stops short of interrogating the politics of this emotional landscape or of asking how an understanding of the political work of emotions in 1990s society might have a bearing on matters.

Helpful in this latter regard is Stjepan Meštrović's sociological theorizing of a 1990s Western society characterized by postemotionalism. Meštrović complicates postmodernist thinking by rehearsing an idea of contemporary Western society as "postemotional":

> It is a society in which people do not react to what, in an earlier era, would have been stirring occurrences and crises. Rather, individuals have become blasé, allergic to involvement, yet intelligent enough to know that the events are significant, and perhaps even to know that in an earlier era individuals would have responded with deep emotional empathy, or equally deep emotional antipathy, to particular individuals, and to the events surrounding them.[24]

The postemotional type is, then, one "who knows so much, but is able to feel, genuinely, so little."[25] The key word here is "genuinely," if one accepts Meštrović's findings that, courtesy of the "culture industry," what we now have is "[a] new hybrid of intellectualized, mechanical, mass-produced emotions."[26] For when the "packaging of emotions" operates to such a degree that it blocks any kind of personal "autonomy," then we risk being out of touch with our own feelings.[27] We are, as it were, unable to feel our way to thinking for ourselves. Here, also, I think of Churchill's *This is a Chair*, populated by postemotional types unable to feel genuinely in either personal or political matters.

If the 1990s can be characterized as a "postemotional society," then the emotional, experiential form of plays such as *Blasted* can be argued as a counter-cultural response to the difficulty of genuinely being able to feel. While it does not necessarily follow that experientially styled, in-yer-face theatre politicizes the postemotional characterization of contemporary society (i.e., I am not laying claim for *all* experiential, in-yer-face theatre as working in this particular way), it does propose this as a possibility. While the outraged theatre reviewers at the time of the play's Royal Court premiere sought to manufacture "emotional antipathy" to *Blasted*, their journalistic crafting of horror and outrage missed a genuine *feeling* for the affective political territory of the play that resides, I would argue, in the way it "blasts" both postemotionalism and postfeminism.

Kane, like Churchill, was concerned with how to move spectators from the position of witness who stands by,[28] who might be shocked, but who fails to *feel* through the fabric of an emotional overdose of media-orchestrated "horrors," such as Ian's reporting of the "slaughtered British tourist Samantha Scrace."[29] When *This is a Chair* begins, the first Brechtian title reads: "The War in Bosnia."[30] Media coverage of the war in Bosnia, which Meštrović offers as one of two media moments that show postemotionalism at its "apex,"[31] affected Kane's writing of *Blasted*.[32] It heightened her awareness that emotive broadcasting would not translate into political action to put a stop to the genocide. As in Churchill's play, where the linguistic sign-posting "The War in Bosnia" has no significance for a London couple rearranging a date because the woman has "doublebooked" herself,[33] Kane sought to capture the inability to feel genuinely committed to taking action.

Blasted moves through the social realism of the opening hotel scenes in which the audience is the bystanding witness, through the rape and abuse of Cate to the shattering of the realist form (echoed in the design for the Royal Court's revival in 2001 that "blew" the realistically conceived hotel set away) in a manner that experientially serves to pull the audience inside mass rape as a weapon of war. As Kane explained, "[t]he play collapses into one of Cate's fits, putting the audience through the experience they have previously only witnessed, which is a direct parallel to the truth of the war raging outside."[34] "Putting the audience through the experience" is an emotionally charged strategy that "presses" upon spectators to feel their way to thinking about the dehumanizing violence the play represents. Of course, not *all* spectators will feel the same way, and certainly the critics' adverse responses to the premiere of *Blasted* reflect a resistance to how Kane envisaged the affectivity of her dramaturgy. However, my own experience of seeing the Royal Court's 2001 revival of *Blasted* on the theatre's main stage (rather than the Royal Court's intimate studio space where it premiered) was certainly one that left me at the end of the performance with the physical sensation of being unable to move, and of feeling emotionally exhausted by what the production had put me through. I remember quite distinctly feeling almost unable to applaud the performers, and of thinking that somehow the convention of applause felt "wrong." This was not because I felt that the production was bad, but because the assault on my senses was such that applause returned the audience to a "normality" I simply was not feeling.

This kind of assault on the audience is experientially purposeful in its attempt to break the inability to feel a responsibility for the sufferings of others. In terms of the characters, the loss of altruistic feeling is represented in Kane's portrait of Ian as the tabloid journalist who "hacks" out sexist, racist, and homophobic abuse. Captured, tortured, and sexually violated by the Soldier, Ian is forced to listen, to bear witness to the Soldier's experiences of war. These are, however, experiences he claims he cannot report – they do not sell papers. "Covering [his] ... own arse,"[35] Ian fails to uncover feelings and a sense of responsibility for the "affairs" he sees as "foreign" to his (national) own.

Violating the compositional "rules" of realism by infiltrating the domestic-hotel realism with her increasingly surreal presentation of the atrocities of war, Kane also captured the male-occupied territory of the female body – both in Ian's abusive treatment of Cate, and in the refiguring of heterosexual rape, as the Soldier, in turn, rapes Ian. When the violence begins, it begins with the rape of a woman;[36] feeling the violent affects of Ian's sexual bullying of Cate, and seeing these through to their unstoppable, escalating, epic conclusion, gives emotional weight to *seeing* a world increasingly lost to a violent, masculinist, phallocentric symbolic order.

Kane's starting point for *Blasted* – older guy rapes younger woman – points to a connection with feminism's longstanding objections to rape. This feminist connection is amplified if one looks at her three early, unpublished monologues collectively titled *Sick*, one of which, "Comic Monologue," is a feminist Brechtian-styled treatment of a woman's experiences of being raped. However, as I have argued elsewhere, Kane put all of this writing to one side, because of wanting to move beyond a second-wave, theatre-as-explicit-feminist style of writing.[37] Crucially, this is not to argue a putting to one side of feminist interests, but rather a concern for how to overcome the feminism fatigue of a 1990s postfeminist society.

"Feminism fatigue," a term I coin as a variation on Meštrović's "compassion fatigue,"[38] occurred as a consequence of, on the one hand, the media's representation of second-wave feminism as having outlived its usefulness, and, on the other hand, its endorsement of "girl power" as a substitute for feminism. Fatigued by the idea of second-wave feminism, a third-wave generation of women were "sold" on the postfeminist promise of personal freedom and empowerment. The issue of rape in the early to mid-1990s is one means of measuring the "apex" of post-feminism, as third-wavers advocated women's rights to sexual empowerment and accused their second-wave "sisters" of being overly invested in an idea of women as passive sexual victims. For instance, capitalizing on the backlash against second-wave feminism, Katie Roiphe, author of *The Morning After*, accused "rape-crisis feminists" of denying women "sexual agency."[39] Feminism fatigue is detectable in Roiphe's writing as she trashes what she perceives to be the worn-out, emotional, second-wave feminist canvas of fear and anger over women's sexual oppression. In her view, the 1990s phenomenon of "date rape" – the idea of a consensual sexual encounter (date) that turns into a violation (rape) – made it possible for feminists to cry "rape" at every opportunity – to play rape as the "natural trump card for feminism."[40] By Roiphe's reckoning, Cate's rape is not rape at all, but sex construed as rape in the light of "morning after" regret.[41]

"Rape-crisis" news was big news during the 1990s. For instance, prior to the O. J. Simpson trial that Meštrović cites as he tracks the apex of postemotionalism, the televised US date-rape trial of William Kennedy Smith in 1991 had the biggest media coverage, making sex wars a newsworthy, newspaper-selling topic. "Rape play girl goes into hiding" was how the tabloid press headlined Kane after the opening of *Blasted*,[42] as though the writer herself was in some way implicated in a real-life rape story – altogether a betrayal of her endeavors to figure rape as a point of genuinely felt connection between "a common rape in Leeds ... [and] mass rape as a war weapon in Bosnia."[43] Making that connection, Kane was neither casting her play in the mold of second-wave feminist theatre of the female victim's story nor joining the third-wave chorus of women as sexually "empowered," pleasure-seeking individuals; rather, in stark contrast to Roiphe's attack on rape-crisis feminism, she experientially figured the "crisis of living"[44] through rape and war.

Important also is Kane's strategy of keeping the rapist Ian at the scene of his crime. Unlike Kennedy Smith, who was acquitted of the rape charge, Ian does not "get off," but is subjected to male rape and torture and "dies" only to remain living the hell of his own masculinist making. Cate survives, but also at the scene of the crime to which she returns, because, in a sense, she has never left – the experience of rape will never leave her. The impression of Cate as a waif-like, vulnerable survivor is what lingers as my memory of the production fades.

In *An Archive of Feelings,* Ann Cvetkovich argues that "[i]n the absence of institutionalized documentation or in opposition to official histories, memory becomes a valuable historical resource, and ephemeral and personal collections of objects stand alongside the documents of the dominant culture in order to offer alternative modes of knowledge."[45] As my memory of the damaged feminine survives, it refuses "official histories" of interpretation that elide the play's conversation with feminism; it "presses" upon the claims I make here for *Blasted* as a play that undoes nostalgic attachments to an old style of feminism *and* detaches from postfeminism's concealment of the enduring power of a masculinist order, in the interests of feminism's renewal. Otherwise, like Cate, surviving the "crisis in living" through a world conditioned and damaged by male violence is the most (best?) that we can hope for.

An experiential genealogy of women's playwriting

Disinterred from in-yer-face-ism, *Blasted* reappears as a landmark play in the context of contemporary women's playwriting, and as seminal to an experiential genealogy of women's playwriting where feeling the loss of feminism presses upon the drama. Such a genealogy can be constructed and traced back through work by other women playwrights from the 1990s that similarly evoked feelings for the loss of feminism as a socially transformative politics. Thinking through an experiential genealogy of women's playwriting, for instance, enables a reconsideration of plays by Rebecca Prichard and Judy Upton, writers who were claimed as exponents of in-yer-face theatre in a way that often elided feminist impressions of their work. Viewed as genealogically connected to feeling the loss of feminism, both playwrights can be seen as in dialogue with feminism – more specifically, as engaging in critiques of girl power as a substitute for feminism.

Less iconoclastic than experimentalists Kane and Churchill, Prichard and Upton were nonetheless concerned with how to *form* an effective social critique. As Prichard observes, if you are committed to scripting socially aware theatre, then you need to avoid writing "social realism which feels like it can affirm or concretize a particular reality" in favor of forms that can "offer some sort of axis for social change, and leave a crack of light open for alternative realities."[46] She elaborates: "If you write really realistic stuff, that's purely realistic and you stick to traditional structures, you give an expectation or pattern that fulfils itself, as if you are saying everything is doomed.... If you do pure social realism, it feels to me as if you are kind of saying this is the way it is and all we can do is despair."[47] Prichard and Upton formed the "despair" of their young working-class women battling with dead-end lives by dramaturgically feeling their way out of what Prichard terms "*pure* social realism": realism that, even while it might serve to raise social awareness through its subject matter, returns an audience to an intellectual place of safety.

In her debut play, *Essex Girls* (1994), Prichard critiqued the loss of feminism in her portrayal of disenfranchised working-class girls. Dramaturgically, she sought to undermine the "traditional structure" of realism through the juxtaposition of two acts that were connected and yet disconnected. Where the opening act, set in the girls' toilets of a comprehensive (state) school, portrays a group of working-class teenage girls worrying about boys, pregnancy, or body image, the second act shows a different older girl coping with single motherhood. While an audience is left to make the connection between the disenfranchisement of the younger and the older girls, with hindsight, Prichard observed that this fell short as an affective strategy for moving audiences to feel the plight of the girls; rather, it "allowed audiences to feel very comfortable in their seats."[48]

In her later play *Yard Gal* (1998), Prichard kept hold of her girls-in-trouble subject matter while more thoroughly letting go of social realism. *Yard Gal,* the story of a gang of "rude gals" narrated by two gang members, captures and captivates through its language of tough-talking urban-speak. People can "stay inside you,"[49] the girls observe at the close of the play, and Prichard's yard gals get "inside" and "stay inside" audiences as their adrenalin-infused style of street-wise storytelling affectively pulls them into the girls' brutalizing experience of life on the streets of Hackney (East London). Performed with intimacy and intimidation in the Royal Court's studio space, without the trappings of realism in either the scripting (a shared narration rather than scenes of conventionally constructed dialogue) or the staging (minimally designed to foreground the performers and their story-telling), *Yard Gal* "pressed" upon its audiences a story of feminine empowerment as a "story that is FI'REAL."[50]

Hailed by *Guardian* theatre critic Michael Billington as the "poet of coastal despair,"[51] given her preference for setting plays in British seaside resorts that have gone to seed, Upton is a playwright whose genealogical connections to feeling the loss of feminism surface in a style of theatre writing that is emotionally charged with anger about young girls' lives laid waste through lack of opportunities. Representing the dark underside of girl power in her girl-gang play *Ashes and Sand* (1994), for instance, Upton portrays the shattered dreams of romance and exotic holidays that, in the "aftermath" of feminism, are all the girls have to hang on to. Their shattered dreams, in turn, shatter (audience) expectations of gender behavior: Upton's in-yer-face girls physically attack men and "rape" a man they have befriended, a police officer onto whom they have projected their romantic fantasies and who, in turn, is psychologically damaged by female violence.

Upton's realism is filmic in style. Scenes dissolve rapidly into each other like a cinematic cross-fade so that, compositionally, *Ashes and Sand* feels like a high-performance car crash waiting to happen. Blood-letting is a release for Upton's girls: self-harming and harming (male) others are their ways of taking out their frustrations on a world over which and in which they have no control. As dreams distort (aided by a mirrored set in the original Royal Court production), so Upton's increasingly surreal dramatic landscape, that "climaxes" in the girls' rape of the police officer, pulls spectators into feeling the loss of feminism that might otherwise have assisted the girls in transforming their lives. Feeling that loss makes it hard to be politically upbeat, but that is precisely Upton's point. Defending Upton's theatre against a perception of her work as lacking a social or political agenda, Rebecca D'Monté argues that the very fact that "Upton is unable to posit an agenda for transformation or for revolution ... in itself becomes a polit-ical message." Representing "the loss of a shared female experience and language seems fitting for an age where equality for women is supposed to have been won," but that, D'Monté summarizes, in turn evidences "a crisis in feminism."[52]

What D'Monté characterizes as a crisis in feminism in Upton's plays, or what I have been tracing here as a crisis produced by feeling the loss of feminism, continues to press upon plays by women in the millennium. More recent additions to an experiential genealogy of women's playwriting include, for example, Irish dramatist Stella Feehily's debut play, *Duck*. Performed at the Royal Court in 2003 in a co-production with Max Stafford-Clark's Out of Joint Theatre Company, *Duck* resumes the girls-in-trouble theme in a style of "dirty" (urban and brutal) realism. A later play by Feehily, *Dreams of Violence* (2009, co-produced by the Soho Theatre and Out of Joint), evinces a more experimental approach. In this play, realism is disturbed by darkly funny dreamscapes, as Feehily dramatizes a feminist activist's struggle to campaign on behalf of the exploited female workforce that cleans the offices of city financiers and to cope with her dysfunctional family.

A dysfunctional upper-middle-class family is the subject of Polly Stenham's debut drama, *That Face*, which took the critics by storm when it premiered at the Royal

Court in 2007. In a twist to the tale of working-class girls in trouble, Stenham's play reveals the cruelty of a privileged class of boarding-school girls and makes monstrous the postfeminist legacy of girl power. Equally, Fiona Evans returns to and updates the subject of the sex wars in her play *Scarborough,* which dramatizes the news-worthy topic of under-age sex. In an uncanny doubling, *Scarborough* first reveals a female school teacher in a sexual relationship with a 15-year-old male pupil, then replays this with the gender roles reversed: the school teacher is now male, the pupil female.[53] Set in a realistically constructed hotel bedroom (in the Royal Court produc-tion, spectators had to perch on bits of bedroom furniture, sit close to the bed, or stand around the sides of the bedroom), the audience was denied their comfort zone of end-on, fourth-wall viewing. This installation of the audience in a moment of theatrical realism – an affective experience of enforced intimacy – served to discom-fort spectators into *feeling* the illicit sexual relations of the bedroom scene.

Close up and personal, the intensely felt intimacies of these later plays are located in the private sphere, where feelings are spiraling out of control into "dreams of violence," sexually illicit relationships, monstrous families, and acts of schoolgirl torture. Realized through a range of experiential dramaturgies, from dirty to uncanny realisms, uncertain and uneasy futures are made visible in the wake of a personal that is no longer political.

Feeling the loss of feminism in a time of terror: *Stoning Mary*

The loss of or crisis in feminism is also cast in the shadow of a world increasingly scarred by regimes of terror and acts of terrorism. This is reflected, for instance, in Churchill's enduring explorations of globalization in *Far Away* (2000) and her political protest of the war in Gaza in *Seven Jewish Children* (2009), both of which position a girl-child (Joan in *Far Away;* a girl we never see in *Seven Jewish Children*) as caught up in and damaged by a dehumanizing fabric of violence and terror. Equally, from a younger, twenty-something writing generation, Lucy Prebble's *Enron* (2009–2010), which I return to in my concluding remarks, presents a relent-less regime of global capitalism in a frightening masculinist and materialist echo of Churchill's 1987 city comedy, *Serious Money.*

Exceptionally, there is one playwright who brings together the epic and the domestic, the terrifying feeling of a world lost to a global tide of dehuman-izing values *and* a feeling for the loss of feminism: debbie tucker green. tucker green made her professional theatre debut in 2003 with two plays on domestic violence and abuse: *Dirty Butterfly* (Soho Theatre) and *Born Bad* (Hampstead Theatre). In 2005, her Royal Court production of *Stoning Mary* made an explicit and angry lament for the loss of feminism, while *Trade,* her treatment of female sex tourism performed by the Royal Shakespeare Company at the Swan Theatre, offered a savagely funny critique of a white, Western, third-wave style of sexual empowerment. The beautiful but brutal poetic style of urban-speak that char-acterizes tucker green's writing has occasioned her reception as a late exponent of in-yer-face theatre.[54] However, as Lynette Goddard insightfully points out, it is important "to understand black women's work within traditions of black cultural production" as having been influential in shaping her theatre.[55] In that sense, tucker green eschews the laddish culture of in-yer-face-ism and is genealogically connected to experiential, socially aware women's writing, though at the same time she also refuses the white, Western traditions of liberal feminism and domestic realism.

Black, female, and angry about the inequalities between Third and First World countries, tucker green distils her anger into trenchant critiques of a Western failure to care for "others." *Stoning Mary* pulled audiences into an experiential mode of imagining "what if" the atrocities, hardships, and injustices happening in parts of Africa were happening here. Performed by a white cast and *"set in the country it is performed in,"*[56] *Stoning Mary* impresses upon audiences the need to be sensitized, rather than desensitized, to problems in Africa, just as Kane had charged spectators of *Blasted* with feeling the crisis in Bosnia.[57] The play is woven out of three narrative strands: a couple who quarrel over a medical prescription for AIDS that can help only one of them, leaving the other to die; the story of a boy soldier; and the stoning of Mary. Each story at first appears to be unconnected to the others, but the connections are gradually made apparent: the boy soldier shoots the quarreling couple, whose daughter Mary kills the boy soldier, whose mother, as the play ends, is the first to pick up a stone to kill Mary.

Stoning Mary reflects a continuing engagement with a cultural politics of post-emotionalism; it reveals how the "compassion fatigue" of contemporary society erodes what Meštrović describes as the *"caritas"* that "binds humanity together." When this happens, compassion no longer means being able to care for others, but taking "pity" on those less fortunate than ourselves: "pity isolates and divides people into those who have the luxury to look down on others versus those who are desperate."[58] As tucker green specifies that the fictional world of the play should be located in whichever country it is being staged in, *Stoning Mary* disillusions audiences of the "luxury to look down on others" by bringing home the lack of *caritas,* our inability to care genuinely for others. Equally, following Ahmed, the play reveals how hate "sticks" to the "other,"[59] and how an emotional hardening toward an enemy "other" impedes the possibility of being able to feel a way out of an "us" versus "them" binary. As tucker green's Husband and Wife, accompanied and prompted by their Egos (a doubling device that serves to highlight the couple's self-centered rather than other-centered feelings), duel over the prescription that can save only one of them, each becomes the enemy of the other. The "stickiness" of words, the rhythms and repetitions of words or truncated lines, create cruel sensations. "If you'd putcha hands – put your hands on me,"[60] the Wife repeatedly urges her Husband, then he might feel how her body has a greater need for the medicine than his. As neither moves to touch the other, as hands (the Husband's) go into pockets, or as the Wife "eyes to the skies it – focus on the floors it,"[61] so the emotional divide between them hardens into a deadly/deathly distance. Each exists in terror of the other becoming the one who will survive. In the Royal Court production, the intimate hostilities of the couple were juxtaposed with the vastness of the playing space (the auditorium was adapted to create a gladiatorial-styled arena), bringing an epic quality to a personal, domestic quarrel.

tucker green's dramaturgy is an aesthetic mix of the personal and the epic, the visceral and the clinical. In contrast to Kane's "pure" experiential, tucker green's experiential combines with disillusioning techniques (for instance, Brechtian-styled titles announce each scene) so that emotional attachments and clinical detachments are both possible. Arguably, this approach might suggest that a "cooler" kind of experiential aesthetic is what is called for, as postemotionalism is affected by the emotional/political temperature raised by the events of 9/11, making terror the new globally *felt* emotion. The kind of experiential assault on the audience that *Blasted* created might be too "hot" for spectators feeling the aftershocks of terror/ism. Hence, different dramaturgical tactics are called for to critique a contemporary lack of *caritas*.

In the presentational and experiential drive toward feeling the lack of *caritas*, tucker green makes explicit hard-hitting feelings about the loss of feminism. *Stoning Mary* figures feminism fatigue, as an imprisoned Mary awaiting her stoning realizes that "not even the women" are going to march for her. In the longest and hardest-hitting speech of the play, Mary asks over and over about "what happened to the womanist bitches? / ... The feminist bitches? / ... The professional bitches. / What happened to them?... *whadafuckabout* them?"[62] None of them have come out to sign her petition – not even her older sister, who gives away her ticket for "stoning Mary" to the corrections officer, can be there for her. Laced through the rhythms of a brutally beautiful poetics of political anger and visually captured in the portrayal of the estranged, alienated intimacy between the sisters is the loss of feminism that makes it impossible to feel genuinely attached to other women. As McRobbie argues: "The loss of feminism, the loss of a political love for 'womanhood' which feminism advocated and encouraged, which also allowed a certain suspension of the self in favour of 'the collective' or 'the communal,' creates new forms of female confinement."[63]

At once a condemnation of the lack of solidarity among women and a lament for the "loss of a political love for 'womanhood,'" Mary's speech can also be read as a condemnation of feminism for creating the false impression of a genuine care and responsibility for women. In such a reading, what is mourned is not the loss of feminism, but the loss of a feminism "we" never had. Interpreted in this way, as bitter as the aftertaste of Mary's speech might be for a feminist spectator such as myself, the play presses the need for a feminism that is genuinely able to care as it critiques the "aftermath" of postfeminism and the escalating terror of the "enemy" that fosters a love of the "selfsame" and a hatred of the "other." tucker green leaves us with the terrifying prospect (reality?) of a world without *caritas*. As the play ends, the stoning begins.

Conclusion: why the "one-eyed view of the world"?

By way of concluding, to come back to where discussion began with Churchill's Muriel in *This is a Chair* and to move forward to the "new forms of female confinement" that McRobbie argues are a consequence of the aftermath of feminism, I want briefly to elaborate on millennial newcomer Lucy Prebble. Debuting at the Royal Court in 2003 with her cyberspace drama *The Sugar Syndrome,* Prebble figured the "illegible rage [of] post-feminist disorders" through her portrayal of anorexic, 17-year-old Dani Carter, who is struggling to cope with her dysfunctional family. From picking over the patriarchal "remains" in this domestic drama, Prebble, as noted earlier, has moved on to the epic canvas of late capitalism in *Enron* (a hit in London's West End, though a failure on New York's Broadway). *Enron* includes scenic vignettes between Big Daddy capitalism (Enron president Jeffrey Skilling) and his young daughter. As the girl-child is taught to count money, blows (capitalist) bubbles about to burst, and looks back at a large television screen of Big Daddy capitalism's rise and fall, this diminutive female figure asks why things are the way they are? From Prebble's anorexic Dani to Skilling's girl-child, both of whom resonate with the "frightening" girl futures represented by the fragile Muriel in *This is a Chair* and figured throughout Churchill's theatre, the vulnerability of the feminine forced to consume, to feed from Big Daddy's dinner plate, is made visible.

The why of the Enron president's daughter could also be the why of Prebble's girl-power generation of women dramatists.[64] Described as "in the vanguard of young women playwrights – including Polly Stenham, Rebecca Lenkiewicz, and Ella Hickson – who have begun to force their work on to the London stage,"[65] Prebble acknowledges, but at the same time finds it hard to account for, the persistent gender inequalities of the theatre profession that keeps women's work out of "main spaces": "it is scandalous, because you are getting such a one-eyed view of the world in your art, in films in particular. Only half of the world is being asked to do the looking, you know." Like generations of women playwrights before her, Prebble adheres to "the idea that there is nowhere a writer, particularly a woman writer, should not go,"[66] as reflected in the move between her debut representation of a disenfranchised feminine and the Enron world of corporate greed. Yet at the same time, her generation, like generations of women playwrights before her, remains constrained by the gender inequalities that mean that there are places/spaces where it is not possible, as a *woman* playwright, to go – or to go in numbers sufficient to challenge the predominantly "one-eyed [male-dominated] view of the world."

Despite these gender limitations, women playwrights continue with their titanic efforts to force their way onto the British stage. Moreover, the cross-generational feminist connections between Churchill and Kane, the disinterment of Kane and tucker green from in-yer-face-ism, and the constructing of a genealogy of experiential women's playwriting from the 1990s onward all argue for contemporary women's playwriting as characterized by *feeling* the loss of feminism. While McRobbie traces the "illegible rage" of a postfeminist feminine in mainstream culture, what all of these women playwrights share in their very different implicit or explicit ways is a commitment to making that rage legible and *felt*.

Notes

My heartfelt thanks go to Jill Dolan and Janelle Reinelt for their invaluable comments and insights that helped with the drafting of this essay, and to Penny Farfan and Lesley Ferris for being such meticulous editors.

1 Ann McFerran, "The Theatre's (Somewhat) Angry Young Women," *Time Out*, 26 October–3 November 1977, 13–15.
2 Heidi Stephenson and Natasha Langridge, *Rage and Reason: Women Playwrights on Playwriting* (London: Methuen, 1997).
3 Ibid., ix.
4 Ibid., xi.
5 Ibid., xii.
6 Quoted in Stephenson and Langridge, *Rage and Reason,* 134.
7 Quoted in McFerran, "The Theatre's (Somewhat) Angry Young Women," 13.
8 Ibid.
9 Ibid. (emphasis added).
10 Sara Ahmed, *The Cultural Politics of Emotion* (Edinburgh: Edinburgh University Press, 2004), 6 (emphasis in original).
11 Angela McRobbie, *The Aftermath of Feminism: Gender, Culture and Social Change* (London: Sage, 2009), 1.
12 Ahmed, *Cultural Politics of Emotion,* 6.
13 Sarah Kane, personal letter to Aleks Sierz, 18 January 1999.
14 A seminal reference point for this is Susan Faludi's *Backlash: The Undeclared War against Women* (New York: Crown, 1991).
15 For instance, a democratic politics arguably is what Churchill had in mind when she described "the kind of society [she] would like: decentralized, nonauthoritarian, communist – a society in which people can be in touch with their feelings, and in control of their lives." Churchill, interviewed by Judith Thurman, "The Playwright Who Makes You Laugh about Orgasm, Racism, Class Struggle, Homophobia, Woman-Hating, the British Empire, and the Irrepressible Strangeness of the Human Heart," *Ms.*, May 1982, 54.
16 Loren Kruger reminds us that the first English translation of *Verfremdung* was "dis-illu-sion" and returns to this in favor of "alienation" as a more accurate means of rendering the sense of *"critical estrangement"* Brecht was seeking; see Kruger, "Democratic Actors and Post-apartheid Drama: Contesting Performance in Contemporary South Africa," in *Contesting Performance: Global Sites of Research*, ed. Jon McKenzie, Heike Roms, and C. J. W.-L. Wee (Basingstoke, UK: Palgrave Macmillan, 2010), 239.
17 Janelle Reinelt, "Navigating Postfeminism: Writing Out of the Box," in *Feminist Futures?: Theatre, Performance, Theory*, ed. Elaine Aston and Geraldine Harris (Basingstoke, UK: Palgrave Macmillan, 2006), 20.
18 Caryl Churchill, *This is a Chair* (London: Nick Hern Books, 1999), 11, 28.
19 Ibid.
20 McRobbie, *Aftermath of Feminism*, 100.
21 Elaine Aston, "Sarah Kane: The 'bad girl of our stage'?" in *Feminist Views on the English Stage: Women Playwrights, 1990–2000*, Cambridge Studies in Modern Theatre (Cambridge: Cambridge University Press, 2003), 77–97.
22 Aleks Sierz, *In-Yer-Face Theatre: British Drama Today* (London: Faber & Faber, 2000), 5.
23 Ibid., 244.
24 David Riesman, "Foreword," in Stjepan G. Meštrović, *Postemotional Society* (London: Sage Publications, 1997), ix.
25 Meštrović, *Postemotional Society*, 66.
26 Ibid., 26.

27 Ibid., 66.
28 In this regard, see Alicia Tycer's highly insightful analysis of Kane's *4.48 Psychosis* in her "'Victim. Perpetrator. Bystander': Melancholic Witnessing of Sarah Kane's *4.48 Psychosis*," *Theatre Journal* 60, no. 1 (2008): 23–36.
29 Sarah Kane, *Blasted,* in *Complete Plays* (London: Methuen, 2001), 12.
30 Churchill, *This is a Chair,* 7.
31 Meštrović, *Postemotional Society,* 125. The second media moment is the O. J. Simpson trial.
32 Like most playwrights, Kane was reluctant to talk about the meaning of her work. On the other hand, she was self-disclosing about the genesis of *Blasted.* For details, see Sierz, "Sarah Kane," in *In-Yer-Face Theatre,* 90–121, esp. 100–101.
33 Churchill, *This is a Chair,* 8.
34 Kane, letter to Sierz, 18 January 1999.
35 Kane, *Blasted,* 50.
36 The relative lack of critical attention to Cate's rape and the manner of its unseen representation is addressed by Kim Solga in "*Blasted*'s Hysteria: Rape, Realism, and the Thresholds of the Visible," *Modern Drama* 50, no. 3 (2007): 346–74.
37 See Elaine Aston, "Reviewing the Fabric of *Blasted*," in *Sarah Kane in Context,* ed. Laurens De Vos and Graham Saunders (Manchester: Manchester University Press, 2010), 13–27.
38 See Meštrović, *Postemotional Society,* 26.
39 Katie Roiphe, *The Morning After: Sex, Fear, and Feminism* (London: Hamish Hamilton, 1994), 84.
40 Ibid., 56.
41 Roiphe's "the-rape-that-never-was" stance feeds into what Solga critiques as "rape's history of cultural disavowal." Solga's persuasive and thought-provoking analysis of *Blasted* argues that through Kane's representation of Cate's unseen rape, "*Blasted* makes not just Cate's rape but the rape's very disappearance one of the central subjects of its political critique"; see Solga, "*Blasted*'s Hysteria," 355.
42 For details, see Sierz, *In-Yer-Face Theatre,* 98.
43 Kane, quoted in Stephenson and Langridge, *Rage and Reason,* 131.
44 Quoted in Sierz, *In-Yer-Face Theatre,* 106.
45 Ann Cvetkovich, *An Archive of Feelings: Trauma, Sexuality, and Lesbian Public Cultures* (Durham, NC: Duke University Press, 2003), 9.
46 Rebecca Prichard, personal communication (e-mail) with author, 23 August 2010.
47 Rebecca Prichard, quoted in Elaine Aston and Geraldine Harris, "Giving Voice(s) to Others," in *Performance Practice and Process: Contemporary [Women] Practitioners* (Basingstoke, UK: Palgrave Macmillan, 2008), 129.
48 Ibid., 124.
49 Rebecca Prichard, *Yard Gal* (London: Faber & Faber, 1998), 55.
50 Ibid., 6.
51 Michael Billington, "Review: *Hamlet/Confidence*: Birmingham Rep," *Guardian,* 26 September 1998, 13.
52 Rebecca D'Monté, "Thatcher's Children: Alienation and Anomie in the Plays of Judy Upton," in *Cool Britannia?,* 93.
53 Originally, the play was performed as just one act. The gender-reversed doubling of the script was introduced when the play transferred from the Edinburgh Festival in 2007 to the Royal Court in 2008.
54 See Aleks Sierz, "'We All Need Stories': The Politics of In-Yer-Face Theatre," in *Cool Britannia?,* 34.
55 Lynette Goddard, *Staging Black Feminisms: Identity, Politics, Performance* (Basingstoke, UK: Palgrave Macmillan, 2007), 185. Goddard specifies "Jamaican poet Louise Bennett, African-American poet-playwright Ntozake Shange, and rapper/singers such as Lauryn Hill, Beverley Knight and Jill Scott."
56 debbie tucker green, *Stoning Mary* (London: Nick Hern Books, 2005), 2.

57 On this point, see also Ken Urban, "Cruel Britannia," in *Cool Britannia?*, 52.

58 Meštrović, *Postemotional Society*, 26.

59 Ahmed explains how "objects become sticky, or saturated with affect, as sites of personal and social tension"; see Ahmed, *Cultural Politics of Emotion*, 11.

60 tucker green, *Stoning Mary*, 3,

61 Ibid., 4.

62 Ibid., 61–62.

63 McRobbie, *Aftermath of Feminism*, 122.

64 See Tim Adams, "I hate to be told somewhere is out of bounds for women," interview with Lucy Prebble, *Observer*, 5 July 2009, available at *http://www.guardian.co.uk/stage/2009/jul/05/lucy-prebble-playwright-interview-enron* (accessed 15 July 2010).

65 Ibid.

66 Ibid.

2 Female Alliances and Women's Histories in Contemporary Mexican and Argentine Drama

Ana Elena Puga

> Who am I?
> Who are we?
> Because although the journey may be individual, the destination/destiny is collective.
>
> > –Patricia Zangaro, *A propósito de la duda*
> > (Apropos of Doubt, 2000)[1]

Individual journeys often lead to collective destinations, or destinies, because of alliances formed along the way. In Latin America, in response to stunning examples of state-sanctioned and state-tolerated violence against women, some extremely effective alliances have been formed by the survivors, as well as by the mothers, and in some cases also the sisters and daughters, of the victims who did not survive. Yet such alliances are sometimes far from perfect examples of utopian power-sharing. Indeed, as Aimee Carrillo Rowe notes, alliances between women are not necessarily always inclusive and transformative. On the contrary, she argues: "Feminism itself is a site of political contestation in which power relations are reproduced along lines of race and class, nation and sexuality."[2] As the work of sociologists Elizabeth Borland and Barbara Sutton on women who participated in protests after Argentina's economic collapse in late 2001 has shown, women from different class backgrounds were able to come together for a common cause and yet remained acutely aware of their divergent economic origins and differing levels of privilege.[3] Borland and Sutton write: "The crisis brought people with diverse agendas and backgrounds together and meant that activists had to handle tensions and negotiate their visions, political histories, and social locations."[4]

I look here at works by four of Latin America's most prominent contemporary female playwrights – three stage plays and one screenplay – in order to consider how they stage the tensions and negotiations intrinsic to the formation of alliances between and among women. Building on Carrillo Rowe, who in turn relies heavily on the work of Chela Sandoval, I define alliances as the conditions under which competition and power struggles are at least temporarily trumped by commonality of purpose, often a purpose that attempts to transform the relationship between an individual and an institution.[5] As Carrillo Rowe writes: "Alliances are the interface between intimacy and institutionality...What kind of power is transmitted through those connections and whose interests are served?"[6] And like Carrillo Rowe, I am just as interested in the limits of female, and feminist, alliances as in their possibilities: Where and why does cooperation break down? What are the obstacles that defeat idealistic dreams of solidarity? Does the above epigraph about individual journeys leading to collective destinations/destinies in fact reflect what Patricia Zangaro and the other women playwrights discussed in this essay demonstrate in their works? And finally, how do these playwrights themselves forge feminist alliances by representing women, particularly women-in-history?

In Mexico, Estela Leñero Franco's *Las máquinas de coser* (The Sewing Machines, 1989) and Sabina Berman's screenplay *Backyard/El Traspatio* (2004) both concern violence against women factory workers. Leñero depicts a small Mexico City sweatshop, with its dividing and conquering of female workers by a male manager, in the hours just before the devastating 1985 earthquake that took some 10,000 lives. Fifteen years later, after three consecutive Mexican presidencies aggressively pursued neoliberal privatization, and after the North American Free Trade Agreement (1994) nourished a massive assembly plant industry on the northern border that in turn spawned record levels of violence against women in Ciudad Juárez, Berman's screenplay critiques a labor environment so dangerous for women that it makes the exploitation depicted in *Máquinas* seem almost quaint by comparison. Directed by Carlos Carrera, coproduced by Berman herself, and distributed by Paramount Pictures in Mexico in 2009, *Backyard* also demonstrates a marked skepticism, maybe even cynicism, about the efficacy of alliances between women to address "femicide" in Juárez.[7]

The Argentine plays discussed here also focus on women's labor and on women's limited room for maneuver, yet they are more intimate and smaller in scale than the Mexican works. If the Mexican works show us women in public spaces so dominated by the demands of labor in ruthlessly capitalist structures that they are denied the "luxury" of healthy private spaces, the Argentine works show us women trapped in more private spaces nevertheless finding ways to make themselves heard in male-dominated public realms. With only a couple of characters each, these all-women microcosmic universes relegate male characters and male-dominated power structures to offstage roles. Written in two different versions with alternative endings, Patricia Suárez's *El tapadito* (The Little Coat, 2004, 2006) indicates ambivalence about the prospects for even a tenuous alliance between two German immigrants in postwar Argentina who were on opposite sides of the Holocaust. By contrast, Patricia Zangaro's short one-act *Tiempo de aguas* (The Rainy Season, 2004) creates a far more optimistic allegorical world in which an older woman and her prospective daughter-in-law forge an alliance across generations that leads to the writing of women into history.

Mexico and Argentina are among a handful of Latin American nations that boast rich dramatic canons to which women have consistently contributed throughout the twentieth and twenty-first centuries.[8] Despite their many obvious differences in styles, genres, themes, and national cultures, with only fourteen years in age difference among them, Leñero (1960–), Berman (1955–), Suárez (1969–), and Zangaro (1958–) form part of a generation of roughly contemporary Latin American women playwrights. All clearly recognize the larger value of alliances between women, even when they lament their fragility or limited efficacy rather than celebrate their tenuous existence. A devastating Mexico City earthquake, the years of killing of women in Ciudad Juárez, the aftermath of the Holocaust, and a flood of biblical proportions – disasters real and imaginary – are represented here from the perspective of female protagonists who find it difficult or impossible to unite to avoid annihilation and erasure from history.

Máquinas: motherhood as collective identity

Estela Leñero wrote her Bachelor's thesis in anthropology on women workers and was inspired to write *Las máquinas de coser* by newspaper accounts of the ruins of sweatshops discovered in the aftermath of the earthquake that shook Mexico City on 19 September 1985. Still, the play is not docudrama or even entirely realistic.[9] On the one hand, the stage directions describe the set in realistic detail as the interior of a run-down clothing factory, the kind of small business known as a *"taller."*[10] On the other hand, they also specify that a child who is responded to only by the women characters moves among a group of at least nine workers. José, the boss, cannot see the child, a boy who seems to be of elementary-school age. The male workers, who are in the minority, can see the child but do not respond to him. Other scenes play out the women's fantasies about romantic dalliances and transform the workplace into a bar for a party. Yet Leñero specifies in the stage directions that while the scenes that give the spectator insight into the interior life of the women represent desires, memories, or obsessions, they should nevertheless be staged in a "totally realistic" manner (9), with the same intensity as the scenes involving their daily factory work. Thus the intersecting realms of work and fantasy constitute two competing realities.

In the realm of work, a system of intense surveillance pits the women against each other. José, the factory supervisor, assigns Cristina, the newest employee, the dreaded task of keeping a notebook in which she is supposed to keep tabs on each worker's rate of production, the degree to which she makes mistakes, and various other statistics useful as ammunition when it comes time to fire someone. If any alliance is forged under this routine of surveillance and control, it is an alliance against Cristina on the part of the other women, who of course resent her role in their exploitation. The notebook emblematizes a regime of increased surveillance over workers that began to take effect in Mexico after the debt crisis of 1982, when neoliberal adjustment policies curtailed the power of unions and increased pressure to produce at ever-higher rates. At the same time, salaries stagnated and unemployment rose, making it easier to dismiss any worker who protested. Cristina dutifully, docilely records workplace statistics in her notebook in the vain hope that she may one day be promoted to an assignment on a sewing machine, where she might actually produce a useful material good and escape the wrath of her coworkers.

The other ways for women to get ahead in this dystopia include having sex with the boss and undermining each other's job security. José threatens to fire one worker, Margarita, unless she comes in early to have sex with him, a demand to which she reluctantly acquiesces. Two other workers, Isabel and Toña, develop a rivalry over the affections of a male worker that escalates into sabotage of each other's work. Toña in the end manages to get José to fire her rival. Such conditions of impunity, of the tolerance of illegal behavior, which Ileana Rodríguez rightly argues have been exposed by cultural texts that relate the *maquilas*, as the assembly plants are called, with femicide in Juárez,[11] are already denounced in Leñero's play, making it seem prescient of the violence that in the 1990s became an even more prominent facet of the lives of Mexican women factory workers. In *Máquinas*, criminal behavior like sexual coercion and dismissal without cause is indulged in by the male supervisor, José, who in turn derives his authority from a mysterious offstage boss known only by his professional title, "*licenciado*," which is emblematic of the powerful educated class that controls the state and the realm of politics.[12] The bodies of the women become nothing more than machines, like the sewing machines, objects to be used and discarded as necessary, as Marxist analysis reminds us, by the owners of the means of production. The possibilities for alliances among the women are thus limited to the occasional kindness, such as teaching one another sewing skills; more effective horizontal affiliations are impossible.

The sole point of connection for the women in *Máquinas* is the boy, with whom only the female characters relate and interact. The boy appears on stage three times. The first time, as the son of a character named Rachel, he warns his mother that his younger brother is getting sicker and sicker. Rachel nevertheless cannot risk losing her job by leaving work to take him to the doctor. The second time the boy appears, he is Margarita's son, inviting her to play ball with him. The third time he appears, he interrupts the factory routine with play, climbing atop a table, arms out to his sides to imitate an airplane. The three women who bring him down from the table and scold him in a motherly way are minor characters identified only as workers: "Obrera [Worker] I," "Obrera II," and "Obrera III" (81–82). The women's generic names, coupled with the boy's lack of a name, imbue him with allegorical significance as the son of all women workers everywhere. The female characters' desire to care for him romanticizes motherhood as an essentialized point of connection among all women, a point of connection that at least forms the basis of a collective identity, even if alliance or resistance is out of the question. In this regard, Leñero's play is uncannily suggestive of the coalition-building around motherhood that began to take hold in Mexico in the 1990s.

The play's apocalyptic ending, as the earthquake begins and the factory's roof caves in, might seem to suggest that feminist alliances would in any case have been futile against the overwhelming force of natural disaster. The characters that were fired would, ironically, have had a better chance of survival than those who remained inside the factory. Yet I would instead read the final catastrophe as a symbolic expression of a utopian hope for the collapse of the corrupt political system that allowed sweatshops to thrive. The collapse of one-party rule in Mexico was infamously heralded by a crash announced by the government itself during the 1988 election, when it stopped the computerized vote count to manipulate the election results and prevaricated that the system had "crashed." The crash of the Partido Revolucionario Institucional (PRI) (Institutional Revolutionary Party) system that eventually led to its first *acknowledged* electoral defeat in 2000 began in the wake of the earthquake with community-organizing to help the tens of thousands left homeless. While some scholars and activists argue that the solidarity following the earthquake was short-lived and has had limited lasting impact, it appeared at least for a time to live up to the "landmark of social awakening" description bestowed upon it by historian Enrique Krauze.[13] *Máquinas* imagines, and in a sense documents, the last moments before that catastrophic awakening from the perspective of the women workers who did not survive to tell their own history.

Backyard: sterile alliances and reimagining history

Titled with an ironic appropriation of the derogatory term some US politicians use to refer to Mexico, Sabina Berman's *Backyard* focuses not on the small family-owned sweatshops of Mexico City but on the giant corporate network of global assembly plants along the Mexico-US border that, despite their ostensible legality, are clearly implicated in transnational illegality. The liberating potential that neoliberalism held for some women workers has been tainted by the hundreds of killings that it has also unleashed since the early 1990s. Known for her 1990s stage plays that critiqued neoliberalism with lighthearted yet biting humor, such as *Entre Villa y una mujer desnuda* (Between Pancho Villa and a Naked Woman, 1993), *La grieta* (The Crack, 1994), and *Krisis* ([Crisis spelled with a "K"], 1996), in this recent screenplay Berman adopts a far grimmer tone.

Backyard's female heroine, Blanca Bravo, is a 35-year-old policewoman who comes across several potential allies, both male and female, during the course of the action, yet ultimately chooses to take the road of individual revenge. Shortly after she begins to investigate the serial murders of women in Ciudad Juárez, Blanca's own cousin, Juana, a young maquiladora worker, is raped and murdered. Blanca then takes it upon herself to execute both her cousin's killer and another man, a serial killer responsible for the deaths of many other women. The film thus addresses a real-world, ongoing femicide with a fantasy of individual action-and-adventure that neatly solves the situation before the protagonist departs for her next assignment in Merida. It is difficult to ascertain whether the film supports vigilantism or critiques it. Either way, after the satisfaction of onscreen rough justice has faded, real-life lack of justice continues: as of this writing, according to *The New York Times*, about sixty women and girls were killed in 2012 in Juárez, a city with a population of about 1.3 million.[14]

Like the young British women playwrights Elaine Aston describes as "feeling the loss of feminism,"[15] Berman makes her rage legible and felt. Rather than lament a loss of feminist solidarity, however, she instead creates an alternative world in which such solidarity is superfluous and not nearly as powerful or attractive as the thrill of individual revenge. Indeed, the screenplay reveals a deep ambivalence about the value of alliances between or among women.

Blanca's strongest ally is Ester Chávez, a character modeled after the actual director of a non-profit organization, Casa Amiga, founded in Juárez in 1999 to combat violence against women. The historical figure, Esther Chávez, died in 2009 at the age of 76, whereas her fictional rendering is described as over 70, small, fragile, "with the energy of a hurricane."[16] The screenplay depicts Casa Amiga attracting liberal foreign donors, as a visitor from Holland tours the facility and offers to fund the organization for yet another year. In the screenplay, the director of Casa Amiga, like her real-life counterpart, meticulously compiles all the press information on the killings of women in Juárez, something the police failed to do. In the screenplay, however, Chávez has an opportunity that Chávez never had in real life: she shares her records with the policewoman, who uses them to pursue her investigation. Despite her good intentions and best efforts, however, Chávez remains powerless to protect one of her clients, Karen, from being murdered. The do-gooders are not nearly as effective as the pistol-packing Bravo.

What to make of this feminist alliance between two characters, one entirely fictional and one very closely based on an actual person? In "Feminist Performance as Feminist Historiography," Charlotte Canning suggests: "Through the connections between the audience and the performer(s), performed history can actively place the past in the community context of present time."[17] What happens, though, when the historical figure is brought into the present time in a screenplay as the relatively impotent ally of a more powerful fictional character? On the one hand, it may enhance the actual person's fame, influence, and prestige to be featured in a positive light in a widely distributed commercial film. On the other hand, it seems problematic to simultaneously depict the real person's approach to activism as flawed or ineffective, while celebrating the fictional character's flouting of the rule of law as efficacious violence necessary for the attainment of justice. Indeed, until she begins to resort to her less savory tactics, Bravo is also impotent. In one scene, after she accompanies Chávez and the mothers to a memorial service in the desert, she even makes a dark joke about the supposed futility of the efforts she and Ester make: "Now we've perfected the funeral service, Ester. I pick them up, you bury them" (129). With the help of Ester's information, however, Blanca delves further into her investigation, plants evidence to facilitate the arrest of a suspect, and eventually gets her men – not through the corrupt justice system, but through the barrel of a gun. In the rising action leading to the climactic executions, spectators are pulled into stomach-turning scenes of teenage women raped repeatedly, mutilated, and, in the case of Blanca's cousin Juana, asphyxiated. The gruesome detail invites spectators, particularly female spectators, to feel revulsion and rage against the male perpetrators, to identify with Blanca, and to cheer on her Rambo-like antics. The film produces intense affect, yet fails to create what Laura Podalsky, borrowing from Arjun Appadurai, calls "communities of sentiment," global affective alliances that "allow for the transfusion of alternate traditions of feeling," such as those created by films like Lourdes Portillo's documentary about femicide in Juárez, *Señorita extraviada*.[18] Instead, the ending of *Backyard* furthers the opposite of community – an atomized emotional response, an individual anger that precludes alliance. As if to exemplify this atomization, while Blanca conducts her investigation, Ester retreats from the fray and goes to visit her sister in Florida.

Another group of women in the screenplay are depicted as something of a powerless Greek chorus: the mothers of the murdered women, who appear clad in black, say little, and devote themselves to mourning their lost daughters by planting crosses in the desert to commemorate the dead. The relationship between Ester and the mothers is depicted as an even more sterile alliance than the Ester-Blanca partnership. Toward the end of the film, after Blanca has executed the murderous men, Ester returns from Florida to Juárez and, according to the scene description, "continues in the wandering of lost causes" as she joins a public protest composed of women dressed in black carrying placards with slogans such as "No more" and "Not one more death" (178–79). While the mothers of the murdered women and Ester are left behind in Juárez, as if frozen in time and place, the fictional character moves on to her next assignment.

Mother-activists are of course a very real presence in Juárez, as well as in Central and South America. Activist alliances based on motherhood were only hinted at as a dreamlike possibility in Leñero's *Máquinas*; by the time Berman wrote *Backyard*, they had become a historical phenomenon, from Argentina to El Salvador to northern Mexico. Melissa Wright argues that the "politics of mother-activism" couches radical demands within the conservative demeanor of women who have been obliged by government inaction to forsake their domestic roles and claim space in the public sphere:

> Their politics rests on a plea for the government to create the conditions by which they can return home. Thus it is their presence on the street that exposes the social perversion, not because the mothers are socially perverse but because the situation has forced them, against the natural order of things, to leave their homes. In this way, the mothers articulate that their politics is a reaction to a state that neither protects nor holds sacred the patriarchal family but instead creates conditions that force women to leave their homes and look for their children.[19]

Perhaps it is the conservative foundation upon which mother-activists articulate their demands that Berman reacts against when she represents them as a dull background lament to Blanca Bravo's flashier heroism. Bravo, whose last name means "courage" or "fierceness" and whose first name means "white," perhaps ironically invoking purity, makes no apologies for her aggressive tactics in the public sphere. Her choice of career as a police officer and her lack of hesitation to use violence as a means to an end have both traditionally been considered the prerogative of men. Moreover, her ultimate eschewal of alliances in favor of individual tactics has also often been gendered male, particularly in the tradition of the superhero.

Does *Backyard* then imply that we need a Lone Ranger of a super-woman to fight fire with fire, intervene in history, and save the innocent daughters of Juárez from evil men? Or does it merely indulge in a respite from historical reality, a fantasy of "wouldn't it be nice if it were this simple"? One might argue that Berman poses an ethical dilemma, asking spectators to consider whether Bravo's ends justify her means. But building on the observations of Priscilla Meléndez, I would contend that while some spectators might be provoked to soul-search, in the end, the perspective of the film comes through clearly in the voice of one of the characters, the radio show host Peralta, who lauds Bravo: "Maybe you are using twisted methods in a twisted society, but your goals are noble" (163). Whether on the factory floor or in the streets, the screenplay seems to conclude that feel-good feminist solidarity just won't cut it in a world dominated by male cutthroats. Yet even in this very dark screenplay, Berman's attempt to reveal the plight of the Juárez maquiladora workers to a wide popular audience itself constitutes an act of feminist solidarity and feminist resistance to a stronghold of US-supported neoliberal globalization. Unfortunately, though the film was Mexico's entry into the 2009 Academy Awards for Best Foreign Picture and was distributed in Mexico by Paramount, it never found a US distributor and so was never widely seen in US movie theatres.

El tapadito: false alliance, revenge, and the scars of history

Like Leñero's and Berman's works, the Argentine plays analyzed here hold out tenuous hope for efficacious feminist alliances. Suárez's *El tapadito*, for instance, centers on a protagonist who at first seeks revenge yet later comes to realize the limits of revenge to make her whole again – physically or psychologically. Written in 2004, the play was first staged in Buenos Aires's Teatro del Pueblo in 2005, under the direction of Hugo Urquijo. Its title means "the little coat" or "the short coat," yet it is important to note that the root of the word *tapadito* is the verb "*tapar*," to cover. Set in 1954, the play involves the cover-ups of the postwar era and unfolds in San Fernando, an actual suburb of Buenos Aires. The action takes place entirely in the attic workspace of an apparently Catholic German immigrant seamstress, Leni, who offers to help her only slightly better-off client, Vera, to escape from her abusive, violent husband Otto, a former Nazi official, and return to her parents in Germany. Yet it turns out that Leni is actually not Catholic or German: she is a Polish Jew who, during the Holocaust, was sent by Otto to a Nazi concentration camp for medical experiments where she was forced to serve as a guinea pig for Nazi scientists. Vera knows nothing about Leni's past with Otto, which makes it easy for Leni to secretly plot revenge: she takes the money that Vera has given her to arrange her ship's passage, pockets the cash, and sends Vera's husband an anonymous note claiming that his wife has taken a lover. With the note, Leni hopes to lure Otto to her attic, where she plans to kill him. But Otto, realizing that his Nazi past has been discovered, instead beats Vera brutally and then takes all of their valuables and flees Buenos Aires.

Suárez wrote two versions of the play with different endings: in one version, staged in 2005 and available online, Vera confronts Leni in the last scene, yet the two women somehow manage to come to an understanding and even agree to live and work together, at least for a time.[20] In another version, published in 2006 in an anthology titled *La Germania*, Vera calls Leni a "shitty Jew" and demands her money back; Leni refuses to return Vera's money, and the play ends in a stalemate.[21] According to Suárez, the latter version is the "real" one.[22] The bleak ending was actually the original but was revised to end on an upbeat for the 2005 production, at the suggestion of the director, Urquijo: "To him it seemed that it had to have a more conciliatory ending, in which both women recognize them-selves as victims of that man. I don't know if that is possible."[23]

As Suárez's reflection indicates, *El tapadito*'s alternative endings demonstrate ambivalence about the prospects for successful feminist alliances in the wake of historical trauma. Even in the more optimistic version, the alliance between the women does not surmount or transcend differences in class or religious identi-ties, but operates in spite of them. And in the more pessimistic version, what appears to be an alliance (Leni will help Vera return to Germany) turns out to be a sham that destroys any semblance of an understanding between the women. Still, as with Berman, I would argue that the feminist alliance that matters most is Suárez's commitment to staging history from the perspective of two types of women who would otherwise have been sidelined or overlooked entirely.

Suárez's work inserts women into two different historical periods, the post-World War II moment of 1950s Argentina in which the play is set and the first decade of the twenty-first century in which the play was written and staged. Argentina was notorious after World War II for how it served as a haven for promi-nent Nazi war criminals, including, most famously, Adolf Eichmann, who lived in San Fernando under the alias Ricardo Klement until he was finally captured by the Israeli secret service in 1960. Suárez has written two plays about Eichmann, *Herr Klement* (2006, with Leonel Giacometto) and *Rudolf*, which was published along with *El tapadito* in the *La Germania* anthology. *El tapadito* diverges from these other Suárez plays about the Nazi era, and from much cultural production about Nazi Argentina, in that it does not focus on the infamous Eichmann, but on the lower-ranking, fictional official she calls "Otto" (though Otto's wife's name, Vera, happens to have been the actual name of Eichmann's wife). More impor-tantly, Suárez does not dwell on the heroic male action-and-adventure story of the pursuit and capture of the Nazi war criminal popularized in narratives such as Neal Bascomb's *Hunting Eichmann: How a Band of Survivers and a Young Spy Agency Chased Down the World's Most Notorious Nazi* (2009) or Uki Goñi's *The Real Odessa: Smuggling Nazis to Peron's Argentina* (2002). In *El tapadito*, women dominate the onstage space, an attic that is very private and yet also public in the sense that it functions as a business and takes in clients from the outside; completely public realms such as streets or cafés, like the male characters, remain offstage. Instead of highlighting the male villain, Suárez focuses on the impact of the villain on the two women who have had significant relationships with him.

This is history from below, from the perspective of anonymous women, with an emphasis on how historical events have shaped their biographies and their bodies. In the version of the play that was staged in 2005, Leni, we learn, had her child stolen from her in the concentration camp and given up for adoption. In the last scene of the play, she opens her dress to reveal a scar that, according to the stage directions, "runs along the length of her body like a worm, it is a very impressive scar."[24] Leni bears the scars of the Holocaust on her body; they mark her as a victim/survivor and serve both to connect her to Vera and to structure a moment of competition with her, as Leni reveals her scar so as to upstage Vera's display of the welts from where Otto has whipped her with a riding crop. To a greater or lesser extent, history is written on the bodies of both women.[25]

For Buenos Aires audiences who saw El tapadito, more recent history must also have been evoked by the display of physical traces of brutality and by the trope of the child taken away from its mother. By 2005 it was common knowledge that during the so-called Dirty War, between 1976 and 1983, an estimated 500 children were stolen from their "disappeared" parents and given to families of police or military officers in illegal adoptions. In El tapadito, the missing child is given a ghostly existence as Leni keeps up the pretense for a while that he is still alive, a teenager now, who is supposedly given to spying on her clients as they change for their fittings. The figure of the missing child imbricates two historical moments, the Holocaust and the post-dictatorship era in Argentina, from the perspective of the mothers who were victimized in both conflicts. While Jews were not explicitly targeted during the Dirty War, they did suffer persecution disproportionately to their representation in the population, and anti-Semitism plagues Argentina even today. Suárez, the daughter of a Jewish mother and a Catholic father, is of course aware of the fraught history of Jews in Argentine society.

Religious difference is perhaps the greatest obstacle to détente between the two characters. Vera, we learn from various disparaging remarks she makes about Jews, has absorbed the anti-Semitism of World War II Germany. Leni at first tries to hide her Jewish ethnicity but eventually gives up the pretense and acknowledges her Judaism. In the 2005 version of the play, Vera's response is hardly a liberal embrace, yet she proposes that Leni repay the money she has taken from her by giving her room and board:

VERA: I don't hate you.
LENI: This house isn't for a lady like you.
VERA: If he hadn't killed them, I would have brought the hens.
LENI: Here?
VERA: What? Now Jews don't eat chicken?[26]

In an attempt to establish a bond with Leni, Vera makes an awkward joke about Jewish dietary restrictions, displaying a sense of humor and taking a stab at friendship with a Jew, an attempt that would have been unthinkable for her character at the start of the action. In addition to religion, social class emerges as a further obstacle to the women's potential bond: "This house isn't for a *lady* like you." In the end, the realization that each woman can contribute to the economic survival of the other sidelines social class distinctions and the two women decide to live and work together, at least for a time. This unlikely coalition recalls some of the alliances forged by women of different classes during protests following Argentina's economic collapse in late 2001. As sociologists Borland and Sutton have detailed, women from different class backgrounds came together in many of the 12,766 street protests staged in Argentina in just the first eight months of 2002.[27]

But even more than class differences, Leni's desire for revenge is the greatest resentment that must be defused in order for the two women to bond. Leni goes beyond wanting to shame Otto, she wants to kill him, yet in the end gives up on that hope: "I thought that in vengeance I could be a perfect machine. What a dreamer."[28] Leni is a woman who would like to kill but misses the opportunity. By failing to accomplish the murder of Otto, she "fails" to make herself a criminal and exclude herself from Argentine immigrant society.[29] Whether she wants to or not, almost against her will, she assimilates to the postwar social order. Even in the second version of the play, in which Leni refuses to come to any sort of understanding with Vera, she still does not manage to take the law into her own hands. While in this sense Leni differs from Berman's Blanca Bravo, this world, like the world of Bravo's Ciudad Juárez, like the world of vigilantes everywhere, is one in which the power of the nation-state seems inadequate to the task of the pursuit of justice. The state never seems to intervene in this theatrical universe: neither of the characters, for instance, ever threatens to call the police.

In Argentina in the 1990s and early 2000s, outraged citizens frustrated by laws that guaranteed impunity to former torturers took it upon themselves to organize demonstrations, known as "escraches," intended to shame former Dirty War criminals who had not been prosecuted. The version of the play in which the women end in stalemate rather than reconciliation, in which differences in religion and class are not circumvented, in which the desire for revenge overcomes any impulses toward reconciliation, is perhaps most consonant with the spirit of those times. Moreover, as in Suárez's trilogy *Las polacas* (The Polish Women, 2002), about young Eastern European Jewish immigrant women in the early twentieth century who were sold into prostitution in Buenos Aires with the collaboration of older women, feminist alliances in *El tapadito* are also constrained by economic realities, as Leni steals Vera's money in part in order to survive. In these works, Suárez shows how not only gender, but also economic scarcity, social class, and religious practices can intersect to subvert any attempt at what Carrillo Rowe calls "coalitional subjectivity," or a sense of belonging-despite-otherness, that might hold the potential to redistribute power.

The Rainy Season: cross-generational alliances

While *El tapadito* raises questions of economic, religious, and class conflicts between women that impede constructive alliances, Zangaro's *Tiempo de aguas* raises questions of generational conflict. By contrast to *El tapadito*, *Tiempo de aguas* is not a realistic play rooted in a particular historical moment or in an actual location.[30] Instead, it is an allegorical work set in a place identified only as a house by the side of a river and a time identified only as the "rainy season." It is a time of floods and crisis, as signaled by the biblical echo in the title, "tiempo" meaning either "time" or "season" and thus bringing to mind Ecclesiastes 3: "To every thing there is a season and a time to every purpose under the heaven."[31] In fact, the title is borrowed from Ramón del Valle-Inclán's Spanish classic *Romance de lobos*, in which a female character in mourning named only "La Mujer" (The Woman) recalls both biblical and Greek tragic lament: "A time of waters!...A time of storms!...A cursed time!"[32]

For Zangaro's two characters, Old Woman and Young Woman, it is a cursed time because they have been cut off from the rest of the world by rising waters. They are separated from their men folk by a flooded valley. The young woman, we learn, is soon to become the old woman's daughter-in-law. The old woman knows how to read and write; the young woman does not but wants to learn, as an antidote to amnesia and a precaution against oblivion:

YOUNG WOMAN: What did you dream?
OLD WOMAN: I already forgot.
YOUNG WOMAN: Why didn't you write it down?
OLD WOMAN: What!
YOUNG WOMAN: If you had written it down you could remember it! I don't know how to write. I am afraid of forgetting everything.[33]

At first, the old woman is reluctant to teach the young woman skills that her father has said he does not want her to acquire, but eventually the old woman agrees and the young woman, in defiance of her father's wishes, begins to write, both for herself and for the other woman, who no longer writes and is slowly even losing her ability to read.

This mysterious short work, just twenty pages long, seems to be about the process of writing itself and about an anxiety of influence, as the younger generation must learn its skills from the older generation yet also has the ability to surpass its elders, or at least to compensate for their inevitable decline. For it is just as the older woman's faculties deteriorate that the younger woman takes up reading and writing. For the younger woman, suggests María Silvina Persino, writing is an act of resistance that serves to construct identity and memory.[34] Taking Persino's insight a step further, I would suggest that when one writes to create memory, one writes history: Zangaro implies that women can learn how to write history from other women. Significantly, Young Woman begins to write with needle and thread, through her embroidery, combining a craft traditionally practiced by women with an occupation traditionally gendered male. By the end of the play, the rising waters – in a catastrophe inspired by nature yet also unnatural in its violent consequences – begin to wash away everything, even the women's traces of themselves. As they run out of firewood and the situation becomes more dire, the younger woman's urge to write increases, though now she wants to write with ink on paper. Her father, she says, has disappeared under the waters. Soon he will exist only through Young Woman's writing, through stories called history, which will make her just as powerful, or more powerful, than he.

Identity, memory, and history passed from generation to generation are also the key themes of Zangaro's best-known play, *A propósito de la duda*. In 2000, Zangaro helped to kick off the Theatre for Identity movement in Buenos Aires with *A propósito*'s cross-generational cast of characters, including grandmothers of the Plaza de Mayo, a young man whose biological parents were "disappeared," the adoptive parents who illegitimately appropriated him, and a chorus of youth that repeatedly posed the question to spectators: "Do you know who you are?" With a very successful run that far exceeded the expectations of its creators, *A propósito* served to educate Buenos Aires audiences about the kidnappings and illegal adoptions that took place during the dictatorship of 1976–1984. Though it would be too much of a stretch to say that the old woman in *Tiempo de aguas* is a Mother, or a Grandmother, of the Plaza de Mayo, she does serve a similar function in a different context, in that she gives a woman from a younger generation the wherewithal to record her own history – even in violation of the law of the father. During dictatorship, the dominant male authorities defied by the Mothers of the Plaza de Mayo were the junta leaders, who forbade public demonstrations of dissent. In a far more delicate, less didactic style than *A propósito*, *Tiempo de aguas* also suggests that older women possess skills that we devalue or ignore at our own peril.

In the developing-world Latin American context, with its uneven modernity and often life-or-death stakes, the texts by Leñero, Berman, Suárez, and Zangaro that I have considered in this essay seem neither postfeminist nor in mourning for a loss of feminism. Instead, regardless of whether or not their authors self-identify as feminists, the texts assume a feminist stance as they question whether solidarity among women can actually save lives and help women find ways to survive, remember, and record their historical traumas. For the most part (with the exception of certain elements of Berman's screenplay), the works themselves constitute models of feminist alliance by how they create and/or promote women's history, offering the possibility of either staging that history for theatre audiences or filming it for a broader audience. The playwrights implicitly ally themselves with the type of women that they are concerned with: marginalized victims of violence. Even as they question, from a feminist position, whether feminism is possible, they demonstrate that it may well be.

Notes

I would like to thank Penny Farfan and Lesley Ferris for their excellent suggestions for revision. I am also grateful to Brenda Werth, who offered several helpful suggestions at the beginning of my research; her own work on Argentine theatre has been inspirational.

1 Patricia Zangaro, *A propósito de la duda*, 1, available at *http://www.teatroxlaindentidad.net* (accessed 1 September 2012); subsequent references to the play will be given parenthetically in the text. All translations from the plays discussed in this essay are my own. Zangaro's use of a single word in the original Spanish, *destino*, includes the meanings of both *destination* and *destiny*.

2 Aimee Carrillo Rowe, *Power Lines: On the Subject of Feminist Alliances* (Durham, NC: Duke University Press, 2008), 2.

3 Elizabeth Borland and Barbara Sutton, "Quotidian Disruption and Women's Activism in Times of Crisis, Argentina 2002–2003," *Gender and Society* 21, no. 5 (2007): 712–713.

4 Ibid., 713.

5 Chela Sandoval, *Methodology of the Oppressed* (Minneapolis: University of Minnesota Press, 2000).

6 Carrillo Rowe, *Power Lines*, 2.

7 While Berman is one of the most prolific and prominent playwrights in Mexico, she has long been a screenwriter as well and moves back and forth easily within the worlds of stage and screen.

8 It is important to note a significant difference between the role of theatre in Argentine and Mexican societies. In Argentina, especially in Buenos Aires, theatre is still central to middle-class cultural life and is attended by people of all ages. In Mexico, because theatre is more peripheral to mainstream middle-class culture, a well-known playwright such as Berman can ensure wider distribution of her cultural production by writing a screenplay for popular film.

9 See Estela Leñero, *El huso y el sexo: La mujer obrera en dos industrias de Tlaxcala* (Bachelor's thesis) (Mexico, DF: CIESAS, 1984) and Eduardo Cabrera, "Mujer e industria en *Las máquinas de coser* de Estela Leñero," *Revista de Literatura Mexicana Contemporánea* 8, no. 17 (2002): 25–33. Cabrera provides an in-depth study of how Leñero's Bachelor's thesis relates to the play. See also Myra S. Gann, "Masculine Space in the Plays of Estela Leñero," in *Latin American Women Dramatists: Theater, Texts, and Theories*, ed. Catherine Larson and Margarita Vargas (Bloomington: Indiana University Press, 1999), 234–242. Gann analyzes how space is gendered in *Máquinas*. Though *Máquinas* has not often been staged, it received a major production in 1994, when it was directed by Luis de Tavira for the Centro de Experimentación Teatral del Instituto Nacional de Bellas Artes in Mexico City.

10 Estela Leñero, *Las máquinas de coser* (Mexico City: Universidad Autónoma Metropolitana, 1989), 8–9; subsequent references to the play will be given parenthetically in the text.

11 Ileana Rodríguez, "Femicidio, or the Serial Killings of Women: Labor Shifts and Disempowered Subjects at the Border," *Liberalism at its Limits: Crime and Terror in the Latin American Cultural Text* (Pittsburgh, PA: University of Pittsburgh Press, 2009), 153–174.

12 "*Licenciado*" or "*licenciada*" is a title of respect used to refer to people who have completed a five-year university course of study that is similar to but more specialized than the US Bachelor's degree.

13 Cited in Anthony DePalma, "The Quake that Shook Mexico Awake is Recalled," *New York Times* 19 September 1995, available at: *http://www.nytimes.com/1995/09/19/*

world/the-quake-that-shook-mexico-awake-is-recalled.html?pagewanted=all&src=pm (access
ed 15 August 2012).

14 Damian Cave, "Wave of Violence Swallows More Women in Juárez," *New York Times* 24
June 2012: A6.

15 See Aston's chapter "Feeling the Loss of Feminism: Sarah Kane's *Blasted* and an
Experiential Genealogy of Contemporary Women's Writing" in this volume.

16 Sabina Berman, *Backyard*, *Gestos* 20, no. 39 (2005): 113; subsequent references to the
screenplay will be given parenthetically in the text.

17 Charlotte Canning, "Feminist Performance as Feminist Historiography," *Theatre Survey*
45, no. 2 (2004): 230.

18 Laura Podalsky, *The Politics of Affect and Emotion in Contemporary Latin American Cinema:
Argentina, Brazil, Cuba and Mexico* (New York: Palgrave Macmillan, 2011), 157–158.

19 Melissa W. Wright, "Urban Geography Plenary Lecture – Femicide, Mother-Activism,
and the Geography of Protest in Northern Mexico," *Urban Geography* 28, no. 5 (2007):
401–425.

20 Patricia Suárez, *El tapadito* (2005), CELCIT, Dramática Latinoamericana, 162, available
at *http://www.celcit.org.ar/publicaciones/dla.php* (accessed 2 September 2012).

21 Patricia Suárez, *El tapadito*, in *Germania* (Buenos Aires: Losada, 2006), 193.

22 Patricia Suárez, personal email to author, 3 September 2012.

23 Ibid.

24 Suárez, *El tapadito* (2005 version), 32.

25 In the 2006 version of *El tapadito*, there is no display of scars and Leni's baby, instead
of being given up for adoption, is killed before his mother's eyes.

26 Suárez, *El tapadito* (2005 version), 34.

27 Borland and Sutton, "Quotidian Disruption and Women's Activism in Times of Crisis,
Argentina 2002–2003," 709.

28 Suárez, *El tapadito* (2005 version), 31.

29 My observations here draw on Josefina Ludmer's insights in her landmark essay on
women who kill, "Mujeres que matan," *Revista Iberoamericana*, 62, no. 176–177 (July–
December, 1996): 781–797.

30 *The Rainy Season* was first staged on 22 May 2004 in Paraná, Argentina by El Yunque
theatre company under the direction of Augusto Carballal. It was subsequently staged in
June 2008 at Teatro Búho in Buenos Aires under the direction of Patricia Casalvieri.

31 King James Bible, available at *http://www.kingjamesbibleonline.org/book.php?book=Ecclesi
astes&chapter=3&verse=.* (accessed 3 September 2012).

32 Ramón del Valle-Inclán, *Romance de lobos: Comedia bárbara dividida en cinco jornadas*
(Madrid: Gregorio Pueyo Editor, 1908), 240.

33 Patricia Zangaro, *Tiempo de aguas* (Buenos Aires: Losada, 2008), 144.

34 María Silvina Persino, "Espacio y opresión en el teatro de Patricia Zangaro," *Latin
American Theatre Review* 40, no. 1 (Fall 2006): 72.

3   Chronic Desires: Theatre's Aching Lesbian Bodies

Sara Warner

"Theater is hard, hard I tell you, especially for women, people of color, and queers. Look at me," exclaimed Hanifah Walidah. "I've got three strikes."[1] Walidah offered this lament in response to my query about the status of her newest play, *Missing*, cowritten with Mecca Jamilah Sullivan, which I saw in a workshop production at the WOW Café in New York in the spring of 2012. An experimental musical drama that follows three women who escape from the slave ship *Trouvadore* in 1795 and magically reappear in the present-day United States as aspiring hip-hop artists, this poignant and imaginative work highlights the "missing" culture and creative voices of Black women from both the historical record and contemporary performance traditions. *Missing* is Walidah's follow-up to her critically acclaimed *Black Folks Guide* (2002), a one-woman show in which the artist plays an entire neighborhood of characters who gather around a card table to gamble and gossip, fraternize and moralize. Tackling the issue of homophobia in Black communities, this dazzling and politically astute production exploring the sexual, economic, and spiritual health of our social fabric earned Walidah comparisons to luminaries such as Anna Deavere Smith, Ntozake Shange, and Zora Neale Hurston. A solo performance with minimal props and technical requirements, *Black Folks Guide* was a darling of the festival circuit for several years, and the attention it garnered resulted in a three-week run at the Producers' Club off-Broadway. *Missing*, a multi-character sonic extravaganza with more elaborate stagecraft, has proven a much tougher sell. Walidah assures me she hasn't given up on this work, but she has decided to focus her energies on other aspects of her career, namely singing and independent filmmaking, arenas in which women have made much greater strides and a talented Black dyke is less likely to strike out.

Some refer to the dearth of employment opportunities and the paucity of diverse representations of women by women as a *crisis*, but this term refers to a *temporary* disruption or destabilization of normal conditions, not a constant or *permanent* state of precarity.[2] Inveterate situations, such as the problem of gender parity, are more accurately described by the term *chronic*, defined here as an ache, as a psychic, corporeal, and/or political injury that has become habitual, routine, or ordinary. *Chronic* implies a radically different temporality than *crisis*, entailing both a distinct sense of duration and a divergent affective intensity. It is typically associated with physical pain (e.g., chronic illness), appetitive incompetence (e.g., chronic alcoholism), and unrelenting social ills (e.g., chronic poverty). As Lauren Berlant has observed, a chronic condition refers etymologically to a disease of time and vernacularly to a condition that cannot be cured, only managed.[3] The chronic is in some ways the most generic form of time, notes Elizabeth Freeman, for *chronic* simply means "of time." It is typically associated, however, with negative temporalities and with aspects of human history that have not interested or that have seemed antithetical to feminism, queer theory, and disability studies: "endurance rather than novelty, pathology rather than transgression, biology rather than performance, duration and sameness rather than repetition and difference."[4] We consciously have lived in and thought about chronic time since AIDS became a survivable disease rather than a death sentence. Yet despite the failure of three waves of activism to effect substantive and sustained transformations in the status of women, we seem reluctant to acknowledge that gender discrimination qualifies as a chronic problem, a constitutive fact of our existence and historical experience rather than a treatable malady. I don't mean to criticize feminism for failing to concede this; rather I want to celebrate and revive feminism's (forgotten?) commitment to failure as a way of being in the world.[5]

If the slow progress of women and long continuance of discrimination in the theatre qualify as chronic, so too do the resistance and resolve of female artists, critics, and scholars who choose to labor in an increasingly inhospitable environment. Many contemporary playwrights, and lesbians in particular, exhibit what we might call a chronic attachment to the theatre. These intrepid souls exhibit a "cruel optimism" about their chances of success in the performing arts. "Cruel optimism" is Berlant's provocative term for an investment in "compromised conditions of possibility whose realization is discovered to be *im*possible, sheer fantasy."[6] It manifests as an incitement to go after "the good life," in this case a career in the arts, even though this path charts for most a bad life that exhausts individuals who nonetheless find their conditions of possibility in an attachment to this (likely unattainable) object of desire. The concept of cruel optimism offers insight into why it is that more women do not leave the theatre (as Walidah temporarily has done), but choose instead to remain devoted to the profession and willing to work in a field that thwarts their flourishing but also establishes them as creative agents who may effect change.

More than any utopian possibility theatre holds for personal and social transformation, it might be fear that motivates women to choose this path.[7] According to Berlant, "the fear is that the loss of the object or scene of promising itself will defeat the capacity to have any hope about anything."[8] In other words, laboring futilely at a goal we probably will never attain (parity in theatre) and a disease we will never eradicate (sexism) is preferable to admitting that there is little hope of reforming institutions, and by extension society, so women playwrights (wittingly or not) develop habits ensuring the reproduction of discrimination as a defense against losing faith in the possibility of change. Drawing upon recent theoretical formulations of queer temporalities by Berlant, Freeman, and others, I explore works by contemporary lesbian playwrights that shed light on why dyke dramatists remain chronically, if not exuberantly, attached to theatre, and why they insist on "dragging" feminist aesthetics, politics, and performance practices developed in the 1970s and 1980s, when gender discrimination was in a state of remission, into the next millennium.[9] I argue here that Lisa Kron's *Well* (2004), Lenelle Moïse's *Expatriate* (2008), and Madeleine George's *Seven Homeless Mammoths Wander New England* (2011) resignify the chronic, detaching it from its association with pathology, paralysis, and death, but also linear notions of progress and normative models of success. Realigning the chronic with unregenerate desires and an obstinate investment in a seemingly outmoded feminist poetics, these artists bend and reshape time in ways that enable us to identify, if not resist, the material, emotional, and corporeal limits that circumscribe women both on- and offstage. I term this approach a degenerate diacritics, by which I mean a mode of scholarly and activist engagement that concerns chronic offenders and that reverts to an earlier stage of culture, development, or evolution in order to put the past in touch with the present so as to reimagine the future.[10]

Chronic fatigue, or, It doesn't get better: Lisa Kron's *Well*

Kron honed her talent and temerity at the WOW Café in New York City's East Village, a crucible for the production of lesbian communities and radical artistic experimentation for over thirty years. WOW gave rise to some of the most important feminist performance artists of the twentieth century, including Peggy Shaw, Lois Weaver, Deb Margolin, Holly Hughes, and Carmelita Tropicana. In 1989, Kron and WOW compatriots Moe Angelos, Babs Davy, Dominique Dibbell, and Peg Healey founded the Five Lesbian Brothers. Unlike many of their dyke peers, the Brothers did not consider their praxis to be antithetical to the social, economic, or aesthetic dictates by which mainstream theatres operate, but their success, while noteworthy, paled in comparison to gay male playmakers such as George C. Wolfe, Harvey Fierstein, Tony Kushner, and Terrence McNally. Kron, who had garnered critical acclaim as a solo performer with *101 Humiliating Stories* (1993) and the exquisite *2.5 Minute Ride* (1997), broke through the glass proscenium in 2006 when her play *Well* opened at the Longacre Theatre on Broadway, but the production, which garnered rave reviews and a number of awards, including two Tony nominations, closed after six weeks due to lackluster ticket sales.

This semiautobiographical play features a Jewish lesbian narrator named Lisa, played by Kron, whose plans to present a scripted "multicharacter theatrical exploration of issues of health and illness both in the individual and in a community" go demonstrably awry when her mother Ann, an inveterate invalid played by Jayne Houdyshell, interrupts the rehearsed scenes, challenging not only Lisa's version of events, but her interpretive framework and theatrical apparatus.[11] Lisa, the character, is troubled by the conundrum of her mother, "a fantastically energetic person trapped in an utterly exhausted body" (15). Assailed by a host of generalized ailments she attributes to allergies, Ann has been confined for much of her life to a La-Z-Boy recliner. At times, however, she exudes a vitality that is awe-inspiring. Ann decided that she wanted her children to grow up in a racially integrated neighborhood, so she set about to create one out of their segregated suburb in Lansing, Michigan. Lisa cannot understand how an ailing housewife could transform herself into a community activist and help heal an entire neighborhood, but not herself. "Why," she asks, "are some people sick and other people are well? Why are some people sick for years and years and other people are sick for a while and get better? Why is that? What is the difference between those people?" (11).

In a direct address to the audience, Lisa says, "I come from a family where everyone is ill. It is the norm. The presumption of illness is so strong that it's *the way we keep time*. People in my family say things like, 'Now I know for a fact the warranty's not up on that dishwasher. I got it the winter I had congestive heart failure seven times'" (13, my emphasis). The entire clan's chronometry is calibrated according to one type of affliction or another. Some members of her family suffer from terminal maladies and "have recognizable, identifiable illness like cancer and heart disease," while others, Ann included, have an undiagnosed chronic condition that Lisa calls "the family mystery illness – the general inability to move, physically cope, to stay awake" (13). Ann prefers "allergies" to the pathologizing medical terms doctors and her daughter use to categorize reactions they do not understand and cannot treat – reactions Ann believes are responses to toxic elements in our environment that no one wants to talk about.

Lisa experienced symptoms of allergies throughout her childhood, but not to an extent that she was incapacitated. In her junior year in college, however, she could not keep up with her work. She told the audience, "I was shocked. I'd always been able to push through on willpower. But that winter I found myself with two options: Go to the [allergy] unit [at Henrontin Hospital]. Or watch my life derail" (19). Lisa left the clinic and managed to finish school, but it wasn't until she moved to New York after graduation that she got better, which she attributes to starting therapy and finding "a girlfriend who cured [her] with sex" (70). Lisa imagines her relocation and coming out to have a telos – a stable, healthy, lesbian identity – but the events of the play actively undercut her homonormative fantasy of sexual evolution and upward mobility. In New York, with its abundance of seitan, sex, and shopping, Lisa comes to conceive of wellness as what follows from living the "right" way, and illness as the result of living the "wrong" way. In other words, health functions as a prescription for "good living" that she achieves by following the "correct" course of action, in this case a series of choices anchored in domesticity and consumption that promise to engender a specific set of behaviors, attitudes, and good feelings. Lisa's language, in particular the suggestion that she made herself better through sexual liberation and the cultivation of a cosmopolitan lifestyle, reflects the individualizing and monetizing precepts of neoliberalism, which imagines wellness as a reward for proper conduct, but also as a good investment. Berlant would call Lisa's "faith that adjustment to certain forms or practices of living and thinking will secure one's happiness" a form of cruel optimism.[12] What the character Lisa fails to see, and as a self-proclaimed progressive queer would be horrified to realize, is that this conceptualization of health is tethered to and predicated on successful normalization. Lisa is blind to the fact that her desires and decisions have less to do with agential choices that run counter to her family's so-called poor lifestyle than they do with the mobilization, by medical and capitalist entities, of psychic and social fantasies that seek to align individuals with the comforting condition of being in good shape.

The discourse of health shapes the terms by which subjects engage in the world through the creation of scripts for how to live right. These scripts can be thought of as what Sara Ahmed calls "straightening devices, ways of aligning bodies with what is already lined up."[13] In *Discipline and Punish*, Foucault demonstrates how institutions pervasively and systematically construct conditions under which citizens administer and govern themselves without necessarily being conscious of what they are doing.[14] Believing that one is or should be well, from this perspective, is precisely the kind of self-disciplining protocol that the nation wishes to inculcate in its subjects. Thus, wellness can be understood as a socially conformist feeling, a state that is held up as an aspiration in order to keep discomfort and discontentment at bay, thereby quelling discord and dissent. In its most nefarious form, the rhetoric of wellness can obscure oppressive power relations, mask the operations of disciplinary regimes, and reinforce social hierarchies. Drawing on Foucault, Ahmed argues that wellness demands adjusting one's body, psyche, and feelings to a world that has already taken shape. If we take the shape of what is given or scripted for us – and this depends on being able or permitted by others to take this shape – we experience the comfort of being in good shape. Every adjustment entails the loss of other possible configurations, a loss that must remain irretrievable if we are to stay well-adjusted.[15]

Lisa's belief that she got better is predicated on a comparison with the past and with other women in her life. Her assessment is based on the patients in the allergy unit and her mother, all of whom fail to become healthy in her eyes. The more Lisa tries to force a distinction between wellness and illness by drawing a line and putting the sick people on one side and the healthy people on the other, making sure her mom is on the former and she the latter, the less convincing this binary is to the actors, the audience, and herself. Lisa's worldview shows signs of cracking when, during a rehearsal of her play, an unscripted character from the past, a Black girl named Lori Jones, rips through a scrim upstage and attacks her, wrestling her to the floor, as she routinely did when they were in school together. Lori calls into question Lisa's rosy memories of racial integration. Fearing that this Black bully would feed into stereotypes and contradict her image of a healthy, desegregated Lansing, Lisa has deleted her from the script, thereby propagating a liberal form of racism borne of oversimplification. Like most repressed desires, Lori returns with a vengeance. "Kick Lori out of the play for acting like a crumb if you want," Ann admonishes her, "but not because she's not an appropriate 'representation'" (56). Throughout the show, Ann reprimands her daughter for glossing over complicated issues in order to create an idealized portrait of her neighborhood's health and a reductionist account of her family's illnesses.

Unhinged by Lori's disruption of the dramatic events and upset by Lisa's treatment of her mother, the cast stages a revolt, abandoning the play and defecting to the part of the stage where Ann sits in her La-Z-Boy. At one point, even the actress playing Ann breaks character, exclaiming, "I can't do it. It's all wrong" (72). Troubled by Lisa's specious alignment of wellness with goodness and disturbed by her moralizing rants against her mother's inability to heal herself, the actress tells the narrator that Ann is not the woman she has constructed in her imagination. Her mutiny forces Lisa to recognize that she has been asking all the wrong questions. With the cast's help, Lisa comes to see that she cannot ignore the elements of her story that are messy, counterproductive, or otherwise unsatisfying to her personally – a point that gets driven home when the actress playing Ann hands Lisa a copy of one of her mother's neighborhood association speeches. It says:

> This organization is about people. It's about busy people and lonely people. Happy people and frustrated people. Young people who want a good life for their children, and old people who want to know that someone cares. People so busy that they don't have time to wonder if anything they are doing is worthwhile, and people who face day after day and have nothing to do but wish that someone might need them. This is the purpose of integration. This is what integration means. It means weaving into the whole even the parts that are uncomfortable or don't seem to fit. Even the parts that are complicated and painful. What is more worthy of our time and our love than this? (76)

As she reads the note, Lisa's rigid and prescriptive worldview is disrupted by and dissolved within her mother's description of integration.

By this point, it is apparent that the character Lisa is a foil and that the playwright is and is not the sophisticated theatre person from New York with a sick Midwestern housewife for a mother who assumes that because she is the narrator she is going to be the one the actors and audience identify with. As Lisa's play within Kron's play goes awry, Ann becomes the one people relate to while the self-righteous narrator proves to be the unhealthy one. In this metatheatrical masterpiece, Kron brings a foundational tenet of lesbian feminism to the masses in this Broadway show – namely that nonconforming women have a history of making others sick by refusing to follow society's prescription for being well-adjusted. Dykes, neurotics, and hysterics are women whose health gets in the way of the wellness of others. Feminism and lesbianism are represented in the mainstream as being caused by an illness and, through contagion, fostering the spread of their disease and discontent. These maladapted citizens are rewarded with the label of wellness for assimilating to or approximating the tenets of hetero- and homonormativity.

In this play, Kron exemplifies Ahmed's assertion that feeling better cannot entail a disavowal or forgetting of discomfort, or else it isn't a feminist form of getting better. Discomfort forms the basis of Ann's politics; it colors her understanding of people and prompts her to become a community organizer. Illness does not index a lack of will or moral failure, as Lisa initially believes; rather, it is a manifestation of the ordinariness of suffering.[16] While Ann's tormenting condition engenders a state of chronic fatigue, it also constitutes an enduring relation of sociality. For her, discomfort functions as a mode of self-consciousness, an awareness of her personal suffering, and as a form of social consciousness, in which the suffering of others disturbs the atmosphere. *Well* offers a feminist understanding of wellness as a mode of chronic discomfort that entails learning to live with, if not seeking out, aching bodies. Without romanticizing illness, the play asks what kinds of worlds might take shape if feeling better were not the aim of politics or if we conceived of feeling better not as an abatement of bad feelings and negative affects but as an enhancement, expansion, and intensification of our capacities to feel. What forms of political and social engagement might we imagine if we change "the way we keep time" by taking the chronic as our horizon? *Well* stages what Kron calls a "carefrontation" in order to direct our attention to the chronic as an integral aspect of sexual and cultural politics (18). As such, it provides enormous potential for thinking about the complexities of queer lives – of lives lived out of sync – in ways that attend to the intricacies of ordinary injustices and chronic modes of resistance.

Fugitive longings: Lenelle Moïse's *Expatriate*

Like *Well*, Moïse's *Expatriate* is a semi-autobiographical play that invites us to consider what it feels like to live with chronic forms of prejudice. It asks what kinds of futurity are possible in a world plagued by seemingly intractable forms of racism, misogyny, and homophobia. Moïse, a Haitian-American playwright, performer, and spoken word artist, wrote, composed, and starred in *Expatriate*, which debuted at the Kitchen Theatre in Ithaca, New York, before moving to an accolade-fueled run at Manhattan's Culture Project and Boston's Theater Offensive. This work follows two friends Claudie (Moïse) and Alphine (Karla Mosley) in a trenchant exploration of desire, Black female sexuality, and creative survival. These young women from a Boston housing project experience what Saidiya Hartman calls "the afterlife of slavery – skewed life chances, limited access to health and education, premature death, incarceration, and impoverishment."[17] Bearing the physical and emotional scars of habituated neglect and indifference, the two friends weather the scene of hopelessness in which they have been cast – a scene punctuated by abject poverty, addiction, a predatory foster care system, and sexual abuse – by engaging in "fugitive dreams" of escape and enchantment.[18]

The cerebral and celibate Claudie retreats into her head, devouring books and music that feed her imagination and enflame her desire for flight, while the precocious and libidinous Alphine seeks solace in corporeal connections, in illicit liaisons that produce both pleasure and pain. Drive and determination propel the protagonists out into the world where they encounter situations that challenge their defenses and unleash their demons. When Claudie earns a scholarship to Juilliard, the women move together to New York, where the charismatic yet needy Alphine finds the attention she craves working as a chanteuse and stripper in seedy clubs. She hitches her star to Claudie's talented but ill-fated twin brother Omar (also played by Moïse), an aspiring rapper and drug dealer, but her world spirals out of control when he dies of an overdose. Distraught at Omar's death, Claudie flees to Paris, where she falls in love with an older white woman. Alphine, strung out and suicidal, joins her friend in France, and the two find success as the singing duo Black Venus.

"Black Venus" was one of the many racially charged appellations given to Josephine Baker by her Parisian fans, and Claudie and Alphine cast themselves in a contemporary version of Baker's *Danse Sauvage* through their choice of this name. Reviving and rehearsing early-twentieth-century history, these more recent expatriates align themselves with a chronic temporality that moves laterally and rearward rather than in a linear progression of racial uplift. Baker's echo is literalized in the musical score, which employs reverb, sonic loops, and other recursive phonic elements in a neo-jazz aesthetic. With Black Venus's rise to fame, the past and present collide, and the band's future is threatened by a host of forces, internal and external, personal and political. Tension builds as Claudie finds sexual satisfaction, artistic inspiration, and spiritual regeneration in her new life abroad, while Alphine's insatiable hunger for adulation from a celebrity-obsessed culture pushes her to the brink. This mounting conflict comes to a head when Alphine insists upon wearing a leopard-print dress from a renowned designer given to her by an admirer. Claudie hates the gown, which she likens to the banana dress worn by Baker in the 1920s. She sees history repeating itself as the public celebrates but also exoticizes Black Venus, just as it did expatriate women of color who found both liberation and nefarious forms of discrimination on European stages in the early part of the twentieth century. She wants to interject their act with a bit of Nina Simone, who found welcoming audiences in France and used her considerable talents as a musical storyteller, or *griot*, in the service of the civil rights movement while refusing to play the primitive. Alphine, who not only needs flattery and favors from male suitors but revels in the power these gifts afford her, willingly enacts the part of the sexualized savage. Unable to bridge this ideological divide, the friends part company, with each woman following her own star.

The rewards the artists reap as solo acts provide a longed-for sense of recognition and security for Claudie, but not for Alphine, who experiences a sensorium-shattering break with reality. She can't seem to figure out what to do when her creativity and energy aren't bound up with day-to-day survival. Alphine's achievements may provide relief from certain forms of suffering (economic and otherwise), but they also induce a permanent rupture in the repertoire of her attachments. Her drug binges and ultimate demise reflect a desperate attempt to maintain the optimism that has sustained her, however fragilely, to this point. Without her one true friend, Alphine finds herself surrounded by people who claim to love her but only want to possess or profit from her. Her disintegration exemplifies the ways in which women who shoulder the burdens of historical injury, institutionalized discrimination, and the norms of white, patriarchal society often numb themselves into nonexistence or, like Claudie, risk working themselves into the ground in an attempt to outrun death, in effect deferring life until they die.

If *Expatriate* effectively dramatizes the violence of existence in the context of deprivation so extreme that the protagonists' "fugitive dreams" are, in some sense, doomed to failure, it also shows us in Claudie an artist who survives the drama of dysfunction that consumes everyone around her, not because she somehow cedes or transcends her chronic attachments and cruel optimism but because she comes to understand, through her compounded losses, how to manage them. While life literally consumes Alphine, Claudie learns to live with injustice, to dwell with the sadness, alienation, and despair of daily life without seeking immediate deliverance from these feelings or transforming them into emotions that may seem, at least on the surface, to be more salutary or more efficacious. Claudie's change of heart may look like resignation, but it encodes another story, one of chronic resistance. In the play's final scene, she debuts her newest hit, "Rebel," an elegy to her brother and best friend. Claudie sings: "Why do beautiful people want to die? / Now the beautiful people are no good to us dead. / I wish you were all ugly and living instead."[19] Claudie laments Omar and Alphine's vulnerability to time. She grieves their passing and mourns for the futures that will never be realized. Wishing they could have kept time differently, Claudie bemoans the fact that Omar and Alphine claimed to be "anti-status quo" but were in fact "anti-life," that they said "fuck the establishment" but then fucked themselves (73). The singer announces that she "will be living instead," that she will rebel against them and the world by bearing the daily grind of discrimination and remaining, against all odds, stubbornly hopeful about the future (73).

In "Rebel," Claudie renders the labor of survival apparent as labor, as work that takes the form of chronic activity. Survival is a creative act that bends and distorts time in order to open up new avenues for subjectivity and alternative forms of sociability. Ann Cvetkovich defines creativity as "a form of movement...that maneuvers the mind inside or around an impasse, even if that movement seems backward or like a form of retreat."[20] Claudie's song needs to be understood not as a refusal of radical social transformation but as a different mode of endurance that remains linked to earlier histories of discrimination, to the fugitive longings and deferred dreams of earlier generations of expatriate women. The play ends with the sole survivor at the crossroads between one habituated life and another yet to be rehearsed. This closing episode stages the possibility that the habits of history might not be replayed or reproduced according to the same old script.

Chronic bonds: Madeleine George's *Seven Homeless Mammoths Wander New England*

Whereas *Well* and *Expatriate* cast a spotlight on the chronic optimism of female artists, George's *Seven Homeless Mammoths Wander New England* concerns itself with another demographic of haggardly hopeful laborers: female academics. An intergenerational group of well-heeled lesbians populate this clever comedy of errors whose plot traverses two overlapping love triangles: one domestic and one prehistoric. The newly named dean of a small, cash-strapped liberal arts college, Cindy Wreen, is under fire after woefully underestimating the reaction that her decision to shut the institution's antiquated, politically incorrect natural history museum would elicit among members of the campus and local communities. This economic quagmire provides the backdrop for a conjugal crisis that ensues when Wreen invites her ex-lover Greer to move back in to her house to undergo treatment for stage-four cancer without discussing this arrangement with her current lover and former student, Andromeda, an anthropology major with a New Age bent and a passion for alternative kinship structures. Mining the stereotype that lesbians never really break up, even after their love affairs are over, George juxtaposes the chronic ties that bind these dykes with Greer's terminal illness. The playwright adds to this cast of conjoined sapphists a soon-to-be unemployed museum caretaker and two immobile human figures in prehistoric dress (but who speak the language of contemporary youth) from one of the dilapidated museum dioramas to create a profoundly quirky sex farce about longing, human evolution, and the perils of monogamy. *Seven Homeless Mammoths* asks profound questions about chronicity, about our time on this planet, the nature of attachments, and the ends of history.

Though Greer and Wreen broke up years ago and have seen each other only occasionally since they parted, they remain deeply committed to one another. Same-sex marriage was illegal when they were together but they would not have wed if this had been an option because they are the kind of lesbian feminists who "object to archaic patriarchal property-transfer ceremonies" and who "feel that even when it has been repurposed, the traditional Judeo-Christian wedding ceremony still contains a history of oppression towards women."[21] When Greer, anxious about the adjustments the others have to make to accommodate her presence in the house, admits that she feels like a charity case, her former lover responds: "How can you say that? How can – you think I would do this out of *charity*? It's turning my whole fucking life upside down to have you here, you think I would do this out of *obligation*? You're here because I *want* you here" (81). Wreen bristles at Greer's suggestion that her actions are born of duty or compulsion rather than love. In this play about debts – economic, social, pedagogical, and amorous – the ties that bind these lesbians have nothing to do with legal marriage, which makes spouses accountable for one another in the same way that the college is beholden to its creditors and the hominids/students in the museum dioramas are responsible to lending agencies for their educational loans.

The chronic modes of attachment that create and sustain lesbian relationships in this play offer vibrant and viable alternatives to traditional marriage, and insofar as they actively subvert the artificial state of monogamy, these bonds are much more optimistic. The script begins with an epigraph from Adam Phillips's 1996 treatise on coupledom and its discontents, *Monogamy*: "Suspicion is a philosophy of hope. It makes us believe there is something to know and something worth knowing. It makes us believe there is something rather than nothing. In this sense, sexual jealousy is a form of optimism, if only for philosophers."[22]

Especially if those philosophers happen to be lesbians. The return of Greer makes Andromeda jealous of the past she shares with Wreen, especially after she comes home from a protest to save the museum and finds the two of them locked in a tender embrace. Greer, in turn, is envious of the steamy sexual relationship her hosts flagrantly and shamelessly engage in, primarily because she never experienced love with Wreen in this way. When Andromeda and Greer act on their complex feelings for one another, after discovering, through a medical-marijuana-induced trip, that they share the same spirit class (in the cosmic cycle of reincarnation), it is Wreen who suffers the green-eyed monster. As Foucault observes in "Friendship as a Way of Life," homosexual desire is the desire for relations with others, "not necessarily in the form of a couple, but as a matter of existence." This kind of relational matrix makes for a discomforting existence insofar as it generates what he calls "a desire, an uneasiness, a desire-in-uneasiness."[23] Rather than tear the women apart, sexual jealousy enriches and fortifies their relationships. Among other things, it prompts each participant to be more open and honest about her desires, while at the same urging the trio to confront the ways in which they take one another for granted.

While George valorizes lesbian relationships, she, like Kron and Moïse, resists the tendency to romanticize queerness as necessarily or inherently transgressive. Being a dyke has perhaps less to do with what makes Andromeda a free radical than her spiritual practice and sincere belief that the television sitcom *Friends* serves as a postmodern paradigm of alternative kinship structures. By the same token, neither Wreen nor Greer, both veterans of second-wave feminism, are particularly progressive; on the contrary, a life in the academy has muffled any revolutionary aspirations these two professors once harbored. As ambitious young feminist scholars, Wreen and Greer (who chose her name in homage to Germaine Greer) believed they could change the world, one student at a time. Things did not work out as planned for either. Having traded the classroom for the conference room, Wreen "accommodate[s] hacks and pedants all day long, entitled alums and bovine foundation functionaries" (130). She finds herself in the compromised position of tearing down a museum in order to erect new dormitories "to house the increasing numbers of increasingly mediocre kids [the college is] increasingly being forced to accept to stay afloat" (8). Whereas Wreen once reveled in the erotics of archive fever, she now blithely orders the destruction of holdings that are deemed out of date and unprofitable. Disgusted with the situation in which she finds herself, she complains to Greer:

> I used to *treasure* a research collection. I used to sit at the heads of seminar tables and conjure worlds. If they would have told me when I first came here to teach that twenty years later I'd be standing in a windowless conference room in front of that gallery of animals, Brooks Brothers animals, arguing about which academic building to turn into a four-star resort for privileged teenagers – I could have taught high school on a Navajo reservation, you know.... I could have trained with Foucault in Paris. I was accepted, I turned down Foucault to come here! (10)

Greer's response – "You chose a certain comfort. It's a reasonable choice" – only makes Wreen feel worse about her shift in values, for discomfort, as we saw in both *Well* and *Expatriate*, constitutes the core of a feminist politics (10).

Discomfort is something the cancer-ridden Greer understands all too well. Philosophy, which she once considered foundational to an ethical life, proves to be of little solace as she faces death. "This rational humanism is getting exhausting," she confesses to Wreen (14). Even before she was sick, however, Greer had lost some of her passion for education and begun, out of habit, to cling to the dogma of academic discourse. Indeed, the seemingly naïve stargazer Andromeda emerges as the true sage in this drama of ideas, if for no other reason than that she retains her wonder about life in the presence of jaded and dispiriting humanists who alternately mock and humor her while trying, in vain, to disabuse her of her faith, which they dismiss as superstition. The student teaches the teachers when she installs herself as Greer's end-of-life doula, creating a vigil plan, a series of rituals, to help her leave this world.[24] In addition to being an anthropology major, Andromeda is a performance artist who understands the efficacy and exigency of this kind of theatrical ceremony. Theatre is a mortal form, one well-rehearsed in entrances and exits. Vigil plans use the mortality of theatre to assist in the transition from life to death and, for Andromeda, rebirth. She tells Greer, "Endings are really important to me, they're like a hundred percent as spiritually significant to me as beginnings. As far as I'm concerned the entire universe is an ouroboros.... My teacher says that beautiful endings not only give rise to beautiful beginnings, they are themselves beautiful beginnings, and that's totally how I see it, too" (25). Though Greer sees her terminal cancer as mortality uncloaked and longs for some kind of control over her death, she resists making a vigil plan.

Undeterred by Greer's objection to ceremony, Andromeda lures her and Wreen to the museum under the guise of performing a ritual for the soon-to-be scattered treasures. She asks the women to join hands and close their eyes while she calls "on the forces of the universe to send down the most gentle dissolving energy to course through this entire building" to "undo the wires that have held our mammoths together for centuries, and let each creature go free to wander the world in a new way." Taking advantage of her captive audience, she adds: "And let the dissolving energy that comes from the very source of the cosmos, so so gently, enter Greer's body and undo the microscopic bonds holding her cancer cells together" (126). At first, Greer is alarmed and insists that Andromeda stop, but with some encouragement she takes charge of the ceremony herself. Unsure of what to do, Greer improvises. She takes a glass, fills it with juice, and passes it for all to drink. Next she wraps it in a napkin and announces that they are going to break the glass, in what is clearly a modification, or queering, of a traditional Jewish wedding ritual.

As the trio stomps the glass, a cascading crash brings up the lights, revealing that the three women are part of a tableau in one of the museum's antiquated dioramas. They are frozen in mid-action and observed, mockingly, by the two hominids/students, now disclosed to be a young Wreen and Greer on their first date. The ritual was supposed to conduct Greer into the afterlife by dissolving her into an ecstasy of atoms and ions in preparation for rebirth. Instead of transporting her to the future, however, the ceremony catapults her forward by way of the past. It's "as if" her relationship with Wreen and Andromeda is just beginning, and in some sense it is. In this scene, we see the future's past and the past's future. History, as Rebecca Schneider and others have argued, is "recurrent (that is, like theatre, capable of being mounted *again*)."[25] In this play, "mounted *again*" has a double meaning as Wreen and Greer not only restage their past, but they do so in the location where they first had sex – the museum diorama (a detail that gives new meaning to the term "institutions of intimacy").[26]

In the strange simultaneity of the museum, the "then" and "now" of planetary history collide and commingle. History is a present tense and an imminent direction that exists (or as Schneider would say "remains") before the protagonists waiting to be (re)discovered. "They're clearly freshly installed," observes Wreen as she surveys the diorama, "and yet they somehow already seem dated" (130). The lesbians, the ones looking and the ones being looked at, will all suffer the same fate; they will become "the victims of progress" (17). Indeed, these dykes, with their desire for communal kinship, chronic attachments to lesbian feminism, and (futile) struggles to oppose the commodification of knowledge, are, George suggests, the "last fragments of a lost world" who appear to us today, at a moment dominated by assimilationist gays concerned with marriage and military service, as a "beloved treasure trove of rare prehistoric skeletons." Like the mammoths and hominids on display, the lesbians are anachronisms – pre-queer relics from the early years of feminism and the gay liberation movement, a dying breed. If so, George asks, can we let this archaic creature "go to its grave un-eulogized by the individuals who loved it?" (17). The scene's promise derives from what our image of "waves" of activism and the rhetoric of "generations" often obscures: the irruptive energy of moments that are not yet bygone and yet not entirely present. George's play keeps lesbians alive (and well) as a meaningful index of sexual subjectivity and social practices. Its characters may be out of sync – existing in multiple registers of dramatic time and historical realness – but this does not mean they are out of date. On the contrary, as living artifacts they have much to contribute to current conversations about time, about its unfolding, our desire to preserve it, and the possibilities for other futures.

It's about time: the chronic activism of 13P

Seven Homeless Mammoths Wander New England reveals history to be something other than a linear chronology, a teleological project of advancement instantiated and perpetuated by normalizing institutions. This work received its world premiere in 2011 at the Two River Theater Company in New Jersey, a venue that serves as a model for innovation and inclusivity, producing multiple plays by women and people of color every season. If even half of the regional theatres in this country operated according to similar principles, we would be well on our way to racial and gender parity. Frustrated by the entrenched discrimination in the American theatre and deeply concerned about the lack of new plays (by anyone, male or female) being produced around the country, George decided to take matters into her own hands. In 2003, she cofounded 13P, a collective (of sorts) of thirteen mid-career dramatists – eleven women and two men – dedicated to staging new work by members of the organization. Uniting under the motto, "We don't develop plays. We do them," this playwright-driven, production-oriented company operated (until 2012) according to a rotating structure in which the (meager) resources of the organization were placed at the disposal of the featured dramatist, who also served as 13P's artistic director during the production of her work.

With no permanent space, no wealthy board members, and a largely volunteer staff, 13P managed to stage, on average, two productions per year of plays that had failed to reach fruition by more traditional means. A chorus of practitioners has sung the praises of this Obie award-winning experiment, from Paula Vogel to Mac Wellman. Polly Carl, of the Center for the Theater Commons and editor of *HowlRound*, hails 13P as "a model for the future of new plays. It ensures that they will actually get produced, and let's face it, that's *radical*."[27] Work mounted by this group includes Sarah Ruhl's *The Melancholy Play* (a chamber piece), Young Jean Lee's *We're Gonna Die*, Erin Courtney's *A Map of Virtue*, and George's *The Zero Hour*, a play about a closeted lesbian writing about the Holocaust, her chronically unemployed, very out, butch girlfriend, and the secrets they keep.

From its inception, 13P's objective was simple and specific: to produce one play by each dramatist and then disband. In fact, the group plotted its implosion at the moment it announced its genesis. This organizational rubric, explains Young Jean Lee, "was the reason why we could take such huge risks – we didn't have to worry about the long term sustainability and growth of the company."[28] For this vibrant, thriving theatre collective to implode, consciously and purposely, at the zenith of its power and influence may seem to many a mistake of epic proportions, but there was no way to change course and continue the experiment without compromising the group's mission and praxis. The goal was not to become an institution but to prompt institutions toward more flexible ways of working with artists.

We designate longevity as the most valuable and desirable future for social movements and artistic organizations, dismiss as a waste of time modes of aesthetic and political engagement that show little or no concern for permanence, and view with suspicion individual or collective action that does not aspire to institutionalization. What distinguishes 13P from most other theatre experiments is that members had no desire to make the organization into a fixture of the theatre world or to reproduce themselves in new inductees. These artists do not labor under the assumption (or is it a delusion?) that the problem of parity in American theatre is solvable. Rather, they accept discrimination for the chronic situation that it is and offer cunning ways of dealing with inequality, failure, and the slowness of social change. Whereas groups such as 50/50 in 2020 advocate fiercely for gender parity (and in this organization's case by a date that its members know is completely and utterly unrealistic), 13P acknowledges the fact that the war on discrimination will never be won, that it cannot be won; it is an ongoing struggle, an endless battle.

Crises can be solved. Chronic predicaments, on the other hand, necessitate chronic forms of action and chronic modes of activism, which is to say ways of being and doing that help us manage and manage to live with incurable maladies. While the production cycle of 13P has come and gone, the collective lives on through an extensive online archive, which they created to demystify the process for other playwrights. Taking a page from the promptbook of direct action groups such as W.I.T.C.H., the Lesbian Avengers, and Dyke Action Machine – none of which believed they would or could end sexism and homophobia – 13P documented, organized, and freely disseminates information to make it easier for others to form coalitions.[29] One of the key differences between 13P and these experiments is that they did not burn out. Like the characters in George's *Seven Homeless Mammoths*, this collective anticipated and staged its own death (with a party at Joe's Pub). 13P's implosion was, to quote George's Andromeda, both a beautiful ending and a beautiful beginning. The group's fleeting existence, coupled with their enduring archive, redefines what success and failure look like in the American theatre by reminding us that there are many ways of keeping time, including the chronic.

Notes

I would like to thank the following people for their insightful commentary on various drafts of this essay: Penny Farfan, Lesley Ferris, Dagmawi Woubshet, Masha Raskolnikov, Lucinda Ramberg, Camille Robcis, Lynne Stahl, Jayna Brown, and Kyla Tomkins.

1 This conversation with Hanifah Walidah took place at the "Queerness of Hip Hop/The Hip Hop of Queerness" conference at Harvard University on 21 September 2012.

2 See Maria M. Delgado and Caridad Svich, *Theatre in Crisis? Performance Manifestos for a New Century* (Manchester: Manchester University Press, 2003).

3 Lauren Berlant, "Slow Death (Sovereignty, Obesity, Lateral Agency)," *Critical Inquiry* 33, no. 4 (2007): 754–80. See her discussion of "crisis ordinariness," which "measures the structural intractability of a problem the world can live with" (762).

4 Elizabeth Freeman, "Chronic Thinking," paper presented to the "Strategic Ruptures" Lecture Series, Cornell University, Ithaca, NY, 23 February 2012.

5 I refer here to the quest for alternatives to limiting notions of success as defined by a sexist, racist, heteronormative, capitalist society; to academic endeavors that merely rehearse what is already known or produce "new" information gleaned by working according to approved methods of inquiry; and to cultural criticism that boasts of tracking new terrain while mapping established archives. See Judith (Jack) Halberstam, *The Queer Art of Failure* (Durham, NC: Duke University Press, 2011).

6 Lauren Berlant, "Cruel Optimism," in *The Affect Theory Reader*, ed. Melissa Gregg and Gregory J. Seigworth (Durham, NC: Duke University Press, 2010), 94.

7 See Jill Dolan, *Utopia in Performance: Finding Hope at the Theater* (Ann Arbor: University of Michigan Press, 2005).

8 Berlant, "Cruel Optimism," 94.

9 For a discussion of "temporal drag," see Elizabeth Freeman, *Time Binds: Queer Temporalities, Queer Histories* (Durham, NC: Duke University Press, 2010), and in particular chapter two, "Deep Lez: Temporal Drag and the Spectres of Feminism."

10 For an elaboration of what I am calling a "degenerate diacritics," see Sara Warner, *Acts of Gaiety: LGBT Performance and the Politics of Pleasure* (Ann Arbor: University of Michigan Press, 2012), 26.

11 Lisa Kron, *Well* (New York: Theatre Communications Group, 2006), 12; subsequent references will be given parenthetically in the text.

12 Lauren Berlant, "Two Girls, Fat and Thin" in *Regarding Sedgwick: Essays on Queer Culture and Critical Theory*, ed. Stephen M. Barber and David L. Clark (New York: Routledge, 2002), 75.

13 Sara Ahmed, *The Promise of Happiness* (Durham, NC: Duke University Press, 2010), 91.

14 Michel Foucault, *Discipline and Punish: The Birth of the Prison*, trans. Alan Sheridan (New York: Vintage, 1977).

15 Ahmed, *The Promise of Happiness*, 79.

16 See Kathleen Stewart, *Ordinary Affects* (Durham, NC: Duke University Press, 2007) and Sharon Holland, *The Erotic Life of Racism* (Durham, NC: Duke University Press, 2012).

17 Saidiya Hartman, *Lose Your Mother: A Journey Along the Atlantic Slave Route* (New York: Farrar, Strauss, and Giroux, 2007), 6.

18 Ibid., 234.

19 Lenelle Moïse, *Expatriate* (unpublished script), 73; subsequent references will be given parenthetically in the text.

20 Ann Cvetkovich, *Depression: A Public Feeling* (Durham, NC: Duke University Press, 2012), 21.

21 Madeleine George, *Seven Homeless Mammoths Wander New England* (unpublished script), 34; subsequent references will be given parenthetically in the text.

22 Adam Phillips, *Monogamy* (New York: Random House, 1996), qtd. in ibid., 1.

23 Michel Foucault, "Friendship as a Way of Life," in *Foucault Live: Collected Interviews 1961–1984*, ed. Sylvère Lotringer (New York: Semiotext(e), 1996), 308–309.

24 This observation is inspired by Maria Goyanes's essay, "The Finite Animal: 13P's End Days," *HowlRound*, 2 October 2012, available at *http://www.howlround.com/the-finite-animal-13ps-end-days-by-maria-goyanes/?utm_source=feedburner&utm_medium=email&utm_campaign=Feed%3A+HowlRound+%28HowlRound.com%27s+Journal%2C+Blog%2C+%26+Podcasts%29*.

25 Rebecca Schneider, *Performing Remains: Art and War in Times of Theatrical Reenactment* (New York: Routledge, 2011), 28.

26 Lauren Berlant and Michael Warner, "Sex in Public," *Critical Inquiry* 24, no. 2 (Winter 1998): 547–66.

27 Polly Carl, 13P Company Overview, available at *https://www.facebook.com/13playwrights/info* (accessed 15 January 2013).

28 Young Jean Lee, quoted in Ben Gassman, "The Imminent Implosion of 13P," *The Brooklyn Rail* (July–August 2012), available at *http://www.brooklynrail.org/2012/08/theater/the-imminent-implosion-of-13p* (accessed 15 January 2013).

29 13P, "A People's History of 13P," *http://13p.org/* (accessed 15 January 2013).

4   Women Playwrights in Egypt

Nehad Selaiha with Sarah Enany

The landscape of women playwrights in Egypt has been inextricably bound up with the historio-political background of the country in the twentieth century, when theatre on the Western model first appeared and with it the concept of "playwriting." Although theatrical phenomena related to rituals and various forms of popular entertainment, including story-telling and puppetry, are known to have existed in Egypt and the Arab world at various stages in history, text-based theatre on the Western model is a relative newcomer, being the result of intensive cultural contact with Europe in the nineteenth century and initially largely confined to the aristocracy and expatriate communities. By the beginning of the twentieth century, however, this class-based bias for the European theatrical model – loosely understood and applied – had become largely established, formalized, and institutionalized to the detriment of indigenous, popular theatrical forms.

Given the class barriers and pervasive religious discourse branding women's liberation initiatives as atheistic and heretical, describing women's demand for equal rights as moral dissolution and a violation of marital duties, and suggesting that dialogue and differences of opinion were seditious and therefore sinful, no woman playwright could be expected to emerge in Egypt without certain changes of attitude toward both women and theatre. These changes were accomplished to a degree during the decades following the turn of the twentieth century due to a number of factors, foremost among which were:

- The emergence of women's liberation movements, led by Hoda Shaarawi (1879–1947) and other pioneers, that championed the rights of women and eventually persuaded "respectable women" to uncover their faces and become active in public life and politics.
- The proliferation of progressive newspapers, literary publications, and women's magazines, and the rise in the number of women contributing to them.
- The increase in the number of schools for girls and, in 1929, the admission of women to the first Egyptian university (Cairo's Fouad University).
- The propagation of the idea of drama as respectable, morally correct, and corrective literature through the translations of many of the classics of Western theatre, including Sophocles' *Oedipus Rex* and Aristotle's *Poetics*, and the introduction, in 1919, by Taha Hussein of the study of Greek and Latin thought and literature at Fouad University.

- State support[1] for theatre and the establishment of the first Egyptian national theatre company in 1935 and its first acting institute in 1944 (after a failed attempt in 1931).[2]

Enter the women playwright pioneers (1922–1952)

The first woman in Egypt to write a piece and call it a "play" was Palestinian-born Mai Ziada (1886–1941). In 1922, she included in her book *Al-Musawah* (Equality) a literary piece titled *Yatanaqashoon* (A discussion) in the form of a dialogue among a group of friends, including women, over the subject of equal rights in general and whether they were conducive to the happiness of humanity. In the following year she wrote a similar piece, *'Ala Al Sadr Al Shafiq* (Tender heart), on the value of mothers' love, this time calling it a play and providing a list of the dramatis personae. A decade later, actress Dawlat Abyad wrote two plays, *Dawlat* and *Al-Wagib* (Duty), the manuscripts of which have been lost. During the second half of the twentieth century, Sufi Abdallah's *Kisibna El-Primo* (Sweepstake), a social drama about the trials and tribulations of the lower classes, was performed during the 1951–1952 season by the recently established Modern Theatre Company at the Cairo Opera House. A copy of the play has survived in the library of the National Theatre.

Women playwrights under the new regime

The first phase: the rise and collapse of the socialist dream (1952–1970)

On 23 July 1952, army units led by Gamal Abdel Nasser and the "free officers" staged a successful coup d'état against King Farouk, forcing him to abdicate and leave the country. A year later, the new regime abolished the monarchy and completely dismantled the old aristocracy. In 1956, women were granted the right to vote, and when the National Union (which replaced the previous parliament) was established in 1968, women were allowed, for the first time in Egypt, to run for political office.

In 1955, Gazibiya Sidqi (1920?–2001), a journalist and prolific fiction writer who had studied at the American University in Cairo, wrote her first play, *Sukkan Al-'Imara* (The tenants), which was a realistic social drama in four acts that reflected the views of the new regime and was, for this reason perhaps, promptly staged in 1955 at the National Theatre. A block of flats, the tenants of which give the play its title, is used as a metaphor for pre-1952 Egyptian society, with its rigid class distinctions, injustices, and prejudices. The same metaphor surfaced a year later in No'man 'Ashour's *El-Nas Elli Taht* (The people downstairs), and then again in his 1958 *El-Nas Elli Foaq* (The people upstairs), and it kept appearing in the realistic plays of the 1960s. Significantly, it is 'Ashour, rather than Sidqi, who is invariably credited with having created this metaphor.

In 1961, Nasser issued his notorious socialist laws nationalizing most industries and private businesses, further limiting land ownership, freezing property and bank accounts, and establishing an economic public sector. Socialism became the official ideology of the regime, and the Socialist Union replaced the National Union as Egypt's sole political party. The regime grew harsher and more coercive during the 1960s, rigidly controlling all aspects of life and turning Egypt into a police state. Censorship of the media, cinema, and the stage was rigorous, and loyalty to the regime, masquerading as "political commitment to socialism," was demanded in return for recognition and acceptance in any field. The result was that almost every field of endeavor became heavily politicized.

More than books and newspapers and to almost the same degree as cinema, radio, and television, theatre was regarded by the socialist regime as an invaluable propaganda organ for disseminating its ideology to a largely illiterate population. Not surprisingly, therefore, theatre enjoyed the dedicated patronage and generous financial support of the regime, which sought to enhance its progressive image by establishing the Pocket Theatre to present the latest European avant-garde and experimental local drama, and it also launched the official *Al-Masrah* (Theatre) magazine to cover all theatrical activities. Furthermore, within a year of the start of television broadcasting in 1960, no less than ten television theatre companies were founded to provide a steady stream of appropriate plays for viewing.

Despite the ceaseless demand for new plays by the television theatre companies, journalist and fiction writer Fawziya Mahran (1931–), a graduate of Cairo University, failed to have her first one-act play, *Al-Buyut* (Homes) (1964), staged. As in Sidqi's *Sukkan Al-'Imara*, the setting in *Al-Buyut* is used metaphorically so that the old, ramshackle family home, which the woman's father built to keep her safe but which ends up being her prison or tomb, emerges as a metaphor not only for marriage and family life under patriarchy, but also for Egypt under Nasser's totalitarian rule.

A year later, in 1965, novelist, political activist, and academic Latifa El-Zayyat (1923–1996), also a graduate of Cairo University, opted for realism and a classical structure in her only play, *Bee' wi Shira* (Buying and selling). Comprised of three acts that depict a twenty-four-hour period and set in a hospital room, the play centers on the moral hypocrisy of a middle-class Egyptian male who decides to have it both ways by marrying one woman for her money and another one, secretly, for love. If we take the hospital as a metaphor for Egypt, in the tradition of Sidqi, and the sick, perfidious male character as representing Nasser or the entire regime, one could interpret the play's message as that (1) despite all his slogans, Nasser effected no real change; (2) that he actually betrayed the common people who blindly trusted him by replacing the old aristocracy with a greedier, more unprincipled and shameless upstart class; and (3) that wealth and power, rather than moral worth and justice, were still the final arbiters in all conflicts. Predictably, the play was not performed and was only published in 1994.[3]

The remaining women playwrights of the 1960s – Laila Abdel-Basit (1940–), an Arabic teacher who worked at the Ministry of Education from 1962 through 1987, and Fathiya El-Assal (1933–), a largely self-taught woman who became a feminist and political activist and earned her living solely by her pen – were luckier in this respect. In 1966, Abdel-Basit's *Waraq... Waraq* (Papers, papers), a realistic one-act play about the evils of bureaucracy and the corruption of the civil service, was staged at the National Theatre as part of a triple-bill called the *Tali'at Al-Masrah al-Qawmi* (The national avant-garde). And in 1969 and 1972, respectively, El-Assal, who had been writing extensively for radio since 1957, managed to get two plays staged: *Al-Murgiha* (The seesaw, or swing) and *Al-Passport* (The passport), both being traditional, realistic social comedies about marriage and family relationships. Later on, El-Assal's socialist ideas and feminist views became more pronounced, leading her to experiment with forms in search of a suitable dramatic mode to accommodate such views without descending into sloganeering.

The second phase: the liberalization of the economy, the erosion of the middle classes, and the rise of Islamic fundamentalism (1970s)

The collapse of the Nasserite socialist/nationalist project was devastating. When Anwar Sadat succeeded Nasser in 1970, he tried to win over the people's support by promising to restore democracy, dismantling the fearful police state Nasser had created, and putting many of its most powerful symbols on trial. His popularity soared after the 1973 war with Israel, in which Egypt won an initial, partial victory, but his peace negotiations created deep rifts between Egypt and its Arab neighbors, between liberals and socialists, and between intellectuals (of all political denominations) and the common people. More controversial still was the sudden transformation of the country's economy from socialism to an unbridled, hastily concocted open-door/laissez-faire economic policy that fundamentally changed the structure of Egyptian society by impoverishing the middle classes, creating a new class of nouveau-riche, socially irresponsible businessmen and leading to a mass exodus of professionals and intellectuals, as well as peasants and workers, to the oil-rich Gulf states. To help win over the people to his new policies and to crush the Nasserites and socialists, Sadat made the fatal mistake of flirting with religion and seeking to enlist the support of the Muslim Brotherhood, the power of which Nasser had ruthlessly curtailed during the 1950s, thus creating, like Dr. Frankenstein, the monster that would eventually destroy him (Sadat).

In such social, economic, and cultural turmoil as experienced in Egypt during the 1970s, "serious" theatre naturally receded, losing most of its playwrights and traditional audiences, and was supplanted by cheap, commercial shows that catered mainly to the newly wealthy businessmen and oil-rich Arab tourists. Sadat's fancied construction of a nation built upon the consecration of science and religious faith was destined to lead to a resurgence of religious fundamentalism and a neglect of the arts. While the National Theatre was preserved and rigorously censored, it no longer received the support of the regime or the media and was left to perish. Not surprisingly, many artists and writers deserted the National Theatre by going abroad or simply keeping silent.

The situation was even worse where women were concerned. During the 1970s, the use of the veil returned in even more extreme forms than during the 1920s, with its concomitant call for women to return to the home in the name of religion. It seemed as if the women's liberation movement started by Shaarawi during the 1920s had doubled back upon itself, relinquished its gains and gone back to square one, and that the battles Egyptian women had fought and won over the decades must all be fought again.

Amina El-Sawi, the celebrated dramaturge (she mainly adapted novels and historical/religious works for stage and television) of the early 1960s, departed Egypt for Saudi Arabia for some years, and when she returned she donned the veil, called herself an "Islamic writer," and devoted her dramatic skills to television religious serials; Abdel-Basit remained silent throughout the 1970s and the following decade, only adapting a foreign play for the Comedy Theatre under the title *Feloos…Feloos!* (Money, money!) in 1989; and Mahran's *Capuche* (1974), about the Palestinian-Israeli conflict, and *Al-Tamathil Aydan Tantahir* (Statues, too, commit suicide) (1977), about the dilemma of the artist in a commercial age, were both published in *Rose Al-Yusef* magazine where she worked, but were never staged and were to be her last plays. Although both are dramas of ideas that passionately express their writer's views and deep-seated convictions, the stage sets Mahran suggests in *Capuche,* as well as many of her stage directions, reveal her deep awareness of the multiple languages of theatre and the value of lighting and sound effects. It is a pity, therefore, that neither this play nor *Al-Tamathil Aydan Tantahir* has ever been tested onstage.[4]

Were it not for Fatma Al-Ma'dool, who wrote, adapted, and directed a string of children's plays, the 1970s would have been completely lacking in new women playwrights. El-Assal wrote two more plays – *Al-Kharsaa* (The mute) in 1972 and *Nisaa bila Aqni'ah* (Women without masks) in 1975 – but failed to get them produced or published during Sadat's reign.[5] (*Nisaa bila Aqni'ah* was eventually staged in 1982 by the Modern Theatre Company, but not before the censor had cut "women" from the title.) Both are a far cry from her two earlier plays. In *Al-Kharsaa*, which used the format of the family saga, together with some agitprop techniques, El-Assal strove to present a comprehensive, panoramic view of the most pressing problems and threats facing Egyptian society, including familial oppression, the resurgence of reactionary values, government and corporate corruption, unemployment, systematic police brutality, the rise of terrorism and religious fundamentalism, the commercialization of sex, and the increasing drug use by young men and wearing the veil (or *niqab*) by young women as a means of escaping the harsh reality of their lives and the sense of impotence and futility.

Additionally, in *Nisaa bila Aqni'ah*, such taboo subjects as female sexuality, the psychological trauma and disastrous long-term effects of female genital mutilation, legitimized rape within marriage, and wife beating were shown onstage for the first time in the Arab world. Here also, and more fiercely than she had done in *Al-Murgiha*, El-Assal lashed out at the ideal of physical beauty sold to women by the male-dominated media and beauty industries, in addition to exposing the moral hypocrisy of society in sexual matters and the process of perpetuating patriarchal attitudes. The play's daring content is matched by an untraditional form, which consists of a number of monologues within the framework of an investigation conducted by El-Assal's persona and involving the enactment of personal narratives, both false and true.

The third phase: documenting the impact of capitalism and globalization (1980 to the present)

On 6 October 1981, Sadat was assassinated by a group of Islamist soldiers, and Hosni Mubarak succeeded him as president of Egypt. Heeding the lesson of his predecessor's assassination, Mubarak immediately clamped down on militant Islamist groups by imposing the Emergency Law, which granted the government extraordinary powers to arrest its opponents without charge and to detain them indefinitely. The militant Islamists retaliated by staging a series of terrorist acts against public facilities, high officials, artists, liberal intellectuals, and tourists, which culminated in the Luxor massacre in November 1997. This situation put an end to the possibility of any real political liberalization; although the regime continued to maintain a "liberal" public façade, allowing some freedoms and public criticism of Mubarak and legalizing privately owned opposition newspapers and, later, television channels, state security was tightened more than ever under the guise of combating terrorism.

While most progressive artists and intellectuals and even moderate Islamic thinkers and conservative political leaders, not to mention the Coptic community, which felt deeply threatened, sided with the regime in its efforts to crush Islamic terrorism and maintain the secular character of the state, they gradually realized that Mubarak's regime had brought about no real change and that, despite outward shows of liberalization, it was as autocratic as that of his predecessor. Moreover, the economic liberalization initiated by Sadat continued apace, encouraging the influence of technocrats linked to multinationals to speed up the globalization of the economy, thus further eroding social justice and forcing the majority of Egyptians below the poverty line, while an elite class of businessmen, working in close collaboration with the regime, enjoyed enormous wealth.

Paradoxically, while corruption, nepotism, cronyism, and graft spread to all aspects of Egyptian life, the Islamization of Egyptian society intensified during Mubarak's reign, with the regime often encouraging it as a safe distraction from economic and political frustration and as an effective weapon to curtail freedom of thought and any radical opposition to capitalism and patriarchy. Indeed, as one observer noted, "Mubarak's principal domestic adversary – and perhaps his greatest asset in selling himself to the West, and to a frightened middle class – [was] the Muslim Brotherhood."[6] Mubarak presented himself to his fellow Egyptians and to the world at large as his country's defense against an Islamic insurgency. Despite this situation, the 1980s and 1990s were the richest in the history of Egyptian theatre in terms of the number of women who wrote for the stage, the number of plays they produced, the quality of those plays, and the critical/media attention they received. While older playwrights like El-Assal and Abdel-Basit produced mature, bold, and relevant plays, a number of talented new women playwrights joined them.

In 1982, El-Assal's *Nisaa bila Aqni'ah* was finally performed after a bitter fight with the censorship, and, in 1989, she published *Al Bayn Bayn* (Betwixt and between), in which women's oppression is once more viewed in a wider perspective, as part of a complex web of interrelated sociopolitical, economic, and ideological forces.

An expressionistic piece with an element of fantasy, *Al Bayn Bayn* centers on an indigent, downtrodden clerk in a factory who succumbs to the temptation of promotion and better wages offered by his boss and who consequently betrays his nature, principles, and girlfriend, and ends up committing suicide. It was not staged until ten years later. Sometime between the performance of *Nisaa bila Aqni'ah* and the publication of *Al Bayn Bayn*, El-Assal wrote her masterpiece, *Sign Al-Nisaa'* (Women's prison), in which she drew on her experiences as a political detainee in 1982 and used real stories she had heard from inmates of the women's prison in which she was incarcerated.

As in *Nisaa bila Aqni'ah* though more transparently, El-Assal wrote herself into *Sign Al-Nisaa'* in the figure of the main character, who, like her, is a writer and active political dissenter, with one daughter and an enlightened, supportive husband. But although El-Assal uses the same formula as in her earlier play – a confessional mode in multiple voices, all female and all oppressed, that refracts the dramatic focus among them and projects their stories as different manifestations of female oppression – the characters in *Sign Al-Nisaa'* are more varied in terms of class and social background and therefore also in language. Their monologues, which reflect the consequences of economic liberalization and the changed structure of society, are played in a richer variety of emotional keys, ranging from the broadly humorous and hilariously sarcastic to the bitterly satirical and deeply poignant. However, the formal similarities between the two plays are so striking that one is tempted to regard *Sign Al-Nisaa'* as a development and expansion of the technique used in *Nisaa bila Aqni'ah*. In both, the structure does not take the form of linear plot progression toward a climax – a male-oriented form according to some feminists – but proceeds, not unlike folk narratives, through calculated interruptions, digressions, and the accumulation of fragments that ultimately make up the whole and create a strong impact. The freshness of the form in both plays is more than matched by the daring and audacity of the content. Indeed, no other Egyptian playwright, male or female, has celebrated with such gusto the female body and its physical appetites and needs, nor has so effectively redefined the personal as political as El-Assal does in these two plays, and particularly in *Sign Al-Nisaa'*.

Sign Al-Nisaa' was not staged until 1994, when Adel Hashim, the same director who had done *Nisaa bila Aqni'ah* at the Modern, directed it at the National, one year after it was published by the state-owned General Egyptian Book Organization (State Publishing House). El-Assal's *Leilat Al-Henna* (Henna night), a one-act play about a long-suffering Palestinian mother who sacrifices her last son to the cause on his wedding night, after losing all her family, friends, and relatives in the conflict with Israel – it was probably written after the Second Intifada (also known as "Intifadat Al-Aqsa"), which erupted on 28 September 2000 – was performed in August 2004.[7]

Abdel-Basit, another dramatist of the 1960s, did not resume writing for the theatre in earnest until the 1990s, when she produced a trilogy of plays – *Thaman al-Ghurba* (The price of exile) (1991), *Ba'd Tul el-Ghiyab* (After a long absence) (1993), and *Mawwal el-Ghurba* (Song of exile) (1997) – about the growing migration of

Egyptian men to the Arab Gulf states in search of work and to make their fortune and its catastrophic effects not only on their psyches and relationships within their families, but also on the national economy and the fabric of society and its culture, mores, and morals. While *Thaman al-Ghurba* projects the theme from the point of view of a wife left behind with the children, and *Mawwal el-Ghurba* (actually written later than the other two plays in the trilogy, almost as an after-thought) presents the point of view of the absent husband, *Ba'd Tul el-Ghiyab* brings husband and wife together, only to reveal how their long separation has changed them and destroyed their relationship. This trilogy ranks as Abdel-Basit's best and most socially relevant achievement in theatre.

Two new women playwrights made their debut during the 1980s. Although Nihad Gad (1935?–1990) belonged to the same generation as El-Assal and Mahran and worked as a journalist in the same magazine as the latter, she was a late-comer to the theatrical scene. It was only after she received her master's degree in drama from Indiana University and married playwright Samir Sarhan that she wrote *Adila*, a one-woman play in one act, in 1981. The play was staged that same year at the state Avant-Garde Theatre, and its success encouraged Gad to write another, using the same formula. This next play, *Mahattet el-Autobus* (The bus stop), however, failed to obtain an immediate producer in the state-theatre sector, so it was published with *Adila* in 1985. When it was finally staged by a commer-cial theatre company in 1986, it was in a new, expanded version, as a full-length play with many characters and renamed *'Ala el-Raseef* (On the pavement).

The heroines in both *Adila* and *'Ala el-Raseef*, although the first is a housewife and the second a schoolteacher, are similar; both are frustrated, materialistic, petty-minded, middle-class, middle-aged women – typical products of the new market economy and consumerist society that emerged in Egypt during the 1970s. While Adila resents her husband's modest income and spends the entire play daydreaming of a future when he will be appointed as a minister, thus trans-forming her into a wealthy society lady, Safiyya, in *'Ala el-Raseef*, spends the best part of her youth in the Gulf region, leading an arid, frugal life, saving up to buy all the modern conveniences and to furnish a luxurious flat in which to be married. Both women uncritically uphold the materialistic values of the new consumerist society and are blithely free of any political concerns; and both have their hopes dashed at the end. Although *'Ala el-Raseef* was violently and viciously attacked by the supporters of both Nasser and Sadat, as well as by feminists who objected to the unflattering images of women these heroines embodied, it was a great success with the public and made Gad an overnight celebrity.

El-Assal's and Gad's view of men as equally oppressed by capitalism and patri-archy stands in sharp contrast to the one adopted by Nawal El-Sa'dawi (1931–). Her play *Isis* is a feminist reading of the ancient Egyptian myth about the murder of Osiris, the god of the fertile valley, by his brother Set, the god of the arid desert, and the arduous journey Osiris's wife, the Goddess Isis, undertakes to collect the parts of her husband's body, which Set had scattered throughout the valley, in order to bring him back to life and have him impregnate her with his future son and avenger Horus. In her introduction to the play, El-Sa'dawi clearly reveals her intention in writing it: in their treatment of the myth, she says, male writers, including Tawfiq El-Hakim in his play *Isis*, invariably adopt a patriarchal inter-pretation of it, presenting *Isis* merely as a faithful wife who has to rely on men to avenge her husband's murder and restore justice. Her play is intended to correct this image.[8]

While preserving the general narrative-line of the myth, El-Sa'dawi's play presents Isis as a strong, rebellious, and deeply learned woman who stands up to the gods Set and Ra' after her husband's death, opposes the patriarchal ideology that they impose on the people in the name of religion, revealing its many lies and unjust prejudices, and ends up leading the people in an uprising against their oppressive regime. The central conflict between the author, disguised as Isis, and the patriarchal culture, embodied in Set and Ra', is represented in black-and-white terms and is depressingly lacking in nuance and dramatic complexity. More disconcertingly, it never seems to move or bring about any real change. To my knowledge, *Isis* has never been publicly performed[9] and is, perhaps, not perform-able – not on account of its structural flaws (worse texts have been performed), but on account of its iconoclastic message and radical views. It is precisely these, however, that make it exciting reading. Its dauntless questioning and intellectual audacity remain unparalleled in any text by an Arab writer, male or female. The same intellectual audacity and radical views caused El-Sa'dawi's later play, *Al-Ilah Yuqadim Istiqalatahu fi Igtimaa' Al-Qimmah* (God resigns in the summit meeting),[10] in which God is questioned by Jewish, Muslim, and Christian prophets and finally quits, to be banned in Egypt and all copies destroyed. Indeed, no other writer in the Arab world, male or female, has been so frequently accused of heresy, apos-tasy, and immorality, or has had so many court cases brought against her for her views and writings as El-Sa'dawi has had.

Critiquing Egypt's cultural heritage – its texts, embedded assumptions, and representations of women – was also the purpose of poet Fatma Qandil (who belongs to the generation following El-Sa'dawi's) in *Al-Laylah Al-Thaniyah Ba'd Al-Alf* (The night following the one thousand and one nights), staged at the Youth Theatre in 1991. Her focus, however, was on Arab folk literature rather than ancient Egyptian mythology, and the character she wanted to rehabilitate was Scheherazade, the heroine of *The Arabian Nights*. Although Scheherazade has appeared in numerous Egyptian plays by male dramatists, sometimes as a symbol of Egypt and even as a revolutionary,[11] in Qandil's play, she not only retains her political dimension, but also acquires a definite feminist one. In this verse drama, Scheherazade finally rebels and decides to cast off her long-inherited robes and denounce both her husband's male chauvinism and his despotic rule. At the end, she is allowed to escape his iron grip and redefine herself as a social and ideo-logical rebel.

No one, however, has gone as far as Nahid-Na'ila Naguib (a trained actress, of the same generation as Qandil, who retired in the 1970s) in ideologically decon-structing the framing story of *The Arabian Nights*. In her *Scheherazade, Sitt Walla Gariyah?* (Scheherazade, mistress or slave?), Naguib takes up the character of Scheherazade and gives it a new, startling interpretation. She begins with the premise that mental and physical coercion cannot breed sane characters. In the harem, leading a life of idle luxury and sensual indulgence, under fear of death for disobedience, women can only rot, she argues. Naguib presents us with a Scheherazade who, after years of imprisonment and impotent inaction churning out silly tales in the court of Shahrayar, has become thoroughly corrupted. She is projected as scheming, lustful, greedy, and morally degenerate. This new image, however repellent, has a lot to justify it in terms of realistic psychology. Needless to say, Naguib's message and her thoroughly negative portrayal of the heroine of *The Arabian Nights* did not make it past the censor, who refused permission for it to be publicly performed. Naguib published it instead, as she had published many other plays before this; in fact, of the many plays she has written, only one – *Itnein fi Na'eem* (Two in bliss), a sociopolitical satire featuring two fetuses in a womb who eavesdrop on what happens in the outside world and, consequently, refuse to be born – has been staged (at the Avant-garde Theatre in 1986). The rest are available in print.[12]

The last new women playwrights of this period are of the same generation as Qandil and Naguib. In 1984, poet Wafaa Wagdi published a lyrical, symbolic play in verse, *Nisaan wa Al-Abwab Al-Sab'ah* (Nisaan and the seven doors), about the plight of the Palestinians and their quest for their lost homeland that draws on a number of legends. Despite some beautiful poetry, the play is dramatically weak, and this is perhaps the reason why it has not been staged so far. Her second play, *Al-Shagarah, Aw Al-Su'ood Ila Al-Shams* (The tree, or climbing to the sun), featuring a group of frustrated young people gathered under a tree and hoping for a miracle to save them, was published in 1993[13] and performed by the Modern Theatre Company almost ten years later, with substantial directorial revisions.

Unlike Wagdi, Nadia El-Banhawi (who studied Greek and Latin in college and has translated several of Beckett's plays) does not call herself a poet; her plays, however, though not in verse, are profoundly poetic in structure, language, and impact. At the center of each play is an existential quest for truth and meaning, undertaken by a reflective and iconoclastic female character (El-Banhawi's dramatic persona) bedeviled by a crushing sense of spiritual desolation and social alienation. All of her plays have an intense personal quality, which perhaps explains their deeply experimental nature. El-Banhawi's first play, *Al Wahag* (The glow),[14] originally called *Al-Mamarr al-Dayyiq* (The narrow path), features a lost soul trapped in an endless maze of dark, circuitous roads and narrow alleys, chased by weird shadows and ghostly figures and vainly searching for a guide to lead her out. When the Savior finally appears, we discover that he has become a cynical, embittered, and disillusioned man who sneers at his useless sacrifice, and the play ends ambiguously with the two disappearing in the sudden flare of a magic lantern. Predictably, *Al Wahag* was first denied a license for public performance because of its iconoclastic representation of the Savior; however, a modified version of it was eventually staged (in 1997) at the National Upstairs.

Staged the same year at the Avant-garde Theatre, El-Banhawi's *Sonata Al-Hob wa Al-Mawt* (Love and death sonata) is set on a lonely seashore and features a female painter – strongly reminiscent of the painter in Virginia Woolf's *To the*

Lighthouse – who struggles vainly to finish a painting that she believes will finally enable her to make sense of her failed life. The sea becomes a symbol of the sense of absurdity that threatens to engulf her, and its waves, as they crash upon the shore, throw at her the debris of broken hopes and relationships and many ghosts – scraps of what she once believed was her life. The sea also haunts El-Banhawi's fictional world of *Al-Lahn Al-Mafqoud* (The lost melody),[15] presented at the Avant-garde Theatre in 2003, which centers on the fragility of human relationships and the essential loneliness of human existence. In the bar of a deserted seaside hotel on a cold winter's night, a chance meeting between a violinist, Elise, and a pianist and budding composer, with wine to loosen the gates of memory, yields two contrapuntal monologues that conjure up ghosts from the past: her former lover, a painter, and his ex-wife, a pathetic creature. Elise and her companion desperately try to escape the past and find a new link to the present, but the more they try to get closer, the farther apart they are drawn by the ghosts of their lost loved ones.

El-Banhawi's most recently performed play, *Ru'a* (Visions), staged at the Avant-garde in 2007, strongly echoes her first play. When the corpse of her long-dead father suddenly materializes, refuses to be re-interred, and asks to be cast upon the waves, Ru'a, already branded as a heretic for daring to question the truth of God and the nature of His justice and still suffering the trauma of a broken marriage, which was her last link with reality, is forced to rethink the meanings of life and death, gradually sliding toward (what is traditionally called) insanity. We last see her dragging this half-dead, half-alive corpse across a bridge and desperately calling upon God for release.[16]

The quest for transcendental truth is at the center of *Rabi'a Al-'Adaweyah*, El-Banhawi's latest play, which dramatizes the life and spiritual journey of the famous Muslim mystic Rabi'a Al-'Adaweyah. The text has not yet found a publisher, and should some reckless director offer to stage it, it is bound to fall afoul of the censor due to El-Banhawi's untraditional portrayal of the mystic's character. Indeed, given the kind of plays she writes, it is surprising that she has had so many of them staged. In this respect, she is more fortunate than most women playwrights in Egypt, who have to fight for years to get their plays staged – and not infrequently they fail. This could partly explain why the next generation of Egyptian women playwrights have not only undertaken their own staging of their plays, but have also sought to create a space for themselves outside the male-dominated mainstream theatre by forming their own independent troupes and working on the fringe.

Enter the woman playwright/director

Although a small number of actresses have directed plays once or twice during the course of their careers, and an equally small number of professional women directors appeared in the 1970s and 1980s alongside women playwrights, the two groups – directors and playwrights – kept strictly apart until the early 1990s, when women artists began combining the two activities, writing and directing their own plays, and often designing, choreographing, and performing them as well. Rather than women directors and women playwrights being separated, a new generation of women theatre-makers write performance scripts rather than plays.

The Liqaa' al-Masrah al-Horr Al-Awwal (First free theatre encounter), a nongovernmental event organized in December 1990 by a group of theatre artists working on the fringe, heralded the rise of an independent theatre movement in Egypt that gradually gathered force, producing scores of independent theatre troupes that have proved themselves to be truly experimental, not only in the kind of work they do, but, more importantly, in their untraditional mode of work and production and their survival strategies. A few of these troupes were founded by talented, inventive, resourceful, and versatile women theatre-makers who, over the years, have produced some very exciting work that has won critical acclaim at home and has been shown at Arab and international theatre festivals and events.

The most important of these theatre-makers are Abeer Ali, who founded the Al-Misaharaty troupe in 1992, Effat Yehia, who founded Al-Qafila (Caravan) the following year, and Nora Amin, who, after acting in other independent productions for ten years, launched her own La Musica troupe in 2000. Although these three individuals differ in their methods and distinctive artistic styles – folkloric/ritualistic/musical, in the case of Ali; expressionistic/transcultural/text-oriented, in the case of Yehia; and physical/autobiographical, in the case of Amin – all of them display a keen common interest in such issues as patriarchal family relationships, freedom of thought and belief, the traditional position of women in Arab societies, and the established roles and images of women.

Al-Misaharaty, the name Ali chose for her troupe, refers to the man who, in the old days, before alarm clocks, traditionally went about the streets before dawn during Ramadan, the month of fasting in Islamic countries, beating a drum to wake up the sleepers to have their last meal before the fast commenced at dawn's first light. The name is emblematic of the troupe's intellectual and artistic orientation, which can be summed up as researching the development of certain themes in Egypt's popular cultural heritage and dramatizing its findings in the form of collectively written sketches, accompanied by period music and songs. The troupe's *Wa La 'Azaa'* (No condolences) (2000), which dramatizes traditional death and mourning rituals in Egyptian villages, is typical of its productions and method of work.

Choosing the theme of death and the traditional village funeral as framework and source of aesthetic inspiration, Ali and her troupe drew upon several sources, including the ancient Egyptian *Book of the Dead*, collections of traditional elegies and lamentations, and studies of folk songs and literature, as well as their own personal experiences. The material was then collectively pieced together, shaped and written in the light of an overall concept provided by Ali, who wrote the final script and also designed and directed it. Besides the many folk songs, choral lamentations, and funerary chants interwoven in the text, she also incorporated bits of relevant contemporary poems. The result was a gently nostalgic perform-ance text, subtly interlaced with earthy humor despite the sad theme, and deeply engaged with contemporary Egyptian reality as viewed through the experiences of the various mourners.

Effat Yehia's performance texts, like Ali's, are usually based on improvisations by members of her troupe around a certain theme or, more frequently, a published source. In its collective method of work, quasi-expressionist style, and feminist thrust, her *Iskitshat Hayatiyah* (Life sketches) (1993), the debut production of Al-Qafila, which consists of a series of sketches concerning a gagged woman tied up in ropes and constantly urged by her male torturer to declare that she is happy, was like a manifesto outlining the troupe's ideological and artistic orientation. *Sahrawiyah* (Desertscape I), a sophisticated satire on the position of women in Egypt throughout history, followed in 1994. Here, the first act of Caryl Churchill's *Top Girls*, which brings together women of different ages and cultures, was used as a launching pad for researching the history of women in Egypt and their images in Arab culture in order to find equivalents for Churchill's characters. Although each of the six actresses was allowed to write her own part, Yehia orchestrated the various parts to produce the performance script.

The same desert setting, a visual metaphor for contemporary Egyptian society, was used in *Sahrawiyah II* (Desertscape II) in 1996, and once again a foreign play, in this case Alastair Cording's *Lanark* (translated by Yehia), served as inspiration and material for improvisation. It was severely cut, modified, and "Egyptianized," but was also infused with contemporary Egyptian poems, old Egyptian songs, and excerpts from Edna O'Brien's *Virginia* (which Yehia had directed in 1992) and Botho Strauss's *Time and the Room*, as well as with many satirical parodies of contemporary Egyptian politicians, preachers, and popular entertainers. The final text, which begins with the creation of the world and structurally resembles boxes within boxes, with each story generating another, presents an image of a doomed society of political charlatans, frustrated lovers, oppressed artists, drug addicts, and lost souls – all suffering from cancer of the skin – and ends with the appearance of the mysterious Creator/Author to write the final, disastrous scene.

Yehia's favorite mode of "writing upon writing" produced, in subsequent years, extensive, drastic adaptations of other foreign plays, including B. M. Koltes's *La Solitude dans les Champs de Cotton*, Claire Flohr's *Veronique, ou la vie commence at 5h.30*, and, recently, Shelagh Stephenson's *Memory of Water* and Marjane Satrapi's comic-strip narrative *Embroideries*. Another interesting experiment with literary texts was Yehia's *Kan Ya Ma Kan* (Once upon a time), written collaboratively with Tunisian actress Amel Fadji and staged in Cairo in 2003. Featuring an imaginary meeting between the legendary Scheherazade and her Greek oppositional counterpart Antigone, and contrasting the former's docile compliance with the latter's willful disobedience, *Kan Ya Ma Kan* ulti-mately suggests that, in the context of any patriarchal culture, whether a woman consents as a rule and succumbs to the dictates of the status quo or instead opts for straightforward opposition, she is doomed.

More than both Ali and Yehia, Nora Amin, an actress, dancer, and choreographer who has also published several novels, collections of short stories, and literary translations, has used theatre as a physical mode of artistic and existential exploration, an intimate register of her memories and experiences, and a way to discover her own subjectivity amid many possible identities and inherited role models. Like many feminists, she believes that the route to female subjectivity lies through the forbidden body – its physicality, desires, traumas, and memories, and, of course, all the taboos inscribed upon it. She therefore relies heavily upon dance and movement as major structural elements in her performances.

In *Al-Dafirah* (The braid), by which Amin launched her La Musica troupe in 2000, she set the tone for her following productions. Defying the traditional idealized image of the mother within Arab culture, Amin also revealed the many complexities and tensions of the mother/daughter relationship in Arab societies. With a minimal spoken text and the imaginative uses of set, costumes, lighting, movements, and gestures, Amin presented a series of haunting images of a mother and daughter cooped up in a tiny, derelict, dark, and windowless room, and hopelessly interlocked, as in a fatal embrace, in a love/hate relationship, with death as their only hope of release. Similar intimate relationships are honestly and sometimes shockingly explored in her other plays, such as the relationship of a daughter to her dead father in *Risalah Ila Abi* (A message to my father) – a solo performance – and the turbulent relationship of a divorced couple in *La Musica 2eme*. Even when Amin collaborates with other artists and allows her actors/dancers to improvise their own words and movements or adapts a well-known play for her own uses, as she did with Ibsen's *A Doll's House* in *Abwaab Nora* (Nora's doors), she invariably interweaves into the performances her intimate thoughts and feelings.

While some highly gifted women theatre-makers of the generation who appeared on the scene at the start of the 1990s have sadly turned away from the stage – such as Rasha Al-Gammal, a painter and set and costume designer who wrote and directed *Afareet Hamza w'Fatima* (The spirits of Hamza and Fatima) in 1995, *Al-Ghaba al-Sa'eeda* (The merry jungle) in 1996, *Bahiya el-Kharsa* (Bahiya the mute) in 1998, and *Taht el-Shagara* (Under the tree) in 2001; and Sarah Nur El-Sherif, who dramatized and directed a popular epistolary verse narrative around the same time – others have appeared on the scene, promising a continuity of the woman playwright/director phenomenon. Women playwrights have recently emerged, such as Laila Soliman and Rasha Abdel-Mon'im, who learned their craft through working as dramaturges, actors, and directors in the independent theatre, while others, such as Marwa Farouk, still develop their texts through close collaboration with theatre companies.

It would, of course, be wonderful if the question "Where do we go from here?" could yield pat answers. The number of women playwrights and theatre-makers in Egypt is still very modest, and would still be modest even if it included all the women who have been involved in television drama and movie scripts. Still, with the harsh economic pressures on both male and female theatre-makers alike and the increasing allure of video and film media, it is a wonder that so many still devote themselves to the theatre. The state-run Youth Theatre is timid and limited in ability and resources, while the Hanager Theatre, which used to offer a venue to writers/directors, was considered too iconoclastic by the state and therefore, under the guise of "fire-safety repairs," was closed for three years, only reopening in 2012. One can only hope that in addition to women playwrights, independent women theatre-makers, both those who are (relatively) established and those who are emerging, will find the energy and wherewithal to carry on; unfortunately, the best and most energetic are also the ones who would rather make theatre than market themselves or find grant-writers – a necessity in this day and age.

Notes

1 The state has continued to support theatre since establishing a state-theatre sector after the 1952 coup, with many theatre companies in the capital and a cultural organization for promoting regional theatre. These official theatre organizations are still in operation today and account for the majority of theatrical productions in Egypt.

2 See Samir Awad, "Qisat Awal Ma'had Li Fan Al-Tamtheel" (The story of the first acting institute), *Al-Masrah* (Theatre magazine) 39 (February 1992): 106.

3 *Bee' wi Shira* (Cairo: General Egyptian Book Organization [State Publishing House], 1994).

4 *Capuche* and *Al-Tamathil Aydan Tantahir* were published in one volume, *Capuche wa al-Tamathil Aydan Tantahir* (Cairo: General Egyptian Book Organization [State Publishing House], 1995).

5 Fathiya El-Assal, *Al-Kharsaa* (Cairo: Al-Thaqafa Al-Gadida Publishing House, 1981), and *Nisaa' Bila Aqni'a* (Cairo: General Egyptian Book Organization [State Publishing House], 2002).

6 Adam Shatz, "Mubarak's Last Breath," *London Review of Books*, 29 May 2010, available at *www.lrb.co.uk/v32/n10/adam-shatz/mubaraks-last-breath* (accessed 25 September 2010).

7 For a description of the play and performance, see Nehad Selaiha, "Blood Wedding," *Al-Ahram Weekly* 704, 12–18 August 2004, available at *http://weekly.ahram.org.eg/2004/703/cu1.htm*; and Selaiha, "Of Silence and Violence," *Al-Ahram Weekly* 757, 25–31 August 2005, available at *http://weekly.ahram.org.eg/2005/757/cu1.htm*.

8 Nawal El-Sa'dawi, *Isis* (Cairo: Dar Al-Mustaqbal Al-Arabi, 1986), 6.

9 Samia Habib mentions a private production by an amateur group in 1998, but I could find no further evidence that such a production ever took place; see Habib, *Masrah al-Mar'a fi Misr* (Women's theatre in Egypt) (Cairo: General Egyptian Book Organization [State Publishing House], 2003), 174.

10 Nawal El-Sa'dawi, *Al-Ilah Yuqadim Istiqalatahu fi Igtimaa' Al-Qimmah* (1996; reprint, Cairo: Madbouli, 2007).

11 Nehad Selaiha, "Faces in the Mirror: Images of Scheherazade on the Egyptian Stage," in *The Egyptian Theatre: Perspectives* (Cairo: General Egyptian Book Organization [State Publishing House], 2004), 213–28. This section incorporates parts of this essay.

12 Nahid-Na'ila Naguib has three collections of plays: *Ahl Al-Markeb, wa Masrahiyyat 'Ukhrah* (The boat people and other plays), 1984; *Kalila wa Dimna wa Ba'd* (Kalila wa Dimna and after), 1988; and *Yawmiyat Mukhbir wa Masrahiyat Ukhra* (The diary of a detective and other plays [including *Scheherazade, Sitt Walla Gariyah?*]), 1998, all published by the Anglo-Egyptian Bookshop in Cairo.

13 Wafaa Wagdi, *Nisaan wa Al-Abwab Al-Sab'ah* (Cairo: General Egyptian Book Organization [State Publishing House], 1984); *Al-Shagarah, Aw Al-Su'ood Ila Al-Shams* (Cairo: General Egyptian Book Organization [State Publishing House], 1993).

14 Published in a collection of plays, together with *Al-Lahn Al-Mafqoud* and two unperformed plays, *Limadha?* (Why?) and *Mashhad Drami* (A dramatic scene); see Nadia El-Banhawi, *Al-Wahag wa Masrahiyat Ukhra* (The Glow and other plays) (Cairo: General Egyptian Book Organization [State Publishing House], 1996).

15 Ibid.

16 Nehad Selaiha, "A Dip into the Dark," *Al-Ahram Weekly* 837, 22–28 March 2007, available at *weekly.ahram.org.eg/2007/837/cu1.htm.*

5   Transcultural Dramaturgies: Latina Theatre's Third Wave

Natalie Alvarez

In an effort to resist the potentially homogenizing effects of the term "Latina," which often elides the diversity of ethnicities that comprise this contested demonym, this essay undertakes a hemispheric perspective in its analysis of the points of contact and schisms that characterize the work of some of the most prominent voices in a new generation of Latina theatre. The essay telescopes its analysis on a cluster of "third wave" Latina playwrights[1] who have risen to prominence in the past decade and whose work registers in distinct ways the impacts of transnational migrations on the formation of a sense of identity and place. In its analysis of representative plays by US playwrights Caridad Svich and Tanya Saracho and Canadian playwright Carmen Aguirre, the essay offers an examination of the transcultural dramaturgies that emerge as a means of capturing cultural collisions and the lived experiences of existing in between and across the shifting borders of race, class, gender, and nation. This investigation also charts these playwrights' uneasy navigations between cultures as they attempt to both upend and work within the dominant culture's aesthetic conventions and means of production.

Undertaking a hemispheric perspective in the analysis of Canadian and US Latina playwrights is strategic. It underscores the complex transnational movements, flows, migrations, and cultural practices that imbricate seemingly discrete and self-contained national spaces and, in turn, complicate any appeals to uniform, totalizing notions of *latinidad* and Latina subjectivity. Not surprisingly, the playwrights featured in this essay have expressed in varying ways their discomfort with the moniker "Latina" and the concomitant pressure of writing to "represent" an ethnic position. Indeed, the performative force of the ethnic category that constitutes in advance expectations about how the Latina is embodied, voiced, and written is precisely what mobilized playwrights such as Aguirre, Svich, and Saracho to begin writing in the first place. In many ways they write to contest and redress the repressive stereotypes of the Latina in the cultural imaginary that have dictated the formation of the Latina subject. In bringing together these three playwrights who write from and through a prism of positionalities and hemispheric relations within the broad rubric of *latinidad*, we can come to understand Latina/o subjectivity as a transcultural position that is constituted in performative acts and moments of enunciation that carry with them an historical "lifeworld" (or *Lebenswelt*) of cultural contacts and conquests. My aim here is to resist the tendency in theories of transculturation to approach it as a structuralism, which risks obscuring its contingency on individual movements, positionalities, and performative acts.

The notion of transculturality and the transcultural subject within the broader context of hemispheric studies offers a theoretical line of flight away from the dualistic and binaristic thinking that often delimits analyses of "border identities" and diasporic subjectivities – dualities that inadvertently perpetuate, rather than effectively undermine, the asymmetrical relation between a dominant culture and the subaltern. Originally coined by Fernando Ortiz in a 1940 study of Cuba, the neologism "transculturation" was conceived as a mode of cultural exchange produced by forces of colonization and globalization in order to resist the discourse of assimilation that pervaded the discipline of anthropology in the late 1930s; transculturation, Ortiz asserted, was fundamental to an understanding not only of Cuba but also, "for analogous reasons," the Americas in general.[2] While the concept of "assimilation" implied the unidirectional impact and imposition of a dominant culture which subsumed the cultures of the colonized, transculturation emphasized instead the *mutual* imbrication, influence, and generativity of colonial contact that result in the production of new cultural formations. Ortiz likens this phenomenon to the genetic composition and formation of a child: "the child may possess something from both parents, but is also always distinct from each of them."[3] The emphasis in this analogy lies in the generation of new cultural formations that are distinct from the originary "source" cultures. Moreover, transculturation is understood as processual and ongoing – comprised of different phases of *de*culturation and *neo*culturation – as the impact of colonization and neocolonizations continues to unfurl.[4]

The "trans" in transculturation suggests a mediation between two cultures that supersedes them both, producing not simply a "third" but a multiplicity of cultural formations and processes. As Silvia Spitta has noted, transculturation is "not a single process, but rather...many different processes of assimilation, adaptation, rejection, parody, resistance, loss, and ultimately transformation of Spanish *and* indigenous cultures."[5] In terms of the impact of these processes on the formation of subjectivity, Spitta adds that the transcultural subject is "someone who...is consciously or unconsciously situated between at least two worlds, two cultures, two languages, and two definitions of subjectivity, and who constantly mediates between them all – or, to put it another way, whose 'here' is problematic and perhaps undefinable."[6] The transcultural subject, while generated processually within cultural contacts that occur in shared time and space, circumvents fixity within an uncertain, ambiguous "here" or, to consider this another way, within the fluidity of an *atopos* that is not a negative structurating force that one seeks to recuperate and recover, but one that generates, propels, and allows a movement forward and, in turn, the creation of new spaces of possibility.

In their analysis of what transculturation offers for the conceptualization of Latina subjectivity, Alberto Sandoval-Sánchez and Nancy Saporta Sternbach gloss over the *trans*cultural as a mediation that supersedes the two worlds, the two cultures, and so on, reducing the transcultural instead to a "model for the

Latina/o bicultural subject."[7] Metaphors of a "bifocal condition"[8] and "bicultural subject" that appear throughout their analysis advance the supposition – and illusion – that one exists between two discrete cultures, as though each exists as a homogenous and unified force, and risk perpetuating, in turn, the asymmetrical binary relation of the colonial encounter that the theoretical intervention of transculturation aims to undermine. If the "heterogeneity, partiality,…and multiplicity that give transculturation its theoretical apparatus" also account for the "fluidity of the transcultural protean subject herself or himself," as Sandoval-Sánchez and Saporta Sternbach go on to capture in more exacting terms,[9] then we must dispense with dualistic metaphors that align with binaristic thinking in favor of the processual multiplicities of transculturation and transcultural subjects in formation. Only then can we begin to fully understand how the transcultural subject is generatively multiple, contextually contingent and situational, and not delimited in advance by a structural dualism.

In this essay, I analyze representative plays by each of the three playwrights – Svich's *Prodigal Kiss*, Saracho's *El Nogalar*, and Aguirre's *The Refugee Hotel* – in order to examine the possibilities of the transcultural as a methodology that allows us to examine questions of subjectivity, as well as questions concerning dramaturgical interventions. Transculturalism, I argue, makes legible not only how the subject is constituted in the "contact zones" of the transcultural process, but also how individual movements and enunciative acts constitute and make possible new transcultural formations. An analysis of these playwrights' dramaturgical strategies reveals transcultural reciprocities evident in how each play negotiates its relationship to the dominant aesthetic of western theatre traditions and its positioning within major theatre institutions or "dominant cultural production sites."[10]

Transcultural subjects in process: Caridad Svich's *Prodigal Kiss*

In *Prodigal Kiss* (1999), the audience encounters the protagonist, Marcela, on "a slim board in the middle of the ocean"[11] singing an invocation to Santiago, Cuba.[12] Within its opening refrains, Marcela is caught in contradictory movements: Santiago is a home to which she is ostensibly returning, but as the song progresses, we learn that she is dreaming of her home, a home to which she cannot return. We encounter the protagonist in mid-journey but in stasis, longing to return home but unable to and instead heading to an unknown destination. The "un-home-ness" of the past is established, not as something the subject is longing to return to, since its recovery is an impossibility, but rather, as a propelling force that drives the movement forward, even if the destination is unknown. Marcela appears on stage as a lone figure in the open playing space that becomes, here, the expansiveness of the ocean, her singing voice attempting to carve out a sense of location, and a sense of self, in this vast *atopical* no-where. Within these opening moments, the play establishes the terrain of the transcultural subject as one that is unstable, shifting, and in process – a subject standing, appropriately, on shifting ocean waters. Svich has emphasized her interest in "the voice in space" in performance and particularly in the ability of song to "[lift] the voice" and establish a "different emotional relationship to the audience."[13] The lyricism of the song establishes an affective relationship between the audience and a performer-protagonist that sets up the conditions for a transcultural encounter in which both audience and performer-protagonist will be effectively impacted and co-generated in the exchange, pointing to how performance, like the process of transculturation itself, "makes room for a reciprocal, two-way exchange through contact."[14] Svich creates a language of a non-place, of one who has left home and cannot return and who has not yet found another – a language of liminality, of the journey, theatricalizing the process of transculturation.

The opening invocation to Santiago, Cuba establishes what will become a hemispheric constellation of Santiagos through Marcela's encounters with other diasporic subjects who have migrated to the United States from various Santiagos in the Americas – Santiago de Chile, Santiago de los Caballeros in the Dominican Republic, Santiago del Estero, Argentina – and from Santiago de Compostela, Spain, which is figured as the "only" Santiago, the "Fi-nis-terre," the "last place on earth before you reach heaven" (22); "[a]ll roads," Marcela learns from a fellow-migrant, Ignacio, "lead to Saint James," whose bones have been laid to rest in the city's cathedral and have become a site of pilgrimage. Later, we learn from her second encounter with a migrant, Coral, on a train to St. Louis, that "[t]here is only one Santiago ... The one in Spain. The rest of us [Santiagos] are stars dropped down from the heavens and scattered over the earth" (48). The positioning of Santiago de Compostela in the colonial motherland as the originary Santiago, from which all Santiagos spring and to which all lead, casts the colonial and neocolonial histories as constitutive of these ongoing transcultural migrations, negotiations, and encounters. Transculturation, while operating as a corrective to the unequal power relations inherent in the structures of acculturation and discourses of assimilation, ultimately cannot transcend or escape these inherited power disparities and the attendant violence they wield.

The violence of the colonial history that has shaped each of the Santiagos, and the neocolonial forces that have prompted each of these migrant's journeys, haunts their encounters, engendering more violence. Marcela's first encounter with Ignacio, hailing from the colonial Motherland of Santiago de Compostela, leads to a violent confrontation when he demands that Marcela give her body to him, assuming she is a *jinetera* (or prostitute) for the taking. In an effort to defend herself, Marcela hits him with her suitcase and he falls to the ground. She opens the suitcase to reveal that it is filled with dirt from her homeland of Cuba, which she pours over him, rubbing it into his face, his hair, his mouth:

[think] you can fuck me over cause I just got off the boat. Well, let me tell you: I got some soil here, I got some soil in here that's got nothing to do with you ... Feel it? This is Cuba. This is that sweet Caribbean ass you want to

fuck... Here. Bury yourself in it. Think of Spain. Cause there isn't a bus or train that can save you. Not even Saint James can save you now. (44–45)

In this gesture of burying Ignacio in the soil, the spectre of the colonial relation is made manifest; the colonial figure is buried in the soil of colonial land. Marcela, here, reverses the unidirectional imposition of the dominant culture over the colonized and the violence of the plundering of colonial lands, making the colonial figure subject to a forced consumption of the lands that were occupied, pillaged, and ravaged. The earth is made continuous with the Cuban body, invoking the bodies that were enslaved by the first Spanish settlers to work the tobacco fields in the sixteenth century, the bodies that worked the canefields in the 1920s and 1930s for American corporations, which had taken control of sugar cane production in the Caribbean islands, and the sexualized *mulata* bodies trafficked in the "masculinist imagination."[15]

Marcela figures the body as a site of transculturation in what Mary Louise Pratt has called the "contact zone," that space of the colonial encounter between subjects "previously separated by geographic and historical disjunctures, and whose trajectories now intersect," but under "conditions of coercion, radical inequality, and intractable conflict."[16] While Marcela attempts to take control of the encounter in a defiant appeal to her national identity, she relinquishes and leaves behind the earth from her homeland of Cuba in the process, symbolically pointing to the thinning of cultural identity and the loss that invariably accompanies transcultural collisions and exchanges. But this loss also propels and "makes lighter" Marcela's movement forward, an inevitable part of the trans-cultural process that ultimately overcomes the colonial imposition and generates new conditions of possibility.

Dramaturgically, Svich employs an episodic structure, and the composition of each scene reflects her stylistic reconciliation of a "literal social realism" with dreamscapes and "dream time" wherein the body "can become another body" and "can mutate in interesting ways,"[17] a feature that theatricalizes one of the central motifs of migration in Svich's *oeuvre*, in which "bodies are reborn in new landscapes."[18] A simple, unadorned realism in the dialogue between characters is interspersed with Marcela's lyrical, expressionistic monologues and moments of song, a stylistic negotiation that situates Svich in the tradition of avant-garde Latin American novelists of transculturation who sought to reconcile a "level of verisimilitude with that of the fantastic in the novel,"[19] but that also places her in the tradition of *teatropoesía* that characterized Latina theatre in the 1980s. According to Sandoval-Sánchez and Saporta Sternbach, in the 1980s Latina theatre turned to a fusion of dramatic text and poetry as a means of expressing "Latina experience within a theatrical discourse." This "commingling of poetry and performance" situated the Latina experience within a context in which its meaning is in development and constantly proliferating. It thereby allowed for a "Latina subjectivity-in-process, a hybridity just beginning to articulate itself in those years."[20] Sandoval-Sánchez and Saporta Sternbach note that while early Latina experimental theatre began by commingling poetry and performance, this tradition "is now one of the major constitutive elements of Latina transcultural discourses, regardless of genre."[21]

Prodigal Kiss also meditates on the transcultural subject-in-process, but rather than giving voice and agency to an early Latina theatrical culture in formation, it discloses both the sense of loss and the generativity that invariably accompanies the transcultural encounter. The play characterizes the transcultural subject as a dissolution of the self that is, paradoxically, in a perpetual process of becoming and in so doing serves as an archive of the development of Latina playwriting, marking the historical turn toward dramaturgies in which stylistic innovations serve a performative function that newly constitute transcultural subjectivities. At the harbor in San Diego, Marcela meets Miriam Mocha from Santiago del Estero, Argentina, a woman in a makeshift wheelchair who wears a blanket pinned with small scraps of paper documenting all the cities she has visited in the United States. Marcela shares her desire to get to New Jersey to visit her aunt, her only living relative aside from her son Ambrosio, whom she left for adoption in Cuba. Mocha offers to help make Marcela presentable for the visit to her aunt and ties a velvet ribbon in her hair. Marcela, hoping to catch a glimpse of herself, looks into the water of the harbor, but she doesn't recognize her own reflection. This lack of recognition incites a lyrical monologue, rupturing the realism of the preceding dialogue, about her own assassination, her own death:

> I've been assassinated by the sky.
> Marcela has died,
> Drowned in the ocean's well,
> Covered in seaweed and stagnant black water...
> Oh to be christened now with another name,
> A name that will fit this sun-patched,
> stone-bruised I
> Who is eternally homesick?
> As befits one from this land
> Where homesickness is a national disease. (116–17)

Entreating Mocha to "christen" her with a new name that "befits...this land," Mocha names her Sharon: "Sha-ron. Sharon, Sharon, Sharon. It tastes funny in my mouth, but if I keep saying it...Sharon, Sharon..." (118). Marcela kisses Mocha's hand and leaves for New Jersey, determined to find a way to get there despite the fact that she has no money. She has lost her identity, but the homesickness or nostalgia, the *algia* or pain for a lost *nostos* or home, drives the acquisition of a new identity that impels her movement forward, a turn that captures the complexity of movements – of de-, re-, and neoculturation – that characterize the transcultural.

Marcela's encounters with fellow migrants from Santiagos in the Americas occur in a series of self-contained episodic scenes, each of which, standing alone, comes to stand for a discrete "contact zone" of encounter, allowing the audience to be instantiated as witnesses to the temporal and spatial co-presencing of subjects engendered by the encounter. We witness the mutual constitution of the characters in this space of contact and, through the accretion of these episodic scenes, the cumulative effect of these encounters on Marcela herself, who, through a kind of signifying chain, comes to embody the transcultural subject-in-process. These episodic contact zones come to function in ways akin to Homi Bhabha's notion of a Third Space, as "contradictory and ambivalent space[s] of enunciation" in which subjects are constituted.[22] While the play focuses on the transformation of the protagonist Marcela herself, the individual scenes, most of which are intimate two-handers, allow us to witness the cogeneration and copresencing of subjects in momentary acts of enunciation.

The mutual co-generativity of these exchanges is critical to an understanding of the transcultural, which aims to redress conceptualizations of colonization as an imposing, dominating force that leaves no avenues for the subaltern beyond assimilation and absorption. Transculturation conceives of cultural exchange not as a one-way phenomenon, but one that is reciprocal, mutually impactful and generative; the "self" and "other" are performatively instantiated and made immanent within these spaces of enunciation. In this respect, the *teatropoesia* that characterized the burgeoning of Latina theatre in the 1980s becomes here the internal language of these momentary encounters within that "Third Space." Svich theatricalizes the "fluctuating movement" and indeterminacy of these sites of enunciation, in which meaning, locutions, symbols are no longer culturally fixed or owned but are instead "appropriated, translated, rehistoricized, and read anew"[23] – acts that are contingent upon one's specific positioning in the moment of enunciation. Importantly, meaning is not predetermined by a structurating force of univocal cultures but arises from and out of individual acts of enunciation, reminding us that transculturation does not operate paradigmatically but as a process that is always situated.

Transcultural selectivity and inventiveness: Tanya Saracho's *El Nogalar*

Even before her joint commission by the Latino theatre company Teatro Vista and the Goodman Theatre for an adaptation of Chekhov's *The Cherry Orchard*, Chicago-based Tanya Saracho was christened the "Chicana Chekhov."[24] Teatro Vista had expressed interest in adaptations of classics from a Latina/o perspective and Saracho had long held that "the most Latino playwright [she] encountered in college was Chekhov."[25] In partnership with the Goodman, Teatro Vista enjoined Saracho to adapt a Chekhov play and the result was a piece inspired by *The Cherry Orchard*, which Saracho cheekily titled *El Nogalar* or *The Pecan Orchard*[26] to reflect a plant variety more indigenous to Mexico. *El Nogalar* (2011) relocates the action in Chekhov's play from Lyubov Andreyevna Ranevskaya's estate in turn-of-the-century Russia to present-day Nuevo León, a northeastern state that shares a nine-mile stretch of border with Texas. Nuevo León is part of what is known as *el triángulo de la muerte* ("the triangle of death"), a corridor of highways connecting its capital of Monterrey with the cities of Reynosa and Nuevo Loredo in the state of Tamaulipas that has become the site of gang warfare between the rival drug cartels Los Zetas and the Sinaloan cartel led by "El Chapo" Guzmán. In Chekhov's play, the social change brought about by the ascendancy of the bourgeoisie threatens old systems of order and displaces the aristocracy. In *El Nogalar,* these circumstances are transposed into the context of criminal cartel activity, positioned as a neocolonial force that is overhauling traditional social systems and the rule of law, and seizing land in a tyranny of criminality. As the character López says, even in the face of his own ties to the local cartel, "we are under an occupation."[27]

The Gayevs of *The Cherry Orchard* become, in Saracho's play, the Galváns, and Madame Ranevskaya, the matriarch and landowner of the orchard, becomes Maité Galván, who returns to Los Nogales from New York City after a fifteen-year absence. The economic downturn, coupled with her lover's depletion of her funds, sends Maité back to her homestead with her US-college-educated, naturalized daughter Anita to reunite with her daughter Valeria, who decided to settle in Los Nogales to oversee the family home and what remains of the servants – Dunia, the maid, and the elderly Fulgencio – in the hopes of marrying López, a family friend and former field worker on the estate with dubious connections to the local cartel. Like Chekhov's Ranevskaya, Maité remains in denial about her dire financial straits and her inability to sustain the orchard, a situation about which Valeria is painfully aware. But in Maité's case, the real threat comes from the encroaching cartels who have annexed "[e]very other piece of land" in the area, according to López, "by force" (78) and have threatened to overtake hers. The seemingly well-intentioned López attempts to bargain with the local cartel chief on the family's behalf in an effort to save the orchard, but like upwardly mobile Yermolai Alexeievitch Lopakhin in *The Cherry Orchard*, López is the only one who possesses the assets necessary to buy out the cartel leader and take ownership of the orchard himself, ultimately betraying the Galváns.

In Saracho's free adaptation of Chekhov's play, the male characters have been set aside, with the exception of López, the play's Lopakhin, who represents the upwardly mobile "*nacos*" (78), a slang term for the nouveaux riches who make spectacles of their wealth to compensate for their low social class. Dunia, the maid, ridicules López for his snakeskin boots and ostentatious use of his Blackberry, but López is also a by-product of the economic conditions in Mexico that have, as Valeria says in the play, "turned good boys, from good families todos mañosos" [vicious; cunning] (78). Affiliation with the cartels has provided men, who were previously disenfranchised and without viable employment, with an opportunity to have a piece of *el sueno Americano* in their own lands without having to cross north of the border, and it is those "who've been waiting to have a little something, the ones who grew up with nothing," Valeria says, who "are the bloodiest and the most cruel" (78). Saracho's decision to focus on the matriarchal dynamics of Chekhov's play by largely dispensing with the male characters reflects the impact of the emigration and cartel crises, and the violence of border cities, on the social fabric with respect to the composition of gender in local communities. When men are not being disappeared by gang warfare, they comprise the largest percentage of out-migration to the United States in search of employment, leaving communities consisting predominantly of women in their wake, in some cases permanently, when they do not succeed in returning from the border crossing alive.

But the border presents the prospect of both opportunity and violence for women as well, as we learn at the outset of the play when Dunia is upset with López for persuading her mother that her aspirations to seek employment at a maquiladora along the border is a dangerous proposition. A young woman venturing alone in search of employment at the maquiladoras (where foreign materials and parts are assembled in Mexico and then shipped back to the United States) is the equivalent, in López's mind, of "putting a sign on your forehead, 'Come kidnap me and rape me, cut me into little pieces'" (72), a brutal reality that, while flippantly captured here by López, is reflected in the widespread massacre of young women maquiladora workers that, since 1993, has surpassed the 370 mark in such places as Ciudad Juarez, where multinational corporations take advantage of the cheap and compliant labor of women seeking to supplement family incomes or acquire a modicum of financial independence. With Dunia's desperate attempts to be industrious and find a way to sustain herself by seeking work along the border set against the return of Maité and Anita, whose family money affords them the luxury of reverse migration during the economic downturn, the play maps with subtlety the transnational movements resulting from interlocking economic and social systems that cut across classed, raced, and gendered lines.

While at the start of the play Dunia's eyes are set on the horizon of the border for a better future, they shift to her feet at the play's conclusion. After learning that López is now the new owner of El Nogalar, Dunia shrewdly begins to seduce him, artfully finding her way onto his lap and then, suggestively, in front of him on her knees, grabbing handfuls of dirt to indicate the promise that the land now presents to them – land they can now touch and own – obviating the need to seek better fortunes north of the border. The play concludes with stage directions for an *"interpretive sound of trees falling"*: *"Now don't go cueing chainsaws because it's not literal,"* Saracho instructs. *"Just make me feel trees are falling. Along with the upper class"* (87). The industriousness and promise of the lower classes finding opportunities at home is what keeps the play's ultimate vision, for Saracho, hopeful: "It ends with the servant getting the house. It's about *el pueblo* – the people of Mexico, who are navigating and doing whatever they can for this bad time to pass."[28]

In the course of charting these navigations and migratory movements precipitated by shifting geopolitical and economic conditions, the play concomitantly captures how these movements impact the formation of transcultural subjectivities. In the fifteen years that Maité has been trying to forge a new life in the United States, she's lost both a sense of place and a sense of self, speaking to the atopic, undefinable "here" that, according to Spitta, troubles the transcultural subject: "These past 15 years since I've been gone I find the world so confusing.

The world is now a version I don't recognize. We don't belong up there, we don't belong down here. Where do we fit? No encajamos. [We don't fit.] There's no place for people like us in the world anymore" (80). Her daughter Anita – described in the character breakdown as "[a] hybrid. Lost" (72) – has spent most of her life in the United States with lingering traces of her family's cultural identity that are now palpable upon her return home, a return that throws her into a radical process of *neo*culturation, leaving her with a sense of incompletion and loss made evident when, drunk on tequila, she asks Valeria to teach her how to "dance Mexican": "Nobody's ever taught me. There are so many things I know halfway. Like I know the beginning or the ending, but I don't know the middle. I'm a half person, Vale…My tongue is a half tongue, my brain too. I'm a half thing" (85). Perhaps aided by the tequila, Anita's desire to embody the family's cultural traditions marks a pivot from the resistance she had expressed earlier toward the pressure to embrace the return "home." Anita's conflicting position-alities in relation to so-called "home" reflect not only the ways in which the process of transculturation undergoes an ongoing and complex movement of de-, re-, and neoculturations; they also speak to the contingency of this process on a subject's situatedness, which determines whether or not transculturation in a given moment enables a sense of immanent agency in resistance or leads to a sense of profound loss. As Diana Taylor emphasizes, transculturation "is not essentially or inherently a resistance theory. It describes a process…. Rather than being oppositional or strictly dialectical, it *circulates*."[29]

Saracho's strategic and selective appropriation of *The Cherry Orchard* is evidence of how the process of transculturation generates artistic interventions. The synthesis of different symbolic registers in the creation of new forms, a process that typifies transculturation, is reflected in her formal negotiation of the new languages that transculturation has produced. In her stage directions at the outset of the play, she is careful to indicate how the performance is to capture the hybrid language that the border has produced; Spanglish or *Espanglés* is neither Spanish nor English, but an altogether different, third language operating on a different symbolic register: "the hybridity of the tongue is important on the border," Saracho writes, "Spanglish and Espanglés can only exist when engendered by the two mother tongues" (72). Light and sound changes throughout the play capture the movement between different registers; there is the "Real World, where char-acters speak whatever they speak" and the "Translated World, where light and sound sort of turn the dial up on the English" (72). But the "Translated World" does not operate in a discrete or "pure" fashion; Spanglish or *Espanglés* pervades it. Consequently, theatricalizing the movement between these two registers makes the audience cognizant of the reciprocal exchanges and losses occurring within theatrical spaces that are themselves transcultural "contact zones," invariably involving acts of transmission and translation. What Taylor says of Peruvian novelist and ethnographer José María Arguedas could be said of Saracho's dram-aturgical strategies in *El Nogalar*: she "yokes two symbolic systems together to emphasize the cultural and historical syncretism of both. And from these two, [she] creates a third, an original cultural product."[30]

Saracho's transcultural dramaturgical strategies also speak to how she negotiates her place as a "Latina" playwright within the broader theatrical culture of Chicago. Saracho was apparently "plucked from a happy fringe career" as cofounder and Artistic Director of Teatro Luna, Chicago's first Latina theatre company, "by the city's larger institutions."[31] Aside from the Teatro Vista and Goodman Theatre commission of *El Nogalar*, Saracho has received commissions to write a play for Steppenwolf's (largely white) theatre ensemble, as well as for Chicago's queer theatre company About Face, for a play about the transgendered Civil War soldier Albert Cashier – commissions that are taking her beyond "Latina/o" subject matter. Henry Godinez, Artistic Director of Teatro Vista, supported Saracho's departure as artistic director of Luna in 2010, in order to expand her potential as a writer and avoid "get[ting] pegged as a writer of Latina monologues."[32] According to Godinez, Saracho is the "first really viable local Latino playwright [they've] had" in Chicago.[33] The increasingly "national role" Saracho is now taking on, according to Steppenwolf's director of artistic development Polly Carl,[34] can be seen as the product of a successful negotiation of the transcultural process that began with a strategic, playful, and purposeful appropriation of *The Cherry Orchard*. As Taylor observes in her reading of Angel Rama's *Transculturación narrativa en America Latina*, transculturation involves a simultaneous process of "loss, selectivity, rediscovery, and incorporation"[35] that shifts the ground upon which hegemonic and marginal cultural forms come into contact. Saracho has appropriated selectively and inventively from Chekhov's play in order to address the immediate political concerns that press upon her community's ongoing historical present, while actively installing herself in Chicago's "dominant cultural production sites," sites that she indelibly impacts and transforms in turn.[36]

The transcultural signifier: Carmen Aguirre's *The Refugee Hotel*

First produced at Toronto's Theatre Passe Muraille in 2009, *The Refugee Hotel* follows the arrival of Canada's first wave of political refugees from Chile in 1974, five months after Augusto Pinochet has come to power following a violent coup that overthrew the democratically elected socialist government under Salvador Allende on 11 September 1973. They have all made the same journey as political exiles of the Pinochet regime and must reckon with their reasons for leaving Chile – a transition that marks the onset of a transcultural process relinquishing previous identities in order to encounter new possibilities and ways of being. They confront the guilt they feel for abandoning the resistance, and attempt to reconcile their previous lives as political resistors with their current ones working in Canada. But their stories are not uniform. While there are points of solidarity and common ground, the trajectories and experiences leading to their arrival in the refugee hotel in Vancouver are wildly disparate; the play complicates any generalized assumptions about the mass migratory movement precipitated by the coup by individualizing its impact, tracing the aftermath of the Pinochet regime on individual subject formation in new cultural contexts.

The play opens with a framing device that situates the narrative as a memory of its central character, Manuelita, who, now in her late thirties, recounts the events of her family's arrival at a hotel in Vancouver, which served as a provisional home to the first waves of Chilean refugees until more permanent jobs and homes could be arranged. Manuelita stands alone centre stage with a suitcase in hand, a mirror image of Svich's Manuela in *Prodigal Kiss*. The audience hears the final phrases of Allende's last broadcast from La Moneda Palace on the morning of the coup before the bombs drop on the building. Manuelita repeats the speech in English accompanied by a lone male *cueca* dancer in the traditional *huaso* (or horseman) dress of leather boots, oversized spurs, *chupalla* or straw hat, and *manta* or poncho, who performs the aggressive and rhythmic foot stomping or *zapateo* typical of the *cueca* – a figure that will recur throughout the play. Over the *zapateo*, Manuelita introduces the historical moment and the events that have precipitated her family's arrival in Vancouver. She joins her family "in the scene," returning to her eight-year-old self and taking the audience back thirty years to her family's first week in the run-down hotel.

Like Svich, Aguirre uses an episodic structure characteristic of early naturalism but ruptures illusionism through the use of the framing device, the recurring presence of the *cueca* dancer, and, significantly, allowing each of the characters not only to be visible to the audience in their individual hotel rooms throughout the play, but to hear and bear witness to the events happening on stage at all times. This staging strategy effectively creates a community of witness that interpellates spectators as witnesses as well, a position that is cued at the outset with Manuelita's direct address to the audience, which plays an important function in the play's broader political context. The creation of a performance space in which the stories of political prisoners, exiles, and the disappeared can be heard is a freighted undertaking and one that mirrors the ongoing investigations of the Comisión Valech, The National Commission on Political Imprisonment and Torture Report in Chile, which continues to collect testimonies of political imprisonment and torture that occurred during Pinochet's regime from September 1973 to March 1990, a regime that would effectively disappear over 3,000 people, torture over 30,200, and exile approximately 300,000[37] – 7,000 of whom would eventually settle in Canada and 17,600 in the United States.[38] Through the course of the play, we learn of the imprisonment and torture of Manuelita's mother, Flaca, a former professor and reputed revolutionary, her father, Fat Jorge, whose nightmares of his time in prison wrench him from his sleep throughout the play, and, in harrowing detail, the methods of torture used against Manuel, a refugee who arrives at the hotel "directly from a concentration camp on Dawson Island, near Antarctica."[39] Isabel, another refugee who arrives at the hotel, is nicknamed "Calladita" (the quiet one) because the horrors she has witnessed have rendered her mute, unable to speak.

Cristina, an 18-year-old Mapuche refugee whose parents have been disappeared, arrives at the hotel with Isabel and soon confesses her cynicism at the apathy of her people who have watched their neighbors be taken in broad daylight: "I've come to the conclusion that our country is a country of cowards" (70). When pressed by Jorge as to why she didn't remain in Chile to join the underground resistance,

Cristina confesses her fear: "Now, you may know a little bit about fear, comrade. But I know a lot about it. I am a Mapuche. We've lived in fear for 450 years" (75). Cristina goes on to allude to centuries of struggle against conquering forces beginning with the Inca, followed in turn by the Spanish and the Chilean government. These words, uttered by the Mapuche Cristina, who was played by the Canadian First Nations actor Cheri Maracle in the 2009 production at Theatre Passe Muraille, became a powerful testimonial of transindigeneity in the Americas, constellating the political violence against indigenous populations in the hemisphere by linking the conditions of the Mapuche with those of First Nations in Canada; the apathy Cristina describes in her country corresponds with Canada's own in the face of its history of de facto apartheid in the treatment of First Nations peoples and reservation lands, and in the legacy of the residential school system. The transnational linkages that occur in the *longue durée* of Cristina's testimonial recur in the epilogue of the play, when we return to the adult Manuelita's present-day reflections on the events that followed that week in the hotel. The receptionist of the hotel, she relays, filled a wall with photographs, not just as mementos of her family's visit and the Chilean refugees who followed, but of the "many, many more refugees [who] came to stay at the refugee hotel. From Guatemala, El Salvador, Vietnam, Iran, Ethiopia, Somalia, Yugoslavia, Colombia, Iraq" (126). The play concludes with a hemispheric perspective that situates the first waves of Chilean political exiles in the broader context of geopolitical forces and neocolonial oppressions that continue to produce global migrations and diasporic communities.

The *cueca* dancer, who reappears at the end of the play and throughout at key moments during the characters' testimonies and nightmares of torture, performs a transnational function bridging the Chilean cultures left behind with the new diasporic cultures in formation. But he also functions as an important cipher of transculturalism. The formation of *cueca* as Chile's national dance is itself the product of a long history of transculturation such that its origins and development are obscure and contested among dance historians and ethnomusicologists. There are over a hundred regional variations of *cueca* in Chile, but the *huaso cueca*, which features the male dancer in the *huaso* dress and which appears in *The Refugee Hotel*, became a national figure, indeed a figure of "national chauvinism" under the Pinochet regime, as Jan Sverre Knudsen argues, designed to promote a unified Chile and suppress regional diversity and political dissidence.[40] A stereotypical, singular form of the *cueca* was deployed as an ideological tool in the project of national identity formation under a totalitarian state. However, the *cueca*, traditionally viewed as a courting dance that occurs in pairs, underwent a significant transcultural evolution in the hands of the resistance. Members of the resistance both within Chile and in exile appropriated the *cueca* in an effort to "liberate the dance from its chauvinistic overtones" and its ideological function within the Pinochet regime, performing the dance without the traditional folk dress and to lyrics that emphasized political issues over the themes of love and country life that typified traditional *cueca* music.[41] Within Chile, the *cueca sola*, performed alone without the traditional dress in front of official government buildings and police stations by the mothers and wives of the jailed or the disappeared, became a charged tool of political protest. The women would perform the dance solo with pictures of their loved one pinned to their clothes, appropriating a form of cultural expression strategically nurtured by the regime as a "wordless, subtle…[and] powerful denunciation of the atrocities committed during the dictatorship."[42]

In *The Refugee Hotel*, the *cueca* dancer appears as a productively ambiguous transcultural signifier. Dancing solo in the form associated with political protest, yet dressed in the traditional *huaso* costume of the national dance cultivated by the regime, the *cueca* dancer becomes both at once and yet something else altogether in this new cultural context. Appearing in the shadows of Manuel's account of the torture methods used against him at the concentration camp, during Jorge's nightmares of his torture while in prison, and during Manuelita's expressions of resistance and solidarity expressed at the outset and closure of the play, the solo *huaso cueca* dancer becomes at once an expression of a Chilean monolithic nationalism and the violence that unifying projects of national identity formation can wield, as well as an expression of political resistance against the violence of a totalitarian regime. But as a figure summoned by political refugees under forced exile in a new country, the *cueca* dancer acquires a particular potency as a figure of the cultural identity that gives them the strength to move forward, suggested by the accelerated strength of the dancer's *zapateo*, but also of an identity that will gradually be relinquished in the process of transculturation in order to encounter new modes of being and new avenues of possibility. How this signifier operates to Canadian audiences who may not be aware of the solo *cueca* dancer's freighted ideological significance invites further consideration of the ways in which reception can itself foster the process of transculturation through acts of appropriation that attempt to create meaning across cultural difference. The *cueca* dancer finally reminds us that the very meaning of transculturation is itself contingent not only on the different cultural contexts in which it is posed but on the individual positionalities of its interpretive uptake. These individual interpretive labors within transcultural contact zones result in the formation of new audiences, momentary collectivities that break down the boundaries mapping the hegemonic and the marginal, the mainstream and the peripheral.

In his analysis of literature in the Americas through the lens of Ortiz, Rama emphasizes the multiple facets of the transcultural – the de-, re-, and neoculturations – that "combine in different ways" and reveal "destructions, re-affirmations, and absorptions" which, in the field of literature at least, lead to "a proportionately higher level of freedom, apparent in the artists' capacity for selection."[43] This capacity for selection emphasizes a degree of agency in the formation of transcultural artistic innovations and, by extension, the formation of transcultural subjectivities, pointing to how transculturalism has served as a means of circumventing narratives of victimization, assimilation, and passivity in the face of colonial oppression. The overarching aim of this investigation has been to resist the tendency in theories of transculturation to speak of it paradigmatically as a structurating force. To do so is to reduce transculturation to a structuralism that precipitates and delimits individual movements and acts, which works against its potential both as a mode of agency and as a generative force that overcomes a colonial imposition – aspects that have characterized the political and theoretical motives behind its uptake in Latin American studies. By examining the work of these "third wave" Latina playwrights, we can come to understand how transculturalism serves as a productively tensile methodology for examining the aesthetic interventions that arise from cultural encounters and collisions in contact zones – interventions that make possible individual sites of enunciation articulating the emergence of transcultural subjectivities-in-process.

Notes

1   Caridad Svich and Anne García-Romero have provided lucid overviews of the successive waves of Latina playwrights that can be traced back to the mentorship and playwriting workshop initiatives of Maria Irene Fornes. The current "third wave" of Latina theatre that began in the 1990s with the work of Quiara Alegría Hudes, Elaine Romero, Cusi Cram, Karen Zacarías, and the playwrights I examine here can be characterized, according to García-Romero, by a refusal of any "monolithic" understandings of cultural identity and theatrical experimentations that arise out of cultural collisions. See Svich's introduction to *Out of the Fringe: Contemporary Latina/Latino Theater and Performance*, eds. Caridad Svich and María Teresa Marrero (New York: Theatre Communications Group, 2000), xii, and García-Romero's PhD dissertation *Transculturation and Twenty-First Century Latina Playwrights* (University of California, Santa Barbara, 2009).
2   Fernando Ortiz, *Contrapunteo Cubano del tabaco y el azucar* (Caracas: Biblioteca Ayacucho, 1978), 97; translations mine.
3   Ibid., 97.
4   Ibid., 96.
5   Silvia Spitta, *Between Two Waters: Narratives of Transculturation in Latin America* (Houston: Rice University Press, 1995), 24.
6   Ibid.
7   Alberto Sandoval-Sánchez and Nancy Saporta Sternbach, *Stages of Life: Transcultural Performance & Identity in U.S. Latina Theater* (Tucson: University of Arizona Press, 2001), 25.
8   Ibid., 21.
9   Ibid., 97.
10 I borrow this phrase from Jill Dolan, *Presence and Desire: Essays on Gender, Sexuality, Performance* (Ann Arbor: University of Michigan Press, 1993), 26.
11 Caridad Svich, *Prodigal Kiss: a play with songs*, *Prodigal Kiss and Perdita Gracia: Two Plays by Caridad Svich* (South Gate: Lizard Run Press, 2009), 18; subsequent references to the play will be given parenthetically in the text.
12 In a 2009 interview with Adam Szymkowicz, Svich indicates that *Prodigal Kiss*, subtitled "[a] play with songs," "was written with the Cuban bolero and guaguancó in mind." Available at *http://aszym.blogspot.ie/2009/09/i-interview-playwrights-part-61-caridad.html* (accessed 23 September 2012).
13 Svich, quoted in Justin Maxwell, "Cartography Lessons with Caridad Svich," *American Theatre* (July/August 2009): 35.
14 Diana Taylor, *The Archive and the Repertoire* (Durham, NC: Duke University Press, 2003), 105.
15 On the mulata body and transculturation, see Alicia Arrizón, "Race-ing Performativity through Transculturation, Taste and the Mulata Body," *Theatre Research International* 27, no. 2 (2002): 136–52.

16 Mary Louise Pratt, *Imperial Eyes: Travel Writing and Transculturation* (London: Routledge, 1992), 7, 6.

17 Svich, quoted in Maxwell, "Cartography Lessons," 35.

18 Caridad Svich, introduction, *Prodigal Kiss*, 12.

19 Angel Rama, "Processes of Transculturation in Latin American Narrative," *Journal of Latin American Cultural Studies* 6, no. 2 (1997): 161.

20 Sandoval-Sánchez and Saporta Sternbach, *Stages of Life*, 58.

21 Ibid.

22 Homi K. Bhabha, *The Location of Culture* (London: Routledge, 1994), 37.

23 Ibid.

24 See Fabrizio O. Almeida, review of *Kita y Fernanda*, 6 October 2008, available at *http://newcitystage.com/2008/10/06/recommended-kita-y-fernanda16th-street-theater/* (accessed 23 September 2012).

25 Saracho, quoted in Rob Weinert-Kendt, "Mexican? American? Call Her a Writer," *New York Times*, 22 March 2011, available at *http://www.nytimes.com/2011/03/27/theater/tanya-sarachos-nogalar-mexican-take-on-chekhov.html* (accessed 22 June 2012).

26 It should be noted that *El Nogalar* more accurately translates as "The Walnut Orchard," but Saracho refers to it throughout the play, and it is generally translated, as *"The Pecan Orchard."*

27 Tanya Saracho, "El Nogalar," *American Theatre* (July/August 2011): 74; subsequent references to the play will be given parenthetically in the text.

28 Saracho, quoted in Kerry Reid, "Tanya Saracho Catching the Wheel: A Mexican-born playwright steps boldly from Teatro Luna into Chicago's larger scene," *American Theatre* (April 2011): 40.

29 Diana Taylor, "Transculturating Transculturation," *Performing Arts Journal* 13, no. 2 (May 1991): 101; emphasis in original.

30 Taylor, "Transculturating Transculturation," 95.

31 Weinert-Kendt, "Mexican? American?"

32 Godinez quoted in Kris Vire, "Playwright Tanya Saracho," *TimeOut: Chicago* 6 June 2010, available at *http://timeoutchicago.com/arts-culture/theater/82931/playwright-tanya-saracho* (accessed 22 June 2012).

33 Godinez, quoted in Weinert-Kendt, "Mexican? American?"

34 Carl, quoted in Weinert-Kendt, ibid.

35 Taylor, *The Archive and the Repertoire*, 105.

36 Dolan, *Presence and Desire*, 26.

37 Comisión Nacional Sobre Prisión Política y Tortura, 1 June 2005, available at *http://www.bcn.cl/bibliodigital/dhisto/lfs/Informe.pdf* (accessed 30 June 2012).

38 Encyclopedia of Immigration, "Chilean immigration," 8 February 2011, available at *http://immigration-online.org/65-chilean-immigration.html* (accessed 30 June 2012).

39 Carmen Aguirre, *The Refugee Hotel* (Vancouver: Talonbooks, 2010), 55; subsequent references to the play will be given parenthetically in the text.

40 Jan Sverre Knudsen, "Dancing *cueca* 'with your coat on': The Role of Traditional Chilean Dance in an Immigrant Community," *British Journal of Ethnomusicology* 10, no. 2 (2001): 68.

41 Ibid., 69.

42 Ibid.

43 Rama, "Processes of Transculturation," 160.

6 Black Women Playwrights Making History: Katori Hall's *The Mountaintop*

Soyica Diggs Colbert

In content and form, Katori Hall's *The Mountaintop* negotiates the legacy of Martin Luther King Jr.'s civil rights leadership and African American drama. Questioning the vertical structure implied through traditional models of kinship, which are thematically pervasive in American drama (in works by Eugene O'Neill, Arthur Miller, and Tennessee Williams, for example), Hall's play troubles the notion of cultural transmission via inheritance or passing down. The formal attributes and themes of the play posit a horizontal model of transmission that situates legacy as something to be contested, crafted, or shaped but never merely received. Engaging with the familiar history of the civil rights movement through an iconic figure, Hall's play not only changes what we knew about civil rights leadership, but it also influences what we can know. Similarly, by signifying on the form of the African American history play, *The Mountaintop* links itself to and distinguishes itself from the black aesthetic practice of recuperation. Hall's work engages a tradition of black playwriting that reimagines historical figures in order to craft revisionary and recuperative narratives and to give voice to histories that may otherwise be forgotten.[1] The act of reimagining is instructive by calling attention to historical narrative as constructed over time and, therefore, enabling collaboration among historians of the past, present, and future.

Set in the Lorraine Motel in Memphis, *The Mountaintop* depicts King's last night alive. Conjecturing what may have been King's final thoughts, reservations, desires, and fears, the play consists of a conversation between King and an enigmatic maid named Camae, who we learn midway through the play is actually an angel of death. Often playful, the conversation between King and Camae centers on the continuation of the civil rights movement after King's death. *The Mountaintop* culminates with Camae describing, in verse, the years following King's assassination, a panoramic video presentation accompanying her description.

Part August Wilson-style mystical realism and part Suzan-Lori Parks-style history play, Hall domesticates King – a larger-than-life figure – to recalibrate the movement he personifies, shifting the emphasis from King as the singular embodiment of the civil rights movement to the constitution of him by way of an unlikely heroine and the audience. The play contemplates the ways we know

King in order to call our attention to the civil rights movement as an ongoing endeavor whose past, present, and future continues to be under necessary revision, reexamination, and production. Moreover, the play's depiction of King in relationship to Camae foregrounds the women who helped to produce the movement and the ways we, as audience members, perpetuate and contribute to civil rights movement history. Hall explains, "It's important to show our saints in a way that makes the great good in us attainable.... By showing [King] struggling, having imperfections – it proves to us we have the potential to do the same."[2] By humanizing King, Hall creates space on stage for another character to participate in shaping the events and meaning of the play and thereby raises the question of how humanizing King provides room within the history of the civil rights movement to tell women's stories.

Hall's work is new to the national theatre scene and thus has yet to receive any critical attention in scholarly publications. Popular critics, however, reviewed the London and New York productions of *The Mountaintop* in 2009 and 2011 respectively. Sam Marlowe wrote: "This two-hander by the emergent US playwright Katori Hall electrified the London fringe venue Theatre 503 in its 2009 premiere.... This inventive and startlingly moving drama ... at its finest is thrillingly intense."[3] Expressing less enthusiasm and questioning the reception of a US play across the pond, *New York Times* theatre critic Ben Brantley quipped, "'The Mountaintop' arrives on Broadway attended by great expectations and the skepticism that some New York theatergoers may feel about British-endorsed, American-themed productions ('Enron,' anyone?)."[4] Brantley also identified the play's inability to bring a greater level of humanity to King as its failure: "Unfortunately, this big-picture drama (and Ms. Hall's big picture is bigger than you imagine) is short on revelatory close-ups. And despite an engagingly low-key performance by Mr. [Samuel L.] Jackson, it never provides the organic details and insights that would make Martin Luther King live anew."[5]

Although Brantley makes some persuasive points, questioning whether "mounting [the play] on this scale turns out to be a bit like spinning gossamer into Dacron,"[6] his simile also highlights which historical figures merit the position of larger-than-life characters and which do not. I would argue that *The Mountaintop* purposefully repositions King as a co-star in the civil rights movement rather than in its leading role. While perhaps unfulfilling for some like Brantley, the play questions the desire to see a great man on a large stage and the disappointment of finding a woman there instead, no less one with supernatural powers. The interplay between Camae and King not only refashions King, but also positions her as a figure central to the movement.

The Mountaintop is at its most forceful when it is Camae's play. King, however, is necessary in order to call forth the conventions of the history play and intervene in the civil rights historiography that would foreground him as an exemplary civil rights activist instead of as a figure in relationship to Camae, a cursing, drinking former prostitute. The version of King presented by the play calls attention to a struggle in the historiography of the civil rights movement over how to position King regarding his legacies and then how to position him in relation to the women of the movement. In doing so, *The Mountaintop* participates in a refashioning of the history play that Parks exemplifies, deforming historical figures in order to reform the audience's relationship to the past and thereby make history. The play builds on a civil rights historiography that Danielle McGuire's *At the Dark End of the Street* extols, foregrounding the essential role of activism fighting violence against black women in shaping the civil rights movement. Moreover, by reframing the audience's knowledge of King and shaping the depiction of Camae through references to her life and untimely death, *The Mountaintop* democratizes civil rights activism by not only positioning women and survivors of sexual violence as key to the ongoing movement, but also by demonstrating, in Camae's final speech, the audience's equal access to the black oral tradition idealized in the church and in King's elocution.

In her introduction to a 2011 collection of her plays, Hall frames the cultural intervention she hoped to make, revealing a number of experiences – her mother's and her own – that inspired *The Mountaintop*. Her mother lived one block from the Lorraine Motel and participated in the first sanitation workers' strike in Memphis on 28 March 1968. Hall recalls, "Within minutes, that march descended into chaos, leaving one person dead and King deeply depressed. But my mother had participated and, despite the defeat, was left inspired by King that her small voice could be heard in order to change the world for the better."[7] Hall then describes her mother's regret about missing King's final speech due to inclement weather and concerns that white supremacists would bomb the Mason Temple. Concluding, she asserts, "I am a baby of the civil rights movement and have benefited greatly from [King's] legacy" (xii). At the same time that Hall asserts an all-too-familiar causal relationship between the activism of the civil rights movement and the post-soul generation's[8] educational and social opportunities, she implies that her play offers some type of answer to the question of "how close are we to the Promised Land" (xii).

Whereas Brantley argued that the play does not offer new insights into King's humanity, locating our proximity to a fuller realization of US democracy must be measured in relationship to the only other character in the play, Camae. Camae not only draws attention to the essential role of women in the movement and the particular gender violence they suffered, but she also foregrounds the necessary collaborations that sustain battles for civil and human rights. Hall's critical framing suggests that measuring our proximity to a full realization of the promise of US democracy requires a re-engagement with history that includes acts of imagination. Put another way, Hall situates the historical recuperation that drama provides specifically and that art enables more generally as fundamental to achieving the promise of civil and human rights for all Americans.

To resist limiting the civil rights movement to King's leadership, Camae must convince King that when he dies the following day, his work will continue. She explains:

> Honey, I know all about your trials and tribulations. I done read yo' blessings file. It bigger than yo' FBI file and that bigga than the Bible. I know it might be hard for you to leave this life, ... yo' family, ... and yo' plans. But you gone have

to pass off that baton, little man. You in a relay race albeit the fastest runner we done ever seen't. But you 'bout to burn out, superstar. You gone need to pass off that baton. (231)

The notion of passing the baton is reprised in Camae's final speech. Passing the baton symbolically represents a collective movement that entails passing on but not necessarily passing down. It requires individual autonomy as it depends on collectivity to achieve the goal of winning the race. It suggests that no matter how fast an individual runner King may be, he cannot run the race alone.

As the subject matter and language of *The Mountaintop* calls to mind the question of succession, it suggests that King's legacy may not properly live on in the practice of passing down but instead must continue through the process of passing on. The language of "passing on" creates a horizontal mode of exchange rather than the vertical and therefore hierarchal means that passing down connotes. Passing on creates an extension – the bodily curving, breaking, and unhinging of a contortionist seemingly freeing limb from joint while remaining tethered to a source. Free yet connected, independent yet reliant, extension allows innovation even as it signifies on a larger body of work, transforming the source and creating different modes of interrelation. The conversation between Camae and King extends King's legacy just as *The Mountaintop* extends the history of African American drama.

History in the making

African American drama is often understood in terms of succession, which seems to account nicely for Broadway production history following the untimely death of August Wilson in 2005. Since his death, a cadre of black women playwrights has filled the commercial vacancy Wilson left as the most frequently produced African American playwright on Broadway. This cadre, including Parks, Lynn Nottage, and Lydia Diamond, as well as Hall, demands a rethinking of Wilson's influence as mutually constituted and constitutive of black theatre of the twenty-first century.[9] While Wilson's drama existed in relationship to and alongside black women playwrights' drama even before his death, the confluence of black women on Broadway functions similarly to Camae's role in *The Mountaintop* in that it calls for a reconsideration of the way we understand the history of a great man. It begs for a re-examination of Wilson's place in theatre history, which is often framed in relationship to his intersection with and departure from a male-centered black arts movement and blues aesthetic and discussed in terms of the types of black plays producers will fund.[10]

Within the context of reading the current work of black women playwrights alongside Wilson's drama, Harry Elam Jr.'s study of Wilson may be transposed to describe the efforts of many black playwrights, including Hall. According to Elam, the critical practice of "(w)righting history" unifies Wilson's drama.[11] Elam explains, "I consciously riff on the meanings of *writing, righting, right,* and *rites* to frame and analyze Wilson's processes of reckoning with the African American past."[12] He elaborates: "Wilson (w)rights history through performative rites that pull the action of our time or even ritualize time in order to change the power and potentialities of the now. The process of (w)righting history necessarily critiques how history is constituted and what history means. It reinterprets how history operates in relation to race and space, time and memory."[13] Revealing the co-constitutive nature of the spiritual and the human realms, Wilson's drama demonstrates the intricate role of ritual in the formation of the everyday. Making room for unfamiliar voices on the Great White Way, Wilson's drama functions in part as an act of recuperation. It serves as a fitting analog to Hall's drama, which uses ritual not only to mobilize the healing quality of recuperation – to recognize, mourn, and document the brutal experience of women in the civil rights movement – but also to revive.

Working alongside, after, and with Wilson, Parks is another key contributor to the theory of how black theatre makes history. Her history plays are of a different sort; they are more aptly described as historiography plays in that they seek to intervene in and challenge the ongoing historical discourse and to reconstitute historical figures by imagining them in situations they never experienced. She does not write about those whom history forgot. Instead, Parks adds chapters to the stories of well-known figures, from Abraham Lincoln to Saartjie Baartman to Hester Prynne. Using historical figures as prototypes for her characters, Parks creates simulacra that destabilize these figures and render their articulation as a matter of historiography that Parks may equally enter into by making dramatic history. In *The America Play*, for example, she creates a Lincoln-like figure but casts him as a black man and calls him the "foundling father." In *Fucking A*, she creates a character named Hester who has an "A" branded into her chest, but in this case, unlike Nathaniel Hawthorne's character in *The Scarlet Letter*, the "A" stands for *abortionist*. By defamiliarizing iconic American figures, Parks reveals the processes of crafting myths and makes that power available to the members of her audience.

Recuperating King

The Mountaintop benefits from Wilson's proactive and healing practice of recuperation and Parks's signature style of revision to produce a history play engaged in negotiating transitions. Set on 3 April 1968, Hall's play enables the possibility of imagining King as a figure in transition. Although King often functions as synecdoche for the civil rights movement, such representations trap him in 1963 at a podium giving his "I Have a Dream" speech and limit the civil rights movement to a shallow desire for African American assimilation and inclusion in the national body. Hall's play instead foregrounds the multiplicities of King's conception of the movement, having him lament his unfinished business once he learns that Camae is an angel of death. He recalls his men charging, "'You splittin' the movement, Martin, you splittin' the movement! You can't focus on war, and poverty, and

Negroes. Choose one!!' But I could not, *will* not choose just – " (227). Ending with a dash to grammatically represent a man at the crossroads, the play recovers King's less frequently represented and more radical political vision. Instead of splitting the movement, King's vision sought to make the movement as interrelated as the parts of the body and as singular as well. He understood that to deny the importance of poverty or war to black people's freedom would be analogous to ignoring a foot infection and assuming that the infection would not spread to the rest of the body. The failure to address one violation of human rights would be to the detriment of all human rights. Nevertheless, to prescribe medicine for a foot infection when the patient has a systemic infection would be equally problematic and dangerous. King's understanding of the civil rights movement required attention to the differences within sameness. It also demanded an understanding of the triangulated relationships that the movement produced, which in turn requires considering racial justice as always "routed through, and in relation to," the status of other human rights.[14]

King's most radical descriptions of the movement foregrounded a struggle for legibility that the complex interweaving of focuses (racial justice, war, poverty) produced and continues to produce in the contestations over how to historicize the movement justly. As Nikhil Pal Singh explains: "just as King's antiwar stance has been minimized or forgotten, so has the steady incorporation of currents of democratic socialism and black nationalism into his thinking. By the end of his life, King viewed the idea of obtaining civil rights for black individuals as an inadequate framework for combating the economic consequences and cultural legacies of white supremacy."[15] Productively calling attention to the idea of a movement as change – the antithesis of stasis – Singh presents King as evolving and therefore the movement as occupying different positions, via King, throughout his life. Therefore, time always triangulates King's relationship to the civil rights movement.

King's philosophical movement – his shift in thinking from his first phase, 1955–1965, to his second phase, 1965–1968 – proved disruptive and dangerous because it resisted the incorporation of the civil rights movement into the narrative of US exceptionalism predicated on diversity and assimilation. But instead of marking the passing of the Civil Rights Act of 1964 and the Voting Rights Act of 1965 as the culmination of the movement, "Civil rights, King argued, were just the beginning of a struggle that revolved around housing, employment, and economic justice, the root struggles of the long civil rights era."[16] King sought to recharge the movement by situating race relations as fundamental to the formation of the United States and therefore extending the movement from the origins of the country to the present. The fluidity and indeterminacy of his notion of the civil rights movement came to the foreground as early as 1961, in his commencement address at Lincoln University. In this speech, King charged: "Each individual has certain basic rights that are neither conferred by nor derived from the state. To discover where they came from it is necessary to move back behind the dim mist of eternity, for they are God-given.... The American dream reminds us that every man is heir to the legacy of worthiness."[17] Tying Americanness, the ethos of the nation's exceptionality, to rights that exceed state conferral, King challenged the United States to meet not only its legal obligations to its citizens but its moral obligations as well. The ethical grounds that King used to supplement his argument emphasized the extra-legal means of redress he sought from the nation-state.

Placing an expansive sense of democracy predicated on human rights and "neither conferred by nor derived from the state" at the center of the movement reframes King as one runner among many in the relay race for freedom. The expansiveness of the vision resists codification and the impulse to confine "the civil rights struggle to the South, to bowdlerized heroes, to a single halcyon decade, and to limited, noneconomic objectives,"[18] which, according to Jacquelyn Dowd Hall, serves to create "the master narrative" that "simultaneously elevates and diminishes the movement.... It prevents one of the most remarkable mass movements in American history from speaking effectively to the challenges of our time."[19]

Set on the eve of King's assassination, *The Mountaintop* positions him as a man advocating for the poor and planning a march for sanitation workers' rights. The play opens with rain pouring down, forming sheets of water that, according to the stage directions, "[slide] down the pane on to the walls" (191). As the storm escalates from rain to thunder and lightning, it serves to punctuate the interaction between King and Camae; at one point, she starts to leave King's room but the boom of thunder sends her back inside. At another moment, the deep roar of thunder and sharp crack of lightning sends King jumping frantically: "Wheew! Thought they got me! *He puts his hand over his chest. He begins to breathe hard*" (204). Within popular historiographies of the civil rights movement, King represents singularity and exceptionality, but his reaction to the changes in weather in Hall's play highlights relationality and position drama as the perfect medium to communicate the collectivity necessary for a movement.

Remembering women's activism

The Mountaintop demonstrates King's vulnerability, thus humanizing an icon who rose to prominence alongside women, including Rosa Parks. The play thereby creates a structure for the narrative that foregrounds Camae's crucial role in the drama. McGuire's *At the Dark End of the Street* begins its narrative revision of civil rights movement historiography with two women: Recy Taylor, a survivor of a brutal gang rape, and Rosa Parks. McGuire reveals Parks as "a militant race woman, a sharp detective, and an antirape activist long before she became the patron saint of the bus boycott."[20] Parks's image has been sanitized for national consumption: rather than a militant and bold race woman, we often think of her as a meek, tired, and passive participant in an event that sparked the movement, but in fact, well before King became the face and voice of the bus boycott, Parks worked tirelessly to bring Taylor's rapist to justice. McGuire argues:

Unfortunately, this King-centric and male-dominated version of events obscures the real history of the Montgomery bus boycott as a women's movement for dignity. The focus on King is so absolute that even today many historians over-look the fact that it was four female plaintiffs, Claudette Colvin, Mary Louise Smith, Mrs. Aurelia Browder, and Mrs. Susie McDonald, who filed the lawsuit that finally ended segregation on public transportation and put teeth into the *Brown* decision.[21]

Rather than eclipse the role of women in general and that of sexual violence survivors in particular, *The Mountaintop* casts Camae as a sexually exploited and overtly sexual character who ushers King through his final hours in order to reframe him as a man in relationship to women activists from all walks of life. The play not only intervenes in the history of the civil rights movement, but it also makes a critical contribution to the historiography, calling attention to the gender politics that continue to inform the characterization of black women activists.

The play answers the call of black feminist critics who challenge the exclusion of women from the history of the civil rights movement and the distortion of the roles women played. Belinda Robnett explains the relationship between the ideal of male leadership that the civil rights movement perpetuated and the brutal practice of vigilante policing of black women through rape. She argues:

> Many women discussed the reasons why they or others supported and promoted Black male leadership and accepted less than formal leadership positions. One of the central explanations has centered on the belief that, throughout history, reprisals have been worse for Black men. The argument is generally made that men were lynched more often than were women. Yet throughout history women also suffered reprisals and were beaten, raped, and, though not as frequently as men, lynched.[22]

Black women's awareness of the ways violence functioned to delimit the impact of male leaders helped to cultivate a movement that recapitulated gender hierarchies and ignored the brutality of women's experience. At the same time, the need to depict not just male leaders but strong, heterosexual family men (part of King's and Malcolm X's iconography stems from the popular perception of them as husbands and fathers) and supportive, chaste, dignified women marks a politics not just of gender but also of sexuality that reinscribes the shame suffered by many victims of sexual violence. Through her figuration as a survivor of sexual violence, Camae questions the purity that subtends the mythical greatness of leaders, harnessing the power of myth even in the midst of her status as survivor.

The play depicts Camae not only as an angel but also as being like Legba, the sexually ambiguous trickster and guardian of the crossroads in Yoruba cosmology who functions as "the divine messenger of the orisás, uniting *aye*, the world of the living, with *orun*, the invisible sacred world,"[23] and who "intercedes on behalf of humans in their appeals to spiritual beings, if appropriately treated and honored, but garbles messages and wreaks havoc if angered."[24]

Camae calls to mind the figure of Legba because she negotiates the point of transition, has a biting sense of humor and mischievous spirit, and figures her power in relationship to her body and sexuality. At one point, King questions Camae: "Where are your wings?" In response, *She points to her breasts* (222). Later he accuses her of using her breasts to lure "men to their deaths" (236).

Camae is as an unlikely figure of transition when viewed solely within the stereotypical social hierarchies of the civil rights movement as rooted in the moral absolutes of Christianity. The play calls attention to the hierarchies by insisting that God is a she – "Black? Mmhm. And PROUD" (234) – and having King correct Camae when she describes Coretta Scott King as an activist. He responds, "Mrs. King," truncating her position in the movement to his helpmate (199). Contrasting with Mrs. King, Camae is a sexual abuse survivor and prostitute who died at the hands of one of her johns only hours before she became an angel and received the assignment, as a condition for employment, to bring King home. The play presents all the reasons Camae might be deemed unfit to play a divine role in order to reveal the impact of a syncretic form of spirituality on the movement, revising the moral strictures that denigrate Camae and bar her, an angel and a Legba-like figure, from being the perfect person for the job. A paradoxical figure associated with divinity and purity as well as trickery and hypersexuality weds Christianity to diasporic belief systems and renders a more expansive spiritual basis for the movement.

As an angel and Legba figure, Camae mediates King's relationship with God as well as with the audience. Camae comes to bring King the message that he has completed his work on earth and to bring the audience a message of work yet to be done. Legba, guardian of the crossroads, "lives at the point where roads converge, which is symbolic of the intersecting lines connecting heaven and earth, east and west, north and south," providing, according to Marta Moreno Vega, "access to knowledge of the past, present, and future."[25] While the imagery of the crossroads invites a spatial reading, Vega also points to the temporal liminality of the site. If, as I claim, *The Mountaintop* draws attention to how we remember King, then the play, through Camae, "makes possible a community of memory constituted through a trans-Atlantic, cross-generational communication between the gods and their servitors, the here and the beyond, the living and the dead."[26] The role of exchange is key because it calls attention to the necessity of interconnection that facilitates civil rights movement activism and enables King's transition in the play.

The sound of leadership

Camae expands the spiritual parameters of the movement, but she also mobilizes the oral tradition to create practices that, in their formal attributes, call for inclusion. The conversation she has with King prompts a consideration of what types of connections will enable a truer realization of democracy predicated not on black people approximating modes of leadership based on masculine, heterosexual norms of propriety, but instead on the individual's ability to mobilize the transformative power of collectivity. Through a play purportedly about King, we access Camae's story so that the space opened up by writing history makes available new forms of historiography. By imagining Camae as a leader, leadership becomes democratized and available to the flawed as well as to the superhuman. Moreover, the play demonstrates the process of crafting the mythical qualities of leadership, showing Camae practicing how she would perform one of King's moving speeches, setting the greatness of the figure at a critical distance from the person. In the play, leadership becomes a myth inscribed with ideal qualities that, like other identity categories, never materialize in an actual person. Nevertheless, just as one can perform blackness, femaleness, and queerness, leadership is a performance that "must be reinvented the second time or 'the nth time' because it cannot happen exactly the same way twice, even though in some instances the 'constancy of transmission' across many generations may be 'astonishing.'"[27] Hall's act of recuperation thus serves to make legible and sustainable an ideal of leadership attenuated from masculinity through a set of practices; in the process, Camae remakes herself and the category of leadership.

Cursing like a sailor and willing to charm King into submission with sexual innuendo, Camae possesses the gift of locution. When King asks her what she would do to drive the civil rights movement forward, she performs a speech that, according to the stage directions, prompts King to issue "well-timed sayings like, 'Well!' 'Preach!' Or 'Make it plain!'" (210). In the production of the play that I attended in New York on 8 October 2011 at the Bernard B. Jacobs Theater, the audience also participated in the affirming call-and-response that the stage directions script.

> Camae (*with a 'King' voice*) Chuuch! We have gathered here today to deal with a serious issue. It is an issue of great paponderance – you like that? – paponderance! ... *[H]ow do we deal with the white man?* ... Abel was slain by his brother Cain and, just like the Bibilical times, today the white man is killing his Negro brethren, shackling his hands, keeping us from rising to the stars we are booooouuuuund to occupy.... To this I say, my brethren, a new day is coming. I'm sick and tired of being sick and tired, and today is the day that I tell you to KILL the white man! (*Sotto voce.*) But not with your hands.... But with your miiiind! (*Back to regular voice.*) ... We should build our own counters. Our own restaurants. Our own neighborhoods. Our own schools. The white man ain't got nothin' I want. Fuck the white man! *Fuck* the white man! I say, FUCK 'em! (210)

The speech begins playfully with Camae standing atop the bed in King's motel room donning his shoes and jacket. Assuming the cloak of masculinity, Camae's costume positions the sermonic form, a rhetorical mode central to civil rights activism, as the province of men. She acknowledges King as her audience by calling attention to her use of vocabulary and their difference in social class. But once Camae articulates the problem "how do we deal with the white man?" she launches into a well-crafted speech of her own that uses repetitions of phrases, visual imagery, allusion, dramatic pauses, and changes in tone to produce a rapt audience invested in the transformational scheme that she will provide. The speech moves from the articulation of the problem and rehearsal of the common ground – describing the generosity "we" have shown and the brutal rebuff issued in response – to a biblical allusion that then introduces a journey of mythical proportions that will result in redemption, in "a new day."[28] The speech then offers two solutions, one of raised consciousness and the other of racial separatism. The final solution of "kill the white man" aligns Camae's thinking with that of black nationalists and calls attention to her physical and ideological differences from King. When Camae begins her speech, her performance through costume and tone suggests that she is imitating the great leader, but once she diverges from his message, she reestablishes herself as the speaker and therefore calls attention to her individuality. In the midst of the speech, Camae demonstrates the transformative power of performance to redefine as it reiterates prior performances. Calling forth and moving to resituate, her performance places King's speech-making in relation to, and, importantly, not restrictive of, her own.

The formal attributes of Camae's speech invite vocal performance techniques that create the opportunity for the audience, through call-and-response, to participate in the transformative vision that Camae articulates. First, the tone of her speech shifts from mimicry of King's voice, to sotto voce, to her own. Second, she creates drama through enunciation; she purposefully pronounces *church* as "Chuuch," elongates the words *bound* and *mind*, and shouts the words *kill* and *fuck*. And third, she deploys familiar imagery and catch-phrases, including exodus typology in the depiction of sojourning in a wasteland with the promise of salvation and the saying, "I'm sick and tired of being sick and tired."[29] Throughout the speech, Camae draws into the action the ambiguous "we" who "gathered here today," including the imaginary audience of her speech but also the audience of the play. By doubling the audience, the speech does not depend on the participation of the play's audience for coherence, but it does provide the opportunity for the theatre to become a communal environment.

Camae's final speech is actually a spoken-word poem, and it ruptures the temporal limits of King's life, recalling events that have punctuated black life and culture in the post-civil rights era. Adding a new chapter to the African American history play, the choice to end the play with poetry recalls Ntozake Shange's influential use of the chorepoem in *for colored girls who have considered suicide when the rainbow is enuf* (1975) as it ritualizes time. The increase in tempo from prose to poetry occurs alongside the acceleration of time in *The Mountaintop*. The majority of the ninety-minute play covers King's last hours of life, compressing hours into minutes. The last scene, however, shrinks decades into seconds, demonstrating theatre's ability to bend time. The manipulation of time foregrounds the importance of King's death as a moment of rupture in American history. Much like Parks's America plays, instead of focusing on the life of the famous man, Hall depicts King's last moments of life in order to recalibrate the focus to the moment of transition. Instead of calling attention to the ground King covers, Hall's play asks where we go from here, making the past an object of inquiry and engagement.

The poem at the end of *The Mountaintop* covers the same historical ground that Hall treads in her introduction, further emphasizing the relational quality of the play's recuperative work. The poem unfolds in a loose chronology, which begins with Camae proclaiming, "Let's take you to the mountaintop" (244), and declaring, "The Prince of Peace. Shot" (244). In the next stanza, she names the places that burst into flames following King's assassination. Moving from specific US cities (Memphis, DC) to the geographically abstract "cities burning," she then moves to an international context by declaring, "Vietnam burning" (244). This movement follows the shifting ground of King's political concerns. But just as the poem seems to move toward a linear progression in the second stanza, it loops back to domestic concerns in the final three lines: "Coffins coming home / Another Kennedy killed / *The baton passes on*" (244).

The second stanza solidifies a relay that contains an external structure of progression while also having an internal structure of return. Therefore, the riotous destruction at home and abroad in Vietnam that follows King's death and at once leads to and anticipates, through the passing of the baton, the Black Power movement is described in the next stanza. In Camae's depiction, the revolutionary impulse of the Black Power movement encompasses gay and women's rights activism, affirmed in her references to the Stonewall riots, Angela Davis, and Assatta Shakur. In specifying where she enters the historiography of the Black Power movement in her final speech, Camae also contextualizes the black nationalist call for separatism that she made earlier. Suggesting that Black Nationalism must not necessarily entail sexism and homophobia, her speech enables a more expansive understanding of that movement as well.

In the next stanza, the terrain of struggle shifts from political unrest to social incorporation, as Camae cites integration in US culture from schools to the media to politics. The triumph of integration comes along with a flourishing of gang and drug culture and the rise of AIDS in the Reagan years. The juxtaposition of the integration stanza with the one that follows, which opens with "Crips / Bloods / Blue / Red / White / Crack / Smack" (245), calls attention to the fundamental dichotomy at the heart of multiculturalism. The poem emphasizes this dichotomy by circling back to the ostensible spread of democracy in the Reagan years: "Berlin Walls / Apartheid falls / Robben Island sets Mandela free" (245). While democracy spreads abroad, gang violence and drug use flourish in the United States. The poem continues to create ironic juxtapositions by pointing to the seeming spread of opportunities for people of color and therefore democracy while also highlighting the concurrent limitations to access and therefore the ultimate contraction of liberalism. Collapsing the dichotomy produced by the juxtaposition, the poem ends with two references that affirm the contradiction at the heart of describing the period from the 1970s through to the 2010s as the post-civil rights era: "Black picket fences /...And Black Presidents!!!" (247). The blackening of American ideals from the symbol of domestic tranquility to the highest public office ironically critiques the promise of the spread of US democracy as it highlights the limitations of national inclusion and the continuous need to pass the baton. Moreover, Camae's refrain "the baton passes on" serves to create a structure that denies completion even as it emphasizes movement. The refrain delimits the individual power of iconic figures (Bob Marley, Bill Clinton, Oprah Winfrey) and notorious ones (Marion Barry, skinheads, and Osama bin Laden), placing them in a list that passes on.

This refrain also renders US history subject to the logic of poetics. What does it mean to present the history of the post-soul generation as a spoken-word poem? Susan Somers-Willett has described the characteristics that distinguish slam poetry, noting that it functions as a nightly competition and that anyone who signs up to deliver a poem may participate. Members of the audience judge the poems and performances, democratizing the distribution and reception of the form.[30] Somers-Willett distinguishes slam poetry from what she describes as the more commercialized spoken-word poetry, but I contend that through her turn to poetics in her collection of drama, from the blues-inflected writing in *Hoodoo Love* (2007) to the signifying in *Saturday Night/Sunday Morning* (2011) to the preaching and spoken word in *The Mountaintop* to the hip-hop verse in *Hurt Village* (2011), Hall develops formal protocols that free her characters to act as leading women in historical narratives that would otherwise render them supporting cast members at best. Hall's use of spoken word thus allows women to play roles usually denied to them, just as slam poetry creates an atmosphere of greater access.

While the purportedly high art of poetry may seem an odd form to democratize the ostensibly low form of theatre, as Tyler Hoffman argues, figures from Langston Hughes to Amiri Baraka have performed their poetry "to connect with an audience that had not been reached by poetry before and to connect those audience members to each other, to forge a politically potent black counterpublic sphere, 'a nation within the belly of white America.'"[31] Bending poetics to create counterpublics, American poets create theatre as a means to connect with audience members, rendering the spectators critics and participants in the making of poetry. While the art can never mandate certain outcomes, the formal attributes of performance poetry invite call-and-response, which shifts the making of meaning from a singular to a collective act.

While *The Mountaintop* does many things well, including using formal devices that attempt to level the playing field between a prostitute-turned-angel and the figurehead of the civil rights movement, the end of the play seeks refuge in theatrical conventions that undercut the power of the historiography the play constructs. As I have argued elsewhere, the casting of Sidney Poitier in Lorraine Hansberry's watershed play *A Raisin in the Sun* changed the dynamic of the play from the women's story to Walter Lee Younger's play.[32] I wonder if the shift in balance also helped make Hansberry's play a classic piece of US drama. Would Hansberry's play have become *the* African American play if Poitier had not hijacked the show? While Jackson did not commandeer the 2011 Broadway production of *The Mountaintop*, his star power and Hall's choice to give the King character the final words of the play seem to encourage audiences to focus attention on him. The play functions more forcefully, however, as a meditation on the relationship between King and Camae because it does not seek to recuperate King's singularity but instead aims to illuminate the histories in which King functioned as one runner among many who held the baton. Camae serves as an ideal figure to take us to the mountaintop because she undermines the gender hierarchies requiring King to hold a singular place in history and a King-like figure to pass on the baton. The play, which does much to demonstrate how art may function to recuperate histories that expose alternative modes of black leadership freely available to anyone, should end with Camae's final proclamation, *"The baton passes on / The baton passes on / The baton passes on / The baton passes on"* (247).

Notes

1 As Cheryl Wall argues, "Black women writers' reading of the African American and American literary tradition produces what Adrienne Rich called a quarter century ago 're-vision – the act of looking back, of seeing with fresh eyes, of entering an old text from a new critical direction'"; *Worrying the Line: Black Women Writers, Lineage, and the Literary Tradition* (Chapel Hill: University of North Carolina Press, 2005), 6. Wall is one of several critics, including Hortense Spillers, Mary Helen Washington, and Hazel Carby, who consider how black women write themselves into history.

2 Qtd. in Nosheen Iqbal, "'I've had two hours sleep!' Katori Hall Was the Surprise Winner at This Year's Olivier Awards," *Guardian* 24 March 2010: 19.

3 Sam Marlowe, review of "The Mountaintop," *Times* 24 March 2011: section T2, 16.

4 Ben Brantley, "April 3, 1968. Lorraine Motel. Evening," *New York Times* 14 October 2011: C1.

5 Ibid.

6 Ibid.

7 Katori Hall, *Katori Hall Plays: 1* (London: Methuen Drama, 2011), xii. Further references to Hall's introduction and to *The Mountaintop* are from this edition and are given parenthetically in the text.

8 Mark Anthony Neal defines "soul babies," or the post-soul generation, as "folks born between the 1963 March on Washington and the [*Regents of the University of California v.*] *Bakke* case [in 1978]" (3). *Soul Babies: Black Popular Culture and the Post-Soul Aesthetic* (London: Routledge, 2002).

9 Sandra Shannon begins to do some of this work in "An Intimate Look at the Plays of Lynn Nottage," which briefly considers Nottage's relationship to Wilson. *Contemporary African American Women Playwrights: A Casebook*, ed. Philip C. Kolin (New York: Routledge, 2007), 185–193.

10 In *The African American Theatrical Body* (Cambridge: Cambridge University Press, 2011), following the definitive work of Harry J. Elam Jr., *The Past as Present in the Drama of August Wilson* (Ann Arbor: University of Michigan Press, 2006), and the illuminating scholarship of Sandra Shannon, *The Dramatic Vision of August Wilson* (Washington, DC: Howard University Press, 1995), I consider the intersection of Wilson's and Amiri Baraka's theatre. In addition, many scholars have examined the role of the blues in Wilson's drama.

11 Elam, *The Past as Present in the Drama of August Wilson*, 1.

12 Ibid., xv.

13 Ibid., 3.

14 Robyn Wiegman, *Object Lessons* (Durham, NC: Duke University Press, 2012), 193.

15 Nikhil Pal Singh, *Black is a Country: Race and the Unfinished Struggle for Democracy* (Cambridge: Harvard University Press, 2004), 3.

16 Ibid., 13.

17 Martin Luther King Jr., "The American Dream," in *A Testament of Hope: The Essential Writings and Speeches of Martin Luther King, Jr.*, ed. James M. Washington (New York: Harper Collins, 1991), 208.

18 Jacquelyn Dowd Hall, "The Long Civil Rights Movement and the Political Uses of the Past," *The Journal of American History* 91, no. 4 (March 2005): 1234.

19 Ibid.

20 Danielle L. McGuire, *At the Dark End of the Street: Black Women, Rape, and Resistance – a New History of the Civil Rights Movement from Rosa Parks to the Rise of Black Power* (New York: Vintage, 2011), xvii.

21 Ibid., 132–133. For more on women's prominent role in civil rights activism, see Darlene Clark Hine and Kathleen Thompson, *A Shining Thread of Hope: The History of Black Women in America* (New York: Broadway, 1998), chapter 11; Paula Giddings, *When and Where I Enter: The Impact of Black Women on Race and Sex in America* (New York: William Morrow, 1984), chapters 15 and 16; and Deborah Gray White, *Too Heavy a Load: Black Women in Defense of Themselves 1894–1994* (New York: W. W. Norton, 1999), chapters 5 and 6.

22 Belinda Robnett, *How Long? How Long? African-American Women in the Struggle for Civil Rights* (New York: Oxford University Press, 1997). 41.

23 Marta Moreno Vega, "The Candomblé and Eshu-Eleggua in Brazilian and Cuban Yoruba-Based Ritual," in *Black Theatre: Ritual Performance in the African Diaspora*, ed. Paul Carter Harrison, Victor Leo Walker II, and Gus Edwards (Philadelphia: Temple University Press, 2002), 162.

24 John H. Drewal, John Perberton III, and Rowland Abiodun, qtd. in ibid., 162.

25 Vega, "The Candomblé and Eshu-Eleggua in Brazilian and Cuban Yoruba-Based Ritual," 164.

26 Sara Clarke Kaplan, "Souls at the Crossroads, Africans on the Water: The Politics of Diasporic Melancholia," *Callaloo* 30, no. 2 (2007): 518.

27 Joseph R. Roach, *Cities of the Dead: Circum-Atlantic Performance* (New York: Columbia University Press, 1996), 3.

28 In the promise of "a new day," Camae's speech demonstrates how, according to Hortense Spillers, "the sermon…provide[s] an imaginative field of inquiry into the strategies of African survival, evinced on the hostile landscape of social and political praxis. We would not exaggerate the case to assert that the sermon, as the African-American's prototypical public speaking, locates the primary instrument of moral and political change within the community." *Black, White, and in Color: Essays on American Literature and Culture* (Chicago: University of Chicago Press, 2003), 254.

29 For more on exodus typology, see Eddie Glaude, *Exodus!: Religion, Race, and Nation in Early Nineteenth-Century Black America* (Chicago: University of Chicago Press, 2000).

30 Susan B.A. Somers-Willett, *The Cultural Politics of Slam Poetry: Race, Identity, and Verse in America* (Ann Arbor: University of Michigan Press, 2009).

31 Tyler Hoffman, *American Poetry in Performance: From Walt Whitman to Hip Hop* (Ann Arbor: University of Michigan Press, 2011), 169.

32 Colbert, *The African American Theatrical Body*, 20–23.

Part II
Conflicts

7   The Gendered Terrain in Contemporary Theatre of War by Women

Sharon Friedman

The Iraq wars and the ubiquitous war on terror have generated numerous theatrical productions in the United States that envision the subjectivities of perpetrators, as well as victims of violence. Theatre critics have observed the "surge" in plays about Iraq and other conflict-ridden nations, as well as "war-story fatigue" that has emerged in the wake of interminable battle.[1] Several playwrights have cut through this malaise and the "ubiquity of media images" that, as Jeanne Colleran argues, "situate spectators before they even enter a theatre" and often result in a "collapse of critical judgment and ethical assessment."[2] These dramatists unsettle familiar perspectives by giving voice to those often silenced or ignored in official stories by politicians and the mass media.

Contemporary theatre about the wages of war has emerged in a range of genres. Anti-war adaptations of classical texts transpose ancient battles and catastrophic consequences for home, nation, and polis to contemporary settings, or move between historical and geographical timeframes to comment on recent events (e.g., *The Antigone Project*; Christine Evans, *Trojan Barbie*);[3] surrealistic theatre conflates twentieth- and twenty-first-century war zones in the haunted memories of its participants (e.g., Naomi Wallace, *In the Heart of America*; Quiara Alegría Hudes, *Elliot, A Soldier's Fugue*);[4] and inventive approaches to docudrama and/or "theatre of the real" transform interviews, journalistic accounts, court transcripts, and personal stories into dramatic texts that question the relationship between "facts and truth."[5] Several of these plays imagine the anguish of the incarcerated and tortured (e.g., Victoria Brittain and Gillian Slovo, *Guantanamo*; Shem Bitterman, *Harm's Way*);[6] others focus on the experience of soldiers, veterans, translators, and journalists (e.g., Gregory Burke, *Black Watch*; George Packer, *Betrayed*);[7] and some are concerned with those whose lives are forever transfigured by horrors they have witnessed or endured (e.g., Jessica Blank and Erik Jensen, *Aftermath*; Michael Weller, *Beast*).[8] A number of plays, predominantly composed by women, focus more specifically on the experience of women in war. For example, Julie Marie Myatt's *Welcome Home, Jenny Sutter*, Helen Benedict's *The Lonely Soldier Monologues*, and Kia Corthron's *Moot the Messenger* dramatize the plight of women soldiers, veterans, and embedded journalists.[9] Lynn Nottage's *Ruined* and Danai Gurira's *Eclipsed*,[10] both produced in 2009, bring attention to sexual abuse, rape, survival sex, and psychological violence toward women in countries ravaged by conquest and conflict between government and insurgent forces.

Political theorists Lindsey Feitz and Joane Nagel use the language of theatre to describe war as "arenas of male sexual aggression, theatres of hypermasculine, heteronormative performance, stages where gender and sexual scripts are enacted and reinforced,"[11] while Krista Hunt and Kim Rygiel have argued that the war on terror is "produced, constructed, and waged on highly gendered terrain."[12] This essay argues that women playwrights from the United States, the United Kingdom, and Canada have created a theatre that submits these performances and scripts of war enacted "elsewhere" to interrogation and scrutiny. One aim has been to make visible women's war stories: the militarization of women and "femininity" in support of the war effort, the dangers confronted by women in areas where there is little distinction between militarized and nonmilitarized zones, and the sexualized dynamics of armed conflict in which women's bodies become weapons of war. Another aim in dramatizing these war stories has been to foreground ideologies of gender inscribed on bodies and transformed into brutal practices in communities engaged in violent conflict, as well as in the structure and culture of the military and its protocols.

The plays under discussion demonstrate not only the multiplicity of theatrical forms and themes in war plays informed by or inflected with feminist critiques, but also the hybrid intentions that constitute their participation in contemporary political theatre as "cultural practice."[13] Political theatre, as defined by Colleran and Jenny Spencer, ranges from "act[s] of political intervention," raising awareness about the plight of a particular population and offering a specific political agenda for the conditions dramatized onstage, to plays that function as civic forums, encouraging audiences to consider competing perspectives, thus provoking a critical and active response from viewers. Even plays that dramatize political issues "covertly" might disturb complacent spectators.[14] For example, characters who give a face to injustices and atrocities often unsettle deep-seated prejudices in audience members who interpret these horrors as by-products of "primitive" cultures, "othered" in terms of race, class, religion, ethnicity, and status in the global hierarchy of power and privilege, rather than as the consequences of poverty and economic and political exploitation in a global marketplace. As Colleran and Spencer argue, theatre performances are "an apparatus for the construction of meaning rather than an index to it" and implicitly demand a reexamination of "official versions of national history"[15] – in this case, accounts of war focused exclusively on the political interests of warring factions, numbers of casualties, and military victory and defeat.

I begin by discussing the synergy between the emerging scholarship on women and war, reports of widespread rape and sexual abuse in war-torn territories, women's increased numbers in the US military and coalition forces in Iraq and Afghanistan and the gendered culture of the military, and theatre by women, particularly during the last decade, that addresses the engendering of armed conflict in specific war zones. I conclude with a reading of Canadian dramatist Judith Thompson's *Palace of the End*, a triptych of monologues that links the stories of those who inhabit distinctly different subject positions within the wars in Iraq to render both its local and global dimensions.

Gender and armed conflict

The burgeoning literature by feminist scholars on gender and war maintains that "flesh and blood" women – soldiers, nurses, comfort women, patriotic mothers, and wives – and ideas about "manliness" and "femininity" sustain the military.[16] Conversely, studies of the specific effects of war-making on women's lives examine the ways in which different groups of women suffer and respond: they are direct casualties in battle; subjects of harassment and rape by military personnel; and in campaigns of ethnic cleansing and genocide, they are victims of rape and enforced impregnation. In oppressive national regimes or conflicts between indigenous groups, women are often targeted and misogyny is employed to extract information, prevent treason, and to shame, intimidate, and unsettle communities. Stigmatized by families and communities, women who have been raped are often cast out to seek asylum elsewhere, and many experience abuse in refugee camps. After reports of widespread and systematic rape in Bosnia between 1992 and 1995 and in Rwanda during the 1994 genocide, the issue of sexual violence triggered developments in international criminal law and humanitarian law. However, it is difficult and dangerous for victims to come forward, for fear of further punishment and shame. To survive or to claim agency in armed conflict, many women have joined rebel forces. Internecine conflicts in Sierra Leone, the Democratic Republic of Congo, and Sudan have not only resulted in widespread rape and the displacement of populations, but also the recruitment of women and children in violent reprisals.[17]

Miriam Cooke argues that the official "war story" reinforces "mythic wartime roles" and narratives, such as "women's need for protection as the reason men must fight" or "outworn essentialist clichés of men's aggressivity and women's pacifism."[18] Cooke points out that women are prominent as "guerilla fighters, [as well] as military targets of bombs and rapes."[19] She notes that history is made up of multiple narratives that "reconstruct events." Most importantly, she dismantles the metanarrative of the war story that artificially divides "beginning and ending; foe and friend; aggression and defense; war and peace; front and home; combatant and civilian," maintaining that "what used to be labeled civilian experience – being bombed, raped, expropriated, and salvaging shreds of living in a refugee camp – some name combat experience."[20] In addition to suffering direct bodily harm, women bear responsibility for the effects of war in their particular roles in the family. Jennifer Turpin details the severe economic hardships confronted by women who must care for children despite the loss of family, work, community, and social structure.[21]

Women are also perpetrators of war. The increasing involvement of women in armed combat by national militaries has generated feminist scholarship on the production of gender and the performance of masculinity in and through institutional policies and the culture of the military. Beginning with the Gulf War in 1991, the past two decades have seen increased numbers of women in coalition forces in Iraq and Afghanistan. At the same time, scandals involving sexual harassment and rape by and within the US military have surfaced. Furthermore, the continuing challenge to policies against gays and lesbians in the US military has led to the scrutiny of ideologies of masculinity, femininity, and sexuality in relation to battlefield conduct. And, of course, the sexual abuse of male prisoners in Abu Ghraib by American servicewomen further complicates any essentialist understanding of the linkages among gender, sexuality, war, and peace. As Angela Davis has observed, the employment of sexuality and misogyny as weapons of war is "available to women as well as men."[22] Feitz and Nagel observe in the Abu Ghraib debacle the intersection of gender, misogyny, race, and sex in the deployment of women "to dominate and eroticize the torture" as they "feminize" (through role reversal) Iraqi male prisoners regarded as racially inferior. They argue that "[w]omen's sexuality has become a tool in an expanded military arsenal, a new form of war materièl [sic]. The new weapon is women's assumed unique sexual power to demean and humiliate enemy men."[23]

Women and war plays

In her essay "Women and War," Alexis Greene observes that in Western culture, war has been assumed to be outside of women's purview, and that when women have written about war, the theatre has not been their "primary outlet."[24] She argues, however, that a confluence of events during the 1950s and 1960s – fears of nuclear war, the intensifying Vietnam conflagration, the anti-war movement, and the women's movement – gave rise to a new generation of women theatre artists who could turn to the emerging not-for-profit theatre community for support in challenging prevailing views about masculinity, violence, and war. Greene identifies plays by women from the 1960s through the 1990s in England, the United States, and Northern Ireland that "deconstruct the concept of wartime heroism, draw a connection between violence in battle and violence in the home, and further investigate the age-old connection between war and sex."[25] Analyzing works by Emily Mann, Lavonne Mueller, Shirley Lauro, Naomi Wallace, Shirley Gee, and Anne Devlin, Greene maintains that these dramatists revise the "canonized narrative of war" that exalts heroism and naturalizes war's brutality.[26]

The past two decades have seen another confluence of events that has generated war plays by women that not only foreground women in war zones in the Middle East, Eastern Europe, and Africa, but also bring a critical lens to violence against women and the performance of masculinity in and through the practices of government and nongovernmental militias. As feminist theatre scholars and practitioners from the United States and the United Kingdom have asserted, the turn toward transnational feminism in the 1990s made "cross-border connections, resistant to the colonial 'othering' of gender, race and nation," and drew attention to both local and global conditions.[27] In "Feminist Futures and the Possibilities of 'We,'" Elaine Aston and Geraldine Harris argue that even as we imagine a "utopic (post)feminist moment[,] ... numerous women practitioners in different countries from different generations have produced vital and challenging works of theatre and performance that address a wide range of pressing social and political problems for women, touching the local and the global."[28]

Women as victims of indigenous conflicts inspired Nottage's *Ruined* and Gurira's *Eclipsed*, which are both based on documentary accounts of women who have experienced or witnessed brutalities. The plays function as acts of intervention that jolt audiences to think about the conditions endured by rape victims, comfort women, and sexual servants in specific historical contexts. *Ruined* (the title refers to the destruction of a woman's genitals and womb) is based in part on Nottage's interviews with Congolese women driven from their families and communities by rape, mutilation, and other forms of violence in protracted armed conflict in the Democratic Republic of Congo, beginning in 1998 and continuing to the present day.[29] Some of these women are doubly victimized – sexually assaulted and impregnated or left unable to reproduce; furthermore, they must endure shaming by male members of their families and communities, who perceive the violation of "their" women as another form of defeat. As Cynthia Enloe argues, "rapes of captured women by soldiers of one communal or national group [are] aimed principally at humiliating the men of an opposing group."[30]

Ruined is set in Mama Nadi's bar/brothel, a refuge in a mineral-rich area of the Congo where groups vie for mines in an unregulated system. The bar is also the site where destitute women survive by providing entertainment and sexual services for warring government soldiers and rebels. As Jill Dolan observes, "caught in the crossfire of men's war," Mama Nadi (Nottage's Mother Courage–like figure[31]) and her girls "find no peaceful refuge."[32] Among the supplies brought to the bar by Christian, a traveling salesman, are two young women seeking asylum. Eighteen-year-old Sophie, "ruined" and continually pained as a consequence, manages to sing "like an angel"[33] at Mama Nadi's behest to both entertain and insulate herself sexually from the men. Salima, a young wife and mother, was raped by soldiers who also brutally killed her wailing child to ensure that they would not be discovered. Subsequently abandoned by her husband, family, and community, Salima finds herself pregnant with the "child of a monster" (70). When her husband, now a government soldier, comes to reclaim her, she protests: "You will not fight your battles on my body anymore" (94). Although both exploited and protected by Mama Nadi, the women find moments in which they imagine finding sustenance in each other to rebuild their lives on the little capital Mama Nadi is able to save.

Gurira's *Eclipsed* stages another war story obscured by headlines of political factions fighting for power and resources in Liberia. Set in 2003 just prior to President Charles Taylor's forced resignation, four women are held hostage by a rebel leader, a member of Liberians United for Reconciliation and Democracy (LURD) during the Liberian civil war. The women, referred to as "wives" of the commanding officer (CO), survive in a compound where they provide housekeeping and sexual services in return for his protection from the random assaults of other men. However, one woman, Raima, finds her way out of bondage by joining the rebel forces as a soldier, and she attempts to take the new "girl" under her wing. In a series of cruel awakenings, "The Girl," as she is called (women in the compound often lose track of their years and parentage), learns that there is little freedom in becoming a rebel soldier except to commit the same atrocities as the men, abduct other women for the CO, and find protection from a powerful male leader. A ray of hope emerges with the appearance of Rita – formerly wealthy, educated, and privileged – who has become a "peace woman" (member of the Liberian Women's Initiative) intent on forging a truce between the warring factions. In juxtaposing scenes with the rebel soldier Raima, Rita offers the women empowerment through the promise of safety and education. Hoping to dismantle the compound households the men rely on to wage war and horde their "loot," Rita finds her mission challenged by the women's difficult choices in an uncertain future. In the ranking system among the wives, based on years of servitude, Helena, the first wife, has a privileged position as number 1, charged by the CO to run the household and divide up the goods. She is reluctant to give up this position, though profoundly tempted by Rita's promise of literacy and freedom. The Girl and Raima would have to give up their guns, symbol of autonomy and empowerment in a continuing civil war. Rita herself has already lost a daughter in this morass, and her ability to protect these women is tenuous. The plea for intervention is clear when a radio report blasts that approximately a hundred women, all dressed in white, marched to the US embassy in Monrovia calling for immediate and direct intervention by the US government, yet the radio voice trails off and the outcome is uncertain.

Both Nottage and Gurira seek to evoke critical judgment as well as empathy. Thus the modified realism of *Ruined* makes use of Brechtian-inspired *Gestus* through the characters' exaggerated and ritualized physical enactment of sexual barter and aggression. The transformation, in alternate scenes, of the makeshift bar by day (with plastic washtubs, a car battery, and a covered birdcage) to a lurid dance hall at night, and the characters' bump-and-grind movements triggered by flashing red lights and blaring music, foreground the performance of gender and sexual play. The mise-en-scène and the ritualized gestures subvert any idealized notions of romantic outposts and tender relations between soldiers and comfort women. In *Eclipsed*, the women's shelter is the site of bullet holes and mortar residue, though organized with areas for cooking, sleeping, and bathing. One woman enters and exits from the CO's quarters (we never see him), putting on and pulling off wigs and wiping his semen from between her legs. Here, too, the performance and the set draw attention to the material underpinnings of sexualized discourse and behaviors enacted onstage, where sex and servitude are exchanged for survival.

Whereas both Nottage and Gurira use the device of a group (collective) protagonist, popular in earlier forms of feminist theatre, to signify a shared condition within a specific historical context, Iraqi American playwright Heather Raffo's *Nine Parts of Desire* (2004),[34] based on her research and intimate conversations with many Iraqi women (including her family) following the Gulf War, uses solo performance to invite audiences to see both the shared suffering and the resilience of women under Saddam Hussein's brutal, misogynist regime and the US-led invasion. Raffo's multiple use of the *abaya*, a traditional Arab black robe–like garment, as she moves from character to character, creates a unifying prop to connect these various personas, but she also uses the *abaya* as a distinguishing sign to denote a subject's particular relationship to Iraqi culture. The characters that Raffo invents and performs occupy different positions in the Iraqi cultural landscape and take varying positions on the US involvement in the country. Thus the performance as a whole does not seem to advocate a particular intervention; instead, audience members are encouraged to consider their own competing perspectives on Iraq in light of these diverse and personalized narratives framed and interpreted by Raffo through poetic prose, religious, literary, and folkloric allusions, and inventive stage imagery. The production notes state that the stage represents "various levels of Iraqi society from the ancient to the modern: crumbling tiles, layers of mosaic, bricks, books, carpets and sandbags." A simulation of a river at the center of the production is "both mythic and functional, a symbol of a life-giving source and of the underworld."[35] The women's monologues invoke the traditions of a culture that audiences might only know through televised images of destruction. The stories, however, pointedly reference the rape and violence perpetrated by Hussein's sons, as well as the particular effects of war on women inhabiting different classes, regions, and political affiliations during the escalating US–Iraq crisis and the bombing of the country.

Above all, Raffo textually embodies multiple personas that subvert any fixed notion of Islamic womanhood and undermine neo-Orientalist notions of women in need of rescue and enlightenment. They point to the complex history of Iraqi women, some of whom were once considered the "female arm of the [Baath] [P]arty" (General Federation of Iraqi Women) and granted civil rights, education, and employment to boost political and economic development, only to be deprived of freedoms during the Iraq–Iran War (1980–1988) and Hussein's embrace of certain Islamic and tribal traditions to consolidate his power.[36] Raffo's personas are composites of women who shared their stories with her: the doctor in Basra who cannot heal the genetic damage in children who have absorbed depleted uranium or chemicals released from the bombings during the Gulf War; the exiled politico who, despite her leftist politics and erstwhile anti-war activities for Vietnam and Chile, supports the US invasion that would annihilate an "enemy of the people"; the celebrated artist and curator of the Saddam Art Center, who may have compromised herself to Saddam's regime at the same time that she represented other women's stories in her haunting nudes and, more specifically, in a painting titled "Savagery"; and, finally, the mother who searches for the remains of her children among the rubble of an explosion outside of the Amiryiyya bomb shelter. Among the charred and fused bodies, she recognizes her daughter Ghada (meaning "tomorrow"), and she becomes known as Umm Ghada (Mother of Tomorrow), though her full name is "dead with them" (32). The device of performing multiple and diverse personas in monologue theatre enables audiences to envision unlikely and unseen connections among individuals. The theatre, as Colleran and Spencer argue, thus has the potential to provide an imagined "intervening space" where these links can become visible and "revisionary projects can be undertaken."[37]

Palace of the End

Judith Thompson's *Palace of the End*[38] creates this kind of revisionary intervening space through a triptych of monologues connecting disparate stories in a complex rendering of the local and global dimensions of the Iraq War and the masculinized, sexualized, racialized, and classed dynamics through which war functions.[39] Incorporating aspects of docudrama and poetic soliloquy into monologue theatre, *Palace of the End* probes the interiority of three public figures who recount vastly different experiences in relation to the effects of the US and British presence in Iraq.

The first monologue, "My Pyramids," was inspired by the media frenzy surrounding US Army reservist Lynndie England, the American soldier photographed in the act of sexually humiliating Iraqi detainees in Abu Ghraib prison in 2003. England was subsequently imprisoned for actions that had been ordered or sanctioned by her superiors, including Specialist Charles Graner, the father of her child, who staged the photos.

The second monologue, "Harrowdown Hill," was drawn from the publicized account of the suicide of Dr. David Kelly in 2003. Kelly, a former UN weapons inspector employed by the UK's Ministry of Defense as an expert on biological warfare, was identified as the source of a BBC report claiming that the British government had exaggerated its assessment of Iraq's weapons program in the lead-up to war. In Thompson's play, Kelly's admission follows firsthand reports of US soldiers' fatal abuse of a young Iraqi girl, daughter of his close personal friend whose entire family subsequently perished in the US military's hunt for insurgents. After a public hearing before the Foreign Affairs Select Committee investigating his role in the media scandal, Kelly was denigrated in the media, often in emasculating terms. Two days later, he was found dead in a wooded area near his Oxfordshire home.

The third and emotionally wrenching final monologue, "Instruments of Yearning" – the designation given to Hussein's secret police – interprets the written narrative of Nehrjas Al Saffarh, a well-known member of the Communist Party of Iraq during Saddam's rise to power in the 1970s.[40] In order to obtain information about her husband, a Communist Party leader, the Baathist police repeatedly raped Al Saffarh in the presence of her sons, and forced her to witness her son's torture in interrogation quarters – the ancient Palace of Flowers that came to be known as the Palace of the End.[41]

Although the narratives of the public figures that inspired the monologues of *Palace of the End* were informed by news stories and written accounts, the characters' ruminations were entirely imagined by Thompson.[42] The invented monologues imagine the personal reflections of these figures – our proxies – whose lives function as a lens onto fateful moral choices during escalating violence in Iraq. Their narratives and the language in which they voice private thoughts also call attention to the institutions, discourses, and ideologies that shape their responses in moments of crisis, as well as moments of reflection. As in other Thompson plays, their choices are integrally bound up in shifting identities and subjectivities that are socially constructed, yet provisional and psychologically complex.[43] The scapegoated female soldier, the remorseful weapons inspector, and the Iraqi mother inhabit many more subject positions as they recount their stories; in three different sets situated side by side, separated only by large fragments of glass, they share this imagined space onstage.

One thread that weaves together the haunting narratives of the three monologues is the gendering of militarization, surveillance, political coercion, and torture that we often overlook in these already-mediatized stories. The monologues ask audiences to imagine the personal ruminations of the torturer and the tortured, both women. At the same time, they point up gender as a primary way of signifying relationships of power, specifically in the protocols of torture in the masculinized military at Abu Ghraib, in the targeting of young Iraqi women in surveillance, and in the gendered disciplinary tactics of Hussein's secret police.

Each monologue represents layers of consciousness. Characters speak in formal or colloquial speech to narrate events or pose questions to the audience; at other times, they are poetically introspective, in the mode of soliloquy, to render interiority. Thompson's hybrid genre invites audiences to imagine the private agonies of each figure, identify with facets of their stories, and witness their confessions. Their direct address to the audience breaks the fourth wall, implicating spectators who attempt to distance themselves from conditions that they feel ill-equipped to alter. Two of the figures in *Palace of the End* have already died before the play begins, and their presence adds a surrealistic quality to the alternate universe of horrific events we think of as happening "anywhere but here." Both David Kelly and Nehrjas Al Saffarh speak to us from the grave, compelling us to hear their stories.

The recurrent metaphoric image in the alternate worlds of *Palace of the End*, both in the language of the monologues and in the mirrors of the set design of the 2008 Epic Theatre Ensemble production, alludes to Lewis Carroll's *Through the Looking Glass*. In his sequel to Alice's adventures, the young girl ponders what the world is like on the other side of a mirror. She discovers a book with looking-glass poetry, "jabberwocky," which she can read only by holding it up to a mirror. Thompson's characters, and by extension her audiences, see through mirrors as well, the characters entering the stage "as if through a looking glass" (5). This alternate universe – this violence elsewhere and within – is only legible through a mirror held up to their moral choices, actions, and inactions, and through a reflection that allows for the appearance of the unconscious, the surfacing of repressed past traumas that complicate reason and subvert denial. Naturalized conceptions of gender in relation to violence are made strange in this mirror as well, surfacing to color every reflection.

Soldier, the speaker of the first monologue, clearly refers to Private First Class Lynndie England, the poster girl for sexualized abuse of Iraqi prisoners at Abu Ghraib. Thompson introduces her monologue with Soldier googling herself to glimpse the six hundred thousand hits that come up at the mention of her name, thus emphasizing the construction of England's gendered identity by a mediated culture. Defining herself against the misogynist discourse about her on the Internet, Soldier rivets on references to her appearance as "ugly" or her attitudes as "feminist" (8), and she recoils at the litany of sexually violent fantasies of punishment she evokes in her detractors. Her response alternates between indignation at her accusers and justification of her actions. She retorts that she is not ugly (indeed, she has been the lover of her supervisor and is pregnant with his child even though he has married another woman involved in the abuse) and, most pointedly, that she is not a feminist (read "man-hating and unnaturally aggressive") (8–9). In any other circumstances, she "respects men and their privates" (12), and offers a rational defense of her sexually abusive actions that clearly alludes to the military's othering of Iraqi men in terms of religion and sexuality. In the effort to gain important strategic information in the company of her superiors, she exploits what she has been taught is common knowledge – the homophobic, misogynist, and religiously and culturally conservative attitudes of the Iraqis – to humiliate the prisoners. Piling up naked bodies in a pyramidal structure and leading a man around by a leash would be doubly humiliating because the perpetrator of these shaming acts is a woman. Presumably Soldier does not see homophobia and misogyny operating in the US military elite, who share these attitudes and amuse themselves by inflicting these forms of torture. As she says: "These [Iraqis] are not men, they are terrorists.... And they had intelligence" (12). Echoing the official response to accusations of abuse, she says, "as far as I am concerned I was doin what had to be done, *to get to the intelligence* and that is, according to their culture, me laughin at their willies was worse than a beatin *way* worse.... I had a smile on my face but this was SERIOUS–INTELLIGENCE–WORK" (12).

Social class, nationalism, and prejudice toward disability intersect with gender in Soldier's account of her journey toward a heroism that turned to disgrace. As a young Dairy Queen worker enticed by what she calls a "Tom Hanks style" (9) recruiter who appeared in her West Virginia town to offer her a way out of impoverishment, her fantasies of aggrandizement have been shaped by media images and stories of iconic women warriors. Women as disparate as the heroine of her high school musical, *Annie Get Your Gun*, the martyr Joan of Arc, and, surprisingly, Palestinian women suicide bombers incite her desire for heroism in battle. Her reveries of glory, however, are interspersed with, and presumably emerge from, memories of degradation, though she dismisses acts of humiliation as "human nature" (16). She recounts participating in the clubhouse tortures and sexual abuse of a lame young woman in her hometown, and her own sexual subordination to Charlie (an allusion to Specialist Charles Graner), who coerced her into having their sexual relations videotaped. However, feelings of remorse accompanied by rapid breathing erupt when she gazes at the looking glass and confronts the horrors of the Iraqi prison that she struggles to repress. Haunted by the soft neck of the "Rakee" (16) she led around by a leash and by the words of the "holy man" – "There is no reason for this" (16) – she commends herself, with ferocious passion, for allegiance to the flag, her American God, and her boyfriend, with whom she vanquished the enemy. She fantasizes that she saw an angel "with eagle wings flying, soaring through Abu Ghraib on that night" (10), a vision that we might read as her desire for transcendence or redemption – an escape from the prison of self. But her angel fails her in her moment of painful recognition, rendered in visceral images of the discomfort she experienced at the very moment of triumph: "I will take a minute to go back through the lookin glass. To those secret nights when my breathing went funny and there was dry ice in my heart and I laughed like I have never laughed before.... Had a cool boyfriend and a whole gang of friends and I said NO to the enemy" (18). Like the eagle and the angel, she "soared through the air" until she "crashed back. Through the lookin glass" (18–19).

Soldier's monologue consists of a tangle of discourses involving debates about the interrogation of suspected terrorists and the deployment of sexuality as an intelligence tool. However, addressing the audience, Soldier indignantly holds us responsible for singling her out and scapegoating her, and for not recognizing the alternate universe she inhabited where her treatment of prisoners was lauded by her peers and supervisors. In her anthology *One of the Guys*, Tara McKelvey asks: "Why were we so deeply troubled at the sight of women humiliating and hurting prisoners in the [Abu Ghraib] photos?"[44] Francine D'Amico argues that it is hardly coincidental that the two soldiers most recognizable to the public during the Iraq War were Private First Class Jessica Lynch and Private First Class England – Lynch portrayed as the damsel-in-distress victim to bolster support for the war effort, and England as the "gender-incongruous" victimizer who pointed to the aberration of women in the military thwarting the war effort.[45] Ilene Feinman argues that, in actuality, women were instructed to "use their sexualized behavior to defile and intimidate the male detainees while their [US] comrades watch, participate verbally, and thus defile both female soldiers and male detainees." There were also accounts of "male soldiers raping female prisoners of war and children who were taken up as prisoners."[46] England received disproportionate attention compared to her male cohorts precisely because female aggression is considered aberrant – doubly perverse – in a system of cultural norms that naturalizes male aggression and the masculinism that shapes the core constructs of military culture. Particularly in a "racially gendered theater of subordination,"[47] widely disseminated photographs of a white woman leading an Arab man by a leash or piling up naked bodies as a form of humiliating domination seemed for some viewers a kind of pornographic spectacle. Thompson metaphorically turns the mirror on her audience, reflecting their horror as they distance themselves from this figure.

Soldier and Nehrjas Al Saffarh, the subject of Thompson's third monologue, represent women as weapons of war, one the "female decoy"[48] of the masculinized military (a cover for sexual and racialized abuses), the other the rape victim of Hussein's misogynist secret police supported, as the character says, by the US government and the CIA in his military coup. David Kelly, the second in Thompson's trio of figures, is the interface between the two women, implicated as he was in arms control, international intelligence, and weapons inspections in Iraq on the road to war. Although it is difficult to imagine anyone more remote from Lynndie England than this Welsh/Englishman, an esteemed and withdrawn microbiologist, he also was subject to a kind of media frenzy about his role in thwarting the war effort. Juxtaposed with Soldier's forced bravado is Kelly's humility, his remorse as he walks through the looking glass and attempts to solve the "riddle" of how to defeat the agents of war, as well as the mystery of his earlier silence and his self-deception: "Have you ever told yourself an unforgivable lie?" (25). He finds a path to redemption through suicide or, as some speculate, by becoming a target for assassination. Like Soldier, though in obverse terms, Kelly recalls the gendered taunts of his detractors, who called him the "mousey scientist," "that sad little Walter Mitty of a man.... a weak man, a meek man [who] just couldn't take the pressure" of public scrutiny by Parliament and the press (23). And like Soldier, his monologue points to sexuality as a weapon of war – in this case, the targeting of a young Iraqi girl by US soldiers looking for munitions in her family's home.

It is not only Kelly's confession that Thompson asks us to witness, but also the horror of his abjection as he sits against a tree in the woods, his pant leg pushed up, a slash at his wrist, blood on his knee, his glasses and watch beside him, and, of course, the empty bottle of pills – the price of speaking out against injustice. Kelly struggles to see his death as a courageous political act and as redemption for his earlier silence, "the greatest sin of our time" (24). As the "ghost of Harrowdown Hill" (30), he will be forever present as a reminder of past deeds repressed and of future responsibility. In his invisibility, he will have a stronger presence than he had in life. However, the strength of his plea to the audience does not come from the position of power and authority that he held in life; as a ghost, he relies on childhood, domestic, and parental images that resonate with the guilt he feels for the family in Iraq. He asks the audience directly:

> Can you imagine, knowing, knowing that a man is torturing a child in your basement, and just going on with your life? Knowing it is happening right under your feet, as you wait for the kettle to boil, as you tuck your own children in bed, as you work in the garden the dim light is always there, the muffled sound of her screaming, you pretend to yourself "It's the crows on the line,"... and you don't tell anyone because you might lose something if you do. (24–25)

Kelly says that hiding in the woods reminds him of a children's book, a child's game, woodland creatures running about, "wildflowers everywhere mad scientist hiding" (20). Perhaps the child within Kelly clamors to return to the self before the mirror, prior to entry into the symbolic order and the Law of the Father. He concludes his monologue with an imaginary conversation with his daughter at an earlier age, morphing into childhood rhymes, reassuring her that she has not really lost him, that he will never disappear.

The final monologue picks up the strands of the previous monologues in what at first appears to be a victim narrative of war and violence – the alternate world on the other side of our looking glass. Al Saffarh is not only Hussein's target, but also part of the "collateral damage" of the war when her home was bombed by Americans. She is Soldier's "other" – the enemy that must be sacrificed, but also the martyr with whom she identifies. In Hussein's terms, she is the unpatriotic mother who must be sexually abused and must witness her son's torture. And with poignant irony, she echoes Kelly's vision of a parent who knows that a child – in this case, her child – is being tortured and does nothing to stop it. Al Saffarh inhabits multiple identities, fragmented and unstable, bleeding into each other: a politico, mother of four, rape victim, and tormented spirit, a ghost who presides over the past, present, and future of a landscape – her home – violent and beautiful.

Addressing the audience, Al Saffarh immediately explains that she is adept at creating her own beauty out of pain, creating discomfort even as she smiles. One of her earliest memories is drawing a daffodil (the meaning of her name) in her own blood. As with all of Thompson's figures, repressed trauma hovers at the border of consciousness. Guilt and horror at her own actions, which violate the norms of motherhood, erupt in the most visceral descriptions of her son's torture as he was tied to a ceiling fan and then thrown onto a roof to die. Her unforgivable sin is that she did not try to prevent his torture by revealing the truth of her husband's whereabouts. She believed the "military saying from ancient times": "To harm this tree, it is unforgivable.... Do not kill a woman, a child or an old man" (45). She sacrificed her son for others' freedom. And, like Kelly, she asks, on very different terms: "Why did I not speak then?" (44). Was it her place to save the resistance? Was it Kelly's place to protect the government? On this side of the looking glass, we ponder these questions. Al Saffarh, too, conjures up a child ghost in the form of her son, a desire, perhaps, for a return to an imaginary realm prior to the rupture with the mother. In her dream, mother and son would fly together, watching over Baghdad until there is finally peace.

Misogyny, violence, and the gendered discourse of war are clearly issues shared by all of the playwrights discussed in this essay, and they do not limit their concerns to conflagrations abroad. I would argue that as Western playwrights rendering gendered violence in war stories situated in Africa and the Middle East, Nottage, Gurira, Raffo, and Thompson all strive for what Sara Ahmed terms "ethical encounters" with distant "others" in ways that avoid a kind of cultural imperialism in appropriating their stories and at the same time distancing them through a lens of "pure relativism."[49] This point is crucial for the depiction of violence against women at a historical moment when US policy makers have used women's rights to justify the invasion of Afghanistan and incite the patriotic spirit by exalting women's sexual freedoms in the West.[50] In staging misogyny in war, these playwrights give attention to the cultural, material, and economic conditions that foment injustices experienced by women and men in a range of circumstances. Aesthetically, the plays experiment with theatrical strategies to evoke "critical empathy"[51] rather than voyeurism – always a concern when representing sexualized violence. They resonate with Wendy Hesford's call for a theatre that asks viewers positioned by the US mass media as "voyeurs or surveyors of atrocities and struggles outside [their] borders" to consider their own "[moral] culpab[ility] for a lack of attention to – and objectification of – the suffering of others."[52] The power of these plays resides in making women's war stories visible where they had been eclipsed, as the title of Gurira's play suggests, and in creating an alternative space onstage that denaturalizes the gendered, racialized, sexualized, and classed dynamics through which war operates for perpetrators and victims. Alice's looking glass is an intriguing metaphor for theatre that enables audiences to reflexively enter into an alternate universe that estranges the familiar and asks us to read the signs by holding our own assumptions up to the mirror.

Notes

I am most grateful to editors Penny Farfan and Lesley Ferris for their careful reading and invaluable suggestions during the development of this essay.

1 Alexandra Alter, "The Surge in Plays about Iraq," *Wall Street Journal*, 31 October 2008, available at *http://online.wsj.com/article/SB122541854683986897.html?KEYWO RDS=Alter+%22The+Surge+in+Plays+about+Iraq%22* (accessed 16 October 2010); Neil Genzlinger, "The Feminine, Touched: War as Women's Work," *New York Times*, 10 March 2009, available at *http://theater.nytimes.com/2009/03/10/theater/reviews/10lone. html?_r=1&emc=tnt&tntemail1=y* (accessed 16 October 2010).

2 Jeanne Colleran, "Disposable Wars, Disappearing Acts: Theatrical Responses to the 1991 Gulf War," *Theatre Journal* 55, no. 4 (2003): 615.

3 *The Antigone Project* included one-act plays by Tanya Barfield, Karen Hartman, Chiori Miyagawa, Lynn Nottage, and Caridad Svich (South Gate, CA: NoPassport Press, 2009); Christine Evans, *Trojan Barbie* (Tasmania, AU: Australian Script Centre, 2007).

4 Naomi Wallace, *In the Heart of America* (New York: Theatre Communications Group, 2001); Quiara Alegría Hudes, *Elliot, A Soldier's Fugue* (New York: Dramatists Play Service, 2007).

5 Carol Martin, ed., *Dramaturgy of the Real on the World Stage* (Basingstoke, UK: Palgrave Macmillan, 2010), 3.

6 Victoria Brittain and Gillian Slovo, *Guantanamo: 'Honor Bound to Defend Freedom'* (London: Oberon, 2004); Shem Bitterman, *Harm's Way* (Woodstock, IL: Dramatic Publishing, 2009).

7 Gregory Burke, *Black Watch* (London: Faber & Faber, 2008); George Packer, *Betrayed* (New York: Faber & Faber, 2008).

8 Jessica Blank and Erik Jensen, *Aftermath* (New York: Dramatists Play Service, 2010); Michael Weller, *Beast* (New York: Dramatist Play Service, 2009).

9 Julie Marie Myatt, *Welcome Home, Jenny Sutter* (Ashland, OR: Oregon Shakespeare Festival Scripts, 2008); Helen Benedict, *The Lonely Soldier Monologues*, in *Plays from Actors Theatre of Louisville: Humana Festival 2005* (New York: Broadway Play Publishing, 2007).

10 Lynn Nottage, *Ruined* (New York: Theatre Communications Group, 2009); Danai Gurira, *Eclipsed* (New York: Dramatists Play Service, 2010).

11 Lindsey Feitz and Joane Nagel, "The Militarization of Gender and Sexuality in the Iraq War," in *Women in the Military and in Armed Conflict*, eds. Helena Carreiras and Gerhard Kümmel (Wiesbaden: VS Verlag 2008), 217.

12 Krista Hunt and Kim Rygiel, eds., *(En)Gendering the War on Terror: War Stories and Camouflaged Politics* (Aldershot, UK: Ashgate, 2006), 3.

13 Jeanne Colleran and Jenny S. Spencer, eds., *Staging Resistance: Essays on Political Theater* (Ann Arbor: University of Michigan Press, 1998), 1.

14 Ibid., 1–3.

15 Ibid., 3.

16 See, for example, Enloe, *Maneuvers*, xii–xiii.

17 Estelle Zinsstag, "Sexual Violence against Women in Armed Conflicts: Standard Responses and New Ideas," *Social Policy and Society* 5, no. 1 (2006): 137–48.

18 Miriam Cooke, *Women and the War Story* (Berkeley: University of California Press, 1996), 15.

19 Ibid., 39

20 Ibid., 4, 15, 41.

21 Jennifer Turpin, "Many Faces," in *The Women and War Reader*, eds. Lois Ann Lorentzen and Jennifer Turpin (New York: New York University Press, 1998), 3–18.

22 Angela Y. Davis, "Sexual Coercion, Prisons, and Female Responses," in *One of the Guys*, ed. Tara McKelvey (Emeryville, CA: Seal Press, 2007), 28.

23 Feitz and Nagle, "Militarization of Gender," 204, 213.

24 Alexis Greene, "Women and War," in *Women Writing Plays: Three Decades of the Susan Smith Blackburn Prize*, ed. Alexis Greene (Austin: University of Texas Press, 2006), 83.

25 Ibid., 84–5.

26 Ibid., 85.

27 Elaine Aston, *Feminist Views on the English Stage: Women Playwrights, 1990–2000* (Cambridge: Cambridge University Press, 2003), 8.

28 Elaine Aston and Geraldine Harris, "Feminist Futures and the Possibilities of 'We,'" in *Feminist Futures?: Theatre, Performance, Theory*, ed. Aston and Harris (Basingstoke, UK: Palgrave Macmillan, 2006), 11–12.

29 Director Kate Whoriskey explains in her introduction to the published text that she and Nottage traveled to an Amnesty International in Kampala, Uganda, where they were able to make contacts for interviews with Congolese women who had crossed the border to escape violence; see Whoriskey, "Introduction," in *Ruined*, x.

30 Cynthia Enloe, *Maneuvers: The International Politics of Militarizing Women's Lives* (Berkeley: University of California Press, 2000), 110.

31 Whoriskey recounts that she and Nottage were drawn to Brecht's style, but that ultimately Nottage found *Mother Courage* to be a "false frame" for her play (Whoriskey, "Introduction," xi). Jill Dolan comments that the "conservative happy ending" compromises the gender politics of the play and the "Brechtian vision of the consequences of war for women"; see Dolan, *"Ruined*, by Lynn Nottage," in *Feminist Spectator*, 16 March 2009, available at *http://feministspectator.blogspot.com/2009/03/ruined-by-lynn-nottage.html* (accessed 16 October 2010).

32 Dolan, *"Ruined*, by Lynn Nottage."

33 Nottage, *Ruined*, 13; additional references to *Ruined*, as are those from the other plays under discussion, are given parenthetically in the text.

34 Heather Raffo, *Nine Parts of Desire* (New York: Dramatists Play Service, 2006), premiered at the Manhattan Ensemble Theatre, New York City, in October 2004.

35 Ibid., "Production Note," 66.

36 Cooke, *Women and the War Story*, 220–21.

37 Colleran and Spencer, *Staging Resistance*, 3.

38 *Palace of the End* (Toronto: Playwrights Canada Press, 2007) was commissioned and developed by Epic Theatre Ensemble and first produced by the 49th Parallel Theatre in association with Open At The Top at the NOHO Arts Center, North Hollywood, California, in June 2007. In 2008, it was given a full production by Epic Theatre Ensemble at Playwrights Horizons in New York City.

39 Hunt and Rygiel, *(En)Gendering the War on Terror*, 3.
40 According to Martin Morrow, Thompson learned about the Saffarh family's history from her Toronto neighbors, Dr. Thabit A. J. Abdullah, an Iraqi history professor at York University, and his wife Samara. Morrow reports that "Nehrjas' monologue is based on a written account of her experiences, which Samara Abdullah translated from Arabic for Thompson." See Morrow, "From Hell: Judith Thompson's New Play Finds Scapegoats and Heroes in Iraq," CBC News.ca, 16 January 2008, available at *www.cbc. ca/arts/theatre/thompson.html* (accessed 26 October 2010).
41 It is worth noting that in the 2008 Epic Theatre production, Heather Raffo, author and actress of *Nine Parts of Desire*, performed this monologue, which certainly resonates with her depiction of the vulnerabilities and resilience of Iraqi women during Hussein's reign and the period of the Iraq War.
42 See "Playwright's Note," in which Thompson explains that "everything other than the real events springs from my imagination" (Thompson, *Palace of the End*, i).
43 See Julie Adam, "The Implicated Audience: Judith Thompson's Anti-Naturalism in *The Crackwalker, White Biting Dog, I am Yours,* and *Lion in the Streets,*" in *Judith Thompson,* ed. Ric Knowles, Critical Perspectives on Canadian Theatre in English, vol. 3 (Toronto: Playwrights Canada Press, 2005), 41–6; and Jen Harvie, "Constructing Fictions of an Essential Reality, *or* `This Pickshur is Niiiice': Judith Thompson's *Lion in the Streets,*" in *Judith Thompson,* 47–58.
44 McKelvey, "Introduction," in *One of the Guys*, 14.
45 Francine D'Amico, "The Women of Abu Ghraib," in *One of the Guys*, 45–6.
46 Ilene Feinman, "Shock and Awe: Abu Ghraib, Women Soldiers, and Racially Gendered Torture," in *One of the Guys*, 78–9.
47 Ibid., 69.
48 Zillah Eisenstein, qtd. in Timothy Kaufman-Osborn, "Gender Trouble at Abu Ghraib?" in *One of the Guys*, 164.
49 Sara Ahmed, qtd. in Elaine Aston, Berry Harris, and Lena Šimić, "'It Is Good to Look at One's Own Shadow': A Woman's International Theatre Festival and Questions for International Feminism," in *Feminist Futures?*, 174.
50 Hunt and Rygiel, *(En)Gendering the War on Terror,* 9–13.
51 Wendy S. Hesford, "Rhetorical Memory, Political Theater, and the Traumatic Present," *Transformations* 16, no. 2 (2005): 111.
52 Ibid., 105–06.

8   Enough! Women Playwrights Confront the Israeli-Palestinian Conflict

Amelia Howe Kritzer

The ongoing conflict between the state of Israel and Palestinians in the West Bank and Gaza Strip has created a set of seemingly irreconcilable oppositions that engage partisans of both sides and would-be peacemakers around the globe. Since the beginning of the Second Intifada, an intensification of violence that began in September 2000 and has cost thousands of lives, concern has grown in non-Muslim Western nations about conditions affecting Palestinians, and condemnation has arisen in response to Israeli actions such as the appropriation of land, killing of volunteers with the International Solidarity Movement,[1] extra-legal executions, and military incursions into Lebanon and Gaza. A number of plays written since 2000 address the intensification of violence, attempting to explain or protest it from the perspective of Palestinians, Israelis, or third-party observers.

The Israeli-Palestinian conflict epitomizes contemporary warfare, focusing on sustained disruption of civilian life rather than decisive military encounters and blurring the distinction between civilian and combatant. In such warfare, women and children comprise a high percentage of casualties. Although these conflicts involve and threaten women directly and indirectly, and despite their increased participation in combat, women do not share equally in decision-making regarding war and peace. Their relative powerlessness is a common concern for women playwrights associated with both Israel and the Palestinians, as well as from outside the region. This essay will consider the contributions of a range of women playwrights who have spoken out on the Israeli-Palestinian conflict, using the empowering but outside-the-mainstream medium of drama to present viewpoints that have been unheard or ignored by governmental decision-makers and influential media institutions, and to give audiences the kind of direct and immediate experience of the conflict that can be created in theatre.

Caryl Churchill's protest

Although not the first play to address the Israeli-Palestinian conflict, Caryl Churchill's *Seven Jewish Children: A Play for Gaza*, which made its debut in readings at London's Royal Court Theatre in February 2009, has achieved landmark status even while generating heated controversy. Composed mere weeks after the start of Israel's two-month military assault on Gaza aimed at ending Hamas rocket attacks on Israel, the ten-minute piece goes beyond conventional criticism of Israel. While questions about the proportionality and lawfulness of Israeli strikes on densely populated Gaza were being debated internationally, *Seven Jewish Children* addressed its uncompromising protest against Israeli militarism to Jews around the world. Churchill boldly confronts Jews with a non-Jewish perspective on their suffering as victims of persecution in Europe, their pride in Israel's creation and development, and their failure to condemn recent Israeli actions. The play's confrontational tone reveals the force of Churchill's need to speak out against Israel's actions. Emphasizing her commitment to action on behalf of Palestinians, she waived royalties from the play, while requesting that funds for humanitarian assistance to Gaza be collected at performances. The play immediately generated controversy,[2] and debate intensified when the BBC refused to broadcast the piece, citing its responsibility to practice impartiality. It has since been performed in the United States, Australia, and Israel. Several recorded performances of the play, including one produced by the *Guardian* newspaper as a protest against the BBC's refusal to air it, have been posted on the Internet.[3]

Constructed as seven discussions among Jewish parents or parental figures regarding what to tell an unnamed offstage child (a different child in each scene, hence the seven Jewish children of the title), the play's scenes follow the trajectory of modern Jewish history. In each one, several adults debate how to present the current situation to the child; alternately, the debate may occur in the mind of one adult.[4] The speaker or speakers present a composite Jewish identity initially based in family relationships, but later increasingly formed by Israeli nationalism and opposition to Palestinians. The absent child in each scene serves a potent and multilayered symbolic function: the idea of a child in harm's way evokes strong emotional identification. As the quintessential guiltless party, a child has the right to live and develop free from harm. Furthermore, the child serves as a poignant reminder of a vulnerable and uncertain future – an issue paramount in the conflict between the Palestinians and Israelis. Awareness that both the present and the future must be guarded creates a seesawing "tell her...don't tell her" motion within each of the play's scenes, as speakers contradict one another or themselves in searching painfully for a simple explanation, a partial truth, or even an outright deception to quiet the questioning child.

Although the script does not specify historical settings, Churchill retroactively provided that framework to an American director, Ari Roth. The first dialogue, she explains, "is set at some time of persecution, which could be nineteenth-century Russia (as I think I was inclining towards when I wrote it) or (as we chose at the Royal Court) thirties Germany."[5] In this scene, the adults need to make the child understand an imminent threat and cooperate in hiding. The threat appears serious, as the fourth line cautions: "Don't tell her they'll kill her" (1). Despite cryptic and even sinister overtones reminiscent of the opening scene of Churchill's *Far Away* (2000), the adults in the first scene represent the straightforward effort of parents and guardians to protect children not only from physical harm, but also from the psychological trauma of being the target of hatred. Fear dominates the scene, though in the Royal Court's staged reading, the neutral positioning of the nine actors and the relatively unhurried pace of the scene seemed to signal a degree of power incompatible with historical accounts of the Nazi genocide. In what will be a recurring pattern, the scene ends without resolving the issue or actualizing the threat.

Subsequent scenes chart a chronological progression of reclaiming autonomy by Jews who survived the Nazi death camps. Scene 2 – set, according to Churchill's correspondence with Roth, "some time after the Holocaust in England (or indeed America)"[6] – portrays survivors debating what to tell their daughter about the deaths of family members, presumably in the Nazi camps. Concerned about tainting her understanding of the world if they reveal the full horror of the program to annihilate the Jews, they consider how to remember the dead, whether to abandon their distinctive Jewish identity, and whether they believe hatred toward Jews to be a present threat. Scene 3, showing "people from England (or America) deciding to go to Israel,"[7] portrays Jews balanced between an increased power of choice and continuing limitation. It starts with "Don't tell her we're going for ever," and continues with suggestions to tell the child "we're going home," "it's the land God gave us" (2). Evidently referring to the treatment of Jews as outsiders in postwar England (and America), one adult says: "Don't tell her she doesn't belong here" (3).

The remaining scenes take place in Israel. Scene 4, representing a Jewish family newly arrived in Israel, alludes to difficult relations between Jews and Palestinians, raising questions of property, ethnicity, and dispossession. Its emphasis on Palestinian opposition to Jewish settlement and its assertion of a "we" and "they" viewpoint implies that the issue of where Jews "belong" has not been settled by the existence of Israel. The uncertainty, however, quickly dissolves in scene 5, set in the aftermath of the Six-Day War, when the adults exult: "Tell her we've won" and "we've got new land" (4). Overlaying the celebratory mood with strong irony, this scene locates the emergence of Jewish certainty in military dominance and the power of ownership. Scene 6, which Churchill has said shows adults answering the questions of a child "from England [visiting] relatives in Israel,"[8] focuses on Israel's appropriation of land and resources. This dialogue marks a moral turning point of the piece, as the adults actively deceive the child, withholding information about the diversion of water from Palestinian fields to Israeli swimming pools, the destruction of Palestinian homes, and lethal responses to rock-throwing children. Rather than confront the morality of such actions, the adults in the scene struggle to gauge the threat represented by Palestinians who "set off bombs in cafes" and "want to drive us into the sea" (5). Concerns for national security take precedence over other considerations, even trust within the family.

Scene 7 evidently takes place during the 2008–2009 invasion of Gaza. In this scene, the adults attempt to shield the child from learning about harm inflicted on the people of Gaza. They speak of censoring and discrediting broadcast news, denying the child any opportunity to view Israeli action in objective moral terms. Their efforts to justify civilian casualties, especially the deaths of children, culminate in the longest speech of the play. Starting as a plea for frankness, this speech becomes an outburst of hatred. The speaker declares that Palestinians "want their children killed to make people sorry for them," insisting, "tell her not to be sorry for them … tell her we're the iron fist now … we won't stop killing them till we're safe … they're animals … I wouldn't care if we wiped them out … we're better haters," and denying feeling anything about Palestinian children "covered in blood" (6) except relief that they are not their own children. Although a line earlier in the scene refers to a cousin who refused military service, this speech represents the silencing of moderate dialogue as militaristic viewpoints have come to control Israeli decision-making. The final three lines reiterate the adults' continuing concern: "Don't tell her that. Tell her we love her. Don't frighten her" (6). This scene warns of an Israeli future shaped by corruption, forced isolation, and extremism.

Taken together, the scenes show a transformation from fear for the life and well-being of one's own child to blind insensitivity toward others, and even to hate-fueled aggression under the pretext of protecting one's own children. Thus, while condemning the dehumanization of Palestinians by Israelis, the play links this attitude to the dehumanization of Jews. The final scene's speech compares Israel's treatment of Gaza with the Nazi treatment of Jews, bypassing historical accuracy in the effort to confront audiences with this shocking notion as a protest against Israeli attacks. The play demands that Israel and its supporters not only face responsibility for the deaths of reportedly more than 1,400 noncombatants in the Gaza campaign, but also understand the kind of future being created by such action.

Controversy over *Seven Jewish Children*

The play's representation of Jewish history and identity, more than its condemnation of Israeli militarism, set off vigorous debate among Jewish critics in Britain and the United States. Novelist and columnist for the *Independent* Howard Jacobson wrote that *Seven Jewish Children* expresses anti-Semitism, arguing that "once you venture on to 'chosen people' territory – feeding all the ancient prejudice against that miscomprehended phrase – once you repeat in another form the medieval blood-libel of Jews rejoicing in the murder of little children, you have crossed over" into a form of hatred "which the haters don't even recognize in themselves, so acculturated is it." [9] American playwright Israel Horovitz echoed Jacobson's sentiments, writing that "[t]hose who criticize Jews in the name of criticizing Israel... step over an unacceptable boundary."[10]

Guardian commentator and author of *The Question of Zion* (2005) Jacqueline Rose contested Jacobson's interpretation of the play, pointing to its "precise and focused... criticism of Israeli policies: control of water, house demolitions, checkpoints and the destruction of olive trees" and its dramatic emphasis on "the drastic deterioration of the situation, and the sense, shared by many, that an injustice is being perpetrated."[11] American playwright Tony Kushner and critic Alisa Solomon, co-authors of *Wrestling with Zion: Progressive Jewish-American Responses to the Israeli-Palestinian Conflict* (2003), co-wrote an opinion piece in the *Nation* urging production and discussion of the play "as widely as possible," especially in light of the cancellation of *My Name Is Rachel Corrie* by the New York Theater Workshop in 2006. Arguing that "anger and distress" are appropriate responses to the conflict, yet acknowledging that the extreme compression of Jewish history and reduction of the conflict to "stinging simplicity" make the play "almost brutally painful," they praise its "incitement to speech and... examination of silence," its attention to "what can and cannot be said."[12] The two agree that lines like "tell her we're better haters, tell her we're chosen people" (6) disturb them, because they reflect misunderstandings of Judaism and obliviousness to the stereotyping of Jews. Nevertheless, they conclude that "to see anti-Semitism here is to construe erroneously the words spoken by the worst of Churchill's characters as a statement from the playwright about all Jews." Praising Churchill's "empathy, tenderness and intimacy," Kushner and Solomon ultimately find hope and even a connection with Jewish tradition in the questions that the unseen girls keep asking.[13]

Responses to *Seven Jewish Children*

Seven Jewish Children prompted several immediate response plays,[14] including two titled *Seven Palestinian Children*. One play of that title, written by Mirna Sakhleh, a young Palestinian woman studying in Britain, gives Palestinians the voice that is absent in *Seven Jewish Children*. This brief piece, also divided into seven scenes, protests the treatment of the Palestinians with an intensity rooted in personal experience. The unseen child functions as a mere device; the monologue speaks directly to the audience, asserting a history of robbery and betrayal. Never mentioning the names of Israel or Palestine, Sakhleh's simplified version of Palestinian history characterizes Israel as "the foreign burglar" (scene 1) or "the thief" (scene 2) and identifies Palestine as the gentle-sounding Jasmine, the youngest of twenty-two siblings who inherited lands from a fabulously wealthy ancestor.[15] Notably, Jasmine directs anger not only at "the thief" who has destroyed homes and farms, imprisoned men, emptied classrooms, and raped women, but also at her siblings, who have failed to prevent or right these wrongs. In scene 3, the speaker says, "Tell her they [the siblings] collaborated with the thief and planned a charade to start a fake fight between them, so Jasmine knows that her siblings are there for her and want to kill the thief! In fact they don't, in fact they won't!" Jasmine has dealt with the conflict at different times by sending children away to safety, accepting a peace agreement, and fighting. Scene 7 concludes the piece by emphasizing the isolation of Palestinians in the Arab world: "Tell her the thief was not the only enemy; tell her the collaborator uncles are also enemies! Tell her because they are only afraid that the thief might steal and occupy their lands, they betrayed Jasmine and sold their little sister for free!"

This set of monologues presents its version of Palestinian experience as a history focused on the tangible issue of land, rather than on abstract issues of power. Claiming simply that land has been stolen, Jasmine demands justice, rather than advocating violence or even explicitly mentioning killing or war. In scene 5, she even expresses willingness to marry "the thief" if that will allow her and her children to "share the land and live together in peace." The play does call for shaming the "siblings" that have not helped Jasmine. While depicting Palestinians as victims, it demonstrates strength by defining wrongs, demanding justice, and claiming kinship with powerful Arab nations. Furthermore, its open-ended conclusion seems to invite dialogue and suggest some possibility of resolution.

Deb Margolin's *Seven Palestinian Children* (2009) has been performed in tandem with some US productions of *Seven Jewish Children* as a means of balancing its viewpoint with an alternate one. A Jewish American playwright and performance artist, Margolin subtitles her work "A Play for the Other,"[16] highlighting her attempt to understand and represent Palestinians. Its sequence of seven monologues poetically expressing a Palestinian mother's fierce love for her young son addresses the audience directly. This mother's back-and-forth debate sets militancy against acceptance. In scene 1, she urges, "Tell him one day he will fight alongside his father," but in scene 2, she cautions, "Tell him to look at the ground...to smile and say *shalom*"[17] in the presence of Israelis. The mother's anger frequently overwhelms her efforts to contain it. She bitterly resents exclusion from Jerusalem, longs for her home – a house "full and big with doors large and small and with windows like paintings" – mourns the killings of relatives and neighbors, reveals both grief and pride in the rebels' deaths of her husband and older son, and wonders whether to tell the child that they are dead or to comfort him with the lie that they have gone away to "get jobs." Through her tenacious love for her child, the mother creates a bond with the audience.

Margolin's play ends, as does Churchill's, with a protracted monologue in which the speaker abandons restraint. Considering the pros and cons of death, the mother finally bursts out in scene 7:

Tell him I don't care any more. Tell him I'd send a rocket if I could I don't want to care anymore. Tell him he is homeless tell him there is nothing to eat. Tell him his father and brother died hungry. Tell him the baby died. Tell him what it is for a mother to see her baby die and have nothing to feed him. Tell him the people who died in the cafes died with their bellies full. Don't tell him. Tell him the world hates the jews and has always hated them. Tell him there's a reason when people hate, when people hate there's always a reason. Tell him everything happens for a reason, tell him his mother believes that everything happens for a reason, tell him his mother knows this his mother loves him *tell him I do it for him he will be taken care of now.*

The final lines, in which the mother urges "tell him to come home... [and] look under the shroud," imply that she engages in a suicide attack.

This monologue centers on the ultimate act of extremism, which epitomizes the despair on one side and fear on the other, feeding and justifying the continuing conflict. In attempting to explain why a mother would choose to commit a suicide bombing, it emphasizes the desperation of Palestinians deprived of homes, sustenance, identity, and autonomy; even more importantly, it points out that the lack of these basic necessities defines and dominates Palestinians. This context makes suicidal violence seem the only meaningful action. The mother hopes that, as the survivor of a martyr, her child will receive food. Hatred of Jews plays only a secondary role in the mother's act of violence; in her final speech, she invokes anti-Jewish prejudice to dehumanize those she is preparing to harm. Although Margolin wrote this piece because of "distress over some of Churchill's generalizations about the Jewish community,"[18] she clearly attributes the mother's suffering to the actions of Israel. This play for "the other" represents the Palestinians in one embattled mother who wants more than anything to return to the life she enjoyed before the conflict. The terrible constraints of the occupation move her toward destruction by depriving her of hope for the future. The play ends, in Margolin's words, with the moment "when one human being is incapable of seeing the humanity in another."[19] Margolin's *Seven Palestinian Children* thus implies that extremism on one side of the opposition produces extremism on the other side.

The conflict from opposing points of view

A common factor among *Seven Jewish Children* and the dramatic responses by Margolin and Sakhleh consists in their advocacy of particular points of view toward the conflict. Rather than calling for or envisioning reconciliation of the opposing sides, each play urges recognition of experiences that define the conflict in terms of harm to one side or the other. Additional plays by women about the Israeli-Palestinian conflict tend to follow this pattern. Betty Shamieh, a Palestinian American playwright and performer, believes that "there is something particularly devastating about being invisible"[20] and has devoted most of her playwriting and performing to making Arab women visible.[21] Her monologue *Tamam* premiered at the Imagine Iraq event organized by the Artists Network of Refuse and Resist in 2002. The young Palestinian woman who speaks this monologue informs the audience that her name, Tamam, means "enough," and says that since she was the seventh daughter, her name announced that her family had enough female children. Tamam explains the family's preference for sons by referring to the conflict: "we in Gaza understand the power of might" and "times like these call for soldiers"[22] – thus implying that warfare reduces the value of women to their society. Tamam becomes a victim in the conflict, as she relates in a sequence of events beginning with the arrest of a beloved and promising younger brother for throwing rocks at Israeli soldiers, continuing with her rape by soldiers when she visits him in an Israeli jail, and culminating with the brother's suicide bombing of a bus in Israel. She concludes by describing the drastic change in her life, as her family's home has been destroyed in retaliation for her brother's act and the agreement for her own marriage has been revoked because of the rape.

This play, like those of Sakhleh and Margolin, presents Palestinians entirely in the context of the conflict, showing their lives engulfed by it. While the narrative expresses Palestinian hopes for a future that includes education, careers, and happy marriages, it depicts a simple and fatalistic pattern of violence that grows more annihilating with each new development. Tamam, like Jasmine in Sakhleh's play and the mother in Margolin's, represents all Palestinians. The femininity of these characters implies a vulnerability and lack of power on the part of the Palestinian people, presenting the primary Palestinian experience of the conflict as suffering, rather than aggression. It gives Palestinian suffering a deeply personal dimension. Tamam, for example, expresses bitterness at being deprived of love, as well as of basic necessities. In the end, she simply repeats her name and the word "enough."

Tamam defines the Palestinian struggle against Israel through two iconic acts: the everyday and relatively harmless rock-throwing through which Palestinian youths defy Israeli authority, and the rare though devastating and media-attracting suicide bombing. Linking the two in a continuum of escalating retaliation, the play offers another explanation of what may lie behind extreme acts of destruction and warns of ever-increasing violence and brutalization on both sides. This play, like Margolin's, emphasizes the disruption and degradation of Palestinian lives by Israeli domination. In depicting direct violence against Tamam, who is raped and deprived of her home and planned future even though she has committed no act against the Israelis, it highlights the injustice of punishing all members of a family or community for the act of an individual. Finally, its focus on extreme violence, coupled with repetition of the cry "enough," calls unconditionally for cessation. Most centrally, this cry refers to Tamam's personal suffering: while demanding attention to the wrongs committed against her, the character Tamam looks to others to alleviate her pain unless she is to follow her brother's path toward ending it.

"Enough" appears again as a central theme in Iris Bahr's 2006 solo play *Dai*, which translates from Hebrew as *Enough*. Bahr is an Israeli American performer, director, and writer who lived in Israel as a teenager and served in the Israeli army. In the play's preface, she notes her long-standing refusal to discuss the Israeli-Palestinian conflict, because "even the most enlightened discourse always seems to descend into a flurry of defensiveness and frustration."[23] In writing this piece, which premiered in New York at the Culture Project in 2008, she sought to recognize the views of both sides and call attention to the variety of positions within Israeli society.

Set in a café, *Dai* encompasses eleven characters, all originally played by Bahr, that form a colorful and often humorous collage of Israelis and non-Israelis and suggests the vibrant life of Tel Aviv. One by one, each character establishes a viewpoint in what turns out to be his or her last words, as the speech is cut off by the explosion of a suicide bombing. These characters offer widely differing views on the meaning of Israel: Uzi, a middle-aged member of a kibbutz,[24] exemplifies stoic commitment to Israel's defense, coping with the permanent hospitalization of an older son injured in military service, the impending military service of his second son, the emotional breakdown of his wife, and his own reserve duty; Shuli, an ultra-orthodox mother of seven from a West Bank settlement, defines Israel in religious terms, as the "God-given birthright" (37) of the Jews; 20-year-old Avivit believes that the drug Ecstasy is the key to peace; and Alma, an Israeli who emigrated to the United States, believes that all Israelis should follow her example, because "[l]ife is more important than an idea!" (31). At the same time, several characters from other nations have been attracted to Israel because of opportunities: a film for the American actress Jessica; converting non-Christians for the American evangelist Trev; money for the Russian prostitute Svetlana; the hope of finding a semblance of family for the orphaned 19-year-old Rebecca from the United States; reunion with a former boyfriend for the German Hendrik; and a career boost for Christiane, a Syrian British television reporter. To Nijma Aziz, a middle-aged professor from Ramallah who serves as the single representative of Palestinians, the café provides the opportunity for respite from the struggles of life in the West Bank.

The characters' observations about the Israeli-Palestinian conflict range from the predictable to the surprising. Uzi considers the conflict a life-and-death struggle, saying that "[t]he Arabs put down their weapons, no more war, we put down our weapons, NO MORE ISRAEL!" (22). The reporter

Christiane accuses Israel of "severe human rights abuse and mass *murder*" (8). Nijma compares the relationship between Israel and the Palestinians to "a bad marriage" (69) in which each side blames the other. Svetlana likens the Israelis to "wounded animals" who strike at the nearest target, because of the trauma of being "hated since the beginning of time" (49). Avivit thinks that leaders on both sides have "too many memories, too many scars" to end the conflict, and promotes a huge party with free Ecstasy to bring young people from the two sides together "through common enjoyment, not common suffering" (65). Both the ultra-orthodox settler Shuli and the Christian evangelist Trev regard the Palestinians as obstacles to the fulfillment of their central religious expectations. Those focused on purely personal goals ignore the conflict until it literally explodes in their faces.

The theme of hope connects these disparate lives. Hope takes many forms, both personal and political, among the characters, but transcends their divisions and serves as the primary energy in the play. The pragmatic Svetlana describes the Israelis as people who "have hope in something they know is impossible" (49), echoing the idealistic Uzi's comment about Holocaust survivors who came to Israel: "After such trauma the brain floods the body with hope, beyond reason or rationality, otherwise it will just die!" (22). Every character pursues some sort of dream. Most poignant is Nijma's plan to share the tranquility she has found in her weekly visits to Tel Aviv with her increasingly militant son Youssef. She wants him to develop "a cohesive Palestinian identity," but more than anything wants to give him hope; and to show him "a life of normalcy and prosperity" (70), she has asked him to join her here for coffee. She smiles with pride as he enters the café and pauses near a young woman, but then, in horror, realizes that he is in the act of detonating a bomb. Ironically, the suicide bombing forces ultimate unity on lives that otherwise had little in common.

The structure of *Dai* creates a metaphor of ordinary life in Israel disrupted and irrevocably changed by Palestinian violence. Grounded in an Israeli perspective, most of the monologues express a range of trivial and weighty concerns. The Palestinian woman, however, speaks only about the conflict, emphasizing the limitations it has forced on her, from being enclosed by a wall to being surrounded by posters picturing martyrs. While the characters identified with Israel refer to or demonstrate the strong and even irrational force of hope, whether they carry the legacy of persecution or anticipate Armageddon, the Palestinian's monologue speaks of the power of despair. Nijma wants to prevent her son being "sucked in by his friends' anger and thirst for blood" (70), but she has become isolated from other Palestinians to the point where she feels comfortable only during her weekly visits to Tel Aviv. Youssef, though named, does not appear or speak; thus the play does not attempt direct representation of the despair, hopes, or aspirations of young Palestinians. Although it hints at the possibility of positive change through Nijma's belief that Palestinians can create opportunities for themselves, it ends on the fatalistic note of the seemingly inevitable suicide bombing. The cumulative emotional shock of the repeated explosion creates a reactive barrier that cuts off the potential of thinking beyond continuing violence.

The sense, absent in other plays, of everyday Palestinian life that existed before the occupation and continues, though disrupted by the violence, emerges in a recent solo performance piece, *I ♥ Hamas and Other Things I'm Afraid to Tell You*, which debuted at the 2008 New York Fringe Festival. Jennifer Jajeh, an American actor, writer, and producer whose parents are from Ramallah in the West Bank, wrote and performs the monologue. On a bare stage backed by a screen on which slides are projected, Jajeh begins by remembering an elementary-school exercise in which pupils shared information about their ethnic origins. She alone could not match her origin with a nation on the classroom map. Jajeh explains that this episode initiated her quest for identity. Displaying the confident and informal style of an affluent American, she overturns expectations that associate Palestinians with powerlessness and victimization. By means of a light-up board captioned "Ask a Palestinian," she humorously incorporates scripted questions and answers into the narrative, simultaneously playing to and defusing the audience's potential discomfort with her message. Having described herself as descended from the family of Christians who founded Ramallah in the 1400s, Jajeh teases the audience with the revelation that she has been sleeping with a Jewish male. The sleeping partner, however, turns out to be a cat named Judah, previously owned by the mother of a Jewish friend.

After this lighthearted introduction, Jajeh narrates and enacts episodes from her journey to the West Bank in 2000, at the beginning of the Second Intifada. She finds a sense of belonging in Ramallah, enjoying the familiarity of its cooking smells and tastes; but instead of affirmation of her identity, she experiences a new kind of otherness. Her appearance, unmarried status, and inability to speak Arabic brand her as an outsider and lead people to ask where she is from – the very question that prompted her journey. The initial visit leads to a second, longer sojourn, but by then, life in the West Bank has become difficult. Long lines at checkpoints prevent easy trips to Jerusalem to go to clubs or pick up sushi; the university no longer provides a sanctuary; violence is close at hand. Nevertheless, Jajeh provides sympathetic and often humorous glimpses of daily life and ordinary concerns. She develops a relationship with a man who is Muslim; when he brings up the subject of conversion, she rejects the idea, because, as she says, "I have my own religion I don't believe in."[25]

Violence increasingly dominates the second half of the play. In one episode, Jajeh films the action at a checkpoint, documenting the long waits and random harassment to which Palestinians are subjected when they enter Israel. Presumably protected by her US citizenship, Jajeh confronts an Israeli soldier and sparks a protest; she exults in the cheers of Palestinians until she realizes that they are chanting "Espaniola," evidently thinking that she is Spanish. At another time, she persuades a very reluctant male friend, who is determined to avoid trouble, to take her to an area known for its flare-ups of violence. She observes children throwing stones at Israeli soldiers and is hurried away by her friend as the soldiers open fire, killing a boy. Jajeh's experiences radicalize her, and at the end of her narrative she confesses that she can now imagine blowing someone up. She also finally feels a strong connection to her family and its unique history. This connection, expressed with wistful pride toward the past, concludes the monologue, as Jajeh cradles in her arms a huge book that, she reveals, contains the genealogies of Ramallah's original settlers.

Jajeh's monologue places her personal experience and concerns in the context of the Israeli-Palestinian conflict – the individual at times colliding with the political. She does not downplay her commitment to an acting career, her religious difference from the Muslim majority in the West Bank, or her enjoyment of being single and independent, but at the same time, she omits a great deal from the narrative, including her feelings about returning to the United States and any exploration of the implications of her newfound admiration for Hamas. Nevertheless, the piece counters Palestinian invisibility and makes a credible protest against the monolithic view of Palestinians common in the United States. It provides audiences with a glimpse of history, culture, and everyday life in the West Bank, as well as explaining how the conflict disrupts the lives of Palestinians. As a personal story presented in a confidential style and leavened with self-deprecating humor, the monologue draws the audience in and promotes empathy with Palestinians who are neither two-dimensional victims nor suicide bombers.

Naomi Wallace's visions of dialogue

The plays discussed thus far make clear the passionate desire for an end to violence expressed in the insistence on "enough"; however, their pattern of emphasizing the viewpoint and experience of one side limits their potential for bridging the deep divisions between Palestinians and Israelis underlying the violence. In *Fever Chart*, Naomi Wallace, an American playwright, moves beyond the cry of "enough" to find and make visible the fragments of shared experience that might provide a starting point for peace. Wallace developed this trilogy of one-act plays about the Middle East, including two about the Israeli-Palestinian conflict,[26] over a period of two years in theatres in the United States and the United Kingdom. The trilogy was first produced in its entirety in 2008, at New York's Public Theater. Subtitled *Three Visions of the Middle East*, her plays employ a dream-like landscape and theatrical style to draw the audience's attention beyond the entrenched oppositions of the conflict. The surreal scenes, with their lyrical language, invoke actual events,[27] but do not attempt to mimic or use them as reference points in an argument. A mood of sadness pervades both plays with the Israeli-Palestinian conflict as subject, in contrast to the tone of anger and impatience common to other plays about the conflict. Both also feature a trio of characters, a choice that undermines the either/or pattern of the binary opposition between Palestinian and Israeli positions.

"Vision One: A State of Innocence" takes as its setting the ruined Rafah Zoo, which was demolished in 2004 by the Israeli army.[28] The characters include Yuval, an Israeli soldier serving as a zookeeper, Um Hisham, a Palestinian woman, and Shlomo, an elderly Israeli architect. Yuval worries about the zoo animals, because it seems that pieces of them disappear each morning, only to reassemble by afternoon. Um Hisham provides a gentle, maternal presence; Yuval hears her singing quietly and demands that she stop. Their verbal exchange, while pointed, does not lack humor: when Yuval asserts that "you want to throw me in the sea," Um Hisham counters, "I just might. But I can't get to the sea. Seventeen and a half checkpoints keep me from it" (9). Shlomo, the architect, gives an impromptu lecture on "Homa Umigdal, the Wall and Tower" (11), to which he blissfully attributes the development of Israel. Shlomo is a vampire of sorts who feasts on destroyed Palestinian homes and villages. When informed of a "fresh ruin in the Salahaddin district" (15), he runs off to find it, but returns disappointed after finding the site cordoned off, because an Israeli soldier was killed there.

Through cryptic questions and exchanges, the play gradually assembles its central narrative. The undefended zoo and many of its animals were crushed by sixty-five-ton tanks. Yuval was killed by a Rafah sniper, because he paused, saw Israeli soldiers beating Um Hisham's husband, called a halt to the beating, and then accepted the cup of tea she gratefully offered him. Um Hisham's daughter Asma, a girl who loved the zoo, numbers, and her pet pigeons, was killed when the Israeli army demolished the family's home in retaliation for Yuval's death there. Asma, the animals, and even Yuval, who never wanted to be a soldier, perished as innocent victims of the conflict. Um Hisham repeatedly refers to having "something that belongs to" (18) Yuval's mother; it turns out to be his final three minutes of life, which Um Hisham shared as she cradled him in her arms. She expresses kinship with Yuval's mother: "We had pieces of life in common. In our children. Our children were our pieces of life. Now we have pieces of death. In common" (22). The connection between Um Hisham and Yuval reveals an intimate, though painful interrelationship between Israelis and Palestinians. Their emotional though unsentimental memory of mutual generosity, coupled with recognition of the resulting mutual disaster, overturns the familiar formulae invoked in the conflict and exposes the absurd inadequacy of conventional responses. With one party to this mutual experience dead, the dialogue can go nowhere, but the imagined moment opens a space of possibility for the audience to consider.

"Vision Two: Between This Breath and You" takes place in a medical clinic in West Jerusalem. Again, a Palestinian parent confronts a young Israeli. The middle-aged father, Mourid Kamal, appears as the clinic is closing for the day, but insists on speaking with Tanya Langer, a 20-year-old nurse in training. The third character, Sami, a custodian, symbolically clears away the detritus of injury and illness with his mop, offering a humorously hopeful take on his job that invokes the Jewish myth of the golem: "With what this mop gathers I could build, particle by particle, out of abandoned parts, an entirely new human being!" (29). Tanya, the play reveals, has been partially reconstructed by receiving a lung transplant to treat her cystic fibrosis. Mourid, after years of detective work, has tracked her down to inform her that her donated lungs came from his 12-year-old son Ahmed, who was shot by Israeli soldiers. Mourid wants to somehow communicate with the part of his son still alive inside Tanya. She resists this idea and even taunts Mourid by suggesting that his son participates in her sexual affairs, but eventually shares with him a recurrent dream that seems connected with a childhood trauma experienced by Ahmed. Rejoicing at this indication that an aspect of his son survives, Mourid helps Tanya recover from a fit of breathlessness. Touched by his generosity, she asks him why he is helping her, and he replies: "Because this is not the only world.... Because you are. My son" (52–53). Through the recognition of shared vulnerability and the need for hope in the face of death, the two experience mutual understanding in the instant "where exhalation ends, before the next breath begins" (51).

Wallace's plays protest with vivid images the madness of war and the death of innocents, but they also go beyond protest to attempt the rehumanization of each side to the other; deconstructing the conflict's dehumanizing separation and alienation of the "other," the plays highlight instead "pieces of life" (22) shared by richly characterized individuals on opposite sides of the conflict, but with interests and experiences outside it. In both plays, a connection that transcends death mediates the impulse to destroy the "other." The Palestinian mother in "Vision One" mourns two deaths: that of her beloved daughter, and that of the Israeli soldier bound to her inextricably, though involuntarily, by his final kindness. Tanya in "Vision Two" incorporates and depends on the lungs of the dead Ahmed; and as she has accepted the extension of life, she also comes to accept relatedness to him and to his father in an encounter made more urgent by their knowledge that she is nearing the end of the transplant's efficacy.

Both plays acknowledge violence and loss without portraying revenge as the inevitable response. Using a consciously theatrical style, surprise reversals of assumptions, witty humor, and third characters functioning as a kind of wild card, the plays clear away habitual responses to the conflict, replacing them with a dream-like indeterminacy that obscures concrete aspects of the dispute to permit the emergence of a strong sense of the human potential for giving to, helping, and loving others. Attempting to provide an alternative to the despair that fuels violence, Wallace's plays suggest the possibility of communication between Israelis and Palestinians, though without diminishing the difficulty of actually making a connection.

In a time when electronic media coverage of the Israeli-Palestinian conflict largely fails to counteract public weariness in Western countries, the plays considered in this essay seek to move the conflict to the forefront of the international political agenda, reaching the public via alternate routes even within theatre, including rehearsed readings, solo perform-ances, production within a larger event, and distribution on the Internet. All employ a tone of urgency, and many use shock tactics to communi-cate the sense of crisis. They succeed, at least temporarily, by personalizing the situation through arresting and sometimes unforgettable characters. The real time and unrepeatability of the performances create a sense of urgency that may induce audience members to set aside their defensive distance, engage with the situation, and give serious thought to the moral and political issues involved. Such engagement may have a strong imme-diate impact, but the challenge remains to shape a future of peace, justice, and reconciliation.

Notes

1　The most widely publicized of these killings was that of the 23-year-old US volunteer Rachel Corrie, who was run over by an Israeli army bulldozer on 16 March 2003 while nonviolently resisting the destruction of a Palestinian home. The verbatim drama *My Name Is Rachel Corrie* (2006), edited by Alan Rickman and Katharine Viner, is the best-known play dealing with the Israeli-Palestinian conflict.

2　Even the reviews generated controversy, with *Guardian* critic Michael Billington drawing heavy criticism for his comment that the play shows "how Jewish chil-dren are bred to believe in the 'otherness' of the Palestinians"; see Billington, "Royal Court Theatre Gets Behind the Gaza Headlines," *Guardian,* 11 February 2009, available at *http://www.guardian.co.uk/stage/theatreblog/2009/feb/11/royal-court-theatre-gaza* (accessed 16 August 2010).

3　The *Guardian*'s recorded production is available at *http://www.guardian.co.uk/stage/video/2009/apr/25/seven-jewish-children-caryl-churchill* (accessed 16 August 2010).

4　Churchill states in the published text that "the lines can be shared out in any way" and that the scenes "may be played by any number of actors"; see *Seven Jewish Children* (London: Nick Hern Books, 2009), 2; subsequent references will be given parenthetically in the text. The online version of the play produced by the *Guardian* uses a single actor.

5　See *The Theater J Blog*, correspondence between Caryl Churchill and Ari Roth, 24 March 2009, available at *http://theaterjblogs.wordpress.com/2009/03/24/* (accessed 17 September 2010). Roth, who was preparing *Seven Jewish Children* for perform-ance by Theater J in Washington, D.C., had e-mailed Churchill a list of questions about the play, and she e-mailed her replies.

6 *Theater J Blog.*

7 Ibid.

8 Ibid.

9 Howard Jacobson, "Let's See the 'Criticism' of Israel for What It Is," *Independent*, 18 February 2009, available at *http://www.independent.co.uk/opinion/ commentators/howard-jacobson/howard-jacobson-letrsquos-see-the-criticism-of-isra- el-for-what-it-really-is-1624827.html* (accessed 16 August 2010). The deep current of anti-Semitism within British society undoubtedly complicates efforts to contextualize and understand the play.

10 *The Theater J Blog*, 19 April 2009, available at *http://theaterjblogs.wordpress. com/2009/04/19/a-new-response-play-to-7jc-by-israel-horovitz-what-good-fences- make/* (accessed 22 September 2010).

11 Jacqueline Rose, "Why Howard Jacobson Is Wrong," *Guardian*, 24 February 2009, available at *http://www.guardian.co.uk/commentisfree/2009/feb/23/howard- jacobson-antisemitism-caryl-churchill* (accessed 23 July 2010).

12 Tony Kushner and Alisa Solomon, "Tell Her the Truth," *Nation*, 26 March 2009, available at *http://www.thenation.com/article/tell-her-truth* (accessed 17 September 2010).

13 Ibid.

14 Theater J, which brought Churchill's *Seven Jewish Children* to the United States, invited responses from Jewish playwrights. In addition to Deborah Margolin, whose play is discussed in this essay, Israel Horovitz wrote a response, *What Good Fences Make* (2009), which he offered royalty-free, with the suggestion that a collection be taken for the One Family Fund, a charity aiding children wounded in attacks on Israel. Horovitz's play is available at *http://theaterjblogs. wordpress.com/2009/04/19/a-new-response-play-to-7jc-by-israel-horovitz-what-good- fences-make/* (accessed 22 September 2010).

15 Mirna Sakhleh, *Seven Palestinian Children*, in *Palestine Telegraph*, 11 May 2009, available at *http://www.paltelegraph.com/index.php?option=com_content&view=art icle&id=799:seven-palestinian-children&catid=85:diaries&Itemid=148* (accessed 23 August 2010); subsequent references to the play will be to this edition.

16 The concept of "Writing the Other" was introduced by playwright and teacher Betty Shamieh in a series of workshops that encouraged Jews and Arabs to write monologues from the other's point of view.

17 Deborah Margolin, *Seven Palestinian Children*, in "Reb Barry's Blog," available at *http://www.neshamah.net/reb_barrys_blog_neshamahn/seven-palestinian-children. html* (accessed 17 September 2010); subsequent references to the play will be to this edition.

18 Monica Hesse, "'Jewish Children' Comes to D.C. Already Upstaged by Controversy," *Washington Post*, 17 March 2009, available at *http://www.washing- tonpost.com/wp-dyn/content/article/2009/03/16/AR2009031603255.html* (accessed 23 August 2010). The article discusses Churchill's and Margolin's plays, which were performed together at Theater J in Washington, D.C.

19 Ibid.

20 Betty Shamieh, "The Art of Countering Despair: Naomi Wallace," *Brooklyn Rail*, May 2008, available at *http://brooklynrail.org/2008/05/theater/the-art-of-counter- ing-despair-naomi-wallace* (accessed 23 August 2010).

21 Shamieh's works include the solo-piece *Chocolate in Heat: Growing Up Arab in America* (2001); the drama *Roar* (2004), about a Palestinian American family in

1990s Detroit; and *The Black-Eyed* (2005), about four Palestinian women from different eras.

22 Betty Shamieh, *Tamam*, in *Talk to Me: Monologue Plays*, ed. Eric Lane and Nina Shengold (New York: Vintage Books, 2004), 473.

23 Iris Bahr, *Dai (Enough)* (Evanston, IL: Northwestern University Press, 2009), vii; subsequent references to the play will be given parenthetically in the text.

24 The *kibbutzim*, or communal farms, were established by the Zionist founders of Israel. They constitute a politically left factor in Israeli politics.

25 Jennifer Jajeh, *I ♥ Hamas and Other Things I'm Afraid to Tell You*, performed at Bedlam Theatre, Minneapolis, 19 February 2010.

26 The third play, a monologue titled "Vision Three: The Retreating World," deals with the war in Iraq and is therefore not discussed in this essay.

27 Wallace's note to the published version reads: "*The Fever Chart: Three Visions of the Middle East* is based on true events" (*The Fever Chart: Three Visions of the Middle East* [New York: Theatre Communications Group, 2009], 2); subsequent references to the play will be given parenthetically in the text. In a review of the play for the Egyptian English-language weekly *Al-Ahram*, Egyptian critic Nehad Selaiha identifies the event that inspired "Vision Two: Between This Breath and You" as the shooting of 12-year-old Ahmed Khatib by Israeli soldiers in a raid on the Jenin refugee camp, and the subsequent decision of his parents to donate his heart, liver, kidneys, and lungs for transplant into six Israelis; see Selaiha, "Politics Centre-stage," *Al-Ahram* 889 (20–26 March 2008), available at *http://www.weekly.ahram.org* (accessed 17 September 2010).

28 The small zoo was rebuilt with international donations and reopened in 2005.

9   Women Playwrights in Post-Apartheid South Africa: Yael Farber, Lara Foot-Newton, and the Call for *Ubuntu*

Yvette Hutchison

Described by Jane Taylor as a "founding theatrical event, a metaphysical 'tournament of value,'"[1] South Africa's Truth and Reconciliation Commission (TRC) publicly and performatively renegotiated memory and history, facilitated the hearing of specific stories related to apartheid in public, and attempted to redefine contemporary social values in terms of forgiveness and reconciliation. The TRC's chairman, Desmond Tutu, suggested that this process could be achieved through *ubuntu*: the acknowledgement that "a person is a person through other persons," which includes acknowledging that we are "diminished when others are humiliated or diminished, when others are tortured or oppressed."[2] *Ubuntu* is an African formulation of humanism and socialism which claims that humanity is defined by the degree to which we accord equal dignity and personhood to all people, regardless of class, race, gender, or status; we cannot be human separately from one another, we are connected, and what each of us does affects the world. In this analysis, I want to consider how South African playwrights Yael Farber and Lara Foot-Newton have contributed to the endeavor of negotiating *ubuntu* in a country comprised of diverse and divided people.

The TRC was an important watershed for South Africa, but its mandate was specific and limited. Although the Commission carefully analyzed the "context in which conflict developed and gross violations of human rights occurred,"[3] it did not address the everyday brutalities of apartheid or deconstruct gender formulations and it only addressed institutional violence in special hearings. While it is important to acknowledge that the Commission achieved much, not least the breaking of silences and acknowledgement of the realities of apartheid, it is also important that it not be perceived as having dealt with or resolved all South Africa's issues with its past. Plays like Jane Taylor's *Ubu and the Truth Commission*,[4] the Khulumani Support Group's *The Story I'm About to Tell*,[5] and Antje Krog's *Waarom is die Wat Voor Toyi-Toyi Altyd so Vet?* (Why are those who toyi-toyi in front always so fat?)[6] demonstrate the degree to which individuals and the society as a whole are still haunted by the past, as well as the significant role theatre continues to play in confronting it.

In 1999, Temple Hauptfleisch pointed out that women have profoundly influenced the shape of South African theatre, but that "most of these women operated mainly in the private and commercial world, for ... the state-funded theatre organizations have hardly ever allowed women into prominent positions of power. Thus these women were used, their creativity tapped – but their control of the system limited."[7] To some extent, this situation was due to the fact that theatre was perceived as a public and political space in which primarily men spoke and protested against apartheid, with women in supporting roles. Post-apartheid South African theatre has shifted away from almost exclusively male-centered and male-authored plays to include more female voices.[8] This shift in the theatre aligns with a larger shift in South African politics.

Women have profoundly influenced the nation's transition to democracy, entering parliament in large numbers, playing important roles in defining one of the most liberal constitutions in the world, and becoming involved in large-scale law reform that "has managed to create very women friendly legislation to promote gender equality."[9] At the same time, South Africa has been challenged by the need to build a nation from the extreme racialization of apartheid, high levels of gender violence, and one of the highest increases of HIV/AIDS infections in the world, with varying levels of poverty among at least 40 percent of the population. The paradoxes of the "new" South Africa are exemplified in the fact that it has one of the most progressive constitutions in the world, but also "the worst known figures for gender-based violence for a country not at war."[10] The gap between the constitutional and legislative prohibitions against discrimination and the lived reality of many people in South Africa is significant.

Corlann Gee Bush has argued that the great strength of women's movements, and feminism, has been the "twin abilities to unthink the sources of oppression and to use this analysis to create a new synthesizing vision."[11] Clearly, considerable "unthinking" needs to occur in order to "create a new synthesizing vision" for all in South Africa. As South African theatre has shifted from a sociopolitical context in which "it was almost considered politically incorrect to depict the personal because it somehow seemed to detract from larger political issues" to one in which individuals can "write plays that are dealing with real community issues and communities made up of people,"[12] women playwrights are playing a key role in the "unthinking" and revisioning process. In what follows, I will consider how playwrights Farber and Foot-Newton have used theatre to expand on the TRC process, to encourage ongoing public engagement with diverse, ubiquitous, and often disavowed stories, and to thereby propose new ways for South Africans to interact.

Yael Farber: facilitating empathetic engagement with the past

Farber is an award-winning South African director and playwright who has written three testimonial plays in collaboration with the original performers whose lives they represented – *A Woman in Waiting* (1999), *Amajuba: Like Doves We Rise* (2002), and *He Left Quietly* (2003) – as well as *Molora* (2007),[13] which draws on the framework of the *Oresteia* to explore the TRC from the perspective of "the common everyman and everywoman,"[14] here represented by the Ngqoko cultural group of the Transkei. In each of these plays, Farber explored the experiences and memories of the performers, which she then reworked into a text that was performed by the performer-testifiers back to their own communities in the first instance and to wider audiences later. This process transformed personal narratives beyond specific experiences to reach people who had not necessarily shared such experiences or engaged with such stories. The process thus extended the embodied recounting of memory begun at the TRC, combining South Africa's workshop tradition with processes of community theatre and thereby facilitating ongoing engagement with the past while providing a methodology for processing the trauma of individuals and engaging diverse communities in and beyond South Africa.

The first play, *A Woman in Waiting*, traces actress Thembi Mtshali-Jones's memories of being separated from her parents as a child because they worked in the city and of how later, when she lived with her mother, she was "hardly ever home – working day and night in the 'kitchens'" (54). Later, the cycle repeats itself as Thembi must herself leave her baby in order to go to work. The everyday horror of apartheid is communicated in her memory of Mr. Boss's outrage at her using his toilet, and her mother's humiliation is dramatized when the "large suspended dress" that is used in the play to represent her "starts to droop and slowly crumples to the ground" (58). Another powerfully evocative image is that of Thembi's mother's annual gift of shoes, which are always too small because she has measured the child's feet a year ago, to suggest how much of the child's life the mother has missed while caring for other peoples' children. This image may evoke memories of audience members' children's first shoes, and perhaps the contemplation of what it would mean to be away from a child for an extended period of time.

Farber's second play, *Amajuba*, was the result of a commission by the North West Arts Council to work with the Council's five resident actors to create a piece "culled from the lives of the cast, lived in the shadow of Apartheid's dying years."[15] In this play, Tshallo Chokwe, Roelf Matlala, Bongeka Mpongwana, Phillip "Tipo" Tindisa, and Jabulile Tshabalala tell their stories, which Farber describes as being "five 'small' stories from the millions untold."[16] Bongi recalls being abandoned in an abjectly poor community with her alcoholic but beloved grandfather and suffering constant hunger and despair. Roelf's experiences of racist abuse in Soweto and the Pedi community in Pietersburg because he is of mixed race highlight the effect of apartheid upon all South Africans, resulting in oppressed people discriminating against other marginal groups because of their race or ethnicity. Tipo explores the personal effects of forced removals on his family, which led to his father abandoning the family and Tipo becoming embroiled in the resistance movement, where he "saw things...that kids shouldn't see" (146). Jabulile explores the ubiquitous violence of life in the townships, where her cousin was killed by a stray bullet; she herself had to leave her home and family when a gang threatened to rape her. Tshallo's story juxtaposes his dream of escaping poverty by becoming a soccer star with the realities of his experiences as a youth in the struggle movement. Here again, Farber finds images to facilitate empathy for experiences that may be alien to many in the audience. For example, she helps us understand Tshallo's experiences as a youth activist by citing his fear of the dark, which most people have experienced, and then recounting how now he is beyond fear. Such details highlight the cost of the struggle against apartheid in human terms, as well as the ongoing need to "look back" on the "years that shaped" youths like Tshallo (173). Notably, although *New York Times* reviewer Charles Isherwood praised the play generally, he suggested that some of these sentiments "skirt banality."[17] Isherwood's comment suggests that perhaps the need to "look back" can only really be understood by societies who have lived through extended periods of trauma, an idea supported by Adrienne Sichel when she overtly links remembering and healing in her review of the play.[18] Isherwood's statement further suggests the significance of the banal in relation to regimes of oppression. In the context of remembering trauma, Hannah Arendt remarked that Adolf Eichmann's testimony reflected neither guilt nor hatred, and that "the grotesque silliness of his last words" summed up the "banality of evil."[19] In *Amajuba*, Farber dramatizes the everyday evils of apartheid policies that were experienced by the majority of South Africans but that were not acknowledged in the TRC hearings.

Farber's play *He Left Quietly* is based on the experiences of Duma Kumalo, who was sentenced to death in 1984 on a false charge of taking part in the murder of a town councilor in Sharpeville. In March 1988, Kumalo had been measured for his coffin, had his final meeting with his father, and eaten his last meal when his sentence was deferred under international pressure. In *He Left Quietly*, he appears almost as a ghost. The play extends his thirty-minute testimony before the TRC and his performance in the Khulumani Support Group's production of *The Story I Am About to Tell* (2001) in order to juxtapose his personal trauma alongside questions of culpability, as demonstrated by the last performance of the play before an audience of judges and prosecutors, some of whom had been serving at the time of Kumalo's trial. *He Left Quietly* is constructed differently from the other two plays, although it draws on Kumalo's memories and he himself performed in it. Here, Farber created the characters of Young Duma, who enacts much of the narration, and a Woman who represents the white community. The title is drawn from Duma's experiences with teenage activist Lucky Payi, who helped him process his brother's death, read Peter Abrahams's *The View from Coyaba* to him through the bars of his cell,[20] and "taught me how to face dying.... how to be free."[21] When it was Lucky's time to die, Duma says, "He left quietly" (223). The stories give faces and details to the unspeakable horrors of death row under apartheid. There is much emotion in the play, particularly concerning loss, which Farber again focuses through the central image of shoes. Throughout the play, Duma dreams about the shoes he bought just prior to his arrest, but at the end of the play, the shoes remain untouched and he gives them away, saying "I am no longer the man who once walked in those shoes. Give them to someone who has miles to go!" (236). The shoes remind us of the prison room full of the shoes that represent the "more than four and a half thousand people who were hanged" in South Africa between 1910 and 1989 (213), which in turn invokes images of the piles of shoes remaining after the Jewish Holocaust. They also call for us to stand metaphorically in Kumalo's shoes and answer the same charge of complicity "by the Law of Common Purpose," which requires that we acknowledge that "we all conspired in that man's death," and that, by extension, we must all bear responsibility for South Africa's past (209, 225).

Critic Fintan O'Toole stated of the performance that "Kumalo's own presence as narrator and actor takes the piece far beyond the realms of artistic imagery. It is inescapably real." In O'Toole's words, "Farber has given it the deliberation and distance of a ritual," resulting in a piece that "becomes almost literally haunting."[22] Active engagement on the part of the audience is crucial to the efficacy of Farber's plays, as is dramatized in Duma's first encounter with the Woman, who "sits inconspicuously in the audience":

> Duma: Where is home – if you are just here to watch? What country are you
> running to – if you are just a bystander here? ... A guest...
> Woman: I'm not running...
> Duma: You are in or you are out. (190–91)

Much later, the Woman asks, "What we do with such knowledge?" Duma replies, "This is our history. We all come from this broken place. Either you are in or you are out. But if you choose to be in – you must partake" (234).

Mark Sanders has noted that applicants' requests to the TRC were both material (for help to find the bodies of victims and for support for funeral rites) and psychological (for "mournful commemoration" or the "official and public acknowledgement" of personal loss and "a massive refusal to mourn the dead of others").[23] Farber's plays facilitate public acknowledgement of loss as audience members listen, empathize, and, according to Farber, heal themselves: "Without a listener who believes and empathizes with you, you are dislocated from – yet deeply shaped by – your own story. To own the events of one's life and share these memories is to reclaim one's self and offer your community, your witnesses a collective possibility to do the same."[24]

While facilitating empathetic engagement, Farber simultaneously highlights complex issues relating to history and hegemony, as is evident in the narratives spoken in the performers' various mother tongues. Farber argues that "[t]here's a fundamental connection between the psyche of the country and the languages that people speak. The denigrating of indigenous languages through colonialism is a psychic violence."[25] Thus, the inclusion of mother-tongue narratives in the plays highlights this historic hegemony experientially as audience members may be temporarily unable to follow the narrative:

> When the actor speaks in the vernacular, the actor is deep in their integrity, while the audience is momentarily an "outsider" who misses out. When the actor breaks from the vernacular, and returns to English – the audience no longer takes this for granted, but is aware that this storyteller is reaching out in a language imposed upon them – which is a profoundly generous act.[26]

This dramaturgical strategy simultaneously highlights the problems of the past while literally enacting a potential form of reconciliation, which audience members can reciprocate by listening empathetically and acknowledging their place relative to the narrative.

Farber's plays signal the need for ongoing mourning in South Africa and celebrate "the inexplicable hope that has continued to burn in South Africa's people."[27] Symbolic ritual and song are key to these processes. All the plays include songs and hymns, often to connect disparate stories and facilitate the communication of unspeakable experiences affectively. For example, at the end of *Amajuba*, the five performers acknowledge that they "cannot leave things in the dust without a decent burial. No matter how small." A symbolic ritual follows that signifies both a burial and a resurrection. Using biblical referents, the performers take handfuls of dust and chant "ashes to ashes, dust to dust" in their various languages, while Tshallo makes the titular statement, "From the dust – Like doves...we will rise" (175–76). The performers ritually wash, cleansing themselves of the past, and chant "We are like doves" (178) before reiterating their signature song and the theme taken from the title *Amajuba*, meaning *those who spring back or rebound*. The dove and water invoke the holy spirit at Christ's baptism and resurrection, suggesting that the characters will rise above these painful memories as individuals and that the audience can share their hope.

Farber's play *Molora* draws on Aeschylus' *Oresteia* and Sophocles' and Euripides' versions of *Electra* to explore the paradoxical need for social stability through structured reconciliation in the face of embodied memories of past violence. As well, the play is framed by songs and rituals drawn from traditional Xhosa culture. After the women stop Elektra from perpetuating the cycle of violence, a Xhosa diviner ends the play by praying to the ancestors for help in the battle to stop crime and killing and in speaking truth. Here, Farber suggests that we must draw on whatever spiritual frame is appropriate to engage with and expiate individual and communal trauma and pain.

Many of the songs that Farber uses in her plays were included either in testimonies or in response to them at the TRC. Fiona Ross has argued that, rather than being forms of "aestheticizing testimony," these songs tapped into oral forms that were implicitly related to the liberation movement in South Africa and that, insofar as they were widely known, they "invited audiences to participate with them in the performances of memory and meaning, and drew audiences with them in the testimonial process."[28] Songs aid affective engagement with narratives that audience members have not personally experienced and thereby facilitate empathy, which is crucial to *ubuntu*.[29]

South African playwright Peter Hayes stated in an interview about his 2009 play *Ncamisa*, about the brutal 2006 murder of Zoliswa Nkonyana by a group of young men because she was a lesbian,

To really effect political change, the amount of lobbying and activism needed is greater than what we can do in a play. I think what theatre can do is create a very intimate exchange. Prejudice arises from ignorance and fear and when you're sat in the theatre to hear an actor tell a true story – at some stage in that performance they will look you in the eye and it starts eroding the fear. That's as much as I can hope for in a play, that we can attack the prejudices. You can't hate somebody that you know.[30]

In Farber's work, the emphasis on persons telling their own stories calls for understanding and empathy for people whose histories and memories may be different from our own in a period of transition and sociopolitical reconstruction.[31] In this way, she calls both for understanding and for a cooperative revisioning of how individuals see and interact with one another, thus expanding on the work begun at the TRC.

Lara Foot-Newton: challenging cycles of violence and fear

Foot-Newton has moved from being a director, producer, and adapter of other peoples' work to writing and directing her own plays. Her first play was *Tsephang: The Third Testament* (2003), which began in her garage, was first performed in a scout hall near Pretoria and then moved to larger venues in South Africa, London, Amsterdam, and Ottawa. Since then, Foot-Newton has written *Karoo Moose* (2007) and *Reach!* (2007) and co-created a number of other plays. In her work, Foot-Newton challenges essentialist constructions of masculinity while facilitating her audiences' engagement with examples of violent experiences that are often unspeakable and disavowed in South Africa. In doing so, she suggests that there are many and complex reasons for violence, but that, in perceiving and engaging with them, we can begin to "unthink" the legacies of apartheid and imagine how to achieve *ubuntu* in South Africa.

Tshepang is based on the actual 2001 rape of a nine-month-old baby, Siesie, by her mother's lover, Alfred Sorrows. Siesie's nurses nicknamed her Tshepang (Hope) because her recovery from the consequent internal damage was miraculous. Foot-Newton wrote the play as part of her Master's degree at Witwatersrand University, after spending a year researching the story's sociopolitical and historical background with actor Bheki Vilakazi. Tshepang's story had a profound effect on South Africa: as Foot-Newton has stated, "Once the story of baby Tshepang hit the headlines, the scab was torn off a festering wound and hundreds of similar stories followed. Each story was equally horrific."[32] Her dedication specifying that the play is "based on twenty thousand true stories" refers to South Africa's annual statistic for child rape. The mind cannot engage with twenty thousand such stories, so Foot-Newton uses this one to reflect upon what may lie behind equivalent acts of violence, asking what these acts mean for each individual in the audience and for the society as a whole.

One of the challenges of *Tshepang* is that its circumstances may seem to reinforce the sense that many destructive behaviors have become overwhelmingly associated with descriptions of masculinity in general and with the stereotype of

African men as "violent sexual predators."[33] I argue, however, that one of Foot-Newton's distinctive contributions as a playwright is how she deconstructs essentialist approaches to masculinities in South Africa by contextualizing destructive behavior within particular experiences of apartheid while also asking audiences how we can all contribute to changing these patterns.

Tshepang begins in the dark, with an insistent, rhythmic grinding sound. As the lights go up, we see Ruth, Siesie's mother, sitting with a pile of salt on some animal skins, rubbing the salt into the skins. She has a small bed tied to her back with a blanket. Her partner Simon, who is Alfred's cousin, sits next to her in front of a rusty steel bed and tells the entire story, acting all the characters with compassion and reminding both them and us of who they are and how they have come to be as they are. Ruth remains silent until the very end of the play.

Simon's first speech introduces the central issues of the play: the relentless heat, the fact that people "like to drink here," and the idea that "nothing ever happens here. Nothing. Niks."[34] This statement is repeated like a refrain throughout the play, suggesting an existential hopelessness and the reasons for it. The characters' sense of purposelessness, of drifting, is explained historically: for example, community member Trompie's "drinking vaalwyn [very poor wine]" (20) refers to the "dop" (drink) system, whereby laborers were paid with liquor rather than money, which perpetuated low self-esteem, domestic violence, and an inability to challenge injustices under apartheid. The consequence of this iniquitous economic practice is illustrated in the account of Trompie's ridiculous failed suicide attempts (21–22). Other examples of the community's plight include Tshepang's grandfather Dewaal, who sits and untangles fishing nets although he lives far from the sea and never goes fishing (23), and the policeman, who "smokes dagga [marijuana]" and "sits on his fat arse and does fokkol" (25). Foot-Newton uses comic irony to highlight the socio-psychic consequences of years of social, economic, and political oppression that have left these people without agency, seeking oblivion in wine, sex, sleep, or death.

It is significant that sex is included in this list of anodynes. In his introduction to *Tshepang*, Tony Hamburger notes that the descriptions of sexual encounters in the play are "presented as anonymous, indiscriminate and disconnected from human contact but associated with annihilation, oblivion";[35] as Simon says, "first you naai [fuck], then you die!" (32). Here, sexual encounters are not interpersonal encounters; women are merely human receptacles into which the men empty their mental anguish. Simon describes his and Alfred's sexual experiences with Sarah, whose brother sold her for five cents, while she got a comic and chewing gum: "[we] had to finish our business...before she had turned three pages of the comic.... if we didn't finish in time...her brother Petrus, for an extra two cents, would let us continue in half a loaf of white bread" (26). Here, Simon hardly differentiates between the girl's body and the loaf of bread. This incident explains Sarah's lack of engagement with Tshepang's rape: we are told three times that she "did nothing when it happened. Just lit a match and walked out of the room" (20, 25, 42). The incident further suggests that both men and women have been brutalized by the socio-economic conditions of apartheid.

The view of women as functional objects that men use to meet their physical or psychological needs is exacerbated by the historical "houvrou" arrangement. As Simon explains, a "houvrou is a woman that you keep, but she's not your wife. But here it is better to have a houvrou, because you can't get rid of a wife. A houvrou you can let go" (20). This arrangement highlights women's personal and economic vulnerability and to some extent explains why Ruth hesitated to tell the police that it was her boyfriend who raped her child, since, as Simon reveals, he was "[t]he one that brought her food and clothes. The one that brought her drink…She was too scared to tell them because she was his houvrou" (42). It also explains Alfred: Simon recounts how Alfred was beaten almost to death by his father's "very young houvrou called Margaret" when he was three years old, because he had wet himself laughing (28–29). Simon describes Alfred thereafter as "[n]either here nor there. Not good. Not bad. Very quiet. Like he was always remembering the time with the broom, and the broken bones" (34). This incident dramatizes the consequences of cycles of oppression: men brutalize young women, who fear being thrown away and so in turn hurt small children, who grow up and rape babies. The play does not ask us to sympathize with Alfred, but it does suggest that he is more than an aberration and that his action arose from extended and complex cycles of abuse and violence that have dehumanized both men and women.

The socio-economic background that frames *Tshepang*'s exploration of masculinity, sexuality, and gender relationships is signaled in the set design, where the bed, pile of salt, and a small-scale model of the town form a triangle around which the events are narrated. According to designer Gerhard Marx, "This 'small town' consists of a number of simple houses arranged to resemble the stark grid of government housing projects. During the performance these houses are used to 'enter' the town, to establish the couple's relationship with the town (far enough to be outside, close enough to observe)."[36] Such housing "grids" were created during apartheid to segregate by race and class and, as Steven Robins notes, they remain "firmly intact in the new South Africa."[37] This situation suggests that, while racial policy has changed, the lived realities of many people have not. Thus, the personal domestic space on stage in *Tshepang* and the events that occur within it are connected spatially and historically to the wider sociopolitical context by the model of the town.

This stage space works in conjunction with the symbolic use of everyday objects to suggest the complex causes of the violence that characterizes the wider society that is the context for the play's action. Thus, the broom that is used to beat Alfred is used against a loaf of bread in Simon's re-enactment of Siesie's rape (42). Beds are emblematic of the trauma and violence that have destroyed Ruth's life and deprived her of her child. There are three versions of this "burdened" object in the play: the literal bed, which Simon and Ruth cannot replace because they are so poor; the miniature bed that Ruth carries on her back in place of her absent child; and a miniature bed "found beneath one of the small houses"[38] when Simon narrates his discovery of Ruth's self-mutilation and which he carries to hospital as a substitute for her body. Marx suggests that the bed "stands in stark contrast to the crib in which the baby Jesus lay," an image evoked in the play "by

Simon's carvings of the nativity scene" as "an idealised image of the family struc-ture, in dismal contrast to that into which baby Tshepang is born."[39] These uses of everyday objects in the play bring together our awareness of rational causality with more affective responses invoked by the events associated with them in the play.

This greater sense of understanding may shift an audience away from an initial sense of clear outrage and horror, articulated in the play by the Johannesburg newspaper reporter Maureen de Witt, to appreciate Simon's response to de Witt's coverage of the rape:

Shame that you are so ugly, lady. Shame on you! Shame on all of you! Who do you think you are? Coming here and pointing your cameras and your accusa-tions. Pointing your painted ugly fingers at us. Where were you, where were you? What are you doing here? Get out of here! Take your cameras and get out! This town was raped long ago. This town was fucking gang-raped a long, long, long, long time ago! Shame on us? Shame on you, shame on all of us! (40–1)

Hamburger's introduction to *Tshepang* raises questions regarding what playwrights intend when they engage audiences with unaccountable horrors:

Are the writers seeking to excuse the inexcusable? Are they suggesting that understanding can undo the social and personal ills? Are they offering to pardon infant rape and the rapist(s)? Their theatre puts us, the audience, in danger. The jeopardy is that our clarity about where evil resides, where to lay the blame, is threatened. The blurring of boundaries between good and evil troubles us. We can only condemn if we are free of guilt, collusion or association.[40]

In *Tshepang*, Foot-Newton argues that everyone – men and women alike – from this community and beyond is implicated by the socioeconomic structures that have determined South African history and society. As Simon's response to Maureen de Witt makes clear, the play asks each person to analyze their part in this story and to consider what we need to "unthink" in order to change these patterns so that we can see people as people and thus realize a truly "new" South Africa.

Central to this shift is finding a position between condemnation and abso-lution. Simon's nativity carvings and the play's subtitle *"The Third Testament"* challenge the binary images of an Old Testament god of vengeance and the New Testament depiction of Christ-like love and forgiveness. This "third testament" is a challenge to South Africans to find a way through the cycles of violence provoked by poverty and sociopolitical brutalities that have devalued people so that they do not see the humanity in other people, not even a child; all they want is oblivion. Yet although baby Tshepang is a provocation for people to acknowl-edge and break the cycles of violence, hope does not lie in her. Rather, it lies in Simon, who narrates the child's mutilated body, Ruth's distress, and the stories of the other people who have been brutalized by the past; who sculpts his nativity figures; and who assures Ruth that he "will stay with her" rather than joining his friend at the tavern (45). This assurance interrupts Ruth's endless rubbing of salt into the skins. She stands, looks into the distance, and quietly says, "Tshepang," meaning "hope" or "saviour" (45). In Simon, Foot-Newton offers audiences a new vision of masculinity and humanity for South Africa, significantly from a black male perspective.

Whereas in *Tshepang* Simon is key to challenging stereotypes of men and violence in South Africa, in Foot-Newton's second play, *Karoo Moose* (2009), "the key redemptive quality," as critic Brent Meersman has observed, "lies in its format. Each performer in the ensemble acts several roles.... In playing male and female, adult and infant roles, the actors through their performances deconstruct and debunk the patriarchal constructions of black masculinity."[41] *Karoo Moose* is much less forgiving than *Tshepang* in its exploration of violence and the abuse of children in contemporary South Africa, and it gives the female protagonist Thozama far greater agency than Ruth, who is both silent and burdened by guilt.

The play centers on Jonas and his family: his daughters Thozama and Quinnie and son Thabo, who are tormented by the gangsters Khola and David, and the children's grandmother, Grace. Jonas's family is paralleled by the white van Wyk family, for whom Grace works. The daughter of the van Wyks, Sarah, has committed suicide because her father has sexually abused her, and the van Wyks' son Brian befriends Thozama. The play frames violence against racial injustice, as Mr. van Wyk accidently kills Jonas's wife but is not held accountable. Jonas's desperation is such that he gambles with gangsters who then threaten him with violence until he finally agrees to give them his fifteen-year-old daughter in lieu of the money he owes them.

Foot-Newton uses ritual to frame her analysis of the hidden causes of violence and child abuse and offer an exorcism of sorts, but instead of presenting a final celebration of communal values, *Karoo Moose* issues a warning if the audience does not take note and act. At the start of the play, the actors "ritualistically enter the space one by one," carrying objects that will be used metaphorically during the performance: a net, a beer bottle, a belt, a cabbage, a wheelbarrow, moose horns, a washing pail, and a drum.[42] They walk in a circle, ritually preparing the space and the audience. The frightened moose, which is not indigenous to South Africa, represents the unknown onto which people project their fears: the children speculate as to whether it "eats children" (9, 22); Grace insists that it heralds "disease, drought, fire" and that "[i]t's going to eat our lives" (9); Mrs. van Wyk accuses it of eating a neighbor's Scottish terrier (12); and the narrator promises a frightening story of "the young girl Thozama and the wild, unimaginable and terrifying beast" (7–8). This animal embodies all the social and economic problems that facilitate oppression and violence against all in this society – men, women, and children.

Foot-Newton engages her audience with what is unspeakable through symbolic objects that evoke visceral affective responses without realistically re-enacting the violence, as is most evident in the symbolic performance that signifies Thozama's rape. Before the rape, Thozama's father Jonas and the gangsters Khola and David are watching soccer together, a pastime associated with the performance of male identity. After being violently threatened by the men, Jonas calls Thozama into the room and Khola gives her a roll of humbugs – an appropriate signifier of impending child abuse, suggesting the familiar warning to children not to take sweets from strangers. Khola then kicks a drum, representing tradition, out of the way, puts Thozama into a washing pail, takes up his net, which could be either a fishing net or a goal net, and undoes his belt. He covers Thozama with the net and then he, David, Jonas, and a fourth actor play soccer around her, shouting, "Pass! Substitute! etc." (28). They take off their shirts as the game inten-sifies and start taking shots at Thozama's body with the ball, as if aiming for the goal posts. She cringes like a frightened animal. Toward the end of the scene, they start singing "Shosholoza," a song commonly sung at soccer matches. Ironically, the song is about news coming with the trains carrying migrant workers from faraway places. The song thus suggests some of the antecedents of South Africa's violence, as people were dislocated from their homes and communities to live in the harsh conditions of mine compounds, where women became objects to satisfy men's sexual needs.

Foot-Newton parallels Thozama's story with that of sixteen-year-old Sarah van Wyk, who hanged herself because her father – the farmer who killed Thozama's mother – "used her like a goat" (39). Through this parallel, the play shifts the discourse on sexual violence away from issues of race to underlying issues of male hegemony, the performance of power, and the control of women. The men justify themselves to Jonas by saying that "someone has to teach her to be a woman" (27), and Jonas denies his culpability by accusing Thozama of "asking for it, it was your fault, walking around here like a slut" (34). The relationship between rape and normative female behavior is made clear later in the play when Thozama warns Khola to stay away from her younger sister after seeing her with a roll of humbugs and when he punishes her outspokenness by stealing and raping their baby.

The community as a whole refuses to act on the children's behalf: Thozama's grandmother Grace simply hands her an adult's dress and tells her, "You are a woman now" (30), suggesting the inevitability of the experience of rape for a girl. Similarly, Grace and Mrs. van Wyk either pretend that Sarah's abuse "didn't happen," or they say that it was "God's will"; as Grace explains, "The pain is too much. We try to forget" (41). Thozama, however, challenges the silences and cycles of violence and abuse, insisting: "We shouldn't be quiet about these things" (41). It is the children who revolt and throw the chopped cabbage, which represents Thozama's rape, at the moose before Thozama slits its throat, cooks it, and eats it, "while the boys stare at Thozama, the blood, the knife" (32). This act empowers Thozama to stand up to her father the next day and then later to the gangsters when she "ritualistically calls on the MOOSE by smearing her body with wet earth," a signifier of preparing for participation in a ritual in South Africa, and then "takes on the power of the beast" to challenge Khola (60). Significantly, her father comes to her aid and takes responsibility for Khola's death, thereby redeeming himself. This ritualistic confrontation suggests that we can and must challenge cycles of violence and helplessness and defend ourselves and our families. The play strongly argues that change is possible. Just as the white policeman Brian has rebuilt a scrap car and taught Thozama to drive, and just as their cross-racial relationship blooms, so other changes are possible. The closest *Karoo Moose* comes to a final valedictory celebration, however, is in the image of the children of the village, represented by sunflowers dressed in bright clothing, waving goodbye to us from the back of a truck. They are united in their rejection of abuse and the play ends with the warning that if the adults will not protect them, they will leave and the village will die.

Foot-Newton's third play, *Reach!*, references child abuse, but its focus is on wider post-apartheid issues, asking what other things we need to "unthink" in order to achieve *ubuntu*. Realist in style, *Reach!* ponders unemployment, racial prejudice, children losing parents to HIV/AIDS, and parents losing their children to crime or emigration. Above all, it is about fear. As the central character Marion says, "It's a pathology really, fear" – a "[s]tuck feeling. A paralysis."[43] This feeling is inspired by the sense that life in South Africa is precarious and that violence is ubiquitous, an idea that is further explored through the character Solomon, a young unemployed man who witnessed Marion's son's murder. Solomon explains that he remained silent because he feared that the murderers "would have sent their friends to kill me. Hang me, or burn me, or rape my sister or even my grandmother. They are like dogs that take the meat from the table. They feel nothing" (62). Solomon's silence has resulted in both him and Marion being ill, but as both characters overcome their fear and speak to one another, they are able to progress: Solomon gets a job and Marion plans a visit to her daughter in Australia. *Reach!* thus extends Foot-Newton's earlier explorations of how people can overcome racial, generational, and even traumatic distances by revising the principles they have set and live by, reaching out to one another as human beings despite cultural differences, preferences, and memories. Ultimately, the play suggests that if we refuse to be paralyzed by fear, we can overcome it and the various divisions of the past.

Foot-Newton's and Farber's power as playwrights lies in their ability to engage with post-apartheid South Africa's complex realities and to acknowledge the legacies of the past without suggesting that those legacies are inescapable or inevitable. They compassionately explore the reasons for silence and violence, but call for these patterns to be challenged and changed by our acknowledgement of the humanity of each individual. In this way, they exemplify André Brink's view that "[a]rtists...are not agents of power, but campaigners for invisible values no human being can live without."[44] Farber and Foot-Newton provide ways for audiences to engage with disavowed or contested subjects in the context of South Africa's renegotiation of its history, including its gender politics. In facilitating the contemplation of what is unspeakable, they enable the rehearsal of different ways of being and interacting and thus of achieving *ubuntu*, inviting us to become fully human, despite previous inhuman experiences, by recognizing others as human too.

Notes

I wish to acknowledge that research support for this essay came from a grant awarded to me by the Leverhulme Trust, though the research was not conducted by or for the Trust.

1 Jane Taylor, "Reform, Perform: Sincerity and the Ethnic Subject of History," *South African Theatre Journal* 22 (2008): 9.

2 Desmond Tutu, *No Future Without Forgiveness* (New York: Image, 1999), 31. The concept is further explained by Ramose B. Mogobe in *African Philosophy through Ubuntu* (Harare: Mond Books, 1999) and his two essays "The Ethics of *Ubuntu*" and "The Philosophy of *Ubuntu* and *Ubuntu* as Philosophy," in *Philosophy from Africa*, ed. P. H. Coetzee and A. P. J. Roux (Oxford: Oxford University Press, 2002), 324–330 and 230–238, respectively.

3 Truth and Reconciliation Commission of South Africa, *Final Report*, vol. 2 (London: Macmillan, 1998), 4.

4 Jane Taylor, *Ubu and the Truth Commission* (Cape Town: University of Cape Town Press, 1998).

5 Performed in 1999, unpublished.

6 Performed in 1999, unpublished.

7 Temple Hauptfleisch, "The Background: Reza de Wet and the South African Literary Establishment," *Contemporary Theatre Review* 9, no. 1 (1999): 55.

8 Among the women who have impacted South African theatre are Vanessa Cooke, Reza de Wet, Fatima Dike, Susan Pam Grant, Juanita Finestone, Jeanne Goosen, Janice Honeyman, Phyllis Klotz, Gcina Mhlope, Muthal Naidoo, Jennie Reznik, Irene Stephanou, Janet Suzman, Clare Stopford, and Jane Taylor. New post-apartheid playwrights include Nadine Naidoo, Krijay Govender, Devi Sarinjei, and Malika Ndlovu, as well as Yael Farber and Lara Foot-Newton. Relatively few of these women are published, however, and, with the exception of Dike, none of them are black. This situation may be due to the fact that many women work in community-based theatre such as the Mothertongue project (*http://www.mothertongue.co.za/*), the Zanendaba Institute of African Storytellers (*http://www.zanendaba.co.za/about.html*), and the Sibikwa Arts Centre. These community-based projects focus on embodied and oral forms of theatre that is collaboratively created and in which the text is only one dimension.

9 Amanda Gouws, *(Un)thinking Citizenship: Feminist Debates in Contemporary South Africa* (Aldershot: Ashgate, 2005), 1.

10 Helen Moffett, "'These Women, They Force Us to Rape Them': Rape as Narrative of Social Control in Post-Apartheid South Africa," *Journal of Southern African Studies* 32, no. 1 (March 2006): 129.

11 Qtd. in Amanda Gouws, ed., *(Un)thinking Citizenship: Feminist Debates in Contemporary South Africa* (Aldershot: Ashgate, 2005), 1.

12 Miki Flockemann, "On Not Giving Up: An Interview with Fatima Dike," *Contemporary Theatre Review* 9, no. 1 (1999): 19, 24.

13 These dates indicate first performances.

14 Yael Farber, foreword, *Molora* (London: Oberon Books, 2008), 7.

15 Yael Farber, "A History of the Text and Production Development," in Yael Farber, *Theatre as Witness: Three Testimonial Plays from South Africa: A Woman in Waiting; Amajuba: Like Doves We Rise; He Left Quietly* (London: Oberon Books, 2008), 89.

16 Yael Farber, *Amajuba: Like Doves We Rise*, in Farber, *Theatre as Witness: Three Testimonial Plays from South Africa: A Woman in Waiting; Amajuba: Like Doves We Rise; He Left Quietly*

(London: Oberon Books, 2008), 91–2; subsequent references to the play will be given parenthetically in the text.

17 Charles Isherwood, "'Amajuba: Like Doves We Rise': Apartheid's Private Pain Becomes Group Art," *New York Times* 26 July 2006, available at *http://theater2.nytimes. com/2006/07/26/theater/reviews/26dove.html?_r=0&adxnnl=1&adxnnlx=1349444682-cY-GiGj/jw3hvUJCURIpdKA* (accessed 4 October 2012).

18 Adrienne Sichel, "Remembering and Healing," *The Star*, 3 July 2001, available at *http:// www.farberfoundry.com/amajuba-press.html* (accessed 4 October 2012).

19 Hannah Arendt, *Eichmann in Jerusalem: A Report on the Banality of Evil* (New York/ London: Penguin Books, 1994), 252.

20 Abrahams is a South African novelist who lived in exile in Britain and Jamaica. This novel chronicles four generations of a Jamaican family and their experiences with racism.

21 Yael Farber, *He Left Quietly*, in Farber, *Theatre as Witness: Three Testimonial Plays from South Africa: A Woman in Waiting; Amajuba: Like Doves We Rise; He Left Quietly* (London: Oberon Books, 2008), 221, 222; subsequent references will be given parenthetically in the text.

22 Fintan O'Toole, *"He Left Quietly,"* *Irish Times*, 29 November 2002, available at *http:// www.farberfoundry.com/he-left-quietly-press.html* (accessed 4 October 2012).

23 Mark Sanders, *Ambiguities of Witnessing: Law and Literature in the Time of the Truth Commission* (Johannesburg: Witwatersrand University Press, 2007), 49.

24 Yael Farber, interview with Amanda Stuart Fisher, in Farber, *Theatre as Witness: Three Testimonial Plays from South Africa: A Woman in Waiting; Amajuba: Like Doves We Rise; He Left Quietly* (London: Oberon Books, 2008), 24.

25 Ibid., 25.

26 Ibid., 26.

27 Yael Farber, director's note for *Amajuba*, in Farber, *Theatre as Witness: Three Testimonial Plays from South Africa: A Woman in Waiting; Amajuba: Like Doves We Rise; He Left Quietly* (London: Oberon Books, 2008), 92.

28 Fiona C. Ross, *Bearing Witness: Women and the Truth and Reconciliation Commission in South Africa* (London: Pluto Press, 2003), 175n4, 35.

29 Farber describes her role as writer as being to "transport" an audience "from indifference to empathy, from their own limited perspective to deep inside the interior landscape of another person's world," (interview, *Theatre as Witness*, 20).

30 Jo Caird, interview with Peter Hayes, "Brief Encounter With ... Ncamisa! Kiss the Women," 8 October 2010, available at *http://www.whatsonstage.com/interviews/theatre/off-west+end/ E8831285243428/Brief+Encounter+With+ ... +Ncamisa!+Kiss+the+Women+.htm* (accessed 14 May 2012).

31 Farber's plays thus expand the use of verbatim testimony in South African protest theatre beyond signaling veracity and articulating silenced or disavowed experiences in a dangerous political context. For a more detailed analysis of verbatim theatre in the South African context, see Yvette Hutchison, "Post-1990s Verbatim Theatre in South Africa: Exploring an African Concept of 'Truth,'" in *Dramaturgy of the Real on the World Stage*, ed. Carol Martin (Basingstoke: Palgrave Macmillan, 2010), 61–71 and "Verbatim Theatre in South Africa: 'Living theatre in a person's performance,'" in *Get Real: Documentary Theatre Past and Present,* ed. Alison Forsyth and Chris Megson (Basingstoke: Palgrave Macmillan, 2009), 209–223.

32 Lara Foot-Newton, author's note, *Tshepang* (Johannesburg: Witwatersrand University Press, 2005), vii.

33 Moffett, "These Women," 132–35.

34 Lara Foot-Newton, *Tshepang: The Third Testament* (Johannesburg: Witwatersrand University Press, 2005), 19; subsequent references to the play will be given parenthetically in the text.

35 Tony Hamburger, "*Tshepang*: A Morality Play?" in Lara Foot-Newton, *Tshepang: The Third Testament* (Johannesburg: Witwatersrand University Press, 2005), 8.

36 Gerhard Marx, designer's note, *Tshepang*, x.

37 Steven Robins, "At the limits of spatial governmentality: a message from the tip of Africa," *Third World Quarterly* 23, no. 4 (2002): 671.

38 Marx, designer's note, x–xi.

39 Ibid., xi.

40 Hamburger, "*Tshepang*: A Morality Play?" 4.

41 Brent Meersman, "*Karoo Moose* (Baxter Theatre)," 14 October 2007, available at *http://realreview.co.za/tag/lara-foot-newton/* (accessed 6 October 2012).

42 Lara Foot-Newton, *Karoo Moose* (London: Oberon, 2009), 7; subsequent references to the play will be given parenthetically in the text.

43 Lara Foot-Newton, *Reach!* in *At this Stage*, ed. Greg Homann (Johannesburg: Witwatersrand University Press, 2009), 40, 42; subsequent references to the play will be given parenthetically in the text.

44 André Brink, *Reinventing a Continent: Writing in South Africa* (London: Secker and Warburg, 1996), 58.

10 Writing Across Our Sea of Islands: Contemporary Women Playwrights from Oceania

Diana Looser

The past fifty years have witnessed the development and proliferation of written drama by indigenous playwrights throughout the Pacific Islands region. While individual sites have varied in terms of the scope, scale, and period of dramatic production, this phenomenon has been dynamic and widespread, and motivated largely (especially in its early phases) by a postcolonial sensibility. In many different ways, artists throughout the region have created plays that foreground Pacific philosophies and practices; co-opt and rework the form, rationale, and representational strategies of Western theatre; and attempt interventions into their broader social milieus. Over the years, this output has become more varied, encompassing an increasing range of concerns, experiences, cultural perspectives, and dramaturgical techniques to register the region's historical vicissitudes and contemporary complexities. In a situation common in theatre globally, men's voices have tended to dominate; nevertheless, from the beginning female dramatists have made an influential – even pioneering – contribution to this discourse. In Guam, Linda Cruz's *White Lady on the Bridge of Maina* (1969) was an early Chamoru play that formed the basis of the first Chamoru opera, *Like'we'ake* (1971);[1] and in Papua New Guinea (PNG), the plays of Nora Vagi Brash produced from the mid-1970s pricked the conscience of the newly independent nation, posing critical questions about PNG's future direction and its responsibilities to its culture and constituents. Victoria Nalani Kneubuhl shaped the local tenor and international circulation of Hawaiian drama with a career that began in the early 1980s; and in Aotearoa New Zealand, Māori women played key roles in forging an indigenous theatre movement, from their involvement in performative self-determination protests and Māori theatre groups of the 1970s and early 1980s through to the emergence of individual playwrights like Roma Potiki, Renée, Rena Owen, and Riwia Brown during the later 1980s.

Since the 1990s, there has been a flourishing of Pacific women's playwriting and performance. This development is due to multiple factors (most of which are not unique to Oceania), including greater regional resources for education, training, and theatrical production; increased opportunities to encounter work by local and foreign playwrights through touring theatre companies, festivals, residencies, and exchanges; and the broader diffusion of feminist discourses, which have made the representation of women's experiences a more pressing issue and have stimulated a greater encouragement and market for such projects. This chapter offers a regional survey of prominent female playwrights whose work has been produced during this period, highlighting a body of work that has received very little critical attention. In so doing, I acknowledge that there are many influential dramatists working throughout Oceania who are not indigenous – Leilani Chan, Jean Betts, Jo Randerson, Vivienne Plumb, Pip Hall, Lauren Jackson, Lorae Parry, Fiona Samuel, Lynda Chanwai-Earle, and Jo Dorras, to name only a sample – but for reasons of space and focus, this discussion will concentrate on Pacific Islander women of Māori, Cook Island, Niuean, Samoan, Hawaiian, and Tahitian heritage. This overview does not set out to catalogue every female Pacific playwright in the region or to discuss every one of her plays. Its purpose is to assay some of the key established and emergent voices and works as a way of identifying the major trends, concerns, and strategies that have defined this corpus over the last twenty-five years, while demonstrating its stylistic and cultural reach.

One of the principal challenges in taking this approach is how to muster an area of such geographic expanse and elasticity, cultural and linguistic diversity, and sociopolitical variability into a comparative, regional framework. Indeed, the notion of a regional identity and its ideological, material, and ontological implications has been a complicated and continuing debate in Pacific Studies; as Helen Tiffin and Graham Huggan note succinctly, "Oceania" is "as much the name for an ongoing cultural project as a geographical label."[2] My readings of these plays are attentive both to the epistemic, thematic, and dramaturgical particularities of each dramatist's oeuvre, and the political, aesthetic, genealogical, and cultural affiliations that maintain ties between different playwrights in common sites and across imposed boundaries. Accordingly, this chapter highlights the playwrights' unique corpora, as well as their collective contribution to a wider "oceanic imaginary." A politicized construct designed to counteract Eurocentric paradigms and global hegemony, this ideological approach, in Subramani's terms, treats "Oceania as a complex, multilayered stage" on which islander scholars and artists might reinscribe "their own epistemologies. These would at once involve the critique of oppressive systems of thinking... and entail an exploration into 'Oceania's library' (the knowledge its people possess)."[3] This essay explores how local drama accentuates certain contours and nuances of this regional imaginary, concentrating especially on the ways in which the modern region is reflected in and energized by the plays' profound negotiation between cultures, forms, and worldviews. Consequently, this survey foregrounds Pacific women's playwriting as a significant and revelatory component of Oceania's cultural production and of contemporary world theatre.

Māori theatre in Aotearoa New Zealand

Aotearoa New Zealand is the nucleus of theatrical production in Oceania. As one of the region's most populous metropolitan states, New Zealand's infrastructure supports a vibrant theatre economy with considerable resources for training, creative development, and performance. There is a substantial tradition of work by indigenous Māori playwrights, as well as a growing range of work by other Pacific Island dramatists – a growing demographic that reflects New Zealand's neocolonial purview and its role as a major destination node of the postwar Pacific diaspora. Māori theatre practitioners have had increasing visibility since the early 1970s as part of a cultural renaissance tied to broader self-determination goals (*tino rangatiratanga*), in response to a dominant Pākehā (European) culture. By the late 1980s and early 1990s, there were a number of female playwrights whose work rejected pastoral stereotypes and tabulated the fraught legacies of colonialism and contemporary realities for urban Māori, as in Rena Owen's *Te Awa i Tahuti* (1987), Riwia Brown's *Roimata* (1988), *Whatungarongaro* (1990) by Roma Potiki and He Ara Hou ensemble, and *Te Pouaka Karaehe* (1992) by Renée.

The most prominent female Māori playwright of the past two decades has been Briar Grace-Smith (1966–), whose career was instrumental in helping usher Māori theatre into the mainstream during the 1990s. While Grace-Smith has experimented with a range of styles and subjects in her dramas, major works such as *Ngā Pou Wāhine* (1995), *Flat Out Brown* (1996), *Purapurawhetū* (1997), *Haruru Mai* (2000), and *Potiki's Memory of Stone* (2003) exhibit a constellation of related themes and techniques that comprise her most defining contribution to Māori playwriting and to New Zealand theatre more generally.

All of these plays are complexly plotted dramas characterized by their mythic, epic quality and their imbrication of the past and the present, the numinous and the mundane. In this sense, Grace-Smith's works represent a shift away from Māori theatre's earlier agitprop presentations and raw, urban dramas toward subtle analyses of Māori concerns played out on emotive, intimate terms, favoring narrative and magic realism over critical social commentary. The settings for these plays frequently include small Māori communities in rural locales. The focus is typically on a group of people in a dislocated, unorthodox, or ad-hoc family structure who suffer some loss or burden as the result of a past transgression or unfinished business that must be acknowledged and set right in order for the characters to move forward productively. These stories are sometimes affirmative, sometimes more ambivalent, but there is usually the capacity for the characters to derive redemption from the tragic actions or sacrifices of the past. The human action is lent symbolic significance and particularized meaning through Grace-Smith's recurring technique of using Māori mythology as an allegory or narrative counterpoint, enabling her plays to operate on several simultaneous levels. These mythic motifs set the quotidian struggles of the present and recent history within a more holistic cosmological scheme, and are inherently relevant to Grace-Smith's fashioning of the form and function of her plays to express a specifically Māori rationale and approach. Formally, the plays intercalate Māori dialogue, song, chant, ritual, and practices like weaving, carving, and whaikōrero[4] into the plays' structure and process, extending and troubling the Western frame to create a new theatrical form that pursues an intricate dialectic between tradition and modernity as a foundation for contemporary indigeneity.

Several of these elements can be cast into relief through a closer reading of *Purapurawhetū*, performed in New Zealand, Canada, and Greece and widely acknowledged as a *locus classicus* of contemporary New Zealand drama. Here, the setting is the depressed coastal community of Te Kupenga (the net), blighted because of the unacknowledged murder of a young child, the favored son of a local whānau (family) who was destined to bear the name of an honored tīpuna (ancestor) but was drowned by his jealous older brother, Matawera, before he could receive it. Cold, nameless, and alone, the child's spirit emanates an unremitting sadness, especially for his father, Hohepa – now an old man – who searches for his son on the seashore everyday. While material rejuvenation comes to the village in the form of a new wharenui (meeting house) funded by Matawera (now an aspiring politician), true healing comes about only with the return of the child's mother, Aggie-Rose, after a forty-year absence. In the guise of an old woman, Kui, she narrates the story of Te Kupenga's turbulent past to a young weaver, Tyler (adopted by the community as a boy after being found abandoned in an Auckland cinema), who incorporates this story into the tukutuku panel[5] that he is creating for the wharenui. As a result of these actions, the sins of the past are recognized, the child's spirit is able to break free of his watery bonds, accept his rightful name, Awatea, and take his place among the stars in the night sky. Ultimately, Tyler is named the family's successor instead of Matawera and accedes to the title of the family's land, confirming personal mana[6] and community commitment as more important than biological ties.

While this is a poignant and redemptive narrative on its own, it is how the story is structured dramatically that gives Grace-Smith's play its fuller significance. The play's title, *Purapurawhetū*, is also the name of the particular pattern for the tukutuku panel that Tyler weaves for the wharenui, depicting the stars that represent the souls of deceased loved ones watching over us. Tyler, however, finds himself unable to complete the panel (and thus the wharenui) until he learns the specific stories that lend it local import for the community. The answers to these questions are embedded in Kui/Aggie-Rose's ōhākī (dying speech), which she delivers gradually throughout the play; the action segues fluidly between the 1990s and the 1950s as the story emerges and as Tyler weaves the content of the ōhākī into the pattern. Tyler's process of creating the panel that contains the play's story is a literal drawing together and ordering of the plot as it unfolds, while serving as a metaphor for the theatrical production's working of diverse discursive and material strands into an artistic whole. As a visual representation of oral history for the community's future members, moreover, the panel offers a symbol of cultural continuity, and constructs an orienting pattern by which the play's variously deracinated characters can find purpose and meaning.[7] Grace-Smith's reflexive interweaving of form, leitmotif, and dramatic content is a prime example of how the Western theatrical framework might be invested with a Māori kaupapa,[8] demonstrating indigenous ownership of the medium and engendering new modes of expression.

Grace-Smith's major plays have served as cardinal points in the development of a specific style of contemporary Māori drama. Their formal hybridity and emphasis on generative renewal have posited new ways of knowing and practicing Māoritanga while reconfiguring the form and function of theatre in Aotearoa New Zealand. Grace-Smith's has hardly been the sole women's voice, however, with female playwrights like Riwia Brown pursuing alternative experiments in Māori theatre during the 1990s. Brown became strongly involved with Māori theatre in the early 1980s and wrote a series of pioneering plays in a predominantly realist vein (*Roimata*, 1998; *Te Hokina*, 1990; and *Ngā Wahine*, 1992) before expanding into film and television projects. Brown's play *Irirangi Bay* (1996) marks an aesthetic departure from these earlier works. It shadows familiar themes like the troubled legacies of the past, the destructive implications of colonialism, and the intrusion of the spirit realm into the everyday world, but repositions them on a melodramatic, surreal, and darkly comic plane. Brown structures the play with a cinematic geometry, investing it with the brooding temper and heightened stylization of film noir and incorporating short scenes, jump cuts, and stage directions that imply cinematographic techniques like the close-up, the split screen, and the dissolve. Hone Kouka notes that *Irirangi Bay* was a controversial play when first produced because it eschewed expectations of what a "Māori play" should be, but argues that the work should be acknowledged as a "watershed" in its divergence from epic, mythic, and spiritually moving dramas.[9]

Set in 1957, the play reveals the disastrous outcomes for a newlywed couple, George (Māori) and Mary (Pākehā), who renovate a seaside villa in a bay near Auckland. According to local legend, the area is afflicted by the makutu (curse) of Irirangi, a nineteenth-century Māori woman who had an illicit affair with a British army captain. Banished by her husband's tribe and rejected by her lover, Irirangi was brutally gang-raped by drunken soldiers who beheaded her mixed-race baby, and died cursing the land that caused her suffering. The makutu is borne out repeatedly on subsequent inhabitants of the land, such as the pregnant Catherine, whose secret Māori heritage is so shameful to her husband Earl that he poisons her and hangs himself. Mary's growing obsession with uncovering this history parallels her flourishing Huntingdon's disease; after discovering her own pregnancy and the fact that George married her to get back the land that her father took from George's family, she ties George up in his funeral suit, sets the house alight, and slits her wrists. The final tableau features the ghostly Irirangi, Catherine, and Mary linked in the embers.

Whereas this course of events is almost overbearingly gothic, the play's postcolonial politics are integral to its rationale and effects. The perennial issue of land dispossession resurfaces, as does the fear of ethnic miscegenation, both of which index an intractable residue of distrust between Māori and Pākehā based on a long legacy of confrontation and resistance, as Irirangi's tragedy from the New Zealand Wars period reveals.[10] George's comment, "if every tragic event was marked by spirit unrest, then there would be no place in this entire country to find peace,"[11] specifically situates the play's concerns in a broader context that acknowledges the violent histories of the nation-state. Throughout, the implications of racial prejudice are carried to their grotesque limits, with any generative potential commuted by the deaths of children as infants or *in utero*, bereft of the redemptive afterlife that Grace-Smith's work extends. Elsewhere, more quotidian permutations of racist attitudes (white patients shunning George's surgery, for instance) prompt critical reflection on how far New Zealand has actually come in its race relations. *Irirangi Bay* might thus be interpreted as rehearsing topoi widespread in the Māori theatre canon, but with an original voice and stylistic perspective that diversifies the corpus at the same time that it advances its wider goals.

New approaches in Māori women's playwriting have also been introduced by a younger generation of dramatists born in the 1970s and 1980s, including notable writers Whiti Hereaka and Miria George. Hereaka (1978–) has authored several works that chart new dramaturgical territory and exhibit broad stylistic and thematic variegation. Comedies like *Collective Agreement* (2005) and the existential farce *I Ain't Nothing But* (2006) inject a shot of levity into Māori drama's rather serious mien, while the philosophical two-hander *Rona and Rabbit on the Moon* (2011) reaches into the realm of the fantastic with its depiction of characters drawn from Māori and Chinese interpretations of lunar pareidolia. These works reflect the artistic freedom shared by several young Māori playwrights to experiment with new subjects and categories. In complement, Hereaka's *Te Kaupoi* (2010) is more strongly politicized and racially grounded, and is indicative of a concurrent trend that returns to the political themes of earlier Māori theatre, focusing once more on detrimental colonial attitudes, ethnic conflict, and human rights breaches. In part a response to perceived regressive government policies and a social climate that threatens advances made toward indigenous sovereignty, this tranche of plays provokes New Zealand society to reexamine its identity and commitments.

Te Kaupoi is set in an Orwellian New Zealand of the future, several years into a repressive government regime that has repealed Māori parliamentary seats, labeled meetings as conspiracy, banned tribal customary practices, branded Māori as "terrorists," and quelled any protest with violence and detention. With racist logic taken to its extreme, the country exists in a climate of intimidation and military surveillance. The sole voice of dissent comes from Te Kaupoi (The Cowboy), whose pirate radio station interrupts official news broadcasts with strident messages for Māori to band together to regain their sovereignty and freedom. The action revolves around three Māori characters on a farm in the central North Island: Mary, an ex-nurse and (former) member of a resistance cell; her son Zeke, a rodeo rider; and Sarah, a young woman found viciously assaulted and dumped on the farm, who is nursed back to health by Mary, gains her trust, and begins a relationship with Zeke. Sarah discovers that Zeke is in fact Te Kaupoi, and together they plan a revolutionary uprising for Waitangi Day.[12] On the day of the planned insurrection, however, Mary and Zeke are betrayed by Sarah, who turns out to be an undercover officer in the government's "Operation Cuckoo." Mary and Zeke are arrested, and Sarah is gunned down by Mary as troops raid the house.

Hereaka's depiction of this dystopia is dominated by a starkly realist aesthetic: the short scenes and taut, fast-paced dialogue create an atmosphere of exigency, and there is austere desperation in the raw physicality of bodies bound, beaten up, drugged, and shot, and in portrayals of sex and menstruation. These scenes are intercut with flashbacks that reveal Sarah's ambiguous motives as she is prepared for her mission: is she a willing participant, or a chilling example of the power of society's disciplinary strategies to turn vulnerable Māori against their own? This rather depressing parable is, however, more than a cautionary tale, raising profound questions about the tactics and goals of Māori self-determination. *Te Kaupoi* contrasts two methods of opposition: the passive resistance advocated by Mary, who plants native trees for future generations, and the radical action of Te Kaupoi/Zeke, who dismisses the conciliation of his parents' generation in favor of unequivocal sovereignty that must be seized, not negotiated. In this way, Hereaka rehearses issues regarding Māori sovereignty that reach back to the nineteenth century; indeed, despite its futuristic setting, the play's emphases on oppressive Crown control, passive versus active resistance, rebellious prophet figures, and "rebel" versus kūpapa (government-allied) Māori ghost the dynamics of the New Zealand Wars. Correspondingly, these themes reach back to the earliest phases of Māori theatre, echoing Harry Dansey's groundbreaking play *Te Raukura* (1972),[13] whose open-ended comparison of indigenous resistance methods from the Wars period offered potential exemplars for an incipient Māori protest movement of the 1970s. *Te Kaupoi*, then, is a complex work that brings together past lessons and future fears as a means of evaluating present choices.

A bleak imminent vision of New Zealand with perilous implications for Māori is also the subject of Miria George's political polemic, *and what remains* (2005). George (1980–), of Māori and Cook Islands descent, is a fresh, influential voice in Māori/Pasifika playwriting, having produced a body of work that has toured New Zealand, Australia, Hawai'i, the United Kingdom, and Canada. Prompting an incendiary public response because of its polarizing depiction of the nation's bicultural partnership, *and what remains* takes place in the (then) near future of 2010 when the Māori population has been forcibly expunged from New Zealand. Mary, a young Māori woman waiting in the International Departures Lounge at Wellington Airport, is the last to leave, faced with the choice between exile overseas or mandatory sterilization if she stays. The accompanying characters in International Departures are metonymic representations of New Zealand's multi-cultural milieu: the affluent and abrasive Ila, a cosmopolitan executive of Gujarati Indian heritage; the Samoan man, Solomon, a hard-working graphic designer about to embark on his first overseas trip; and Anna, an Iban Malaysian janitor at the airport who dreams of traveling abroad – all of whom call New Zealand home. This ethnic cleansing thus extends only to Māori, although Ila's repeated and prescient question, "Who's gonna be next?"[14] points to the precarity of not belonging to the dominant cultural imaginary.

Their conversations, which take place around and about the grief-stricken and mostly mute Mary, express differing degrees of justification, ignorance, and moral outrage about the persecution of Māori, yet no one offers any solution or even any real solidarity. Mary's Pākehā partner, Peter, arrives at the airport to persuade her to remain, yet this conversation ends in an impasse, symbol-izing the Māori–Pākehā relationship as a messy break-up replete with misunder-standing. The dialogue verges on the expressionistic and has a repetitive, circular quality; all outgoing flights are delayed, creating an atmosphere of protracted suspension that adds ironic accretions to the characters' discourse on staying and leaving, belonging and exclusion. One of the play's ultimate ironies is that all the non-Māori characters eventually decide to stay in New Zealand, and it is only Mary who boards her flight. The pain that this uprooting entails for Mary is rendered most powerfully in nonverbal ways; in one scene, Mary reveals her suitcase to be full of soil, planting her feet in it in a desperate attempt to transport with her some home ground.

And what remains is a young playwright's provocative artistic response to neoliberal government policies and conservative social stances of the mid-2000s, taking their implications to acute ends to posit the paucity of a nation without its indigenous presence. That migrants are "at home" in New Zealand while the tangata whenua[15] are rendered a diasporic population ironizes New Zealand's relationships to its overseas neighbors, yet at the same time acknowledges the imbricated networks – genealogical, material, administrative, and affective – which bind Māori and other ethnic groups in New Zealand to a wide and intricate range of international cultures and locations, complicating dichotomies between indigeneity and diaspora, locality and globality. Indeed, some of George's other plays (*Urban Hymns*, 2009; *Sunset Road*, 2012) are notable for moving beyond Māori/Pākehā binaries and intra-Māori interfaces to engage a broader range of ethnic and cultural identities and to register New Zealand's connections to a wider world. In particular, *Sunset Road*'s Cook Islands characters, memories of island homelands, and theme of migration to Aotearoa share much in common with a growing number of works by Pacific Island migrants and their descendants, which, since the 1990s, have inflected and enriched New Zealand's theatrescape, representing the country's changing demographics and mobile regional affiliations.

Performing Niu Sila: Pacific Islander theatre in New Zealand

Whereas Māori playwriting also treats themes of memory, travel, displacement, and sociocultural readjustment (just as migrant Pacific Islander work is also invested in questions of indigenous identity), Māori drama has tended to concentrate on issues of sovereignty, the legacies of colonialism, and the conditions of being tangata whenua, while works from the broader Pacific diaspora examine homeland/hostland dialectics within a more specific transnational frame, often focusing on the tensions between the characters' home cultures and life in "Niu Sila" (New Zealand). These themes, for example, resonate in the work of Dianna Fuemana (1973–), one of the leading playwrights to infuse new Pasifika perspectives into theatre in New Zealand and internationally. Of American Samoan and Niuean descent, Fuemana's professional career began with *Mapaki* (1999), in which diasporic themes of dislocation and loss of identity have their locus in a personalized story of domestic violence, and which broke new ground as the first play to present Niuean culture and language on stage in New Zealand. Fuemana's oeuvre covers a range of styles and themes, but she is best known for a series of works written for solo performance that have been produced in New Zealand and abroad.

Like the Cook Islands, Niue falls within New Zealand's neocolonial ambit, whereas American Sāmoa falls within that of the United States, and Fuemana's works pull in both directions. This transnational circuitry is particularly marked in *Falemalama: From Sāmoa to Niue to New Zealand and Back Again* (2006), in which Fuemana draws on family history for her subject matter, offering a compelling interpretation of her mother's life journey between American Sāmoa, Niue, New Zealand, and the US West Coast from the 1940s to the 2000s. *Falemalama* stages a profound and intimate examination of one of the many women's stories that comprise the broad Pacific diaspora and contribute to Oceania's diverse culturescape but remain largely unacknowledged in dominant accounts. The principal interlocutors are Tien (short for "The End"), the youngest daughter of Falemalama, and the Storyteller, who together share the narration of Falemalama's story, while a range of accompanying characters are also activated by the performer. Slipping mutably between temporalities and locations, the piece charts a difficult life: Fale's childhood abuse and neglect in American Sāmoa, an early first pregnancy and the external adoption of her eldest son, marriage and multiple childbirths, the restrictive social mores of her husband's family in Niue, and the family's migration to New Zealand and their struggle to make a home there. Throughout, Fale's independence, bravery, and kindness are balanced with mistakes and self-destructive behaviors that often alienate the family she has built, yet the play closes redemptively with Fale's eventual reunification with her long-lost son in Seattle and the family's final reunion in New Zealand.

In depicting this story, Fuemana suffuses the solo performance form with intercultural elements, employing live music that blends Western orchestration with Pacific instrumentation such as the fala (rolled mat), pātē (log drum), and foafoa (conch shell) to evoke various places, periods, and emotions; traditional songs from Sāmoa and Niue sung by the Storyteller that induce patriotism, pride, and nostalgia; and physical sequences like the Samoan dance that comprises forty-two movements to represent and celebrate Fale's descendants across Oceania. Poised between memory and imagination, Fuemana's tribute is an intricate evocation of identity across time and space, foregrounding the contradictions, pressures, and rewards experienced by Pacific women within the diaspora, while its multinodal transpacific trajectories displace the homeland/hostland dyad with a more nuanced view of the relationships between migration, location, and "home."

The vicissitudes of unorthodox Pacific women, along with the redress of stereotypes, find counterparts in Makerita Urale's *Frangipani Perfume* (1997), which was groundbreaking as the first play in New Zealand by a Pacific Island woman with an all-female cast.[16] Urale, who was born in (Western) Sāmoa and emigrated to New Zealand as a child in the 1970s, is one of numerous Samoan practitioners who have dominated the Pasifika performing arts scene since the early 1990s – a cohort that includes dynamic Samoan women playwrights Fiona Collins, Louise Tu'u, Erolia Ifopo, and Anapela Polataivao. Urale's play, however, remains a landmark in New Zealand theatre and has been performed internationally.

In *Frangipani Perfume*, three Samoan sisters, Tivi, Naiki, and Pomu, feel the keen contrast between life in the Islands and in New Zealand, working as night-shift cleaners to support an invalid father. Multiply marginalized by gender, ethnicity, immigrant status, and occupation, they are the invisible workers whom Pālagi (white people) never see. Surrounded by the smell of urine and cleaning products, they dream of the richly scented oils made by the women back in Sāmoa, and long for the homeland of their childhoods, which exists for them in half-remembered, idealized images. The play exercises multivalent theatrical tactics to express the sisters' affections, rivalries, and fears, while activating various themes relevant to immigrant/Pacific women: obligation to the family patriarch, sexual expectations and prohibitions, religious mores, conflicts between work and home life, and the sustenance of women's traditional skills. All the while, the play represents its subjects as intelligent, vivacious, politically aware, and unrestricted by conventional domestic parameters. Progressing in a series of nonlinear snapshot scenes, the play's complex syncretism creates a fluid and dynamic performative space in which Urale can experiment with gendered identities through scenes of dialogic realism, as well as through visual displays of the Polynesian body that critically deconstruct colonial practices and clichés.

In particular, *Frangipani Perfume* tackles fetishized Western representations of island women as "dusky maidens," subverting the figure of the sensual, long-haired, bare-breasted Polynesian beauty who connotes availability and allure in passive symbiosis with her island environment. The three sisters slip in and out of their identification with the dusky maiden throughout the play, at times consciously embodying it as a part of a sustaining fantasy that helps them cope with the drudgery of their everyday lives, at other times teasing the audience into confronting their own exotic fantasies, and sometimes taking the trope as a point of discursive departure. In this last case, the dusky maiden is often deployed critically as testimony to the history of sexualized oppression that Pacific women continue to bear; in one scene, the sisters offer a revisionist appraisal of Margaret Mead's anthropological construction of the sexually free Samoan girl, exposing Mead's conflation of imperialist politics and touristic promotion.[17] The dusky maiden also exists in parallel tension with more modern and proactive identities that the women inhabit. Pomu (also known as Hydrogen), whose name means "bomb" in Samoan, aspires to be a physicist, and her fascination with science and atomic power recalls broader discourses of colonial dispossession engendered by American and French nuclear testing in the Pacific. In *Frangipani Perfume*, the dusky maiden is an imagined identification that is refigured in the moment that it is recalled and that is ultimately recuperated as a symbol of empowerment, on Pacific women's terms, maintaining affirming ties to cultural heritage while reflecting a pan-Pacific postcolonial consciousness.

If Fuemana's *Falemalama* articulates the historical role that Pacific women have played in building New Zealand's multicultural society, and Urale's *Frangipani Perfume* is about women finding ways to survive the hardships of their contemporary milieu, then Courtney Sina Meredith's *Rushing Dolls* is about women succeeding in that brave new world. In her first published play, Meredith (1986–,

Samoan, Irish, and Cook Islands descent) depicts a new breed of ambitious, educated, and trailblazing Māori/Pacific women, centering on two cousins in their early twenties, Cleopatra and Sia'lei Felise. Cleo (Samoan) is a successful poet with a burgeoning following who aspires to a career with an international event-management company and a post in Berlin; Sia (Samoan/Māori/Tongan) is a fine arts graduate and a thriving multimedia artist. In contrast to an offensive "Girl" doll that the women encounter in a gallery exhibition, portraying another prevailing stereotype of the pregnant, teenage, downtrodden brown woman, Cleo and Sia identify as "rushing dolls," the confident elite of the future: "Fearless and babyless. No jail time and no handouts. No fucking excuses," and poised "on the cusp of glory."[18]

Whereas the sisters in *Frangipani Perfume* recede into the realm of dreams to ameliorate their materially circumscribed existence, the cousins in *Rushing Dolls* have risen from their modest origins to realize their dreams. Charismatic, connected, and cosmopolitan, Cleo and Sia patronize art galleries, upscale restaurants, artists' soirées, and striptease joints, give television interviews, and deliver inspirational speeches to high school graduands. In Urale's play, Naiki's possible lesbianism is a confrontational issue; here, Cleo is openly bisexual and in a relationship with a white woman. In contrast, moreover, to the homeland as a nostalgic retreat of memory and fantasy, Cleo and Sia seek to reinvest in Sāmoa and the broader region, meeting with representatives of the Samoan government to negotiate a multimillion-dollar project to stimulate the local economy. The play eschews romantic island images: "no breezing trees and caramel sand / no coconut truths spilling over woven fans / no plans of making love to the land."[19] Instead, the world the women inhabit as visible, active participants is "Urbanesia," Meredith's neologism for the energetic, urban, polyglot culture of contemporary Auckland that brings the island and the city into profound collision, and acts as the crucible of new global identities. The play's experimental form expresses this atmosphere through the women's sassy, edgy patois, interleaved with the richly textured lyricism of the performance poetry that constitutes Cleo's inner expression. Although the familiar pull of family obligations and the overwhelming pressure of ambition threaten to derail the characters at times, Meredith's new vision of contemporary Oceania dramatizes the aspirations of a bold, emergent demographic whose members know at once where they come from and where they are going.

Regional connections beyond New Zealand

These diasporic Pacific Island plays link the remembered past with globalized identities of the present, forging new networks in their form, their content, the playwrights' mixed genealogies, and the international routes of their circulation. A transnational web of Pacific Islander artists is especially evident among Samoan practitioners, who have expanded and refracted Samoan culture through their connections with various worldwide locations. Women playwrights and performers have been an essential part of this network, including, beyond New Zealand, members of the Polytoxic ensemble in Australia and the Gafa Arts Collective in the United Kingdom, as well as Victoria Nalani Kneubuhl in Hawai'i.

Kneubuhl (1949–, Samoan, Caucasian, and Hawaiian descent) is one of Oceania's foremost playwrights. During her thirty-year career, she has made a substantial contribution to the local essence and international scope of theatre in Hawai'i, with productions of her works throughout the United States, Europe, Asia, and the Pacific. Kneubuhl's plays, which span Samoan and Hawaiian concerns, are predominantly historical dramas presented in an epic style, fusing documentary research and artistic imagination to interrogate the processes, practices, and legacies of American colonialism in the Pacific, and incorporating transversal questions of gender and ethnicity.[20] Her highly compressed format is marked (like that of Grace-Smith) by permeability between past and present, spiritual and quotidian; and favors multiple roles for actors, often with a chorus to elaborate the action, and simple, flexible staging that capitalizes on the theatre's spatial and psychological elasticity. Kneubuhl frequently uses humor and farce to help address serious issues, acknowledging the tenacity of repressive attitudes and stereotypes while working to dismantle them. The Samoan and Hawaiian works both contribute to a multiethnic genre of "Local" theatre in Hawai'i that has become especially notable since the early 1970s, but the plays with Samoan characters and themes tend to feature a lighter tone and a stronger degree of metatheatricality and interculturalism. The Hawaiian plays are more earnest, reflecting their association with, and investment in, a kanaka maoli (Native Hawaiian) sovereignty movement, and – like Māori theatre in New Zealand – pursuing questions of indigenous rights, self-determination, land and resources, and the cultivation of precolonial practices.

Kneubuhl's approach to dramatizing historical material adopts a fluid temporality in which spirits, characters, or scenes from the historical or remembered past may intersect with the present. In *Ola Nā Iwi* (1994), a young woman liberates a set of Hawaiian bones from a German museum and is aided in her quest by the spirit of the bones, who turns out to be a revered figure from Hawai'i's nineteenth-century past; elsewhere, monologues delivered by Victorian phrenologists and bone collectors add intertextual irony to the play's critique of the appropriation of indigenous artifacts. In *Emmalehua* (1996), the protagonist, Emma, reclaims her hula practice and her sense of cultural identity in a rapidly Americanizing Hawai'i of the 1950s with the guidance of her grandmother's spirit. *The Holiday of Rain* (2011), meanwhile, offers a complicated concoction of postcolonial historiography and science fiction. Switching between Pago Pago in 1916 and in the twenty-first century, Kneubuhl uses the conceit of time-travel to deconstruct the racist and misogynist clichés of Somerset Maugham's famous story, "Rain" (1921).[21]

As in *Emmalehua* and *Ola Nā Iwi*, Kneubuhl's plays typically illuminate broader historical moments from the intimate viewpoints of selected female characters, providing necessary cultural and gendered alternatives to the approaches of conventional Western historiography. *Fanny and Belle* (2004), for instance, channels the turbulence of the *fin de siècle* through the extraordinary and markedly parallel lives of Fanny, the American wife (later widow) of Scottish author Robert

Louis Stevenson, and her daughter, Belle Osbourne, taking the period of their lives in Vailima, Sāmoa, as a dramatic through-line. Similarly, *The Conversion of Ka'ahumanu* (1988) examines the period of cataclysmic change occasioned by the breakdown of the Hawaiian belief-system and the coincidental arrival of Christianity in the 1820s via the domestic interactions of five American missionary and Hawaiian women. Many of Kneubuhl's works are also significant for their positioning of Hawai'i and Sāmoa within a global nexus, whether in the international intrigues of *Ola Nā Iwi*, the diverse peregrinations of the characters in *Fanny and Belle* and *The Holiday of Rain*, or the women's intercultural encounters in *The Conversion of Ka'ahumanu*, emphasizing the islands' historical and contemporary connections to, and impact on, a wider world. Kneubuhl's is a rich and influential oeuvre, bringing the grounded and the fluid, the indigene and the traveler, and the cultural past and its tumultuous present into nuanced and provocative tension.

Whereas Kneubuhl's plays encompass broad geographical and temporal territory, Lee Cataluna's broad comedies focus mainly on contemporary life in Hawai'i, celebrating the characters, situations, locations, and practices that comprise the uniquely "Local" culture created from the sustained interactions between Hawai'i's varied ethnic communities. A newscaster and journalist, Cataluna (1966–) began her prolific playwriting career in a scriptwriting class run by Kneubuhl during the mid-1990s. Plays like *Da Mayah* (1998), *Aloha Friday* (2000), and *Super Secret Squad* (2002) are written in Hawaiian Creole English ("Pidgin") and are characterized by physical and verbal comedy, in-jokes and emic references, and a focus on the struggles and desires of ordinary people, often with a satirical edge to prompt critical social examination.

Cataluna's first play, *Da Mayah*, offers a useful illustration of these themes and approaches. Sandralene Leialoha Ferreira, "one middle-age Portuguese-Hawaiian-Albanian, five-time married, former women's wrestling promoter and part-time plus-size swimsuit model,"[22] is the long-suffering administrative assistant to Lester Perez, the inept and corrupt mayor of Hilo. Sandra's efforts to protect Perez's shady dealings for the community's benefit see her drawing on her family contacts to hire a bumbling hit-man to assassinate the mayor's rival, but when Perez joins forces with his former enemies, Sandra finds herself out of a job. Fortuitously, Perez and his cronies die horribly after eating poisoned pasteles from a local lunch wagon, and Sandra becomes the mayor. Here, the slapstick series of events becomes a vehicle for a political satire that critiques the hypocrisy and venality of elected officials, pointing to their community responsibilities and championing the kind-hearted underdog. Cataluna's inclusive community vision fosters solidarity among her Local audiences, expressing and reinforcing a distinctive island culture that reflects Hawai'i's specific histories and preoccupations.

While Cataluna's work weaves its patterns from Hawai'i's multiethnic social fabric, the plays of Tammy Haili'ōpua Baker (1972–) draw directly on the rich resources of Native Hawaiian mo'olelo (legends, stories) with the aim of sustaining and revitalizing traditional material. In 1995, Baker established the Hawaiian-medium theatre company, Ka Hālau Hanakeaka, which has taken the

Hawaiian language in new discursive and geographical directions with a series of pioneering dramas based on mythic themes that have toured extensively throughout Oceania. Baker's English and Pidgin plays blend traditional stories from Hawai'i's precontact past with modern Western dramatic forms in order to make Hawaiian material accessible to a wider, contemporary audience, employing a highly physical style that incorporates hula, chant, and song. *Kupua* (2001), for example, comprises two short plays, *Ka 'Enuhe (The Caterpillar)* and *Ka Puhi a me Ka Loli (The Eel and the Sea Cucumber)*, which deal with kupua (shape-shifters), anarchic spirits that inhabit the forms of animals or human partners, and enervate their targets. These ribald, sensual dramas deploy myth pedagogically, reminding contemporary audiences about caring for the well-being of family members, self-responsibility and restraint, and the importance of balance and the dangers of excess, thus accentuating the present social relevance of traditional tales.

Théâtre Océanien: women's playwriting in the French Pacific

Baker's experiments with writing plays in vernacular and colonial languages have counterparts in the work of other regional practitioners, including Valérie Gobrait, one of the most prominent female playwrights in Tahiti. The Polynesian languages of Hawaiian and Tahitian (Māʻohi) have more in common than the colonial languages that separate the two archipelagos, as Tahiti is part of the francophone Pacific. Pacific literature in French – a dynamic minority in a predominantly anglophone region – remains largely untranslated into English and tends to circulate within alternative local and international networks, but a comparative analysis reveals themes, concerns, and approaches in common with anglophone playwrights. Gobrait (1967–), who was born in Tahiti and spent several years studying in Paris, has created two major productions in Māʻohi as part of an indigenous literary self-determination initiative, and has also translated these works into French to increase her readership and to develop her dramaturgical style by working bilingually.[23] Like Baker's corpus, *Te 'a'ai nō Matari'i/La légende de Matari'i (The Legend of Matari'i,* 2000) draws from the realms of mythology and ancient history; set in the era when migratory explorers first settled in the islands of the Pacific, the play tells of the god Matari'i (associated throughout Polynesia with the navigators' star) and the initiation quest that he gives to his twin sons. Epic, poetic, and symbolic, featuring a chorus, traditional chants, and the art of 'orero (oratory), *Matari'i* revives indigenous epistemologies within a modern dramatic framework, while evoking a regional sensibility in its citation of the ancient voyaging networks that subtend a vast oceanic interculture and form a historical complement to modern-day forms of migrancy.

Gobrait's subsequent work, *Te vāhira'a fenua/Le partage de la terre (The Sharing of the Land,* 2001), shifts direction back to the land and toward contemporary, realist family drama, presenting a skillful anatomy of intergenerational conflict in modern, urban Tahiti. Mr. Taripo, a retired fisherman and plantation worker, organizes a family meeting to formally bequeath his ancestral family land to his three grown sons – a project that he has been working toward since his wife's death many years earlier. On the evening of the meeting, however, his conversations with each son (an overworked civil servant; an unemployed, alcoholic voyeur who neglects his wife and children; and a delinquent drug-dealer) reveal the deep cultural and emotional gulfs between them. The father's astonishment, guilt, and dejection are exacerbated as family tensions rise, capped by the eldest son's surprise announcement that Taripo is to be evicted from the home he has occupied for fifty years to make way for highway expansion, and that the compensation money will fund his lodging in a retirement home. Left all alone and totally disillusioned, Taripo gets drunk and conducts the inheritance ceremony to the empty room. When the public notary arrives to legalize the paperwork, Taripo makes the final decision to stop the proceedings and nullify his bequest. Gobrait's minute analysis of twenty-first-century island life breaks through the persistent mythos of Tahiti as a Rousseauesque paradise and exposes it as subject to the same socioeconomic and cultural concerns as many contemporary societies. Beyond its domestic implications, the play's ambivalent conclusion foregrounds concerns that surface in various Pacific Island and other postcolonial plays – the link to the land, the dignity of elders, and how extant notions of value, genealogy, heritage, and identity might negotiate the imperatives of modernity – speaking to common investments that connect regional playwrights beyond their discrete cultural archives.

Conclusion: new Oceanic imaginaries

From magic realism to gothic melodrama, from ancient mythology to dystopian futurescapes, from social analysis to science fiction, from perilous acts of history to quirky comedies of the present, and from island village life to the urbanesian identities fashioned in the major metropolises of an expanded Oceania, contemporary Pacific Islands women playwrights have adopted a broad array of theatrical strategies to explore and express the polyvalent intricacies of the region's experiences. Drawing inspiration from various Pacific cultures as well as many different playwrights and experimental artists worldwide, the works included in this conspectus demonstrate a sophisticated stylistic and intercultural heterogeneity. At the same time, this corpus is bound together by shared artistic techniques, themes, ideologies, and locales that speak to a wider regional sensibility: related experiences of colonization and migration; recurrent questions about indigeneity in the contemporary world; correlated concerns about the identity and representation of Pacific peoples; mutual influences of island and oceanic geographies; and links forged via diasporic and (neo-)colonial networks as well as by precolonial and genealogical connections. Epeli Hau'ofa's foundational concept of Oceania as an interconnected "sea of islands"[24] foregrounds the geopolitical and conceptual space that these dramatists write across – a task that involves a bridging of boundaries but also a reinscription and repositioning of knowledge. The playwrights discussed here conjure an oceanic imaginary that presents a critical alternative to Eurocentric paradigms while registering the constantly changing face of Oceania in its ebb and flow between different cultural forces, and represent a significant contribution to women's writing and to global theatre.

Notes

1 Peter R. Onedera, "Theater in a Chamoru Sense" (unpublished paper, prepared for Art and Culture in Micronesia, Micronesian Studies Graduate Program, University of Guam, 1999), 3.
2 Graham Huggan and Helen Tiffin, *Postcolonial Ecocriticism: Literature, Animals, Environment* (London: Routledge, 2010), 54.
3 Subramani, "The Oceanic Imaginary," *The Contemporary Pacific* 13, no. 1 (2001): 151.
4 Speechmaking, public oratory.
5 A woven latticework panel in a wharenui (meeting house) that embeds the history and stories of the community for subsequent generations.
6 Bearing, prestige.
7 For an elaboration of these points, see John Huria's excellent introduction to *Purapurawhetū* (Wellington: Huia, 1999), 8–19.
8 Idea, mission, purpose.
9 Hone Kouka, "Introduction," in *Ta Matou Mangai: Three Plays of the 1990s* (Wellington: Victoria University Press, 1999), 27.
10 The New Zealand Wars (sometimes referred to as the Land Wars) were a series of campaigns fought between British soldiers and various Māori tribes in several locations throughout the country during the middle third of the nineteenth century. Representations of the Wars and their multivalent after-effects are recurrent themes in Māori drama.
11 Riwia Brown, *Irirangi Bay*, in *Ta Matou Mangai*, 116.
12 February 6, marking the anniversary of the Treaty of Waitangi, signed in 1840 between the British Crown and various Māori chiefs. Contradictory interpretations of the bilingual Treaty have been a source of dissension since the time of its signing, and Waitangi Day has become a common platform for protests regarding sovereignty and social parity.
13 Harry Dansey, *Te Raukura: The Feathers of the Albatross* (Auckland: Longman Paul, 1974).
14 Miria George, *and what remains* (Wellington: Tawata Press, 2007), 5.
15 Indigenous people, literally "people of the land."
16 David O'Donnell, "Introduction," in *Frangipani Perfume/Mapaki*, by Makerita Urale and Dianna Fuemana (Wellington: The Play Press, 2004), i.
17 See Margaret Mead, *Coming of Age in Samoa: A Psychological Study of Primitive Youth for Western Civilisation* (New York: William Morrow, 1928).
18 Courtney Sina Meredith, *Rushing Dolls*, in *Urbanesia: Four Pasifika Plays*, ed. David O'Donnell (Wellington: Playmarket, 2012), 296, 279.
19 Ibid., 298.
20 There are some exceptions within Kneubuhl's oeuvre. *The Story of Susanna* (1998), for instance, has a female focus but not an overtly Pacific one.

21 See W. Somerset Maugham, "Rain," in *The Trembling of a Leaf* (Melbourne: Heinemann, 1935), 234–95.

22 Lee Cataluna, *Da Mayah*, in *He Leo Hou: A New Voice – Hawaiian Playwrights*, ed. John H. Y. Wat and Meredith M. Desha (Honolulu: Bamboo Ridge Press, 2003), 157–58.

23 "Valérie Gobrait," Interview, *Les Nouvelles de Tahiti*, 22 May 2009, available at *http://www.lesnouvelles.pf/article/a-laffiche/valerie-gobrait* (accessed 2 March 2013).

24 Epeli Hau'ofa, "Our Sea of Islands," in *A New Oceania: Rediscovering Our Sea of Islands*, ed. Eric Waddell, Vijay Naidu, and Epeli Hau'ofa (Suva: University of the South Pacific, 1993), 2–16.

11 Ecodramaturgy in/and Contemporary Women's Playwriting

Wendy Arons and Theresa J. May

Ecodramaturgy is theatre and performance making that puts focus on ecological reciprocity and community.[1] The concept is derived in part from the Earth Matters on Stage (EMOS) playwrights' festival, which calls for ecologically themed new plays that "respond to the ecological crisis and that explore new possibilities of being in relationship with the more-than-human world."[2] Such responses might include illuminating issues of environmental (in)justice; putting an ecological issue at the center of the action; interpreting "community" to include the nonhuman and/or the land as characters or agents; and (re-)imagining intersections between nature and culture. Ecodramaturgy refers not only to the sensibilities and strategies employed by playwrights, but also to the critical approaches taken by scholars and directors as they (re)read or (re)stage works to foreground ecological themes. In this chapter, we trace some of the ecodramaturgical currents that have informed women's playwriting over the last two decades. The "in/and" in our title signals our dual deployment of the concept of ecodramaturgy as something that resides in the work itself and that is (also) a critical strategy.

Coming of age during second-wave environmentalism, ecofeminism, and an era of environmental justice, contemporary women playwrights have contributed to the conversation about the ecological health and well-being of our planet and the beings that inhabit it.[3] Their work is ecodramaturgical when they deal with issues of social and ecological justice; when they reveal how larger ecological, political, and economic forces affect motherhood and family and point out the intergenerational consequences of environmental devastation and degradation; and when they put focus on biology, exposing the interconnectedness of the human with the nonhuman world at microscopic and macroscopic scales.

In what follows, we examine these interconnections in contemporary women's playwriting from a methodological perspective that draws on literary ecocriticism, ecofeminism, and queer ecology. Literary ecocriticism concerns itself with the study of the relationship of literature to the natural world. In its attentiveness to the ways in which literature of the past has figured or stereotyped nature (as resource, as romanticized backdrop to human activity, as wilderness, and so forth) and to the ways nature writers have attempted to revise received notions of nature, ecocriticism can be seen to play a role analogous to that of feminist criticism, which similarly unpacks how literature has reinforced culturally constructed ideas of gender and celebrates the strategies used by feminist writers to revise those ideas. Ecofeminism ties together ecocriticism and feminism in explicit ways, seeking to discern and deconstruct "important connections between how one treats women, people of color, and the underclass on one hand and how one treats the nonhuman natural environment on the other."[4] Karen J. Warren notes that "[w]hat makes ecofeminism distinct is its insistence that nonhuman nature and naturism (that is, the unjustified domination of nature) are feminist issues."[5] Ecofeminism draws into feminism's circle of interest a whole array of ecological and environmental issues that impact the social, political, economic, and, above all, material and bodily well-being of women and their families. Lastly, queer ecology is a theoretical approach that aims to reconceptualize the relationship between humans and nonhumans through focus on the fact that biology does not recognize firm, bright boundaries between inside and outside, male and female, life and nonlife, or between and within species.[6] In his essay "Queer Ecology," Timothy Morton argues that because we share DNA with every other life form, we are always and already part of a collective – "We have others – rather, others have us – literally under our skin."[7] In place of human exceptionalism against a nonhuman world, queer ecology would conceptualize egalitarian difference among species. Queer ecology has provocative implications for imagining both the human and the nonhuman in art, literature, and performance, suggesting that we "treat beings as people, even if they turn out not to be" because of our ethical responsibility to both ourselves and them.[8] Ecocriticism, ecofeminism, and queer ecology thus provide powerful lenses, vocabularies, and modes of analysis for identifying the ecodramaturgical threads that weave through contemporary women's playwriting.[9]

Intersections of social and ecological justice

Issues of environmental justice are front and center in Cherríe Moraga's 1992 play *Heroes and Saints*, which tells the story of a California migrant-labor community struggling to voice protest against the toxic agricultural practices that have spurred a local epidemic of birth defects and fatal childhood cancers.[10] Symbolizing the deleterious effects of chemical-input farming is the teenaged Cerezita, a disembodied head, victim of the environmental pollution that is robbing the play's impoverished Chicano/a community of its genetic future. We are prompted immediately to ponder the impossibility of the survival of a head that lacks a body, and, during the course of the play, to extend that wonder to the possibility of the survival of the community as a whole (and, by extension, the human species) as faceless corporations poison the soil and water that produces food. But Cerezita's status as a headless body also asks us to consider the inverse of her condition – the one thing even more impossible to imagine than a head without a body is a body without a head – and thereby spotlights the false dichotomy that allows for humans to rationalize a destructive exploitation of the environment. That is, it is our insistence on maintaining divisions between matter (body, nature) and thought (mind, culture) that lies at the root of our dysfunctional relationship to the environment that sustains us. Thus, in the play's semiotics, the "presence-of-absence" of Cerezita's body is multivalent: it is not only stark material evidence of the impact of toxins on the health and well-being of workers and their families but also a metaphor for a society that denies the body, privileges the abstract over the material, and severs "nature" from "culture." While Cerezita possesses all of the attributes philosophers have traditionally mustered in support of their claims for human exceptionalism – language, abstract intelligence, spiritual feeling, empathy, imagination, creativity – her bodilessness signals precisely how disastrous that conception of the human relationship to the nonhuman world has proved to be. A genetic dead-end, she symbolizes not only her community's loss of its future but also potentially that of humanity as a whole. She is a warning: we cannot continue to treat the natural world as an exploitable resource for, and backdrop to, human activity and expect to continue to survive as a species.

Consequently, while the play begins by focusing attention on the plight of the immediate victims of environmental injustice – farmworkers – who are sickened by their exposure to pesticides and fertilizers, it also quickly makes clear that "their" struggle is "ours." Moraga's image-rich play makes connections between grapevines and the bodies of children: in a horrifying gesture of protest, the workers hang the bodies of their children, who are believed to have died as a result of pesticides, on crosses and place them in the fields among the trellised grapevines. As Linda Margarita Greenberg observes, within the action of the play, this public display of dead children "highlights the problems of environmental abuse of the Chicano/a farmworking community that the pastoral vision of California agriculture masks,"[11] but the visual parallel between the crosses bearing the bodies of dead children and those bearing the pesticide-sprayed grapevines also metaphorically reconstitutes the material–ecological meaning of the Catholic sacrament of Communion. Catholics believe that bread and wine become the actual body and blood of Christ. Here, the grapes become blood, and if they are covered in poison, that blood is poisoned. We all participate in an ecological communion. The body of the earth and the bodies of the workers (and by implication all those who consume grapes or any other megacrop of California's industrial agriculture) are "one in the flesh," as the Catholic Mass says.

Moreover, in *Heroes and Saints*, violence against the environment is also closely linked to gender violence. While environmental injustice is not exclusively a gendered concern, Moraga calls attention to the fact that the victims of environmental injustice are usually the poor and the disenfranchised, and that women – especially minority women – make up a large percentage of those categories. In Moraga's play, it is women's bodies that bear the brunt of the effects of the toxic chemicals sprayed on the fields, and it is primarily women who must care for the dying children they bring into the world as a result. As Greenberg observes, "rather than placing politics outside the body, the play integrates seemingly exterior sociopolitical problems with female and queer identities that might otherwise shift to a depoliticized private space."[12] Moraga equates environmental injustice with other forms of gendered violence: the abuse of the land, its transformation into sterile "dirt," is paralleled by and made analogous to the "sterilization" of the community through the loss of its current generation of children; the abandonment of Cerezita's family by her father is echoed by the indifference of the consuming public to the cost, in human lives, of industrial agriculture; and the sociopolitical dynamic that allows the wider public to marginalize and effectively dismiss a community of "others" by ignoring the disease that plagues it is replicated by Cerezita's gay brother Mario's self-exile and eventual infection with AIDS. By theatricalizing the interconnectivity between land and body, by putting marginalized (i.e., female, queer, disabled, minority) bodies and the land in simultaneous space, Moraga demonstrates the ways in which violence against the "other" and violence against the natural world share root causes. Foreshadowing works such as Lynn Nottage's *Ruined* (2008), Moraga asserts the interdependence of peace and justice advocated by Vandana Shiva, who observes that "[p]eace lies in nourishing ecological and economic democracy and nurturing diversity. Democracy is...the power of the people...to determine how their natural resources are owned and utilized, how their thirst is quenched, how their food is produced and distributed."[13] Moraga's play offers a perceptive and powerful expression of Shiva's argument that the ecological devastation wrought by global development that appropriates resources, including human labor, for the profit of multinational corporations is a form of violence that strikes marginalized and poor communities the hardest.

A similar preoccupation with the transnational effects of environmental injustice is evident in *Ruined*, which poignantly demonstrates how, in an age of corporatized global markets, global–ecological issues become etched in human bodies, lives, and homelands, and in which the material world betrays our interdependence, connection, and complicity in cultural, social, and ecological crises that seem remote. Seen through an ecodramaturgical lens, *Ruined* calls attention to the ways in which the global marketplace, in putting increased pressure on key resources, threatens local ecosystems and the species – including humans – they sustain. The violence at the center of *Ruined* arises in part from the demands of this market – a so-called "free market," but one that is hardly free for the many people and communities in the world whose land and labor are mined in order to manufacture the goods on which that market depends. *Ruined* reminds us that we touch others, and are touched by them, in every moment of each day.

From the start of play, the land is alive, not only as refuge for the rebels, veiling acts of violence, but also as the repository of memory and indigenous knowledge. The play points to the colonial past and its impact on indigenous forests, peoples, cultures, and languages in the opening scene, when Mama tells Christian about a gray parrot who only speaks pygmy because "Old Papa [Batunga] was the last of his tribe. That stupid bird was the only thing he had left to talk to.... He believed as long as the words of the forest people were spoken, the spirits would stay alive.... [W]hen that bird dies this place is gonna lose part of its story."[14] Nottage links the loss of indigenous cultures and traditional knowledge to the human and ecological devastation of the current neocolonial era. Recalling Papa's conviction that "as long as the forest grows a man will never starve," Mama bitterly summarizes the connection between geopolitical power and access to the land and its resources:

> When I was eleven, this white man with skin the color of wild berries turned up with a piece of paper. It say he have rights to my family land.... Poor old Papa bought magic from a friend, he thought a handful of powder would give him back his land.... Everyone talk talk diamonds, but I... I want a powerful slip of paper that says I can cut down forests and dig holes and build to the moon if I choose. I don't want someone to turn up at my door, and take my life from me. (27)

Here, the economic imperatives of transnational neocolonial corporate profiteering have ruptured indigenous belief and history, cultural and spiritual connection to ancestral lands, and, at the most basic level, the ability to take sustenance from the land's abundance.

Uganda and the Democratic Republic of Congo are nation-states born in the wake of Europe's exploitative colonization of Africa in the eighteenth and nineteenth centuries, and modern patterns of targeted violence in response to neocolonial pressures of the global marketplace reveal how colonized people adopt and adapt the world view, values, and behaviors of the colonizers. Kate Whoriskey, who directed *Ruined* at the Manhattan Theatre Club in 2009, notes that "the men and boys who raped were themselves victims of unspeakable violence" and that "they spend the rest of their lives terrorizing and destroying others."[15] The predicament of these Congo rebel soldiers is a global–ecological one. As one rebel in the play tells it, the Congolese government trades minerals for wealth, even when those minerals destroy the fabric of land and society:

> how do we protect ourselves...? How do we feed our families? Ay? They bring soldiers from Uganda, drive us from our land and make us refugees...and then turn us into criminals when we protest or try to protect ourselves. How can we let the government carve up our most valuable land to serve companies in China. It's our land. Ask the Mbuti, they can describe every inch of the forest as if were [sic] their own flesh. (78)

Ruined gives literal meaning to rapacious capitalism and the ways in which armed conflict rips at the fabric of bodies, family, community, and land. Far from being merely the setting for the play, the land is at the epicenter of what has happened to the women in *Ruined*. Echoing the violence used by colonial explorers, some of whom cut off hands of those who refused to provide free labor for the European rubber trade, rebels' acts of violence against women are more than acts of humiliation and domination. Repeated acts of rape "strip women of their wombs," robbing them of the ability to procreate, killing the very possibility of motherhood, family, and community, and destroying the human ecology along with the nonhuman ecological systems of the Congo.[16]

Like Moraga, Nottage calls attention to the way environmental injustice leads to the tragic and violent end of genetic lines at the local level; at the same time, her play also implicates us, its global audience, as we may wear African diamonds on our fingers or carry conflict minerals from the Congo – coltan, gold, tungsten, tin, tantalum – in the digital devices in our pockets.[17] To call our attention to this interconnectivity, Nottage's Harari brags, "I handle mostly minerals, some precious stones, but I have contacts for everything. My mobile is always on" (78). By putting focus on the vital role of nonhuman matter in human conflicts – coltan, in this case – the play reveals a landscape of material–ecological consequences in the lives and bodies of women and asks us to attend to the potential agency of the things that we conjure into being, buy, use, circulate, and eventually discard. In her book *Vibrant Matter*, Jane Bennett makes a connection between recognizing the "vibrant materiality" of things and our ethical responsibility to others:

> If matter itself is lively, then not only is the difference between subjects and objects minimized, but the status of the shared materiality of all things is elevated.... Vital materialism would thus set up a kind of safety net for those humans who are now ... routinely made to suffer because they do not conform to a particular (Euro-American, bourgeois, theocentric, or other) model of personhood.... Such a newfound attentiveness to matter and its powers will not solve the problem of human exploitation or oppression, but it can inspire a greater sense of the extent to which all bodies are kin.... And in a knotted world of vibrant matter, to harm one section of the web may very well be to harm oneself.[18]

An ecodramaturgical view of Nottage's play does not minimize the suffering of women in the Congo and elsewhere, nor does it conflate women's bodies and the body of the land. Instead, it shines light on the interrelatedness of systems of violence, oppression, and ecological devastation and puts focus on the ways in which we all are knotted into those systems, tied together by the things we consume and the economic, cultural, and physical impact the manufacture and disposal of those things has on others.

Transnational ecological intimacies

Ismail Serageldin, vice president of World Bank, claimed in 1995 that "[i]f the wars of this century were fought over oil, the wars of the next century will be fought over water."[19] Kia Corthron's *A Cool Dip in a Barren Saharan Crick* (2010) theatrical-izes cultural, religious, economic, and ecological meanings and uses of water in the lives of an American family, Pickle Carter and her daughter H.J., and the Ethiopian exchange student, Abebe, who has come to live with them. Like Nottage's *Ruined*, *Cool Dip* explores transnational intimacies, probing at the edges of how "political conflicts over resources are hidden or surpressed," either falsely framed in terms of jobs versus the environment, or camouflaged as ethnic or religious conflicts.[20]

Corthron deploys a series of reversals and parallels in order to bring seemingly remote issues surrounding water – that is, the importance of local control of resources and grassroots involvement in problem-solving – close to home for an American audience. The play begins as Abebe encounters running water and plumbing for the first time in his host family's home; although he, of all the characters, is aware of the value of water, he cannot resist the temptation to flush the toilet repeatedly and experience the small miracle of water-on-demand. The Maryland town where the Carters live is in the midst of a drought, requiring people to "turn off [the] water three hours a day," but at other times water is "in the pipes every time you turn them."[21] In Ethiopia, Abebe tells us, the situation is different: "There is much much much water in Africa. Unfortunately sometimes it is not in the right places. Or the dry season becomes drier. Or the water is unclean" (16). For Abebe's village, the solution is a "primitive dam solution" that "requires the community to work together" to provide a "bulwark against drought" that not only sustains farming in his home village but also frees a few of the girls (traditional procurers of water) to go to school (17). What the US family can take for granted, the play drives home, is the reliable infrastructure that equitably delivers clean and safe water to their communities and homes, even during a water crisis. But this complacency blinds them (and, by extension, us) to the dangers of the commodification of water, dangers Abebe has already experienced firsthand, through the deaths of his mother and siblings from water-borne disease. When Abebe hears news from his stepbrother Seyoum that a World Bank-funded mega-dam is coming to his village, Pickle sees it as a positive development, but Abebe understands immediately that it will wrest local control of a vital resource from the community. In virtually the next breath, Pickle announces the "good news" that a "water bottling plant's finally gonna go through! Jobs!" a development that Abebe presciently sees as *"[t]errible news!"* not only because of the "[t]ons of plastic waste! Tons of fuel to deliver! Minimal health testing!" but also because it will deed ownership rights of the town's beautiful public spring to a private corporation (23). Similar stories of the privatization of water and the cost to local communities are threaded throughout the play, leading our attention back and forth from familiar locations to far-off places, as we learn of people struggling to maintain access to the water commons in Mississippi, Ethiopia, Tennessee, Cambodia, Russia, and Brazil. What connects Abebe's village, Pickle's Maryland suburb, and all of these other places is the insidious ideology that pits jobs and development against the environment: even toward the end of the play, when the environmental and economic consequences of the Nestlé bottling plant have become patently clear (diesel exhaust and noise pollution from the trucks, the disappearance of local waterways and wetlands, and the paucity of full-time, stable employment provided), Pickle and her family continue to remain oblivious to the dangerous slippery slope toward private ownership of water that is happening not only in far-flung spots of the globe, but also close to home.

The commodification of water is not only a loss of a public commons affecting health, communities, livelihoods, and quality of life; it is also, the play argues, a spiritual loss, a loss of a conduit to the divine. The play links the human need and "right" to water to our spiritual sustenance, as Abebe performs "rites" of water on the converted. Abebe is studying to be a Christian preacher until he concludes that his knowledge as a water ecologist is perhaps the more crucial skill in his homeland. But in America, he is intent on "saving...Americans" (58). Returning to a crick in Tennessee in which he baptized his first American converts, Abebe finds that the water has dried up, and recognizes that the commodification of water has done irrevocable physical and spiritual damage to the soul of the land, just as it has in his homeland: "You cannot cross the same river twice. The first time I crossed, there *was* the wide crick, waist deep. And I baptized them, two new converts receiving Christ, a *miracle!* But when I returned to the crick to baptize H.J., when I returned to the miracle.... Gone" (84). The play reminds us that in nearly all faiths water quenches both body and soul; that the rivers of Ethiopia – the Jordan and the Nile – are the mythic nascent waters of civilization; and that water is the unique miracle that makes all life possible. While the play's argument for water as a God-given right asserted by all faiths may seem frail in the face of ecological/economic practicalities, the inclusion of the long-standing spiritual significance of water becomes an invitation to consider larger ethical questions, such as the "right" of "creation" to maintain the integrity of its geologic and ecological processes, and the ways in which human cultural identities – including spiritual identities – are rooted in the nonhuman domain.

Like *Cool Dip*, E.M. Lewis's *Song of Extinction* (2009) provides an intimate and personal exploration of transnational ecological connections. Weaving together such disparate and far-flung elements as the Khmer Rouge, the Bolivian Rainforest, a family coping with cancer, and the transformational power of music, Lewis personalizes the scientific concept of "extinction" in ways that the poster-species campaigns of environmental organizations have been trying to do for a generation. In the play's transnational reach, the potential loss of species and ecosystems, the loss of a young mother to cancer, and the loss of family, community, and culture to genocide enfold us in a pan-geographic loss. These losses, the play argues, are not separate; and they may share more than heartache. Extinction, the character Khim Phan explains, is hard to grasp because it is an abstraction, depersonalized by data and rates of loss over time. But Khim, a high-school science teacher who fled the genocidal killing fields of Cambodia's Khmer Rouge, understands something of extinction. Khim tries to console his student Max, a 14-year-old boy whose mother is dying. Through juxtaposition, the play illustrates that while geopolitical in its causes, species extinction, like genocide, is as personal as losing your mother to cancer; its heartbreak is without equivocation; there is no turning back the clock; no second chance; it is an event that forever changes the landscape of life.

Lewis's play not only encourages us to experience connections between genocide and species extinction on an emotional level, it also helps us to see how skewed and unjust economic priorities contribute to devastating ecological imbalances. Max's father Ellery, a rainforest biologist, sees the imminent extinction of his beloved subspecies of *Dynastinae strategus* as the consequence of violence to the land propelled by political and economic pressures, and accuses Gill Morris, the land developer who wants to deforest the bug's habitat, of "genocide." Gill gives what many would recognize as a "rational" response: the loss of the insect is overweighed by the gain of much-needed employment for Bolivian workers and an "infusion of 7.9 million dollars into the Bolivian economy, not to mention what it will do for ours" (16). Throwing Ellery's words back at him, Gill points out that "[t]he word 'genocide' refers to people.... You want to put two hundred fifty Bolivian workers out of a job and let them starve to death because of a bug?" (14). From Gill's short-term economic perspective, the cost–benefit calculation leads to an obvious, pro-deforestation conclusion. Ellery, on the other hand, recognizes the long-term consequences of Gill's actions: deforestation will lead not only to the extinction of his "bug" and to the unintended and unanticipatable effects of its removal from the ecosystem, but if managed as unsustainably as Gill and his like do, it will eventually lead to our own extinction as well. As in *Heroes and Saints* and *Cool Dip*, the illogic of purchasing jobs at the cost of the environment and the false opposition that capitalism posits between sustainability and profit are here thrown into stark relief.

The emotional center of the play is Lily, Max's mother, diagnosed with stomach cancer and, more than any other character in the play, facing her own imminent extinction. We first meet her in a scene in which she is given less than a week to live. Lily is the very real, unique, and irreplaceable woman who brought Max into the world, and a symbol of what connects us to every other species on earth. We are born of biological stuff, we share that stuff with everything else, we get it from our parents and pass it to our children. Eve Kosovsky Sedgwick has urged a loosening of the anti-essentialist rhetoric in feminist theory, and this return to the material has opened renewed conversations about the kinds of perspectives that the site of motherhood affords.[22] Motherhood can be seen as an organizing index not only of individual experience, but of community and of transglobal events such as dislocation, diaspora, war, environmental injustice, and the ways in which late capitalism rides on the backs of women, children, and families worldwide. Sedgwick's invocation is of particular significance in the ecodramaturgy of works such as *Song of Extinction* and Chantal Bilodeau's *Sila* (2011), in which mothers figure as central characters. An ecodramaturgical view focuses on the ways motherhood is contingent in an ecologically damaged and dislocated world. But the project of motherhood is not only an index of local and global–ecological health, it is also a strategy deployed in the face of destruction/dissolution. Both plays reconfigure motherhood as a *verb*, as a site of agency in the world, a kind of work that extends to characters that are not necessarily woman nor human. As we saw in *Heroes and Saints*, motherhood can be a site from which to expose the local/global forces of catastrophic change (cancer, war, pesticides, global warming). But motherhood also represents a mode of individual and collective action with the potential for *response* to such ecological challenges. In *Song of Extinction*, science teacher Khim takes up the task of parenting Max through his mother's death, and Ellery must ultimately put parenting his own lost child over the high stakes of his scientific research. Each of these plays reaches beyond the bounds and bonds of mother–child relationships to implicate global–ecological forces that play havoc with the project of motherhood and to demonstrate how mothering/ motherhood across both species and gender constitutes an ecological project that radically subverts and reorganizes the priorities of late western capitalism and the globalized marketplace.

Interspecies connections and queer ecology

Motherhood as both sociopolitical–ecological site and radical strategy are evident in Bilodeau's *Sila*, which, to an even greater extent than *Song of Extinction*, focuses on the ways human and animal cultures are co-habitational and ecologically related. Two of *Sila*'s central characters are a mother and daughter polar bear; their story is counterposed against that of a First Nations Canadian family of grandmother Leanna, a climate change activist, her daughter Veronica, a poet, and Veronica's teenaged son, Samuel. In the course of the play, both families suffer devastating loss: the polar bear Mama loses her Daughter when they are cut off from the land by cracking ice and forced to swim further than the Daughter's endurance can sustain, and Leanna loses Samuel to suicidal abuse of drugs brought on by the stresses imposed on the native community from loss of identity and sense of place. Bilodeau stages generational grief in the making, on the part of both humans and bears who suffer from the accidental impact and random violence of changes set in motion by human colonization not only of each other but also of the nonhuman world. As an example of "theatre of species," *Sila* invites us to reconceive our connection to other animals through our shared embodiment and shared experience, offering an expanded under-standing of relationship, responsibility, family, community, and home.[23]

Parenting – especially "mothering" – is a central concern in *Sila*. In particular, the play demands that we confront the question of how to teach and prepare our children to navigate a disintegrating world. The mothers – Leanna, Veronica, Bear – ought to do more than mothers have done in the past, not only teaching their children the old ways, but also helping them cope with a world that is breaking apart – underfoot and under paw – families and ice flows, climate patterns, cultural certainties. But the mothers fail. The depressing truth of Bilodeau's play is that our children stand to inherit unknown challenges of devastating proportions, and we are collectively not only in deep denial but also immobilized by the magnitude of what we burden them with. *Sila* dramatizes this condition by opposing Veronica's sudden loss of speech upon hearing of her son's death with Mama bear's eloquent grief. As if Veronica's voice could be transferred to Mama, the polar bear grieves in a tongue that can touch us: "Where did I go wrong, how did I fail, what did I do, what didn't I do, why didn't I see this, why didn't I prevent this...."[24] Like Inuit artists who put human parts inside animals,[25] Bilodeau has put English text in the bear's voice; it is a transference of skin and exchange of breath, giving voice to the wail of all mothers, all parents, who have lost a child – or stand to lose an entire generation of children – to unfathomable changes that crack and tear at the structures that sustained their lives. *Sila* exposes the ecological stakes of motherhood, imaginatively extending its sociopolitical valence beyond the embodied connection between one female and her offspring to the next generation of all species on the planet. Demonstrating how "theatre of species" underlines the shared contingencies that impact humans and nonhumans in equal and unpredictable ways, *Sila* presents the problem of preparing our offspring for the unknown effects of climate change as a shared challenge for all species.

The ecodramaturgy of *Sila* resonates within a tradition of feminist writing that puts focus on embodied and emplaced ways of being and knowing. Much as early radical feminist writing invited women to confront shared experiences of the female body, in paralleling the pain experienced by the bear mother and the human mother, the play asks us to embrace the commonality of human and nonhuman flesh and suffering. And by siting the action both literally and figuratively "on thin ice," in a landscape cracking and shifting under the pressures of climate change, the play evokes indigenous and *mestizo* understandings of place as inextricable with both being and knowing. Gloria Anzaldúa has theorized *la frontera* as a place where identity is mutable, continually negotiated, fluid. Unlike a fixed boundary that divides nations and species, *la frontera* makes no claims that exclude, but instead draws connections that include and embrace.[26] In *Sila*, the Baffin Island region appears as a new kind of *frontera*, one that is permeable to Inuit, Western (Canadian–American–German), scientific, governmental, animal, and mythic/spiritual realms. As a result, the play pushes our sense of intertribal and international boundaries beyond ethnic, civic, and national identities. Its *frontera* defies attempts to draw a bright, hard line not only between the "us" and "them" of indigenous versus white, colonized versus colonizer, or Canadian versus German, but also between the "us" and "them" of human versus nonhuman. For the Mama and Daughter polar bears constitute a kind of metaphorical nation within the play's *frontera*, and as Mama teaches her daughter the ways of their people, it becomes clear that they are members of a larger community with rights to the place they call home, whose needs and interests imperfectly converge with other inhabitants of that place (a point that is cogently made when the two bears kill and eat a hunter because melting ice has made it impossible for them to hunt the seals that are their usual prey).

The play thus draws an analogy between the "rights" of bears (and, by extension, other nonhumans) and those of historically disenfranchised humans (e.g., women, minorities, immigrants), a move that pulls the play into the orbit of queer ecology, which theorizes just such an expansion of the definition of personhood. Morton observes that "[t]reating nonhumans as people is a political choice that faces the vulnerability and responsibility towards other beings in which we are entangled."[27] *Sila*'s positioning of polar bears as a "nation" among others competing for resources in a shifting and changing borderland – where shared DNA is subjected to the evolutionary pressures of environmental change – is an example of the queer ecological use of theatre to honor our ethical and moral responsibility to, and interdependence with, the whole extant range of "people" – beyond just the human variety.

Directly engaging with Morton's work on queer ecology, Shonni Enelow's play *Carla and Lewis* (2011) similarly horizontalizes relations between humans and the nonhuman world.[28] In both content and form, *Carla and Lewis* grapples with the challenge of making art about climate change. The plot centers on the efforts of an art curator, Elsa, to create a performance/art installation called "The Amina Project" that is aimed at raising public awareness about climate change through a series of art-mediated Skype conversations between gallery-goers in the United States and climate refugees in Bangladesh, among them "Amina," a victim of climate-change-induced flooding featured in the *New York Times*. Elsa recruits Kamna Banerjee, "a feminist mixed media artist who lives in Dhaka," for the Bangladesh side of the installation, and Carla and Lewis, two American artists recently returned from Berlin, for the New York side.[29] Environment pressures evolution, Darwin tells us, and *Carla and Lewis* seeks to theatricalize those pressures and show how, in an age of climate change, humans are no different from other animals in the need to adapt and change, or surrender to extinction. Thus, a central figure in the play is the mud landscape, which is continually morphing and evolving, birthing things and beings ("crocodiles, malaria, rotting wood, rats preening like birds, dead fish, computer parts, trees that are illegal immigrants, Amina") out of its ooze as it encroaches into the apartment building where Elsa and her friend, a scientist studying the effects of climate change on the DNA of water fleas, both live (1). Presented as both a physical reality and as a landscape of the artists' creation, the play's ecosystem blurs distinctions between reptiles, mammals, viruses, plants, objects, and humans, democratizing and horizontalizing their status and thereby pulling us toward what Morton describes as "the ecological thought": "a practice and a process of becoming fully aware of how human beings are connected with other beings – animal, vegetable, or mineral."[30]

The mud invading Elsa's and the scientist's apartments is also an absurd analog that allows the play to explore the psychology of denial that obstructs action on climate change. When Carla and Lewis first come to Elsa's apartment, she explains, "Over the summer there was construction and they ruined the insulation. I've called and called but the landlord won't fix it…. It's a little damp, I know. It's just the insulation. I'm working on getting it fixed" (11). Both Elsa and the scientist are in denial about the scope of their living situation – their apartment floors are "covered in mud," but instead of taking direct action to solve the problem, they just keep calling the landlord fruitlessly. The refusal of anyone "in charge" to address the rising mud is a microcosm of humanity's collective inability to take responsibility for the problems it has caused. Through this substitution of the hyperlocal for the global, the play makes clear how illogical and ineffectual our response to climate change and its effects has been.

In addition, by siting the mud invasion within the walls of Elsa's apartment, the play literally brings home the displacements and habitat losses that climate change has already begun to impose on humans and nonhumans alike. No one would willingly live in an apartment with a floor covered in mud and a landlord who refuses to take care of the problem, unless there is "nowhere else to go," a dilemma faced by climate refugees of all species. Elsa still has a choice to move. That choice is not available to climate refugees like Amina (who notes that "we're all poor people. We don't have anywhere to go" [1]), to the water flea that is the subject of the scientist's research, or – thinking beyond the confines of the play itself – to the polar bear, the poster-animal of climate change, also often described as having "nowhere else to go."[31] The action of the play is repeatedly punctuated by:

Actor 1: HUMANS! LEAVE YOUR HOMES!...

(The weather changes). (4)

But where (some) humans *can* "leave their homes" in response to changing weather, many other species cannot. Trees and other flora do not displace readily: a species of flora as a whole might be displaced to new areas if the climate changes, but individuals of that species will likely perish when their traditional ecosystem no longer provides the conditions for their survival. Individual fauna have more mobility, but they also often occupy highly special-ized niches within a given (climate-dependent) ecosystem: as the play high-lights, many keystone species (like the *Daphnia pulicaria* the scientist studies, which is a keystone predator) are extremely vulnerable to changes in tempera-ture and climate, with wholly unpredictable consequences. The scientist warns: "What happens to the Daphnia? What happens? I'll tell you what happens. THE WORLD ENDS.... That's it. And there's nothing we can do about it except take a front row seat and watch it expire!" (19). At a certain point, the play makes clear, leaving our homes will not save humans either, even those of us with the mobility that "first-world" income and technology provides. "We" cannot escape the effects of climate change any more than polar bears or water fleas or impoverished Bangladeshis can.

Carla and Lewis thus stages queer ecology's understanding of human/nonhuman interconnectedness by shining light on the many ways we share transglobal contingencies with other things and beings. At the same time, the play also directs our attention, as present, living, breathing audience members, to our own imbrication in and with our environment. In the opening of the play, an Actor (who is also the Landscape) greets audience members by asking about both their macro-interaction with the environment on the trip to the theatre – "Did you take a train to this theatre? Did you see any rats?... Did you walk to this theatre?" – and their micro-interactions: "Were you able to remove enough oxygen from the air? Did you feel the vapor saturation of the air? Did your breathing make you lose too much water?... Did the passive diffusion of gases to your heart provide enough for total circulation?" (2–3). Then, in the next direct address to the audience, the Actor underscores our enmeshment in our immediate environs, situating us first as humans whose consciousness sets us apart from nonhuman others but then almost immediately highlighting the extent to which, as Morton notes, "[w]e have others – rather, others have us – literally under our skin."[32]

> Hello people, hello kind, wise, rational, self-aware people, welcome to this play. This is the scene in which we introduce the world and its landscape, which is of course this theatre: its flora and fauna, its technological machinations, and its natural and man-made ornamentation. Over here, you see, there is a stairway, otherwise known as risers, on which there are approximately 80 metal chairs. The metal is aluminum, the silvery white member of the boron group of chemical elements. It is the most common element in the earth's crust. Plants ingest it in their food, the soil, as do animals, who ingest plants. You ingest it. (4)

The idea that what constitutes the chairs we are on is also "in" us should give us pause to consider how much of the environment that we traverse, use, ignore, exploit, and pollute is also always-already in the process of being incorporated into us (just as one day each of us will become part of it), and to recognize that we cling at our peril to the notion that humanity and its culture is separate from what we imagine as "Nature."

Ecodramaturgical work by women playwrights is as diverse and varied as the places and ecological situations from which their stories have emerged. Space has not permitted us to treat all of the plays by contemporary women playwrights whose work engages ecological issues, including (to name but a few) works like Marie Clements's *Burning Vision,* which invokes indigenous perspectives to press environmental injustices beyond the human; Anne Galjour's *Alligator Tales,* which abounds with the use of animal life to foreground interspecies concerns and contingencies; Caryl Churchill's *Far Away,* which ends with an interspecies war that, in its inclusive absurdity, renders nonsensical any conviction that humans are separate from or superior to the nonhuman world (or that culture is somehow separable from nature); C. Denby Swanson's *Atomic Farmgirl,* which brings to life the story of an American town poisoned by nuclear testing; Emma Adams's *Ugly,* which depicts a post-climate-change world starkly divided into ecological winners and losers; and Catherine Banks's *Bone Cage,* which draws parallels between the stripping of the land and the sapping of a community's spirit.[33] These plays, in addition to the works we have discussed in this chapter, invite us to consider theatre's vital role in making visible untold stories of locally felt environmental and health impacts of a globalized economy; in resituating motherhood as both a site of ecological interconnection and strategic response to the juggernaut of eco-hostile global development; and in making vibrantly present the ways in which land and person, human and nonhuman, beings and things are permeable and enmeshed in one another. Rupturing a failing world view that has enforced (and policed) a cognitive separation between mind and body, human and animal, and nature and culture through a taxonomy of difference that asserts the primacy of the human, these plays ask us to consider not only our interdependence with other species, but also the very foundations of thinking and feeling on which we have heretofore based that primacy.

Notes

1 The term "ecodramaturgy" originally appeared in Theresa J. May, "Kneading Marie Clements' *Burning Vision*," *Canadian Theatre Review* 144 (Fall 2010): 5–12.

2 EMOS was cofounded by Theresa J. May and Larry K. Fried, was hosted by Humboldt State University in 2004, the University of Oregon in 2009, and Carnegie Mellon University in 2012, and will be hosted by the University of Nevada, Reno, in 2015. See *http://emosfestival.wordpress.com/* (accessed 26 February 2013).

3 Second-wave environmentalism refers to the environmental movement of the late twentieth century, which has been characterized by an increasing awareness of the magnitude of human impact on earth's ecological systems, as well as the interdependency of nature and culture. See, for example, Richard Gottlieb, *Forcing the Spring: The Transformation of the American Environmental Movement* (Washington, D.C.: Island Press, 1993). Comparatively, first-wave environmentalism refers to the early-twentieth-century wilderness movement associated with John Muir, Gifford Pinchot, and others, and leading to the conservation movement of early and mid-century.

4 Karen J. Warren, introduction, *Ecofeminism: Women, Culture, Nature*, ed. Warren (Bloomington: Indiana University Press, 1997), xii.

5 Karen J. Warren, "Taking Empirical Data Seriously," in *Ecofeminism*, 4.

6 Timothy Morton, "Guest Column: Queer Ecology," *PMLA* 125, no. 2 (2010): 274.

7 Ibid., 277.

8 Timothy Morton, *The Ecological Thought* (Cambridge: Harvard University Press, 2010), 74. For an expanded discussion of the theatrical implications of queer ecology, see Wendy Arons, "Queer Ecology/Contemporary Plays," *Theatre Journal* 64, no. 4 (December 2012): 565–82.

9 See, for example, Arons, "Queer Ecology/Contemporary Plays"; Theresa J. May, "Beyond Bambi: Toward a Dangerous Ecocriticism," *Theatre Topics* 17, no. 2 (September 2007): 95–110; and Theresa J. May, "Greening the Theatre: Taking Ecocriticism from Page to Stage," *Journal of Interdisciplinary Studies* 7, no. 1 (Fall 2005): 84–103.

10 Cherríe Moraga, *Heroes and Saints*, in *Contemporary Plays by Women of Color: An Anthology*, ed. Kathy A. Perkins and Roberta Uno (New York: Routledge, 1996): 230–61. See also May, "Beyond Bambi."

11 Linda Margarita Greenburg, "Learning from the Dead: Wounds, Women, and Activism in Cherríe Moraga's *Heroes and Saints*," *MELUS* 34, no. 1 (2009): 166.

12 Ibid., 172–3.

13 Vandana Shiva, *Water Wars: Privatization, Pollution, and Profit* (Cambridge, MA: South End Press, 2002), xv.

14 Lynn Nottage, *Ruined* (New York: Theatre Communications Group, 2009), 8. For all plays discussed, initial citations appear in the endnotes and subsequent references are given parenthetically in the text.

15 Kate Whoriskey, introduction, *Ruined*, by Lynn Nottage (New York: Theatre Communications Group, 2009), xi.

16 Ibid.

17 See Chris Gaylord, "Conflict minerals: Genocide in your gadgets?" *Christian Science Monitor*, 24 February 2011, available at: *http://www.csmonitor.com/Innovation/Responsible-Tech/2011/0224/Conflict-minerals-Genocide-in-your-gadgets* (accessed 15 April 2013).

18 Jane Bennett, *Vibrant Matter: A Political Ecology of Things* (Durham, NC: Duke University Press, 2010), 13.

19 Shiva, *Water Wars*, ix.

20 Ibid., xi.

21 Kia Corthron, *A Cool Dip in the Barren Saharan Crick* (New York: Samuel French, 2010), 10, 8.

22 See Eve Kosovsky Sedgwick, *Touching Feeling* (Durham, NC: Duke University Press, 2003).

23 On "theatre of species," see Una Chaudhuri, "The Silence of the Polar Bears: Performing (Climate) Change in the Theater of Species," in *Readings in Performance and Ecology*, ed. Wendy Arons and Theresa J. May (New York: Palgrave Macmillan, 2012), esp. 50.

24 Chantal Bilodeau, *Sila* (unpublished play, 2011), 64.

25 The origins and meanings of such "transformation pieces" in Inuit art are complex; often artwork depicting an animal becoming human (or vice versa) is linked to shamanism. See *http://www.iadb.org/EXR/cultural/canada/canada19.htm* and *http://www.inuitartzone.com/inuit_art_transformations_s/50.htm* (accessed 3 May 2013)

26 See Gloria Anzaldúa, *Borderlands/La Frontera: The New Mestiza* (San Francisco: Aunt Lute Books, 2007), Ch. 1 and 7.

27 Timothy Morton, "Ecologocentrism: Unworking Animals," *SubStance* 37, no. 3 (2008): 84.

28 The play emerged out of "The Ecocide Project," a collaborative "research theatre" endeavor spearheaded by Una Chaudhuri at New York University. Una Chaudhuri, "The Ecocide Project's *Carla and Lewis*," Program Note, 2011: 7.

29 Shonni Enelow, *Carla and Lewis* (unpublished play, January 2013), 1.

30 Morton, *The Ecological Thought*, 7.

31 See Chaudhuri, "Silence of the Polar Bears," 46.

32 Morton, "Guest Column," 277.

33 For discussion of the ecodramaturgy of *Burning Vision* and *Alligator Tales*, see May, "Kneading Marie Clements' *Burning Vision*" and May, "Greening the Theatre"; on the "ecocidal free-for-all" at the end of Churchill's *Far Away*, see Una Chaudhuri, "Different Hats," *Theater* 33, no. 3 (2003): 133.

Part III
Genres

12 Making the Bones Sing: The Feminist History Play, 1976–2010

Katherine E. Kelly

> [T]heatre, for me, is the perfect place to "make" history... because so much of African-American history has been unrecorded, dismembered, washed out, one of my tasks as a playwright is to... locate the ancestral burial ground, dig for bones, find bones, hear the bones sing, write it down.
>
> –Suzan-Lori Parks[1]

The dramatic search for a past

This essay will attempt to show an affinity between the thinking of Western feminist historiographers from the 1970s forward and the creative work of selected feminist playwrights who have used the drama to "make the bones sing." Both of these communities – writers of history and writers of drama – recognize the living nature of the historical record and feel an urgency to reform the pasts assigned to women. Historiographers use theoretical and conceptual language to conduct their work, while playwrights use imagery and embodiment. In spite of their different languages, styles, and media, feminist historians and dramatists share a desire to recover the silenced histories of women. In juxtaposing later twentieth-century models of feminist historiography and drama from England, the United States, and Canada, this essay documents expressions of a felt need to reimagine women's past lives as a first step toward living a more just present and future.

This selective survey covers a sampling of dramas produced in a handful of geographic locations to document an ongoing, locally specific struggle to write and perform women's pasts. It also pays tribute to the promise of dramatic performance for implicating a community in that struggle, for inviting it to witness both the search for and the discovery of a revised history. The drama offers an alternative or supplement to narrative history for those driven to look back; it brings an audience along to serve as fellow-seekers or, at the very least, sympathetic onlookers to the framing of a collective memory. Historiography, on the other hand, charts the conceptual ground rules for avoiding the pitfalls of history-writing so that revised histories do not substitute one kind of blindness for another. From the

1970s forward, these two kinds of efforts have proceeded simultaneously – history-making and history-performing – with each illuminating the other's motives and assumptions.

The emergence of feminist historiography and the feminist history play

In 1976, historian Joan Kelly not only revealed the hidden assumptions of traditional Western historiography but also formulated their feminist alternative. As Kelly described it, the work of feminist historians provoked a rethinking of historical periodization, categories of social analysis, and theories of social change.[2] Her influential essay "The Social Relations of the Sexes: Methodological Implications of Women's History" describes three ways in which feminist historiography had begun to reshape historical thinking: (1) women's history began to emerge as distinct from that of men; (2) some historians claimed that women comprise a social category by virtue of their sex and that historical change must therefore address changing relations between the sexes; and (3) some feminist historians identified property relations as determining the sexual division of labor and the sexual order. Under patriarchy, they argued, women function as the property of men in producing and raising children.[3] For Kelly, the promise of a feminist historiography extended to remaking the entire enterprise of writing history, some of whose basic assumptions were proving to be either limited or flatly wrong.

While historians and theorists were framing new assumptions for writing women's history in academic journals and books, mid-1970s playwrights on both sides of the Atlantic and on other continents, notably socialist-feminist Caryl Churchill in England, began experimenting with new methods for staging women in historical time. Churchill created two history plays in 1976, *Vinegar Tom* (with Monstrous Regiment) and *Light Shining in Buckinghamshire* (with Joint Stock).[4] Anticipating what would eventually become Churchill's signature use of double time, a device for setting the past in dialogue with the present, *Vinegar Tom* sets the action in the mid-seventeenth century, but interrupts it with songs from the Edwardian music hall – structurally separating, in Brechtian fashion, the early modern treatment of witches from twentieth-century commentary on that treatment. In *Light Shining in Buckinghamshire*, Churchill and her collaborators revisited another period of critical change – the years during and after the Second Civil War – as narrated by Marxist historian Christopher Hill.[5] The play takes its title and action from the Digger movement that sought to redistribute land to those willing to work it for sustenance. Ranters, a second contingent in the play, proclaimed all Christians equal through the saving power of grace. Both the Diggers' and Ranters' attempts to create a more just world fail by the play's close. *Light Shining* ends inconclusively, with the Ranter Claxton reflecting: "There's an end of outward preaching now. An end of perfection. There may be a time."[6] Churchill meets the revolution's failure head-on in the play, while leaving an opening at the conclusion for a renewed effort to change the economic and political system shown to have harmed so many.

In *Cloud Nine*, first performed and published in 1979,[7] Churchill shifts the focus from the almost-revolution in *Light Shining* to the intersection of imperialism and sexual politics by using the device of two time periods, as she did in *Vinegar Tom*. In act 1, set in the late nineteenth century, she uses farce devices, such as gender and racial role-switching and doubling, comical songs, and direct audience address, to present the potentially serious though in performance hilarious premise that colonial and sexual oppression operate in similar ways. Her innovation in staging history in this play emerges from her rejection of linear, date-focused history in favor of a thematically driven political historiography, enriched by comedy as an ironizing prism for viewing the past. This approach extends to the time-jump between acts 1 and 2. Churchill treats chronology irreverently in this jump, warning the reader/spectator: "Act Two takes place in London in 1979. But for the characters it is twenty-five years later."[8] Placing Victorian mother Betty in the context of consciousness-raising London of the late 1970s focuses both the potential and the failures of 1970s-style sexual liberation. While the performative displays of sexual role-switching and cross-dressing from act 1 disappear here in favor of earnest (and endless) self-exploration and self-seeking, occasional moments of history pierce the characters' fog of self-development, as when a dead soldier (Lin's brother?) visits the séance held by Edward, Lin, and Victoria. Here, historical reality enters suddenly as a ghost and disappears just as quickly. By the act's close, the hilarity of act 1 has been replaced with the confusion and delusion of act 2, but Victorian Betty promises hope for the future as she makes a friend of her son's lover.

Cloud Nine coincided with the English translation of Foucault's critique of the repressive hypothesis in *The History of Sexuality*,[9] and her treatment of sex in the play indirectly resembles his argument that Victorian sexual repression produced, rather than suppressed, a greater knowledge of sexuality out of its will to know, name, and consequently control it. If, as Foucault argued, attempts to "know" sexuality have gradually expanded since the eighteenth century, then Churchill isolated in the later Victorian period a significant moment of such expansion in the emergence of late-Victorian sexologists, and mapped it on the colonial family, a microcosm of empire. But Foucault's usefulness was being questioned by late 1980s feminists. If power constituted the subject, if Foucault's historical method of genealogy assumes that identity categories are created by multiple discourses, they asked, then how can individuals or identity groups be imagined to resist, reform, or resituate their relationship to power? In *Cloud Nine*'s figuring of this dilemma, the key image is the blur or the identity-in-transition. Churchill's uses of parody and irony signal her characters' resistance to the determining force of power. The dynamic characters in *Cloud Nine*, most obviously Edward and Betty, travel between identities, and in that way they can be imagined to elude power.

Kelly's powerful challenge to traditionally male-focused historiography found expression in Churchill's feminist history plays. History told from women's, especially from working-class or plebeian women's, points of view creates a past sometimes overlapping with, but often distinct from, that of men. Historical change as represented by the brief ascendancy of Diggers, Ranters, and millennialists during the failed Civil War includes a changed relation between the sexes, a brief period of reciprocity and mutual exchange after which patriarchy resumed its hold on history. As a socialist-feminist, Churchill took care to show the mutually reinforcing norms of private ownership and patriarchy, temporarily dismantled by digger takeovers of discarded spaces and the village commons. The vulnerability of older, single women in *Vinegar Tom* – women without the protection of property and male sponsorship – drives home the root causes of witch hysteria in "poverty, humiliation and prejudice."[10] In answer to the celebrated question "Did women have a Renaissance?,"[11] Churchill and Kelly both presented a grim portrait of the lives led by ordinary women during the period that has traditionally been celebrated as the pinnacle of Western achievement and the flowering of Western art.

Rediscovering race in feminist historiography and the history play

By the 1980s, a criticism had been launched within the US feminist community by women of color, identifying white feminists' failure to see their distinct reality. In 1988, Elizabeth Spelman published *Inessential Woman: Problems of Exclusion in Feminist Thought*, in which she warned against "an additive analysis of the various elements of [women's] identity" by which gender oppression takes precedence over oppressions of race and class.[12] Spelman's argument for the intersection of racism and sexism asked that feminists first set aside claims that one form of oppression is more fundamental than another, such as the claim that "sexism predates racism" or that "sexism is the cause of racism."[13] She suggested thinking about these two forms of oppression not as separate burdens, but as distinct and interlocking experiences. Most importantly, the sexism experienced by white women is qualitatively different from that experienced by, for example, black women, who share the experience of racism as well as racial pride with black men. White feminist historians in the United States could no longer presume to speak for all women.

A critical consensus began to emerge in the 1990s, claiming the triple role of race, class, and gender in understanding women's histories as a new feminist orthodoxy. Black feminists in the United States and elsewhere were developing their own feminist languages and traditions, drawing on black writers, theologians, artists, and intellectuals to shape its expression. In the theatre, black feminist writers and performers began to tell forgotten stories of their past and to present onstage the conditions that had led to their present situation. One such artist, actress/playwright Anna Deavere Smith, played back to audiences the words used by those directly involved in recent violent racial conflicts in US cities. Smith's series of one-woman docudramas, collectively called "On the Road: A Search for American Character," captured moments in the American landscape where American character(s) manifested themselves. Her docudramas qualify as "historical" in the sense that they attempt to *make* history, to use the subjects' own words to create a comprehensive record of viewpoints at conflict in the present, whose origins and unfolding might otherwise become distorted by what Robert Sherman refers to in the play as the "lousy language" used to think about race in the United States.[14]

For Smith, neither performance nor documentation is static: "The spirit of acting is the *travel* from the self to the other.... the search for character is constantly in motion. It is a quest that moves back and forth between the self and the other" (xxvi–xxvii). Smith made Churchill's blur a foundation of her method. In *Fires in the Mirror* (performed in 1992, published in 1993), she reinvents the history play as a series of monologues from interviews with participants in violent outbreaks of racial conflict – in the work discussed here, the black–Jewish conflict that followed the death of a 7-year-old Caribbean American boy in Crown Heights, Brooklyn, and the retaliatory death of a young Jewish scholar, Yankel Rosenbaum.

Smith's one-woman shows reveal clearly how a performance of citizens' words through the body of an actor/intermediary offers an account and an experience of history unavailable through other media. Her method for capturing history relies on repeating a series of participants' stories of what they did and saw during the race riots. In the case of *Fires in the Mirror*, she first interviewed a cross-section of people involved in the Crown Heights racial riots and then performed the resulting monologues herself, using their words. As the performer, she does not mimic her subjects, but presents herself *"as an empty vessel, a repeater"* (xxv), and they emerge in her performance of their unique use of words and their unique enunciation. The ethical stance taken by Smith charges her with a responsibility not only to transmit her subjects faithfully but also to capture their negotiation of the peculiarly US tension of what she calls "identity in motion" (xxxiv). Smith pays careful attention to the gender performances of her subjects, even capturing a monologue in which a young, black female rapper demands respect from male rappers, only to be told by her black girlfriends that she's "Men bashin'" (37).

Smith dedicates her display of the differences separating the black and Jewish communities in *Fires* to the uneasy divisions within those communities, signaling a new awareness among feminist artists and historians of their own potential blindness to the workings of power at those places where race, gender, class, and ethnicity intersect. The kaleidoscope of monologues in Smith's drama discourages a single interpretation of wrong or justice; instead, the monologues encourage an awareness of the multiplicity of events and their perception, preventing both closure and ethical certainty. The only certainty to emerge from the production is the need to witness the viewpoints of the conflict's principal actors.[15]

Suzan-Lori Parks's surrealist history drama *The America Play* (written 1990–93, performed 1994) pokes holes in accounts of Abraham Lincoln by playing up the absences and silences in US history. Where Smith makes history through her multi-vocal recording of citizens' (mis)understandings of a racially divisive event, Parks pulls apart a constellation of defining moments in US race history (often clustered around the figure of Lincoln), exposing contradictions, gaps, lies, and holes in a record traditionally represented as a full account of a series of known causes and known effects. Parks's history is not that of white America, but the collective past of African Americans – a deep history, characterized by silence and absence – a "hole." Her characters, represented as a family, consequently find themselves obsessed with history, with forging a link to the national past. The link takes different forms for each of them. For "The Foundling Father," the patriarch of the family, the link is embodied by acting. He makes his living by reenacting Lincoln's assassination scene in an amusement park known as "The Great Hole of History." Patrons pay a penny for the privilege of playing the part of John Wilkes Booth, entering a darkened room, selecting a pistol, and shooting "Lincoln" in the head while shouting an epitaph attributed to Booth ("Sic semper tyrannis!") or another of their choosing. Also called "The Lesser Known," the father pegs his identity and his livelihood to performing the hero he resembles. For his wife Lucy – named, perhaps, for the skeletal remains of one of our earliest near-human mothers, hailing from Africa – history consists of the secrets told to her by the dying. As a "Confidence," a keeper of the secrets of the dead, Lucy knows to be skeptical of history, which she has learned often amounts to a series of lies or fakeries told to boost self-importance. She consequently warns her son Brazil to respect plausibility: "Keep your story to scale."[16] Brazil's name, explained in the play as having been adopted from the Brazil nut (along with the nut's racist nickname), would also seem to refer to the country where more than a third of all African slaves arrived and where some of those slaves eventually formed secretive Maroon communities that fought back against slave owners. An African slave was thus more likely to end up in Brazil than in any other single nation, but once there, could have joined an organized resistance to slavery.

In act 2, after waiting thirty years for news of The Foundling Father, Lucy and Brazil have decided to follow him westward, where he traveled to create a replica of the eastern Great Hole amusement park (itself an "exact replica of the Great Hole of History") (174). The western Hall of Wonders displays objects from the past, including objects belonging to her former husband, now presumed dead. Lucy becomes the driving force behind creating the western version of the Great Hole, repeatedly ordering Brazil to "DIG!" (181). In this respect, and in her role as Confidence, she has assumed leadership of her family, preserving privacies and overseeing the hunt for her own past and the past of her community.

Lucy resorts to clichés though she also operates as a creative force, digging for bones and hearing the bones sing. Throughout the play, she holds a trumpet up to her ear, listening. She withholds much of what she hears from her son (and the reader/spectator), telling him only that they are "Stories too horrible tuh mention" (187). These buried stories are the unspoken, unofficial history haunting the play's surrealist language and gesture, distorting its uneasy comedy with an unmentionable legacy of suffering and horror. And they are stored, together with the dead's secrets, in Lucy's mind.

Parks's work unfolds through an aggressive blend of comedy and suppressed horror, resulting in an idiosyncratic mixture of mockery, ebullience, and dread that leaves readers and spectators in a state of confused/amused discomfort. *The America Play*, like Smith's docudramas, does not treat gender or sex oppression as a burden separate from racism; rather, its commentary on the relationship among patriarchy (and its narrative, the Great Man theory of history, by which the past amounts to the achievements of individual, uniquely powerful men), performance, and race draws attention to the overlap of race and gender as a place where power is articulated. Lucy both claims and mocks her dutiful attention to her husband, whom she calls the greatest "Faker" (impersonator) she has known: "Your Father was uh faker.... One of thuh best. There wuduhnt nobody your Fathuh couldn't do" (180). She dutifully raises her son to take up his father's family's occupation of gravedigger, assigning him the role of "Digger," but she carefully monitors his storytelling, correcting his tendency to exaggeration. She teaches her son to keep the secrets of the dead, but to doubt their truthfulness. She doubles for Parks, keeping her ear to the ground, listening for the songs sung by the bones of the dead and selecting those she will pass on.

The America Play insists on the performative quality of history-making. The Foundling Father and his family forge their identity, their story, their relationships derivatively from a series of mythic accounts of white culture, and they realize this identity through a self-parodying performance – "fakin'." In this sense, Parks's drama demonstrates a contradiction among the circular repetition of history, the elusiveness of historical truth, and the solemn role of the historian, or Confidence.

Parks has compared her writing to jazz composition, warning spectators away from expecting a linear narrative or a moral lesson. The Foundling Father impersonates (fakes) history by repeating white history in whiteface, even staging his own funeral at the play's end and reappearing on television after he dies. Lucy holds within her memory the secrets and horrors of their collective past. As a historian, she listens and gathers stories from bones; she keeps the unrepresentable stories to herself; and she honors the dead by preserving their secrets for twelve years. When the play closes, Lucy and Brazil welcome the visitors to their new Hall of Wonders, with the newest wonder – the corpse of The Foundling Father in his coffin – as an item of special interest. The play has come full circle, so that the Digger for curiosities, the Faker of Lincoln's assassination, the would-be object of emulation has himself become an object of historical curiosity. Parks's feminism speaks through her attention to race and class: Lucy was not born but made a black woman, a Confidence (by mistake), the Lesser's Lesser (by patriarchy), and the son's digging teacher (by "choice"). Like Churchill's neo-Victorian fantasy and Smith's docudrama, Parks's surrealist history makes no formal or thematic claim to telling a truth, but is instead driven by a belief that a kind of contingent truth can be revealed by negation, through the re-presenting of a search for the historical past. In this sense, Parks's history play undertakes to put on display – literally and parodically – a shared, recognizable series of past events and persons significant to the African American community, but rendered through her sardonic response to the historical distortions of racism.

Feminist history as a useable past

Feminist history has recently become available to women theatre artists and their spectators as a selective retrieval of past events that, from the vantage point of the present, opened a door – perhaps briefly – on the possibility of building a women's community. A cluster of recent feminist history plays written over the past decade has returned repeatedly to the useable past offered by the late nineteenth and early twentieth centuries as a period of possibilities – sometimes short-lived or even false, but clearly imagined and inspiring – for many groups of women.

In Lynn Nottage's *Intimate Apparel* (2001), the search for love motivates Esther, a 39-year-old African American seamstress. Loosely based on the life of her spinster great-grandmother, who moved alone to New York in 1902 and lived as a devout Christian, sewing ladies' undergarments, Nottage sets her play in a 1905 New York boarding house, where Esther sews elegant corsets for well-paying customers. When she receives a letter from George Armstrong, a young Barbadian worker on the Panama Canal who has been told about her by the deacon's son at her church, Esther shares the letter with two of her clients – one a wealthy white socialite, the other an African American entertainer/prostitute named Mayme. Soon George is declaring he will travel to New York to marry Esther. He arrives an illiterate, scruffy, and unpolished laborer, and they both find themselves disappointed. They marry nevertheless, but George soon turns to prostitutes, especially Mayme, for pleasure and distraction. When Esther realizes he has been lying to her, she leaves him and returns to her sewing machine and life as a woman who will become a single mother.

Both Esther and George had representative experiences for their time, but their stories were unlikely to be told unless at the hands of a teller who sees value in the faceless, nameless many who populated US cities in the early twentieth century. At the close of the first act, the stage directions specify that Esther and George stand downstage and "look out at the world. There is a flash – as from an old-fashioned flash camera. The sepia-toned image is captured. A projected title card appears above their heads: 'Unidentified Negro Couple, 1905.'"[17] At the end of act 2, as Esther sits alone at her sewing machine, "[t]he lights shift, creating the quality of an old sepia-toned photograph. As the lights fade, a projected title card appears about Esther's head: 'Unidentified Negro Seamstress, ca. 1905.'"[18] Nottage has chosen a publicly unexceptional though privately remarkable woman as her heroine, motivated to fill up one small corner of the black hole of history.

An urgent sense of the importance of companionship and connection underlie the play's tale. Two friendships offer striking evidence of the complex social landscape of this intimate play, the kind of complexity associated with third-wave feminism and its negotiations of postcolonial diasporas, as well as gender, class, and racial differences. Esther has become friends with a Jewish fabric merchant, with whom she shares a deep appreciation for the beauty and richness of well-made fabric and trim; and she shares her hopes and disappointments with Mayme, the prostitute who unwittingly takes her husband as a client. Both friendships are unlikely though life-sustaining; they spring not from shared experiences, but from a shared sense of beauty and imaginative sympathy. These can form the basis for feminist alliances in the face of difference.

In her 2007 history play *Age of Arousal*, Canadian playwright Linda Griffiths celebrates and revises the suffrage movement from the vantage point of a third-wave feminist at the beginning of the twenty-first century. Griffiths captures the ambivalence of contemporary white feminism when she describes the "delicious" time-travel she enjoyed while researching her play: "I've always been a bit of a Merchant-Ivory slut, dreaming my way through ... hours of ... costume drama – but I felt guilty at the same time."[19] In her play, Griffiths refuses nostalgia, however, preferring to reimagine the first wave through the revisions of the third. This contemporary play about the suffrage movement takes back and revises that movement, acknowledging lesbian love and attending to class differences that first-wave feminists have been charged with having ignored.

Age of Arousal conflates the period of the New Woman (ca. 1885) with the militant suffrage era (1906–14), treating precise chronology with a calculated irreverence typical of recent historical dramas. The play also borrows from a work of fiction, George Gissing's novel *The Odd Women* (1893), on which Griffiths loosely patterns some of the play's characters and scenes. Susan Kingsley Kent's historical analysis *Sex and Suffrage in Britain: 1860–1914* further helped Griffiths to connect the discourses of sexuality and suffrage during the period covered by her drama. In a deliberate departure from the conventions of realism, Griffiths includes a dialogue experiment she had begun in earlier plays. "Thoughtspeak," what she calls "wild, uncensored outpourings" of speech, a "verbal eruption from the depths of self" (13), occasionally erupts between conventional lines of dialogue, like spoken subtext. Thoughtspeak dislodges the spectator from an automatic identification with the characters' psychology, while framing the Victorian setting with a modern attitude. Thus in an early scene, as both Mary and Rhoda sense that their lives will change in unforeseen ways, each thinks about her tie to the other:

Mary: I've filled her head, done nefarious acts to her body –
Rhoda: Too timid to find my own body till she opened its secrets.
Mary: The icy breath of change.
Rhoda: Nothing has changed. (32)

The doubleness of thoughtspeak echoes Griffiths's hybrid style and plot, which she has described as a bridging of the avant-garde and the populist. The play's rearrangement of historical chronology offers one example of using fantasy to direct emphasis in the historical past. By conflating and even reversing New Woman events from the 1880s, such as the advent of typewriting and independent living for unmarried women, with narrated events from the later suffrage era, such as the forced feeding of imprisoned suffragists, Griffiths relegates the campaign for the vote to a heroic past and focuses her characters' energies on struggling for economic independence and sexual self-understanding, issues resonant with today's audiences.

Griffiths's characters range from ages 21 to 60, in class from upper-middle to lowest-middle, and in sex and politics from resigned spinster to advocate of free love to passionate lesbian. A solidly middle-class lesbian couple – one a veteran suffrage campaigner and 60-year-old founder of a progressive school for secretaries, the charismatic Mary Barfoot, and the other her 35-year-old lover Rhoda Nunn, a zealous, loyal, and passionate New Woman – form the hub of the play's political and erotic passions. Over Rhoda's objections, Mary agrees to train the impoverished Madden sisters – Monica, age 21, the provocative, "naturally sexual" sister whose sexuality leads her to a "revolutionary perspective" ("free lovism"); Virginia, age 40, alcoholic ex-governess who wishes to dress like a man; and Alice, age 46, a "deeply conservative" ex-governess who has resigned herself to poverty and chastity but comes to love the typewriter (23). The final character, Everard Barfoot, plays the part of a New Man, sympathetic with the New Woman's experiments though not above encouraging an affair with Monica. Everard's love for Rhoda and her attraction to him tests her dedication to her life's work for women and becomes symbolic of the play's central conflict. In rejecting marriage to Everard, Rhoda determines to devote her life to improving women's future, offering the activist's alternative to marriage. Griffiths's manipulation of the events in the forty-five-year period (1885–1930) brings the play closer to today's feminists, whose critique of the first wave it both recognizes and mitigates. Citing Germaine Greer, Griffiths slightly revises early feminist activism to appear as a practice that "allow[ed] [women's] differences dignity and prestige."[20]

In another recent history play, *Her Naked Skin* (2009), Rebecca Lenkiewicz memorializes the militant wing of the suffrage movement. Lenkiewicz was inspired by historical writing about the movement, especially Midge Mackenzie's *Shoulder to Shoulder*, a documentary account of the suffragettes and the source for the 1970s television documentary by the same title. Like Griffiths, Lenkiewicz also read novels of the period, among them Radclyffe Hall's *The Well of Loneliness* (1928), the first novel to offer a personal narrative of a lesbian love affair and the source for the lesbian romance in the play.

Her Naked Skin was the first play by a woman to premiere at the National Theatre's thousand-seat Olivier stage, a feat that attracted critical attention from conventional theatre critics and feminists, much of it mixed or tilted toward the negative. The play's critical reception illustrates the aesthetic and political pitfalls of attempting an avowedly historical feminist drama on a large stage. Critics assailed Lenkiewicz for offering too much sensational, gratuitous lesbian sex; too little suffragette history; an unbelievable "upstairs–downstairs" romance between a working-class machinist and a titled suffragette; characters without political principles; music and production values "so slick...that [they] only served to highlight the play's sterility";[21] and a title meant to titillate rather than illuminate. A small number of critics praised the production for bringing attention to the suffrage movement, for using the romance to reveal the class disparities that eroded its political efficacy, for vividly portraying the stalwart women who sacrificed for the cause, and simply for offering the first play by a woman to claim a large stage at the National.[22]

The play opens with Emily Wilding Davison preparing to attend the King's Derby of 1913, where she will proceed to throw herself in front of the king's horse as he rounds Tattenham Corner. As she exits the set en route to the race, grainy newsreel footage of the derby appears on a large screen and a booming soundtrack takes us to the corner where Davison steps out and is run over by the horse. With this documentary opening, Lenkiewicz signals that her approach to representing the suffrage era will loosely follow (albeit more closely than any of the other plays discussed here) the detailed texture of recorded history. She is not attempting a documentary, but, with the exception of *Fires in the Mirror*, she includes in her play more historically based scenes than the other works discussed. Citing the coincidence of the publication of Hall's novel,[23] Lenkiewicz decided to humanize that history, in part by developing the doomed romance of Lady Celia Cain and young machinist Eve Douglas, and in part through staging scenes of parliamentary meetings, graphic prison scenes of force-feeding, husband and wife disagreements over participation in the cause, and scenes of suffragettes discussing the costs of their participation. The romance between Eve and Celia develops in the act 1 prison scenes and is lopsided from the start. Eve is new to the movement and very young, while Celia, more experienced politically and sexually, relies on her allure as a privileged woman to draw Eve to her. It would seem that Lenkiewicz created Celia with a vague resemblance to the historical suffragette Constance Lytton, an aristocratic woman who avoided special treatment in prison by masquerading as working-class seamstress Jane Wharton. Eve and Celia together may have been inspired by Lytton's two identities. In the drama, Celia uses Eve to complete a kind of fantasy in which she can live an alternate new life outside the confines of her marriage, her title, her children, and suffragette discipline.

By the close of act 1, Celia and Eve are deeply involved in a sexual romance that Celia breaks off early in act 2 to avoid losing her title, marriage, and home. In the second act, as Celia continues to work for the movement, Eve goes on a hunger strike and is force-fed. She attempts suicide after Celia's rejection, but recovers and becomes engaged to a watchmaker. War is about to be declared and Celia has planned to return home to her husband, but when he appears she realizes that she cannot resume her married life. Earlier, Celia had confessed to her husband, "I can't change…I have tried. To make a good marriage. I just don't really know how."[24] At the play's close, however, she has been changed by her work with suffragists so that she cannot return to her old life. Lenkiewicz has not concluded the play on a triumphal note, but Celia's shift from titled wife to displaced woman predicts the positive changes that will come for women generally, both as they win the vote and as the class system weakens its hold on power.

Female sexual discovery and same-sex desire fuels another contemporary feminist history play set in the 1880s, before Freud and at the dawn of electricity: Sarah Ruhl's slyly comic *In the Next Room or the vibrator play* (2009). Written in a style described as "non-linear…realism"[25] and characterized as a "low-key" though "daring" extension of the comedy of manners,[26] Ruhl's play portrays the visit of a purportedly hysterical Mrs. Daldry to Dr. Givings, who treats her symptoms with a new electrical tool – a genital massage device that will help release the magnetic fluid in her womb by achieving a healing orgasm (or "hysterical paroxysm" in the language of the day). The doctor's wife Catherine, a frustrated and neglected woman whose husband treats her with the blind indifference of an abstracted scientist, becomes curious about the vibrator, which she can hear operating through the wall of their living room, adjacent to her husband's operating theatre. The deadpan humor resulting from the characters' decorous pursuit of symptomatic relief and from the doctor's presumption of the separation of emotion and arousal gives Ruhl's drama a hilarity that would seem out of place in any of the other plays discussed here.

The portrait of Dr. Givings wryly captures the prejudice of nineteenth-century male physicians on the subject of women's sexuality. In this sense, it resurrects early psychotherapy and sexology as disciplines that produced harmful "knowledge" of sex and gender. But the vibrator helps the patients in spite of Dr. Givings's pronouncements about its purpose. Part of the play's humor arises from the gap between the characters' scientific explanation of the device's therapeutic effects and the audience's post-Freudian dismissal of that interpretation. Act 1 concludes with the meeting of Mrs. Daldry and Mrs. Givings, who demonstrate the device for each other and unleash a force that will cause havoc in act 2.

The second act opens with the visit of Leo Irving, a young painter, to the operating theatre. Leo explains to Dr. Givings that when his Italian wife left him, his whole body turned against him, especially his eyes. No longer able to paint, he seeks a cure for his hysterical symptoms. After the doctor's assistant Annie helps him apply the Chattanooga vibrator to Leo's anal cavity, Leo experiences a paroxysm and is once again able – indeed compelled – to paint. In a series of errors echoing *A Midsummer Night's Dream*, whose fairy dust has been replaced by electric vibrations, Leo pursues and compulsively paints Elizabeth, the married African American nurse hired to breast-feed Mrs. Givings's baby, while Mrs. Daldry pursues Annie, the nurse who first helped administer the device on her, and Mr. Daldry pursues Mrs. Givings, who pursues her unresponsive husband, the doctor.

Ruhl's play treats gender, patriarchy, and race relations as comically artificial and arbitrary, with a few exceptions. Mrs. Givings, Ruhl's twenty-first-century gloss on nineteenth-century womanhood, emerges as the play's comic heroine, her energy springing from her sexual yearning and sense of adventure. She embodies the aggression of comedy by exposing hypocrisy and relentlessly pursuing love, and yet, in an abrupt shift in tone, Elizabeth describes her feelings about the Givings's infant daughter after the death of her own infant son: "When I first met [your baby] all I could think was: she is alive and Henry is not.... The more healthy your baby got, the more dead my baby became. I thought of her like a tic. I thought – fill her up and then pop! You will see the blood of my Henry underneath.... I hope every day you keep her ... you remember the blood that her milk was made from."[27] Following this speech, Mrs. Givings *"touches Elizabeth's elbow. Elizabeth pulls away and exits."*[28] The moment passes, but in this tribute to the black women who supported white middle-class mothering in the 1800s,

Ruhl's otherwise comic play somberly recalls the physical tie between black wet nurses and white children and gestures hopefully toward a shared respect between black and white women in today's world.

Throughout the play, the milk-poor Mrs. Givings is linked with gardens and fertility, and at the play's close, she breaks out of the two-room set, leading her husband to the Edenic garden where they undress each other, lie down, and make angels in the snow. Thus Ruhl recasts the middle-class white woman as a sexual-ized being unintimidated by technology and undeterred by scientific objectivity. Feminism of necessity has always had a sense of humor. Ruhl's *In the Next Room* looks at a recent moment in the history of sexual technology among the middle classes and finds in it an ironically and sometimes hysterically funny tale of female awakening, sharing, and resistance to oppression.

Conclusion

Recent feminist playwrights listen to the bones of their ancestors, hear them sing, and write it down. Knowing where to find those ancestors and trusting to recog-nize them as kindred spirits has corresponded with the intellectual work done by feminist historiographers. As a performance of the past, the feminist history play uncovers what has been hidden, straightens what has been twisted, and/or recalls what has been forgotten about the past of women's communities. A history play does not replicate the work of history writing, which records events for the purpose of answering "truthfully" the basic questions of who, what, where, and when in relation to those events; it invites the audience to know again – to undo and redo – the past in the present of performance and in the absence of the scien-tific truth claims made by official history. The mode of the history play can run the gamut from documentary accounts of events taken directly from participants' testimonies, to metaphorical interpretations of historically recorded events, to deliberately rearranged versions of "officially" recorded events, to the drama-tizing of ignored or overlooked though historically accurate events and persons. The feminist history play necessarily cuts across the grain of traditional history, which, by default, assumes the experiences of men to be normative.

In foregrounding gender, race, class, ethnicity, marital status, and sexual orientation as historically actual and significant categories of human identity and experience, the feminist history play is motivated to look under, over, and behind the official version of how events happened in the past. The long asso-ciation of history with the "real" might seem to predispose the feminist history play to adopt the conventions of realism in creating story, setting, and char-acter. However, determined to trouble the traditional telling of past events, most of the plays discussed here choose unfamiliar, experimental, or hybrid forms of language, setting, character, and narrative to defamiliarize audience expectations of the performed event. The feminist history play embodies a contradiction: it has emerged from a critical, sometimes angry, sometimes contemplative response to oppression within and exclusion from the national story, but it is also skeptical of the completeness and truth of any historical narrative, including its own. Thus the feminist history play offers itself as a provisional, sometimes ironical, and often open-ended commentary on the desire to know the past, to inherit a past, and the likelihood that such knowledge and inheritance is imperfect.

Notes

The author would like to thank the editors for their help in clarifying the argument.

1 Suzan-Lori Parks, "Possession," in *The America Play and Other Works* (New York: Theatre Communications Group, 1995), 4.

2 I am following Sue Thomas (in her edited volume *The Feminist History Reader* [New York: Routledge, 2006], 1) in placing the announcement of feminist historiography with the publication of Joan Kelly's "The Social Relations of the Sexes: Methodological Implications of Women's History," *Signs: Journal of Women in Culture and Society* 1, no. 4 (1976): 809–23, where she presents the three categories of historical thought described here as undergoing profound revision. While Kelly published the *Signs* essay under the hyphenated last name Kelly-Gadol, historians usually refer to her as "Joan Kelly," as I will in this essay.

3 Kelly, "Social Relations of the Sexes," 811–14.

4 Monstrous Regiment was formed as a feminist theatre collective in 1975 by a small group of female and male actors who "wanted to make exciting political theatre based on women's experience" (qtd. in Lizbeth Goodman, *Contemporary Feminist Theatres: To Each Her Own* [New York: Routledge, 1993], 66). The Regiment was socialist-feminist in its politics and was one of the longer-lived of the many feminist performance groups that formed during the 1970s and 1980s, as Goodman's book details. Churchill worked collaboratively with both the Regiment and Joint Stock, a process she has credited with helping her grow and develop as an artist. The Joint Stock Company was founded in London in 1974 by writers and directors David Hare, Max Stafford-Clark, and David Aukin to promote and "workshop" (i.e., use ideas and stories from the actors to inform the script) new plays. It was not avowedly feminist, but Churchill suggested to Stafford-Clark the idea for *Cloud Nine* and it was subsequently developed in workshops with the actors, scripted by Churchill, and became one of Joint Stock's major successes.

5 Brean S. Hammond, "Is Everything History?: Churchill, Barker, and the Modern History Play," *Comparative Drama* 41, no. 1 (2007): 1–23, points to Churchill's use of a December 1648 pamphlet, "Light Shining in Buckinghamshire," as well as Christopher Hill's historical interpretation of the revolution in his book *The World Turned Upside Down: Radical Ideas during the English Revolution* (New York: Penguin, 1984) (6ff.).

6 "Light Shining in Buckinghamshire" pamphlet, 241.

7 Churchill's note in the Methuen 1985 edition of the play included in *Caryl Churchill Plays: 1* explains the complex publication history of *Cloud Nine*. All quotes here are taken from the Methuen 1985 edition (*Caryl Churchill Plays: 1* [London: Methuen Publishing, 1985]).

8 Ibid., 248.

9 Foucault published *The History of Sexuality* in French in 1976; it was translated into English in 1978.

10 Caryl Churchill, "Introduction," *Vinegar Tom*, in *Caryl Churchill Plays: 1*, 130.

11 Joan Kelly, "Did Women Have a Renaissance?" in *Becoming Visible: Women in European History*, ed. Renate Bridenthal, Claudia Koonz, and Susan Stuard (Boston: Houghton Mifflin, 1987), 137–64.

12 Elizabeth V. Spelman, *Inessential Woman: Problems of Exclusion in Feminist Thought* (Boston: Beacon Press, 1988), 115.

13 Ibid., 117.

14 Anna Deavere Smith, *Fires in the Mirror: Crown Heights, Brooklyn and Other Identities* (New York: Anchor Books, 1993), 66; subsequent references to the play and to Smith's introduction to it will be given parenthetically in the text.

15 Gregory S. Jay, "Other People's Holocausts: Trauma, Empathy, and Justice in Anna Deavere Smith's *Fires in the Mirror*," *Contemporary Literature* 48, no. 1 (2007): 119–50.

16 Suzan-Lori Parks, *The America Play and Other Works* (New York: Theatre Communications Group, 1995), 180; subsequent references to the play will be given parenthetically in the text.

17 Lynn Nottage, *Intimate Apparel*, in *Intimate Apparel and Fabulation* (New York: Theatre Communication Group, 2003), 43–44.

18 Ibid., 74.

19 Linda Griffiths, *Age of Arousal* (Toronto: Coach House Books, 2007), 137; subsequent references to the play will be given parenthetically in the text.

20 Griffiths here quotes Germaine Greer (*Arousal*, 8). To be fair to Griffiths, she does present Rhoda as flawed and self-interested. She opposes aiding the three helpless sisters, afraid of her similarity to them, afraid that they can drag her back into poverty. She says in thoughtspeak: "But for a few bits of luck I could be them – I feel the sisters pulling at me, trying to drag me down" (37). It is Mary who insists on equipping them with life-skills.

21 Elizabeth Crawford, "Letter to the Editor: Naked Truths and the Suffragette Movement," *Guardian*, 28 August 2008, available at *http://www.guardian.co.uk/lifeandstyle/2008/aug/28/women1* (accessed 26 October 2010).

22 *Guardian* reviews and letters to the editor referring to *Her Naked Skin* include Viv Groskop, "Sex and the Suffragette," 26 August 2008, available at *http://www.guardian.co.uk/stage/2008/aug/26/theatre.women/print* (accessed 26 October 2010); Crawford, "Letter to the Editor," and Susan Croft, "Letter to the Editor: Naked Truths and the Suffragette Movement," 28 August 2008, available at *http://www.guardian.co.uk/lifeandstyle/2008/aug/28/women1* (accessed 26 October 2010) (both letters were published together); Sally Alexander and Marilyn Finlay, "Letters to the Editor: Theatre Can Still Touch a Nerve," 30 August 2008, available at *http://www.guardian.co.uk/culture/2008/aug/30/theatre* (accessed 26 October 2010); Maureen Green and David Butler, "Letters to the Editor: Theatrical Spectacle and the Suffragettes' Real Achievements," 1 September 2008, available at *http://www.guardian.co.uk/politics/2008/sep/01/women.theatre* (accessed 26 October 2010). The letters by Crawford, Croft, and Butler cite specific weaknesses in the play, while those of Alexander, Finlay, and Green praise the play. In addition, debi withers's review of "Her Naked Skin" appearing in "the f word: contemporary UK feminism," available at *http://www.the-fword.org.uk/reviews/2008/09/her_naked_skin* (accessed 26 October 2010), registers her disappointment with the cliché representations of lesbians in the play.

23 Rebecca Lenkiewicz, "Rebecca Lenkiewicz on *Her Naked Skin*," National Theatre Bookshop Talk, available at *http://www.nationaltheatre.org.uk/?lid=37491* (accessed 26 October 2010).

24 Rebecca Lenkicwicz, *Her Naked Skin* (London: Faber & Faber, 2008), 85.

25 John Lahr, "Surreal Life: The Plays of Sarah Ruhl," *New Yorker*, 17 March 2008, available at *http://www.newyorker.com/arts/critics/atlarge/2008/03/17/080317crat_atlarge_lahr* (accessed 29 October 2010).

26 John Lahr, "Good Vibrations," *New Yorker*, 30 November 2009, available at *http://www. newyorker.com/arts/critics/theatre/2009/11/30/091130crth_theatre_lahr* (accessed 30 June 2010).

27 Sarah Ruhl, *In the Next Room or the vibrator play* (New York: Samuel French, 2010), 80.

28 Ibid.

Performing (Our)Selves: The Role of the Actress in Theatre-History Plays by Women

Lesley Ferris and Melissa Lee

> For me the Theatre is by definition the stage where the living meet and confront the dead, the forgotten and the forgetters, the buried and the ghosts, the present, the passing, the present past and the passed past. There is nothing more Theatre than a great City of the Dead. It is a stage through which all the characters of a story make their appearance, from the most ancient, the most distant in the centuries down to the most contemporary, from the imaginary, the invented, the lost found again down to the real familiars. The dead are not always as dead as we think nor the living as living as they think.
>
> –Hélène Cixous, "Enter the Theatre"[1]

The ghosts of theatre history

The history of the actress in Western culture is fraught with omissions, absences, inappropriate assessments, and outright prejudice. Arriving centuries late to the profession, women have met with hostility, censorship, bans, and working conditions often well below those available to their male counterparts, not least of which was economic security much lower than that of actors. Tracy Davis's historical reconstruction of the actress as a working woman in Victorian society articulates that "conventional subject boundaries are meaningless" in trying to come to terms with understanding the social and historical role of the actress. Using a range of methodologies, she poses her over-arching question: "[W]hy were actresses so equivocal in Victorian society?"[2] Davis divides her book into two sections, the profession and working conditions, to offer a layered and multifaceted argument that considers a range of issues including the gendered divisions of labor, wages, career opportunities, social respectability, costumes, and gestural language that provides a nuanced and convincing depiction of the Victorian actress.

Notably, during the same period considered by Davis, a significant number of plays were staged with actresses as central characters, including Douglas Jerrold's *Nell Gwynne; or, The Prologue* (1833); Eugene Scribe and Ernest Legouvé's *Adrienne Lecouvreur* (1849); Tom Taylor and Charles Reade's *Masks or Faces; or, Before and Behind the Curtain* (1852) and *The King's Rival* (1854); J. Palgrave Simpson's *World and Stage* (1859); Dion Boucicault's *Grimaldi: or, The Life of an Actress* (1864); Watts Phillips's *Theodora: Actress and Empress* (1866); Henry Arthur Jones's *Dancing Girl* (1891); George du Maurier's stage version of his novel *Trilby* (1895); and Arthur W. Pinero's *Trelawny of the "Wells"* (1898).[3] Indeed, the prevalence of these theatrical representations suggests a cultural fascination with the actress, whether this dramatic trope reinforced or resisted her vexed history and equivocal social standing.

This cultural fascination with the actress as a dramatic character has also been a concern to women playwrights from the early twentieth century through to the present day. From Sophie Treadwell's successful Broadway comedy *O Nightingale* (1925) to Virginia Woolf's *Freshwater* (1935) to Alice Childress's *Trouble in Mind* (1955), the actress character has served as a touchstone for a variety of issues linked to gender disparity and aesthetic autonomy. More recent works include Lillian Groag's *The Ladies of the Camellias* (1988), April De Angelis's *Playhouse Creatures* (1993), Elizabeth Wong's *China Doll: The Imagined Life of an American Actress* (1997), Maria Irene Fornes's *The Summer in Gossensass* (1998), Charlayne Woodard's *In Real Life* (2002), Theresa Rebeck's *The Actress* (2002), Pam Gems's *Mrs. Pat* (2006), Liz Duffy Adams's *Or* (2009), Sarah Ruhl's *Stage Kiss* (2011), and Lynn Nottage's *By the Way, Meet Vera Stark* (2011).

Among these metatheatrical plays by women, *The First Actress* by Christopher St. John (Christabel Marshall) serves as a kind of touchstone. Directed by Edith Craig and featured as part of the Pioneer Players' inaugural 1911 London season, *The First Actress* melded the argument for women's suffrage with the history of acting for women. The first part of the play establishes the risks and prejudices plaguing women entering the acting profession. Setting the scene on the stage of Drury Lane in 1661, the play opens at the curtain call of a production of *Othello* as sounds of applause are "mingled with cat-calls, hissing and hooting."[4] Margaret Hughes, the first actress of the play's title and possibly the first woman to play the role of Desdemona, collapses backstage in despair. A fellow actor commiserates with her while simultaneously explaining to her why women are not fit to take the stage.[5] In the second half of the play, an exhausted and defeated Hughes falls asleep backstage; her final words are: "I ought never to have attempted it – I have made it impossible for others – perhaps there will never be – any others – I am sorry for that – very sorry" (11). Hughes then dreams of future actresses, who appear to her while she sleeps. Ten actresses from British theatre materialize on stage, ghostly presences of the future that speak directly to the sleeping first actress: Nell Gwyn (1650–1687),[6] Mrs. Barry (1658–1713), Mrs. Bracegirdle (1673/4–1748), Anne Oldfield (1683–1730), Peg Woffington (1714–1760), Kitty Clive (1711–1785), Sarah Siddons (1755–1831), Fanny Abington (1737–1815), Dorothy Jordan (1761–1816), and Madame Vestris (1797–1856). Each visionary actress counters Hughes's self-defeat with examples of their own successes. The appearance of these future actresses – both as historical characters within the dramatic world and as played by real women performers in the present – contradicts Hughes's worry that she has made it impossible for women to follow her in the profession.

The First Actress also directly references the suffrage pageants of the era that enunciated women's link to their past through the resurrection of historical female figures, particularly Cicely Hamilton's play *A Pageant of Great Women* (1909), also directed by Edith Craig. One of the most produced suffrage plays in Britain, it employed a cast of dozens and an allegorical framework to represent a wide variety of women from various periods of history and from different backgrounds and vocations. In *The First Actress*, St. John reinvented this established suffrage model by focusing on a specific historical moment, profession, and site, showcasing British actresses through a forward-looking past-as-future chronology ending in the present moment in 1911.[7] This metatheatrical approach to the present moment exacts an intersection of character and woman, fiction and fact, that adds another layer of meaning: actresses in the present moment perform actresses from the historical past, a doubling which troubles the theatrical device of character and informs and reframes the present. For example, when the celebrated actress Ellen Terry played Nell Gwyn in the first production of *The First Actress*, Terry's real-life popularity and reputation lent extratextual gravity to the historical fiction of the maligned, forgotten, and incomplete genealogy of actresses who paved her way. While *The First Actress* was part of the Pioneer Players' commitment to the question of suffrage, it was also a celebration of the actress as both a historic and contemporary figure of female artistic autonomy.

Using the suffrage-era lens of *The First Actress*, we focus on two contemporary theatre-history plays about actresses, both set at crucial historical moments for theatre in general and for women theatre artists in particular. The first is April De Angelis's *Playhouse Creatures* (1993), which looks at the pressures facing the first actresses employed on the London stages following the Restoration; the second is Maria Irene Fornes's *The Summer in Gossensass* (1998), set in 1891 London during the time that Ibsen's plays were first being produced in English, a time when there was an expanding number of women seeking employment, as well as an "expansion of the theatrical industry, changing attitudes to theatre, and the gentrification of the upper ranks of the profession."[8] Both plays base their actress roles on actual historical theatre professionals, staging a remembering of the past that transforms the performance space into a site where, in Hélène Cixous's words, "the living meet and confront the dead." According to Gerder Lerner, "The dead continue to live by way of the resurrection we give them in telling their stories,"[9] and the plays discussed here perform a kind of theatrical rebirth in which the present tense overlays and negotiates the performance (and performances) of the past. These theatre-history plays illuminate and interrogate the "roles" of women within two transformative eras by staging the real and symbolic power of the actress as a site for struggle, change, and future possibility.

Playing parts: *Playhouse Creatures*

> To play a faithful wife or an unfaithful wife. A whore, a mistress.
> We play at being what we are. Where's the freedom in that?
>
> —Mrs. Marshall in *Playhouse Creatures*[10]

De Angelis's *Playhouse Creatures* was commissioned and first performed in 1993 by The Sphinx Theatre Company in London,[11] one of several feminist collectives founded during the 1970s, a decade characterized by the rise of second-wave feminism and an interest in theatre "committed to radical change and direct political action."[12] By the time of the play's premiere, there was an increasing intolerance of so-called radical feminist agendas, a cultural backlash that Elaine Aston has called "feminist fatigue." Aston has further argued that the work of some contemporary women playwrights of this period, including Caryl Churchill and Sarah Kane, does not "advocate a 'new' kind of feminism," but, rather, is "characterized by an experiential drive to feeling the loss of feminism."[13] Indeed, this "feeling the loss of feminism" resonates in *Playhouse Creatures*, which raises the question of the status of women in (and outside) the theatre by dramatizing the struggle of actresses for professional acceptance in the late seventeenth century, after women were given royal "leave" to tread the boards. In fact, in 2005, De Angelis would look back on the 1990s, when she wrote *Playhouse Creatures*, and recall this moment of political slippage for women's theatre in terms that reference the feeling of loss that Aston identifies: "Truth be told, women's theatre had become passé.... Even then it felt like writing against the grain of the times."[14] This cultural loss of traction for women and women's issues is given shape in *Playhouse Creatures* by means of the play's haunted playhouse setting. Caught between outmoded parts and plays, De Angelis's Restoration actress-spirits inhabit a liminal space; their displacement performs the instability and uncertainty characteristic of a waning feminist movement, while the haunting itself suggests that our present theatre and women's status within it are still subject to the ghosts of the past.

The Sphinx commission was for a play about the first English actresses written for an all-female cast,[15] a fitting assignment for De Angelis, herself an actress-turned-playwright. In the course of her research, De Angelis realized that the lives and stories of these pioneering performing women had either been hidden from history or presented with a romantic gloss that overlooked professional achievement.[16] For De Angelis, such a lacuna in the historical record certainly spoke to the hegemony of a patriarchal perspective and a concomitant privileging of the experiences and achievements of men. In her re-vision of the actress origin story, De Angelis extricates and centers on the female experience. As set forth by Adrienne Rich, re-vision is "the act of looking back, of seeing with fresh eyes, of entering an old text from a new critical direction."[17] Rich explains: "Until we can understand the assumptions in which we are drenched we cannot know ourselves." Accordingly, she calls the work of re-vision "an act of survival."[18] In its rewriting of history, *Playhouse Creatures* resists the stranglehold of tradition by rousing the ghosts of theatre past, interrogating the cultural assumptions and constructions of femininity that have impeded female progress. In this regard, *Playhouse Creatures* necessarily rubs against conventional historical narratives, offering itself up as a metatheatrical yardstick with which to measure the present moment.

At its heart, *Playhouse Creatures* is a ghost story. Although the main action is set in a playhouse and former bear pit, the play begins and ends in a purgatory with the specters of Nell Gwyn and Doll Common, two theatre women trapped on a nondescript stage without a clear understanding of purpose or direction – the proverbial actor's nightmare. This liminality frames the play proper, a flashback to the Restoration and a depiction of a transitional period when actresses were established in the profession yet still struggled for inclusion. The play's central dramatic conceit of a haunted space invites, recycles, and connects anew the various histories being staged, magnifying the theatre's inherent ghostliness: Cixous's City of the Dead. Marvin Carlson's characterization of the theatre as a "memory machine" exemplifies the theatrical production and circulation of memory, while his concept of ghosting describes how this multi-directional network of infinite exchange touches all aspects of the theatrical endeavor and necessarily informs reception.[19] In its self-reflexive foregrounding of the theatrical experience, *Playhouse Creatures* provides many points of contact within this network of ghostings. Dramatically, the effect is not so much a return to what has come before, but a sense of never having left – of the past resurrected to be critically resonant and recognizable in the present moment. One such recognizable point of contact is the play's actress-doubling, which performs a type of feminist genealogy, a theatrical linking of the dead and the living that questions the changing roles of actresses and women inside and outside of the theatre over time. Dramaturgically, it is a strategy reminiscent of *The First Actress*, which positioned the highly visible and public figure of the actress as a political signifier within the discourses of gender difference in the fight for suffrage.

The play's actress characters are all historical figures and range in age: Nell Gwyn (16), Mrs. (Mary) Betterton (50), Mrs. (Rebecca) Marshall (late 20s), and Mrs. (Elizabeth) Farley (early 20s). Doll Common (60s), a player of bit parts and Betterton's assistant, rounds out the cast of five. The play's fast-paced episodic structure features scenes of the actresses at work, moving between an onstage setting where the women perform in Restoration drama and a relaxed backstage setting where the actresses are "themselves," a chronicling of public and private moments that foregrounds the interplay between sexuality and professional opportunity. Of particular interest to De Angelis is the historical construction of actress-as-whore, a cultural prejudice perpetuated well into the nineteenth century by "lampoons, satires, and gossip" that maintained that "if a woman presented herself on stage, then she would present herself off stage, sexually, as well."[20] The parallel between actress and prostitute in the public imagination was clear: that the actress "consented to be 'hired' for amusement by all who could command the price"[21] stigmatized the actress as lascivious and immoral. Kristen Pullen, however, recognizes a space for female agency within the whore discourse, arguing that rather than being limited by their sexual notoriety, certain women used it to their advantage to further their careers, secure their financial and social independence, and challenge existing notions of female sexuality. In *Playhouse Creatures*, this double-edged construction of actress-as-whore informs the ethos of the playhouse and complicates the terms and conditions of the actresses' employment.

At the beginning of the play, set on a London street in 1670, Farley attempts to carry on where her preacher father, a recent victim of the plague, has left off.

Channeling her father's antitheatrical religiosity, she protests: "The playhouse! That den of defilement! That pit of pestilence!" (6). But speechifying against "heathen decadence" (4) has not earned her a penny; consequently, she is tempted by the prospect of steady income when she learns the playhouse is looking to hire a lady. Unfamiliar with the actress's job description, Farley's main concern (as well as assumption) is "Do they fornicate?" (6). But once a playhouse employee, she is quick to abandon her moral outrage for the perks of her new profession, which include opportunities to augment her playhouse salary by reciprocating the sexual advances of admiring male patrons. An affair with the king, however, is not the boon it seems, providing only a brief and false sense of security; and when pregnancy ends her stage career, she is turned out on the street and must prostitute herself to survive. "Out here I'm a real pro" (49), she declares without irony, explaining how poverty has made her a better actress: "I've learnt things out here. The art of performance. You can't act tired, not for business purposes. You've got to act like you like it. Love it even" (49). De Angelis's portrayal of Farley as both an actress and a whore underscores an economic reality that complicates notions of female sexual agency, lending a double meaning to her status as a professional.

On the other hand, De Angelis's depiction of Marshall's professionalism counters that of Farley's sexual profiteering. Marshall actively resists the whore label, averse to giving over control to a male keeper and thus making business-as-usual difficult. After a disastrous affair with the Earl of Oxford, she is publically punished for her impudence and noncompliance with a custom that sexually subjects the actress to her social betters. Catcalls of "whore" disrupt her performance, and offstage she is accosted by thugs who "rubbed shit into my hair. To teach me my manners" (26). Marshall's express hope is for the freedom to live and work, beholden to no man. Instead, Marshall finds herself at the mercy of an especially vindictive earl who takes a sexual, if unrequited, interest in her. In her ongoing dispute with Oxford, he gets the final word, an accusation of witchcraft that forces the actress into hiding: "They found another word for me," says Marshall, referring to being labeled a witch. "Before I could find one for myself. If they don't get you one way they get you another" (52).

Finally, Gwyn proves to be skilled at the game Marshall eschews and at which Farley fails. Gwyn's early declaration, "I'm an actress, not a tart" (34), betrays an understanding that if a woman is to be taken seriously as an artist, the two identities must be treated as mutually exclusive. Nonetheless, her stage debut has captured the attention of the king, and what was supposed to be a one-time-only visit to the palace turns into a long-term affair, casting the actress in the real-life role of courtesan. At the same time, Gwyn's professional accomplishments in the theatre are unprecedented: she becomes a company shareholder, is given her own private dressing room, and is approached by Aphra Behn, a new woman playwright who has written a part especially for her. Even so, Gwyn does not see a future for herself as an actress. Her failure to "imagine what comes next" (57) is not necessarily her failure alone, but society's failure to empower women economically, socially, politically, and artistically, thus drastically limiting not only women's choices but women's contributions. Consequently, Gwyn willingly resigns from her career to become the king's "protestant whore," as history records she once called herself, a part which was already hers. While Gwyn's choice of domesticity can be read from a position of female empowerment, the degree to which the king's patronage has been a factor in her professional success complicates the notion of autonomy here, calling into question the actress's sense of obligation to her male benefactor and whether this outcome was inevitable from the start. If Gwyn's mentor Mrs. Betterton's fate is any indication, it is not unreasonable for Gwyn to fear that the acting profession holds no future comfort for her. Once the most celebrated actress of her day, Betterton's years of dedication to her craft did not prevent her forced retirement by the company manager, also her husband, to make way for younger women "[w]ith decent legs" (30). Her forced departure speaks to the cultural pressures that regulate acceptable standards of femininity and, in turn, equate youth and sexuality with talent and worth. From Gwyn's royal whoredom to Farley's street-walking and Marshall's defiance, De Angelis stages the complex sexual negotiations that were a feature of playhouse employment for actresses and affected, for better or worse, the quality and trajectory of their lives.

Notably, the first scene to take place in the playhouse setting features the actresses "onstage" in performance, with Farley playing the queen of the Amazons and Betterton and Marshall playing Amazon warriors seeking to avenge their queen's murder. This first staging of performance in the play is purposefully highly contrived and sexually titillating. In her study of the effect that actresses had on Restoration drama, Elizabeth Howe asserts that "[t]he presence of women's bodies on the stage encouraged lurid, eroticized presentations of female suffering, and was designed to tantalise, rather than to attack violent masculine behaviour."[22] The staging of Farley exposed and helplessly tied to a tree as the sexually assaulted queen exemplifies this standard of lurid eroticization. Further, to conclude the scene, the two Amazon warriors bare their breasts as a tribute, an action that contrasts the passive sexual spectacle of the fallen queen but, as De Angelis shows, is ultimately just another means to the same end of sexual objectification characteristic of Restoration drama and playhouse antics.

Throughout *Playhouse Creatures*, De Angelis includes the performance of scenes that seem to be lifted directly from the seventeenth-century dramatic repertory, and yet the Amazon drama and other performed pieces – including prologues, epilogues, and a breeches scene where Gwyn and Marshall cheekily ask the audience for company shares for "playing for your pleasure" (36) – are actually De Angelis's own invention. Ryan Claycomb points out this strategic "consolidation of female voice: contemporary actresses reciting lines written by a contemporary female playwright, lines that reflect the lives of the female characters whose voices this play is resurrecting."[23] Additionally, the invented metadrama functions as a critique of the theatrical and dramaturgical conventions of the era, including the sexual objectification of the actresses and the prescriptive repertory in which they performed. A survey of the actresses' roles here illustrates the mundane and generic nature of female representation: a lusty shepherdess, a dishonored woman, a series of widows, and mythical Muses and Amazons, theatrical parts which do not provide much respite from the roles permitted or forced on the actresses when offstage. While the actresses campaign for the positions of company shareholder and theatrical manager, their real-life roles are restricted to those of dutiful wife, secret mistress, royal whore, and desperate street hooker.

Playhouse Creatures ends with the ghosts of Gwyn and Doll waiting for the epilogue that will conclude the performance, only the speech has yet to be written. Reflecting on her life with the king, Gwyn looks to Doll for reassurance: "Still. I never did nothing I didn't want to. Did I?" (59). Echoing the play's prologue, Doll responds with a story from her childhood about her father, who was the bear keeper when the playhouse was still a bear pit. As imparted by her father, the moral of the story is that even though bears hate to dance for the whip, the more they danced, the better the family ate. Doll concludes with a comment that speaks to Gwyn's original question about living by her own choices: "Playhouse creatures they called you like you was animals" (60). In her re-vision of the Restoration stage, De Angelis considers the ways in which the actresses were simply the next creatures to dance for their keep, ruled by the unseen hand of a male keeper; hence, the play tasks itself with exposing the many forms of this keeper and the reach of this unseen hand. The play's final moment is a tempered celebration of the first women to speak on the stage. Having been roused from the cold and dark recesses of an old and empty theatre, the possibilities of the present moment seem limitless, and Gwyn takes the initiative to make up a curtain speech to be dedicated to Mrs. Betterton. When Doll asks, "What will we say?" Gwyn answers, "Anything. Now we can say anything" (60). The final stage directions instruct, *"They come forward together as if to begin an epilogue. The Lights go down"* (60). It is an equivocal ending that prevents a clear feminist victory. Instead, De Angelis leaves us with a pregnant pause, a moment of anticipation and reflection that insists upon a gendered reading. De Angelis has stated that "[r]eading a play in text or in performance through the lens of gender is in itself a subversive gesture in a critical culture that fails miserably to do so," stressing the importance of representations and critiques that trouble gender on the stage.[24] *Playhouse Creatures* not only troubles gender but demands that the future attend to questions of gender. Moving forward, De Angelis suggests that the responsibility lies with women playwrights like Behn and a program of women writing for women, a strategy not only of words but of yet unplayed parts and performances that will, like this play itself, promote a female perspective and sanction women's voices, bodies, and work.

Producing parts: *The Summer in Gossensass*

We dreamed of an escape....

–Elizabeth Robins, *Theatre and Friendship*[25]

The actresses' demand for "shares" in *Playhouse Creatures* finds a parallel in Maria Irene Fornes's 1998 play *The Summer in Gossensass*. The play is set in 1891 and women theatre artists are still battling for financial and artistic control over the plays in which they perform. Like De Angelis, Fornes based her characters on real-life counterparts, the American actresses Elizabeth Robins (1862–1952) and Marion Lea (1861–1944), both of whom relocated to London with hopes of launching their theatre careers. While performing together in London in a stage adaptation of Dostoevsky's *Crime and Punishment*, Robins and Lea forged a plan to convince established theatre managers to produce a work by Ibsen. Rejected by a number of actor-managers, they then decided to mount their own productions. Robins captured their frustration in an unpublished memoir: "We arraigned the managers, we raged, dreamed, and then more or less awake, began to consider ways and means."[26]

We know from Robins's accounts that actresses of the era were hungry for roles that challenged them in new ways. As she recalled, "the regular Theatre could not content us."[27] She goes on to explain why the theatre of her day was such a source of discontent and frustration:

> We had come to realize how essential to success some freedom of judgment and action are to the actor. The strangulation of this rôle and that through arbitrary stage management, was an experience we had shared with men. But we had further seen how freedom in the practice of our art, how the bare opportunity to practise it at all, depended, for the actress, on considerations humiliatingly different from those that confronted the actor. The stage career of an actress was inextricably involved in the fact that she was a woman and that those who were masters of the Theatre were men. Those considerations did not belong to art; they stultified art.[28]

Hampered and constrained by British theatre's conservative stance in the face of a European theatre undergoing a major transformation both in terms of playwrights' modernist visions and producers' staging innovations, Robins and Lea took the bold step of creating the Robins-Lea-Joint Management. In Robins's words, "We dreamed of an escape, through hard work, and through deliberate abandonment of the idea of making money...."[29] For the two actresses, the "unexplored possibilities of theatre" underscored their resolve. By establishing their management, they made the momentous decision to stage the first English-language production of Ibsen's *Hedda Gabler*.

It is Robins and Lea's moment of "escape" that Fornes captures in *The Summer in Gossensass*,[30] the title of which refers to the summer holiday resort in the south Tyrol in northern Italy where Ibsen wrote *Hedda Gabler*.[31] When asked in an interview with Maria Delgado in 1997 why she chose to write about the first English-language production of Ibsen's play, Fornes explained: "*Hedda Gabler* was the first play I read from start to finish without ever stopping. The dialogue was so clear that it immediately invoked living images in my mind."[32] When she was invited to direct a play of her choice for the 1986–87 Milwaukee Repertory Theatre season, she chose Ibsen's play. Her work with the actors in this production inspired her decision to focus on the genesis of the London English-language premiere in 1891:

> While discussing the play with the cast I discovered that my impressions of Hedda and of the whole play were different from the impressions they had.

They believed that Lovborg was Hedda's love, ... that he is handsome and romantic. And that Hedda was forced to marry Tesman for the sake of stability and financial security. I was amazed. I wondered if they had seen a Hollywood version of the play.[33]

By looking at the first English production, Fornes planned to have the characters discuss the interpretation of the play at the historical moment when it was new and Ibsen was a disturbing, controversial figure. Marc Robinson points out that Fornes believed that certain "meddlesome" readers of the play "had prematurely answered questions that Ibsen meant to leave open – questions about Hedda most of all." Fornes's interest in both the play and its first London production developed from her belief that "Ibsen's protagonist had been softened by generations of actors and directors who had never met a character they couldn't explain."[34]

The play opens with Robins and Lea sitting at a table reading, with books scattered on the table and at their feet. Fornes's two actresses are reading about Ibsen, Norway, and the Bohemian movement in the late nineteenth century. They are trying to understand Ibsen's plays and their impact on their own lives. They have heard about his newest work *Hedda Gabler* and they long to discover it, but it is not yet available in English. They learn that an English-language production is scheduled in London with the role of Hedda going to Lily Langtry, the British music hall singer and comic actress. Both Marion and Elizabeth are dumbfounded but not deterred by this news. Marion subversively gains access to the theatre where the Langtry production is rehearsing. Discovering an empty space and the rehearsal cancelled, she wanders around the theatre, taking in the atmosphere. By a stroke of luck, she finds two pages of discarded script in the wastebasket and brings them home.

Those two stolen pages – the play's first scene between Hedda and Thea – become the centerpiece of Fornes's play when Elizabeth (as Hedda) and Marion (as Thea) read it aloud, three times, in different ways. After each reading, they discuss and interrogate the scene. After the final reading, Elizabeth says of Hedda: "She's capable. She has an interesting mind. But she doesn't use it to be constructive. She uses it to be destructive and to complicate her life and the lives of others. How terrible. But, oh, so interesting" (77). Later she says to Marion: "She is missing a part of herself, and therefore she's missing a part of the world. She is like a person who is colorblind, and therefore is connected to everything but color" (77–78). There is an irony here with this triple reading: this scene, the first moment when Hedda and Thea meet, was likely discarded in the Langtry rehearsal because of Langtry's inability to learn her lines, a fact well-known amongst theatre professionals of the day. The idea that such a fundamental scene, one that identifies the relationship between Hedda and Thea, would be lost when this production opened (which it never did) is horrifying to Elizabeth and Marion. Fornes juxtaposes the reading of the discarded scene with the discussion of another trashed, discarded text – Lovborg's manuscript, which Hedda famously throws into the flames. Both the burnt manuscript and the trashed scene evoke a sense of the fragility of the creative act, but more importantly, they become the impetus for discussion, debate, argument, inquiry. Much of Fornes's work here is the staging of actors engaged in the rehearsal process, and their act of tearing the script apart and putting it back together again is the well-known, much-practiced creative act of table work – character analysis. That level of work on a script was highly unusual in the profession in 1891. Rehearsal periods were very short, actor-managers ran the show, and their main interest was to produce works that featured them in a major male role while ensuring commercial viability.

The narrative of Fornes's script is based on history. In order to set up their management, Robins and Lea raised money by pawning jewelry. Once the meager funding was in place, they organized the translation and acting rights, had a two-week rehearsal period, and opened the production in London in 1891. These two women, as Angela John has noted, "may be credited with changing the course of English drama."[35] Fornes's imagined reclamation of these historical events focuses on the risk-taking ingenuity of two actresses to engineer a triumphant artistic success, an achievement that, while documented and acknowledged at the time, has not been a central concern to scholars of modernism and theatre history until recently. It was not that the actress was written *out* of history: she was absent from its beginnings. Even after women were permitted to perform their own roles on the stage, an active and prevalent prejudice against them flourished, as seen in both *The First Actress* and *Playhouse Creatures*. A key example of this ongoing prejudice is an essay by Goethe, written over a century after women had permission to act publically on most stages in Europe. While visiting Rome, Goethe saw a production in which a male actor took the central female role. The Papal States maintained the ban on women acting anywhere near the seat of Christian power until the last decade of the eighteenth century. Goethe begins his 1788 essay as follows: "The ancients, at least in the best periods for art and morality, did not permit women on the stage. Their plays were organized in such a way that either *women could be more or less dispensed with,* or else female roles were played by an actor who had prepared himself especially for them."[36] This cavalier sense of male power and privilege pronounced by Goethe has reverberated through the centuries in the varieties of prejudice that still continue to this day in the theatre profession with contemporary theatre's lack of equity in terms of opportunity for women as actors, playwrights, and directors.

This historical continuum murmurs in the background of Fornes's play and provides a context for a dramaturgical tripling that parallels the triple reading of the trashed scene. An actress in the present tense (in the 1998 premiere at the Women's Project in New York City, Molly Powell took the role of Robins) plays the character of an actress (Robins) who, in the course of the play, rehearses the role of Hedda Gabler. Instead of "more or less dispensing with" the actress, Fornes retrieves her from the past and foregrounds her, and these three strands – an actress, a character who is an actress, and the dramatic character Hedda – enact theatre's creative process. Additionally, the play's dramaturgical structure stages this process: from the opening scene's research on Ibsen, to a scene in which Robins translates (or attempts to) from a Norwegian copy of the play, to the three moments of table work, to actual performance itself.

The penultimate scene stages the final moments of Ibsen's play: from Hedda's line of acknowledged capitulation – "So I'm in your power, Judge" (93) – to the gun shot and Brack's famous line: "People don't do such things!" (95). This scene is followed by a curtain call – and here is another twist: this curtain call-within-the-play does not double as the curtain call of *The Summer in Gossensass*. Instead, Fornes ends with a leap forward to 1928. The last scene is Robins speaking at the centenary celebration of Henrik Ibsen's birth. Her talk, entitled "Ibsen and the Actress," was published in the same year. The scene begins as follows:

> Elizabeth: (*Reading.*) The reason why I'm here this evening to speak before the Royal Society of Arts on this Twelfth of March 1928, is to... speak to you of the significance of Henrik Ibsen. (94)

Fornes ends her play with this moment of rescue and recovery, a strategy that informs the entire play by claiming this theatrical resurrection as a modernist moment: an actress is invited to speak publicly about her profession at an event that acknowledges her crucial, defining role in theatre history. The text comes directly from the words that Robins wrote and spoke in 1928. In her book *Women, Modernism, and Performance*, Penny Farfan analyzes Robins's performance of Hedda as follows: "Electing to play this repressed, thwarted woman [Hedda] in a controversially sympathetic production for which she and her female collaborator were entirely responsible, Robins introduced the subjectivity of the actress into the formula of theatre production."[37] Gay Gibson Cima states about this same historical moment: "The male critical establishment, particularly in England, grew anxious about the new power assumed by female actors, who not only created a new acting style to portray the principal characters in Ibsen's scripts but also independently produced many of his plays."[38] Cima further explains that "Robins created a style of acting in Ibsen's realistic, narrative plays that allowed her to reveal and critique the roles expected of women."[39] This new acting style that depended upon Robins's critical vision established the actress as a modernist invention, and Fornes captures this defining moment in her play.

Looking back on her theatre career in her memoir *Both Sides of the Curtain* (1940), Robins recalls an interview she had with actor-manager Henry Irving during which she expressed concern about the limited roles available to women. Irving replied: "'Ah... but women have an easy road to travel on the stage. They have but to *appear* and their sweet feminine charm wins the battle –.'" Robins adds, "I had thought we were talking about acting,"[40] and then summarizes the encounter as follows:

> The brief passage with Henry Irving added greatly to the general pressure that would confine women of the stage to the old province outside the stage. The rare exceptions, the great actresses, some of them, had escaped – with the result that lesser women or less fortunate, had been misled. What was wanted of the women of the stage was, first and mainly, what was wanted of women outside – a knack of pleasing.[41]

Irving was simply one of many who enjoined Robins to act in a prescribed way that he perceived to be appropriate for women. Henry James was another. In a letter to Robins about her role as Hilda in *The Master Builder*, James states: "Don't be fantastic – be *pretty*, be agreeable, in the right key."[42] This injunction to please is likewise a central concern of Margaret Hughes in *The First Actress*, who agonizes that she has not pleased the audience, her fellow actors, or Sir Charles Sedley, her "protector." The actresses of her future appear to the sleeping Hughes to tell her of their successes, thus breaking that confining chain of "pleasing" with its pervasive history that has demanded that women please both on and off the stage. Fornes's work continues that rupture by locating subjectivity with two actresses who, in producing *Hedda Gabler*, refuse to use their "sweet feminine charm" to make theatre.

Performing (our)selves: the "Actress of To-Day"[43]

In the concluding moments of *The First Actress*, the final actress to appear to the dreaming Hughes is a theatrical incongruity whereby St. John plays with the concept of mimetic art itself. Western theatre relies on a system in which the actor creates a character of a fictionalized other, but the final role in St. John's play is "Actress of To-day," a generic construction that disrupts conventional theatrical expectations of characters as fixed referents in a seemingly stable mimetic system. In the play's original 1911 staging, Lena Ashwell, a well-known actress and theatre manager, took this role as "herself." Ashwell's presence intentionally broke the frame of conventional dramaturgy: as an actress of her day, she was inside the theatre system but as the "Actress of To-day," a role with no character referent other than herself, she was an outsider to it. Placing the actress-self onstage suggests a new metatheatrical strategy, a modernist moment that stages a neglected subjectivity and envisions the actress as perpetually and knowingly self-reflexive.

The metatheatrical history plays of De Angelis and Fornes adopt this same strategic construction of the actress as always of "To-day" and necessarily self-reflexive in matched critiques that make visible the masculine spheres of power limiting women's sexual, financial, and artistic freedom. In their concluding moments, both plays also echo *The First Actress* by staging the promises of women's future. *The Summer in Gossensass* leaps forward several decades with Robins's 1928 keynote speech "Ibsen and the Actress" underway at a podium; the final stage directions read: "*She is now mouthing words as the lights fade out*" (95). Similarly, *Playhouse Creatures* ends with Gwyn's realization that "Now we can say anything" (60). Robins's silent mouthing of the words the actress authored in real life and Gwyn's step forward to perform an epilogue of her own creation are gestures of anticipation that signal the end of the present performance by referencing a future beyond the current narration. By foregrounding the female voice, a voice that continues to speak and in a sense will not be silenced, these curtain moments stage the promises of female authorship and artistic autonomy, promises that resonate with Robins's real-life realization of "how essential to success some freedom of judgment and action are to the actor," especially the woman actor who operates against a history of objectification and constraint.

Linking performance, women's history, and the actress figure, *The First Actress* innovatively stages the struggle of actresses for professional acceptance through the wisdom of hindsight: the immediacy of the corporeal spectacle of the actress in performance calls attention to the persistent exclusion of women from other arenas of public life. *Playhouse Creatures* and *The Summer in Gossensass* pursue and demand the inclusion of women as active participants in the creative economy of making theatre both by staging actress characters from history and by the act of writing the plays. De Angelis and Fornes align themselves with Rich's perception of re-vision as propelling one's work forward to the future as "an act of survival." In the two plays we have considered here, the lights do not simply black out at the end. Gwyn, with her self-determination to "say anything," and Robins, with her silent but unremitting words, refuse to stop speaking to us. This refusal signals a haunting, a moment when the living confront the dead, an encounter that projects our theatrical ghosts into the future so we can come to terms with our present moment.

Notes

1 Hélène Cixous, "Enter the Theatre," trans. Brian J. Mallett, in *Selected Plays of Hélène Cixous*, ed. Eric Prenowitz (London: Routledge, 2004), 28–29.

2 Tracy C. Davis, *Actresses as Working Women: Their Social Identity in Victorian Culture* (London: Routledge, 1991), xi.

3 Actresses were featured in a significant number of novels as well, including Geraldine Jewsbury's *The Half Sisters* (1848), *Villette* by Charlotte Brontë (1853), George Eliot's *Daniel Deronda* (1876), Mrs. Humphrey Ward's *Mrs. Bretherton* (1884), and Henry James's *The Tragic Muse* (1890).

4 Christopher St. John, *The First Actress* (Lord Chancellor's Play Manuscripts 14, British Lib., 1911), 1; subsequent references to this play will be given parenthetically in the text.

5 For a full analysis of the play, see Lesley Ferris, "The Female Self and Performance: The Case of *The First Actress*," in *Theatre and Feminist Aesthetics*, ed. Karen Laughlin and Catherine Schuler (Madison: Fairleigh Dickinson University Press, 1995), 242–57.

6 The spelling of Nell Gwyn's last name varies, with both Gwynn and Gwynne used in St. John's typewritten manuscript of *The First Actress*. We are using the most common spelling here, which is also the one that De Angelis uses in *Playhouse Creatures*.

7 The only actress to appear in the pageant is Anne Oldfield (1683–1730), who is also a character in *The First Actress*, the fourth future actress vision to appear to Margaret Hughes in her dream.

8 Davis, *Actresses as Working Women*, xiii.

9 Gerda Lerner, *Why History Matters: Life and Thought* (New York: Oxford University Press, 1997), 211.

10 April De Angelis, *Playhouse Creatures* (London: Samuel French, 1994), 51; subsequent references to the play will be given parenthetically in the text.

11 Founded in 1973, The Sphinx Theatre Company had just changed their name from The Women's Theatre Group when *Playhouse Creatures* premiered on 5 October 1993 at the Haymarket Theatre Studio in Leicester. This first production was dedicated to scholar Elizabeth Howe, whose book *The First English Actresses: Women and Drama, 1660–1700* had been an inspiration to De Angelis. In 1997, Dominic Dromgoole asked De Angelis to rewrite *Playhouse Creatures* for a season with Peter Hall's company at The Old Vic. At his request, she added male characters: the Earl of Rochester and the playwright Thomas Otway. She also added one more actress, Mrs. Elizabeth Barry, to bring the cast to eight. The Old Vic version is published in April De Angelis, *April De Angelis: Plays* (London: Faber, 1999), 153–231. We have chosen to focus on the original commissioned play because of its all-female cast.

12 Sue Ellen Case, *Feminism and Theatre* (London: Macmillan, 1988), 63.

13 Elaine Aston, "Feeling the Loss of Feminism: Sarah Kane's *Blasted* and an Experiential Genealogy of Contemporary Women's Playwriting," 19 (in this volume).

14 April De Angelis, "Riddle of the Sphinx," *Guardian* 9 September 2005, available at *http://www.guardian.co.uk/stage/2005/sep/10/theatre* (accessed 30 October 2012).

15 While The Sphinx wanted a small cast of four, De Angelis felt this number was too confining, took a chance, and submitted a play with five women's parts.

16 See April De Angelis, in conversation with Michael Oakley, "Fly: Under *Playhouse Creatures*," recorded 25 July 2012, published on *YouTube* 27 July 2012, available at *http://www.youtube.com/watch?v=4_80zAV5H2A* (accessed 30 October 2012).

17 Adrienne Rich, "When We Dead Awaken: Writing as Re-Vision," *College English* 34, no. 1 (1972): 18.

18 Ibid.

19 Marvin Carlson, *The Haunted Stage: The Theatre as Memory Machine* (Ann Arbor: University of Michigan Press, 2003).

20 Kristen Pullen, *Actresses and Whores: On Stage and in Society* (Cambridge: Cambridge University Press, 2005), 24.

21 Davis, *Actresses as Working Women*, 69.

22 Elizabeth Howe, *The First English Actresses: Women and Drama, 1660–1700* (Cambridge: Cambridge University Press, 1992), 176.

23 Ryan Claycomb, "Playing at Lives: Biography and Contemporary Feminist Drama," *Modern Drama* 47, no. 3 (2004): 539.

24 April De Angelis, "Troubling Gender on Stage and with the Critics," *Theatre Journal* 62, no. 4 (2010): 558.

25 Elizabeth Robins, *Theatre and Friendship: Some Henry James Letters* (London: Jonathan Cape, 1932), 30.

26 Elizabeth Robins, "Whither and How," quoted in Joanne E. Gates, *Elizabeth Robins, 1862–1952: Actress, Novelist Feminist* (Tuscaloosa: University of Alabama Press, 1994), 41.

27 Robins, *Theatre and Friendship*, 29.

28 Ibid., 29–30.

29 Ibid., 30.

30 Maria Irene Fornes, *The Summer in Gossensass*, in *What of the Night? Selected Plays* (New York: PAJ, 2008), 47–95; subsequent references to the play will be given parenthetically in the text.

31 The chapter in Michael Meyer's *Ibsen: A Biography* (New York: Doubleday, 1971) that looks at the genesis of *Hedda Gabler* is titled "The Summer in Gossensass – (1889)." Meyer published a play with the same title in 2001 in *Three Plays About Ibsen and Strindberg* (London: Oberon Books). Meyer's work centers on Ibsen and his meeting with Emilie Bardach, his source for Hedda Gabler.

32 "Maria Irene Fornes Discusses Forty Years in the Theatre with Maria M. Delgado," in *Conducting a Life: Reflections on the Theatre of Maria Irene Fornes*, ed. Maria M. Delgado and Caridad Svich (Lyme, NH: Smith and Kraus, 1999), 248.

33 Ibid.

34 Marc Robinson, "*The Summer in Gossensass*: Fornes and Criticism," in *The Theater of Maria Irene Fornes*, ed. Marc Robinson (Baltimore: Johns Hopkins University Press, 1999), 111.

35 Angela V. John, *Elizabeth Robins: Staging a Life 1862–1952* (London: Routledge, 1995), 19.

36 "Goethe's 'Women's Parts Played by Men in the Roman Theater,'" trans. Isa Ragusa, in *Crossing the Stage: Controversies on Cross-Dressing*, ed. Lesley Ferris (London: Routledge, 1993), 48; italics added.

37 Penny Farfan, *Women, Modernism, and Performance* (Cambridge: Cambridge University Press, 2004), 16.

38 Gay Gibson Cima, *Performing Women: Female Characters, Male Playwrights, and the Modern Stage* (Ithaca, NY: Cornell University Press, 1993), 3.

39 Ibid., 11.

40 Elizabeth Robins, *Both Sides of the Curtain* (London: Heinemann, 1940), 241.

41 Ibid., 242.

42 Robins, *Theatre and Friendship*, 98.

43 St. John, *The First Actress*, 1.

14 Historical Landscapes in Contemporary Plays by Canadian Women

Penny Farfan

Classic theorists of modern drama, from Émile Zola to Raymond Williams, have noted the central relationship between environment and identity in modern drama, while Una Chaudhuri's 1995 book *Staging Place: The Geography of Modern Drama* traces "the imagination of place in modern drama" to find "that dramatic structure reflects deeply ingrained convictions about the mutually constructive relations between people and place. Who one is and who one can be are ... a function of *where* one is and how one experiences that place."[1]

In her 2002 essay "Reading for Landscape: The Case of American Drama," Elinor Fuchs further notes that "[e]very dramatic world is conditioned by a landscape imaginary, a 'deep' surround suggested to the mind that extends far beyond the onstage environment reflected in the dramatic text and its scenographic representation."[2] As Fuchs and Chaudhuri note in the introduction to their edited volume *Land/Scape/Theater*, the term "landscape" encompasses "the multifarious interplay between the land and human adaptations to and of it."[3] Landscape and history are thus inextricably linked, and in Joanne Tompkins's study of space in Australian theatre, "landscape" particularly "signif[ies] locations that correlate with matters of national identity."[4]

Landscape has similarly been a defining feature of Canadian national identity, and "landscape plays" thus serve as a useful entry point through which to begin to articulate the critical work of contemporary Canadian women playwrights. In this chapter, I take as my focus a selection of plays that explicitly "engage the issue of place"[5] so as to consider how key contemporary women playwrights have staged the Canadian landscape in order to foreground new visions of history, place, and identity. Epic in scale, the works that I consider here – Judith Thompson's *Sled*, Djanet Sears's *The Adventures of a Black Girl in Search of God*, and Marie Clements's *Burning Vision* – collectively refigure landscape in order to restage history as it lives in the present moment and so to reshape the social, cultural, and political terrain of contemporary Canada.

Beyond landscape, Canada's officially multicultural status has been crucial to its national identity. *Sled*, *Adventures of a Black Girl*, and *Burning Vision* all expose what Chaudhuri would call the "geopathology," or "painful politics of place,"[6] that underlies the nation's official multiculturalism, staging racial and ethnic fissures and inequities that have marked Canada's past and continue to mark its present and that are thus embedded in the national landscape. In all three plays, female characters figure centrally as the playwrights reconceive nation by staging alternative relationships across cultures that point toward new futures (Thompson and Clements) and by celebrating the continuity of community across generations and beyond individual experiences through connection to landscape (Sears).

"The houses ... look as though they are in the middle of a forest": Judith Thompson's *Sled*

Judith Thompson's 1997 play *Sled* serves as a useful starting point for my analysis, providing a complex portrait of contemporary Canada and suggesting the history of conquest, colonization, immigration, and assimilation that has shaped it.[7] *Sled* moves between a lodge in the forest in northern Ontario and a multicultural neighborhood in the city of Toronto, but in a stage direction, Thompson specifies that the city houses "look as though they are in the middle of a forest."[8] The landscape as described in this stage direction is an expression of Thompson's historical vision, calling attention both to the superimposition of the city upon the wilderness and to how the "civilization" of the Canadian "wilderness" over the course of history has created a wilderness that is other than geographic and that is embodied in the individuals who populate the city. In Thompson's postcolonial history play, and in a variation on Chaudhuri's notion of geopathology or "[t]he characterization of place as problem,"[9] the Canadian wilderness is not the land itself but the traumatized psyches of the people who occupy a landscape marked by a violent history of conquest, displacement, rupture, and loss.

The main plotline of *Sled* centers on the psychopathic murderer Kevin and the consequences of his crimes for various members of the Toronto neighborhood from which he was kidnapped as a child and to which he catastrophically returns during the course of the play. Early in act I, Kevin and his friend Mike disrupt a singer, Annie, while she is performing in the lounge of a wilderness lodge, provoking the violent ire of her husband Jack. Kevin again encounters Annie as she walks in the wintry forest later that night, and purporting to be shooting a moose, he kills her, speaking Norse as he does so.[10] Kevin's uncanny use of an archaic language as he commits murder and takes his victim's dress as a trophy is suggestive of the first contact of Europeans with what is now Canada and casts that first contact as a barbarous moment of brutal conquest. In this sense, Kevin represents an embodied return of the repressed prehistory that is, in Thompson's epic vision, the foundational trauma or "wound ... upon the mind"[11] that continues to haunt present-day multicultural Canada as exemplified in the Toronto neighborhood featured in the play. Moreover, Kevin's early trauma of forcible wrenching from his mother as a kidnap victim is analogous to the violent displacements from mother countries and suppressions of mother tongues and cultures that have defined Canada's development as a nation through waves of colonization, settlement, and immigration. Thus, Kevin functions as a kind of monstrous avatar of Canada's history as a settler-invader nation premised on violence from the earliest moment of European contact with the "new world" and haunted by its violent past through to the postcolonial present.

In scene 2, an elderly neighborhood resident, Joe, reveals that the street where he lives was once a cow path leading to a slaughterhouse that is still in operation (15); and this earlier life as a path to slaughter is made present again when a steer escapes from the slaughterhouse and runs along the street until it is shot down (85–86). The escaped steer that instinctually knows the archaeology of the city and the association of the multicultural neighborhood with a slaughterhouse together clarify how the past is archived in the structure of the city. In "Theses on the Philosophy of History," Walter Benjamin wrote that "[t]here is no document of civilization which is not at the same time a document of barbarism."[12] The steer signals Thompson's interest in the social archaeology or *subtext* of the city as historical document of Canada's barbarism as a settler-invader nation founded upon the violence inherent in the intersected processes of conquest, colonization, immigration, and assimilation. Thus, *Sled*'s main plotline is intercut with meditations on the multicultural histories of the citizens who comprise the Toronto neighborhood to which Kevin returns, and each one of these histories is marked by some form of violence that has been integral to Canada's past. Thompson has used the expression "soul murders" to describe violations that kill the spirit rather than the physical body.[13] In *Sled*, "soul murders" related to the process of "civilizing" the "new world" include Annie's Irish great-great-grandmother's immigration to Canada on a disease-plagued death-ship in the early nineteenth century (30); Joe's boyhood humiliation when his impoverished Italian immigrant mother, widowed and bereft in a new country, forced him to wear her shoes to school (72–73); Jack's shame-driven rejection of his French mother tongue and of the French Canadian foods his mother prepared for him in childhood (42); and the deliberate withholding from Kevin's half-sister Evangeline of the truth of her First Nations heritage (68–69). These "soul murders" resonate with Kevin's physical murders and are as closely associated with the history of Canada as the brutality of the first moment of European contact that is suggested by Kevin's use of Norse as he kills Annie.

At the end of the play, Thompson relocates Kevin and Evangeline from the city to the winter forest, in effect replaying the moment of first contact not as brutal conquest but as a life-producing encounter between half-siblings of different races. Pregnant by Kevin, Evangeline plans to name her unborn baby Annie Northstar, suggesting both a fusion of indigenous and settler cultures and a renavigation of the history that led to the child's conception, which Evangeline describes as an out-of-control ride on a "runaway sled" (84). As Kevin lies dying in Evangeline's arms under the northern lights that illuminated his murder of his friend Mike earlier in the play but that are now represented as benevolent "dancing spirits" who have come for him and his half-sister (109), Annie's ghost, now in a sense a specter from the future, reprises a song that she sang at the beginning and the play ends on an open note as to the nature of the vision enabled through this re-encounter in the wilderness that is contemporary Canada:

> Oh heavenly time of day...
> the fog and the quiet.
> The mist, no sun. I move out of my dream and into
> this day as
> the fog it clears so slowly away to reveal..... to
> reveal...
>> *The Snowy Owl hoots.*
>> *The End.* (109; ellipses in original)

"Heaven is Negro Creek": Djanet Sears's *The Adventures of a Black Girl in Search of God*

Whereas *Sled*'s expansive staging of the Canadian landscape and the history that haunts it encompasses urban and forest settings and multiple ethnic and racial groups, Djanet Sears's 2002 play *The Adventures of a Black Girl in Search of God* takes as its focus the deep history of a particular local landscape and community, but is no less epic in vision and scale, featuring a cast of twenty-one actors in its original production.[14] Sears's play was inspired in part by actual events in Holland Township, a small community outside Toronto, when the municipal council decided to rename Negro Creek Road, which referred to a historic African Canadian community dating back to the years following the War of 1812 when Black Loyalist soldiers were rewarded for their service to the British with land in the area. The town council proposed to replace the name "Negro Creek Road," which it considered to be politically incorrect, with "Moggie Road," commemorating a later white settler in the area. Along with other supporters, the descendants of the Black community from which Negro Creek Road derived its name took issue with this decision, objecting to its erasure of Black history and presence in the area, organizing a protest march along the historic road, circulating a petition to restore the original name, and filing a complaint with the Ontario Human Rights Commission.[15] When a predominantly Black church in the area was defaced with racist slurs some months later, there was speculation that the vandalism was in response to Black activism relating to the renaming of Negro Creek Road.[16] Church leaders elected to leave the graffiti in place "to show that this type of thinking does exist."[17] In addition to these incidents, Sears was further inspired by the controversy surrounding a 1990 exhibition at the Royal Ontario Museum (ROM) in Toronto entitled "Into the Heart of Africa," which represented Africa from the perspective of Anglo-Canadian missionaries and soldiers in the late nineteenth and early twentieth centuries.[18]

In Sears's play, the relationship between the land and the people that have historically lived on it is bodied forth by a chorus – thirteen members in the original production – that performs through sound and movement the elements of earth and water, *"form[ing] the surrounding woods and farmland"* (3) as well as Negro Creek itself, while also functioning as "ancestors" (61), "souls" (88), and the congregation of the local church. The landscape in *Adventures of a Black Girl* is thus a physical, emotional, and spiritual environment, both a "source of life"[19] and a place of return.[20]

The central character in the play, Rainey, has roots in Negro Creek that are long and deep. As Rainey explains, "My Pa's family's lived and died on this bush land – been ours since the war of 1812" (19). In her father Abendigo's words, "Our blood is in this soil" (45). Rainey's daughter is buried amid the wildflowers in the cemetery by Negro Creek, and Abendigo, who is dying, will by his own arrangement be buried in a grave with a view of the creek at the end of the play. As he tells Rainey,

Heaven is Negro Creek. My grandmother left her life in that water. My body will rot in the earth and nurture the land, enriching the soil and more grass will grow and flowers and shrubs. And a cow might eat the grass and a part of me will be in the cow and the cow's milk. And maybe someone on Negro Creek will drink that milk or eat that cow. And the circle will just keep going, and going and going. (94)

At the start of the play, Rainey returns home to visit Abendigo and finalize her divorce from her husband Michael after several years in Toronto following the sudden death of her five-year-old daughter. Unable to accept her daughter's death, Rainey has given up her career as a doctor and is instead pursuing graduate studies in science and religion. She has lost her faith and developed an eating disorder that includes geophagy, especially craving what she describes as "the soft sugary earth by Negro creek [sic]."[21] Rainey returns to Negro Creek to try to fill the emptiness that was created within her by her daughter's death, and by the end of the play she finds solace in the landscape/community that is her ancestral home. As Elizabeth Brown-Guillory has noted, the land in Sears's play is a kind of "healing device."[22]

Following a long-deferred visit to her daughter's grave and a ritual rebirth in the waters of Negro Creek (88–89), Rainey's healing transformation is completed by a secondary plot that has Abendigo and a small band of fellow Black seniors disguising themselves as cleaners, kitchen workers, and chauffeurs to render themselves socially invisible[23] while they perform covert operations to "liberate" racist lawn ornaments, cookie jars, figurines, ephemera, and other artifacts in preparation for their main objective of reclaiming the 1812 military uniform of Abendigo's ancestor Juma Moore, founder of the Negro Creek community, from the storage vault of a museum resembling the ROM. Abendigo explains how the uniform was lost:

Once a year [it] would get a ritual cleaning.... They'd go into the water with it, hold it under, and let the creek purify it. Lorraine [Abendigo's grandmother] had done it for years, but this time.... Well, she was in the water when it happened. The uniform slipped down, out of her hands and she went after it.... They found her downstream when the creek thawed that spring, her hands still gripping that jacket. The authorities returned her body but kept the uniform – said it was the property of Her Majesty's army. (19–20)

Following his team's repatriation of Juma's uniform to Negro Creek, Abendigo's heart fails him and the play culminates in his funeral rites, including burial facing Negro Creek amid the seven generations of his family laid to rest in the cemetery there.

Sears is careful to recognize that the long-standing community of African descent from which Negro Creek takes its name and whose history is in danger of erasure through the act of renaming was itself founded on territory expropriated by the British from the Ojibway First Nation; as Caroline De Wagter notes, "the struggle of African Canadians" is thus situated in the play "within the larger context of colonialism."[24] Still, the strength of Abendigo's sense of continuity with the interlocked history of the land and community of Negro Creek ultimately enables Rainey to find consolation for her lost child. In a revision of the George Bernard Shaw story from which *Adventures of a Black Girl* adapts its title,[25] Sears's protagonist moves from a shattered belief in a god whose master plan encompassed the senseless taking of her little girl to a consoling acceptance of death as part of the grand cycle of life on Earth and as a laying to rest in a special place of communal home. In this sense, and as Jacqueline Petropoulos has noted, the historical landscape of Sears's play is a kind of "hallowed ground" and becomes so "literally...in the end when Abendigo wills his land to the church in order to be buried there."[26]

In the play's epilogue, Rainey observes, "Pa says that heaven is Negro Creek. Sometimes, if you get still, quiet enough, early in the morning or real late at night, you can almost hear her, hear the land singing" (116). In staging Rainey's deep roots and recognition of the relation between history, place, and community, Sears attends to a dimension of the Canadian landscape that has been largely unacknowledged, if not actually erased; as Leslie Sanders has written, in *Adventures of a Black Girl*, Black Canada's "history and its invisibility are brought to light."[27]

At the same time, however, the play includes references to a range of people of African descent from beyond Canada's borders, including Chaka the Zulu warrior (13), Alexander Pushkin and Alexandre Dumas (33), Harriet Tubman (43), Rosa Parks (43), and Martin Luther King (30), among others. Sanders notes that in the original 2002 production of the play, directed by Sears herself,

Three huge blue silk scarves shimmered from the ceiling as the play opened, dropping gracefully to the floor before the action began. As theme, emblem and subject, water was everywhere..., extending the geography of Negro Creek, to the Atlantic itself and to Africa, the source. When the chorus, moving as Negro Creek, beckons to Rainey; when she promises to consign her daughter's dolls to the water; in these moments, a palpable Negro Creek reaches beyond the particular history and struggles that the play addresses. It evokes the river-crossings that saved escaping slaves and the Middle Passage that brought them into slavery....[28]

In this way, Sanders concludes, Sears's staging of Negro Creek pointed toward "a larger imaginary and a deeper root."[29] Thus, while *Adventures of a Black Girl* foregrounds Black presence in Canadian history and the Canadian landscape, it also gestures, through form as well as content,[30] beyond what Rinaldo Walcott has called the "nationally local"[31] toward the broader history and context of African diasporic experience.[32]

"The people they dropped this burning on ... looked like us, like Dene": Marie Clements's *Burning Vision*

While Sears points toward the transnational connections of the Black community of Negro Creek in rural Ontario, the larger landscape of "Canadian" experience is the central focus of Marie Clements's epic 2002 play *Burning Vision*.[33] The play is premised on the fact that the uranium used in the US-manufactured bombs dropped on Hiroshima and Nagasaki during World War II was mined in northern Canada and that the people who lived near and worked in the uranium mine were neither protected from contamination nor warned of the hazardous effects of exposure to radioactive material.[34] Drawing on these historical facts, and inspired in part by Clements's own personal connection to the story through her Native roots in the Northwest Territories,[35] *Burning Vision* demonstrates that the atomic bombs claimed as their victims not only the Japanese citizens of the destroyed cities but also the Canadian men who mined the uranium, the First Nations ore carriers who transported it, the American women who worked as radium dial painters, and the myriad other small players who lived near and worked with or around the "money rock,"[36] as it was called by the Dene community, and whose lives were destroyed by the radiation sickness and cancer that it caused.

Transnational in scope, *Burning Vision* is grounded, literally, in the terrain of Canada, where the "uranium found at the center of the earth" was mined (n.p.). Uranium is personified in the play by the figure of "Little Boy," the code-name for the bomb dropped on Hiroshima but here characterized by Clements as "a beautiful Native boy" (n.p.) whose worst fear is of being "discovered" and "claimed" (20), as happened when the prospecting Labine brothers located and began to mine pitchblende – already known and avoided by local indigenous people (36) – at Great Bear Lake in the Northwest Territories in the early 1930s. A late-nineteenth-century Dene See-er's "burning vision" of the future further grounds the play within the Canadian landscape, rendering the bombing of Hiroshima and Nagasaki from a First Nations perspective and linking the Japanese bomb victims to the First Nations people who were made sick by their exposure to the radioactive ore. As the See-er says,

My voice grew hoarse with the sight of knowing that they would harm my people from the inside.... I sang this strange vision of people going into a big hole in the ground – strange people, not Dene. Their skin was white. Strange.

I followed.... Inside. I followed them down. They were going into this dark hole in the earth with all kinds of metal tools and machines. All sorts of tools that made all sorts of noise deep inside.... I followed them knowing.... They were digging great tunnels.... I looked up inside my vision. I saw a flying bird, big. It landed and they loaded it with things. It didn't look like it could harm anybody, but it made a lot of noise. I watched them digging something out of the hole in the earth and I watched them rise it to the cool sky until it disappeared and reappeared. Burning.

...I wondered if this would happen on our land, or if it would harm our people.

...The people they dropped this burning on...looked like us, like Dene. This burning vision is not for us now...It will come a long time in the future. It will come burning inside. (104–120)[37]

As the play unfolds, the links that the See-er perceives between the Dene and the Japanese extend to the United States as well, as the pretty radium dial painter who licks her paintbrush to keep its tip fine loses her face to cancer. Even "[a]n American bomb test dummy" (n.p.), named Fat Man after the bomb dropped on Nagasaki, reaches across the borders of his cartoon-like bigotry as the moment approaches when the bomb will be dropped on the test site that is his "home." As Clements notes, the dummy "gets more and more human as the bombs draw closer" to him, fearing dying alone and therefore claiming as his family both Little Boy and Round Rose, Clements's version of Japanese American Iva Toguri, who was prosecuted by the US government as the radio propaganda personality Tokyo Rose (n.p.).

These human connections that *Burning Vision* tracks across borders, cultures, races, and sides of the war are borne out through the play's fragmented structure as scenes with different groups of characters across times and places interweave between the shattering bomb detonations that frame the dramatic action (20, 118).[38] Thus, scenes of the Labine brothers' prospecting and mining enterprises abut against scenes of a grieving Dene widow who lost her ore carrier husband to radiation sickness, a Japanese grandmother separated from her grandson Koji during the atomic bombing, a doomed romance between a contaminated miner and the cancer-ridden radium dial painter, the crew of the ship transporting the ore south for processing, the tentative love of the young Métis woman Rose for Koji, who has miraculously fallen from the sky to northern Canada following the blast in Japan, and the allegorical figures of Fat Man and Little Boy, together with Round Rose. Clements's use of the term "movement," rather than "act" or "part," to describe the four sections of the play suggests her almost musical orchestration of the different voices of her dramatis personae to achieve a unified whole from the fractured shards of scenes generated by the production of uranium and the detonation of the atomic bombs.

But the idea of "movement" serves a thematic function as well, as is evident from Clements's emphasis on the elements of air, earth, water, and fire as a structuring principle for the play's four "movements." The first movement, entitled "The Frequency of Discovery" (19), centers on the element of air, broadly construed to include, for example, the airwaves by which television and radio broadcasts transmitted news of the deployment of the atomic bomb, as well as propaganda featuring Tokyo Rose and visual images that constructed viewers' cultural "others," for example, the television Indian Head Test Image that was used in the United States, Canada, and beyond from the 1940s to the 1970s. In Clements's opening stage directions, "the sound of a radio dial glid[es] over stations of scenes into different cultural tones as if stories are sitting on radio waves" (19). In this way, the element of air links what Clements describes as "scenes of the human noise of pain, grief, loss and isolation" (19). Movement Two, "Rare Earth Elements" (42), places emphasis on the globe's surface and depth, as a miner works deep underground while herds of caribou are heard traversing the Earth's surface far above him. From the depths of the planet, Asia seems no further away than the next co-worker; as the miner says, "Being down here is lonely, even if there's other guys it seems the space between us could tunnel to China" (43). The third movement, "Waterways" (75), centers on water as the medium by which the ore was transported south from the mine beneath Great Bear Lake, and the fourth and final movement, "Radar Echoes" (102), focuses on fire as the essential element of the Dene See-er's burning vision of radiation sickness and the atomic bomb. The elemental thematics of Clements's "Canadian" play suggest the unifying experience of human life on Earth and the global effects of the atomic bomb. Tracing the movement of uranium from beneath the surface of northern Canada all the way to Japan, *Burning Vision*, in Theresa May's words, "creat[es] a transnational countergeography that makes previously invisible relationships explicit and meaningful."[39] In doing so, Allison Hargreaves notes, it "radically reframes authorized Western histories of World War II and of the bombing of Hiroshima in particular."[40] In this way, Clements's play corresponds with the compassionate gesture of the Dene elders who traveled to Hiroshima in 1998 for the anniversary of the dropping of the atomic bomb in order to, in the words of Rosie Dolphus, the widow of a Dene ore carrier, "offer comfort" and explain to the Japanese that "we had no idea that rock was so dangerous. To others, to ourselves."[41] The "countergeography" of *Burning Vision* maps such human connections across and beyond the geopolitical boundaries that demarcate nations.

For Clements, the "writing process begins with the land. The land presents itself to her, and then the characters follow."[42] There is a sense, however, in which all three plays that I have discussed here begin with the land in that they are in the largest sense founded upon and framed through the national landscapes within which the histories that have produced the characters have played out and which have at the same time been produced by those characters. Alan Filewod has suggested that "Canadian nationhood is a constantly changing historical performance enacted in an imagined theatre,"[43] while Nadine Holdsworth has noted more generally that "theatre is deeply implicated in constructing the nation through the imaginative realm and provides a site where the nation can be put under the microscope," "generat[ing] a creative dialogue with tensions in the national fabric."[44] As what might be called "state-of-the-nation plays" that "hold [Canada] up for scrutiny and critique,"[45] *Sled, The Adventures of a Black Girl in Search of God*, and *Burning Vision* stage historical landscapes in order to critique but also to reconceive the nation, articulating the roots and effects of violence in all its forms and imagining other modes of interacting; refusing erasure, claiming space, and asserting historical and continuing presence for marginalized groups; tracing networks of connection and shared experience that transcend time and national borders; pointing toward alternative futures through new alliances and forms of rebirth; and representing women as integral to the landscape of Canada's past/present/future. Joanne Tompkins has noted that "[t]he 'space' in the theatre refracts to encompass several dimensions, including the building which houses bodies in real space, in addition to the imagined (and performed) space(s) that those bodies occupy. The venue (simultaneously no place and all places) frames that which is on stage, so that the staged locations intersect with the world offstage."[46] Premiered in some of the nation's leading performance venues, *Sled, Adventures of a Black Girl*, and *Burning Vision* are historical landscape plays that intersect with and intervene in the present context and moment and, in so doing, exemplify the role of contemporary women playwrights in the ongoing act of reshaping Canada's social, cultural, and political landscape.

Notes

1 Una Chaudhuri, *Staging Place: The Geography of Modern Drama* (Ann Arbor: University of Michigan Press, 1995), xi, xii.
2 Elinor Fuchs, "Reading for Landscape: The Case of American Drama," in *Land/Scape/Theater*, ed. Elinor Fuchs and Una Chaudhuri (Ann Arbor: University of Michigan Press, 2002), 30.
3 Una Chaudhuri and Elinor Fuchs, "Introduction: Land/Scape/Theater and the New Spatial Paradigm," in *Land/Scape/Theater*, ed. Elinor Fuchs and Una Chaudhuri (Ann Arbor: University of Michigan Press, 2002), 2.
4 Joanne Tompkins, *Unsettling Space: Contestations in Contemporary Australian Theatre*, Studies in International Performance (Basingstoke, UK: Palgrave, 2006), 5.
5 Chaudhuri, *Staging Place*, xii.
6 Ibid., 15.
7 This discussion of *Sled* draws on my essay "Monstrous History: Judith Thompson's *Sled*," originally published in *Canadian Theatre Review* 120 (2004): 46–49 and reprinted in *Judith Thompson*, ed. Ric Knowles, Critical Perspectives on Canadian Theatre in English, vol. 3 (Toronto: Playwrights Canada Press, 2005), 99–104. *Sled* was first produced in 1997 at Toronto's Tarragon Theatre, a leading venue for the development and production of new Canadian drama.
8 Judith Thompson, *Sled* (Toronto: Playwrights Canada Press, 1997), 15; subsequent references to the play will be given parenthetically in the text.
9 Chaudhuri, *Staging Place*, xii.
10 "*Ek skal skjota ther huorta i gegnum....* Let's shoot her man. Right through the heart" (33).
11 Cathy Caruth, *Unclaimed Experience: Trauma, Narrative, and History* (Baltimore: Johns Hopkins University Press, 1996), 3.
12 Walter Benjamin, "Theses on the Philosophy of History," in *Illuminations*, ed. Hannah Arendt, trans. Harry Zohn (New York: Schocken, 1969), 256.

13 Cynthia Zimmerman, "A Conversation with Judith Thompson," *Canadian Drama/L'Art dramatique canadien* 16, no. 2 (1990): 191.

14 *The Adventures of a Black Girl in Search of God* premiered in 2002 at the du Maurier Theatre at Harbourfront Centre in Toronto in a production by Obsidian Theatre Company, which is dedicated to staging works by Black playwrights, in association with Nightwood Theatre, which focuses on work by women playwrights. Sears directed this first production.

15 Roberta Avery, "Black marchers challenge change in name of road: Negro Creek Rd. called tribute to ancestors," *Toronto Star* 16 June 1996: A4.

16 Roberta Avery, "Vandals deface Collingwood black church with profanity," *Toronto Star* 30 August 1996: A18.

17 Carolynn Wilson, quoted in "Black church isn't removing racial graffiti (Heritage Community Church in Collingwood)," *The Canadian Press* [Toronto] 30 August 1996, available at *http://ezproxy.lib.ucalgary.ca:2048/login?url=http://search.proquest.com/docview /359527795?accountid=9838* (accessed 16 January 2012).

18 The controversy over the ROM exhibition was widely covered in the press. For a sampling of this coverage, see, for example, Bronwyn Drainie, "Black groups protest African show at 'Racist Ontario Museum,'" *Globe and Mail* 24 March 1990: C1; Paula Todd, "African exhibits inspire awe and anger," *Toronto Star* 7 May 1990: A6; Maureen Murray, "Chanting group pickets ROM but respects court injunction," *Toronto Star* 13 May 1990: A3; and Susan Crean, "Africa exhibit added insult to original injury," *Toronto Star* 6 September 1990: A25.

19 Joel Greenberg, review of *The Adventures of a Black Girl in Search of God, Aisle Say (Toronto),* [2002], available at *http://www.aislesay.com/ONT-ADVENTURES.html* (accessed 29 June 2012).

20 For a related analysis of Sears's staging of the relationship between the land and community in *Adventures of a Black Girl*, see Caroline De Wagter, "Land and Cultural Memory: Djanet Sears's *The Adventures of a Black Girl in Search of God* and Diane Glancy's *Jump Kiss: An Indian Legend*," in *Theatres in the Round: Multi-Ethnic, Indigenous and Intertextual Dialogues in Drama*, ed. Dorothy Figueira and Marc Maufort, with the assistance of Sylvie Vranckzx (Brussels: Peter Lang, 2011), 65.

21 Djanet Sears, *The Adventures of a Black Girl in Search of God* (Toronto: Playwrights Canada Press, 2003), 19; subsequent references to the play will be given parenthetically in the text.

22 Elizabeth Brown-Guillory, "Place and Displacement in Djanet Sears's *Harlem Duet* and *The Adventures of a Black Girl in Search of God*," in *Middle Passages and the Healing Places of History: Migration and Identity in Black Women's Literature*, ed. Elizabeth Brown-Guillory (Columbus: Ohio State University, 2006), 167.

23 As Abendigo says, all the team needs to pass is "a little unconscious classification" (15) on the part of the whites from under whose noses they are removing the objects they seek to liberate.

24 Caroline De Wagter, "Land and Cultural Memory," 61–62.

25 The title of Shaw's story is "The Adventures of the Black Girl in her Search for God." In a 2004 interview, Sears explains:

   The title of my new play, *The Adventures of a Black Girl in Search of God*, it's an adaptation, or a revising, of a Shaw title. Shaw wrote a short story about a young girl in South Africa who goes into the wilderness searching for God and finds many versions of God there. It's really more of an intellectual exercise. The piece is interesting, but the title stayed with me. Shaw's story is not really about the black girl at all. ("An Interview with Djanet Sears," by Mat Buntin, Canadian Adaptations of Shakespeare Project, available at *http://www.canadianshakespeares.ca/i_dsears.cfm* [accessed 14 November 2012])

26 Jacqueline Petropoulos, "'The Ground on Which I Stand': Rewriting History, African Canadian Style," in *Signatures of the Past: Cultural Memory in Contemporary Anglophone North American Drama*, ed. Marc Maufort and Caroline de Wagter (Brussels: Peter Lang, 2008), 77.

27 Leslie Sanders, "History at Negro Creek; Djanet Sears' *The Adventures of a Black Girl in Search of God*," in *Testifyin': Contemporary African Canadian Drama*, vol. 2, ed. Djanet Sears (Toronto: Playwrights Canada, 2003), 487.

28 Ibid., 489.

29 Ibid.

30 Sears has stated of the chorus that she "wanted to create a vehicle ... to advance the unity of action within the play," not in a "neoclassical sense" but in the manner of "African story-telling techniques, which I observed over there. Constant movement, gesture, dance and sound – reaching as many of the senses as possible, sometimes without the audience even being consciously aware of it" ("Interview with Djanet Sears: A Black Girl in Search of God," by Robin Breon, *Aisle Say (Toronto)* [2002], available at *http://www.aislesay.com/ONT-SEARS.html* [accessed 27 June 2012]).

31 Rinaldo Walcott, "Dramatic Instabilities: Diasporic Aesthetics as a Question for and about Nation," *Canadian Theatre Review* 118 (2004): 99–106.

32 Brown-Guillory ("Place and Displacement," 167) and De Wagter ("Land and Cultural Memory," 58, 60, 64) also note the diasporic dimensions of Sears's play.

33 *Burning Vision* premiered in 2002 at Vancouver's Firehall Arts Centre, which is committed to the presentation of works that "reflect the cultural pluralism of Canada" and which has, over the past thirty years, "evolved into one of Canada's most well respected cultural hubs"; see Firehall Arts Centre, "Mission Statement" and "Our History," available at *http://firehallartscentre.ca/* (accessed 10 December 2012). The play's original director, Peter Hinton, noted in an interview that Clements has "a very operatic vision for the stage. Her stage directions are wonderfully poetic, they're mythic in scale and many times during the creation it felt like doing opera – poetry and realism collide, time and culture cross paths, and then there is the physical scale of the piece: nine actors. That's very big for Canada" (qtd. in Gaetan L. Charlebois, "Burning Vision mines a sad story," *The Gazette* [Montreal] 4 June 2003: D5.

34 For further details, see, for example, Andrew Nikiforuk, "Echoes of the Atomic Age: Uranium haunts a northern village," *Calgary Herald* 14 March 1998: A4.

35 Clements has stated that she has "always [found it] strange that the uranium that was used to build the first atomic bomb that was dropped on the Japanese in 1945 came from the land of my bones" (qtd. in Rita Wong, "Decolonizasian: Reading Asian and First Nations Relations in Literature," *Canadian Literature* 199 [Winter 2008], available through *Literature Online* at *http://gateway.proquest.com/openurl?ctx_ver=Z39.88–2003-&xri:pqil:res_ver=0.2&res_id=xri:lion-us&rft_id=xri:lion:ft:abell:R04149198:0* [accessed 14 November 2012]). As well, Brian Lin reports:

> While visiting relatives in Fort Good Hope in the Northwest Territories eight years ago, Clements became aware of the story about the discovery of uranium in the area and how the Native people of the area, her extended family, suffered because of it. "You write things you're very passionate about," said Clements. "Having lost a lot of my elders made me hyper-aware and sensitive to radiation poisoning." ("Tuning Into Humanity with Burning Vision," *Raven's Eye* 5, no. 12 (2002): 8, available at *http://www.ammsa.com/publications/ravens-eye/tuning-humanity-burning-vision* [accessed 15 December 2012])

36 Marie Clements, *Burning Vision* (Vancouver: Talonbooks, 2003), 80; subsequent references to the play will be given parenthetically in the text.

37 The See-er and "burning vision" of Clements's play were inspired by an actual see-er described by Dene writer George Blondin in his 1990 book *When the World Was New: Stories of the Sahtu Dene*; see Marie Clements, "Interview with Marie Clements," by Andrea Cochrane, 13 June 2002, available at *http://www.playwrights.ca/portfolios/burningvisioninterview1.html* (accessed 7 December 2012).

38 Rita Wong has noted that narrative in *Burning Vision* "is in a sense torn apart and sundered by the nuclear detonations that begin and end the play" ("Decolonizasian"). See also Robin C. Whittaker, who notes that Clements's "chronotopic dramaturgy enacts an explosive fission on our perception of a stabilized world. In Clements's hands it is a scripted metaphor for the bombing itself" ("Fusing the Nuclear Community: Intercultural Memory, Hiroshima 1945 and the Chronotopic Dramaturgy of Marie Clements's *Burning Vision*," *Theatre Research in Canada* 30, no. 1–2 [2009]: 138).

39 Theresa J. May, "Kneading Marie Clements' *Burning Vision*," *Canadian Theatre Review* 144 (Fall 2010): 7.

40 Allison Hargreaves, "'A Precise Instrument for Seeing': Remembrance in *Burning Vision* and the Activist Classroom," *Canadian Theatre Review* 147 (Summer 2011): 50.

41 Rosie Dolphus, qtd. in Colin Nickerson, "Cancer, remorse haunt tiny village," *Boston Globe* 6 August 1998: A2. For more on the Dene delegation to Hiroshima, see also Deborah Simmons, "Sahtú and the Atomic Bomb," available at *http://www.deline.ca/culture-and-community/deline-stories/uranium/* (accessed 15 November 2012); and Ronald B. Barbour, "Déline Dene Mining Tragedy," *First Nations Drum*, posted 22 December 1998, available at *http://www.firstnationsdrum.com/1998/12/deline-dene-mining-tragedy/* (accessed 15 November 2012).

42 Wong, "Decolonizasian."

43 Alan Filewod, *Performing Canada: The Nation Enacted in the Imagined Theatre*, Textual Studies in Canada 15, Monograph Series: Critical Performances in Canada (Spring 2002): x.

44 Nadine Holdsworth, *Theatre & Nation* (Basingstoke, UK: Palgrave Macmillan, 2010), 6–7.

45 Ibid., 7.

46 Tompkins, *Unsettling Space*, 3.

15

Asian American Women Playwrights and the Dilemma of the Identity Play: Staging Heterotopic Subjectivities

Esther Kim Lee

Young Jean Lee's 2006 play *Songs of the Dragons Flying to Heaven* begins with a disturbing image that might cause audience members to turn away in disgust. A prerecorded voice-over of Lee, who also directed the play, is heard talking and laughing with her friends and then instructing one of them to hit her face hard. Lee is hit multiple times and is heard sniffling yet encouraging the hitting. After a dozen hits, a video of the hitting appears on the back wall. In a 2007 interview, Lee explains that the hitting can be interpreted as a clichéd representation of "Asian self-hatred," but she also emphasizes that the video was an experiment with how a playwright might insert herself into her own play.[1] In the past few years, Lee has emerged as a groundbreaking theatre artist, described by Charles Isherwood of *The New York Times* as "hands down, the most adventurous downtown playwright of her generation."[2] Lee has a unique and original perspective on contemporary theatre, but she is also an Asian American woman playwright who has had to confront, both willingly and unwillingly, long-standing issues of identity, representation, and agency. The racial category "Asian American" does not fit her comfortably and should be an afterthought because the majority of her work does not deal directly with Asian American issues. Still, the label follows her and imposes a set of expectations. *Songs of the Dragons* is her most direct answer to these expectations, and she makes the audience feel her discomfort and pain in having to write about her identity.

Other contemporary Asian American women playwrights have articulated a similar dilemma in writing about identity. Whereas the first wave of Asian American women playwrights[3] dealt directly with identity issues in ways that Lee would call clichéd, drawing on semi-autobiographical history and centering on the politics of representation and resistance,[4] more recent works by playwrights such as Julia Cho and Diana Son, as well as Lee herself, defy conventional categorizations in terms of race and gender and have little to do with autobiographical identity or Asian American history. Son's *Stop Kiss* (1998), for example, is about two women of unspecified race who fall in love, Cho's *Architecture of Loss* (2004) is about family and grief, and Lee's *Church* (2007) is about religion. All three playwrights have in their portfolios more plays with characters without specific ethnic or racial identities than those with specific Asian American references, and when present in their work, Asian American identity functions as one component of a complex combination of influences that shape the characters and dramatic situations. For minority writers, getting recognition for writing on topics not specific to their race, ethnicity, or gender has been read as a sign of success and acceptance, yet Cho, Son, and Lee have all felt compelled to write plays based on their lives and experience. In this essay, I will consider three of their "identity plays" – Cho's *99 Histories*, Son's *Satellites*, and Lee's *Songs of the Dragons Flying to Heaven* – in order to articulate how each playwright writes about her identity as both an Asian American and a woman while at the same time rejecting the limitations and expectations of that identity.

Cho, Son, and Lee do not represent all contemporary Asian American women playwrights, but they are the most produced and influential of the group in the early twenty-first century. The fact that they are all Korean Americans allows a more focused point of comparison within a broader context of Asian American theatre history. As I discuss in my introduction to *Seven Contemporary Plays from the Korean Diaspora in the Americas*, the opening decade of the twenty-first century saw the emergence of a noticeable number of Korean American playwrights.[5] Korean immigration to the United States reached its numerical peak after the late 1960s, and so was much later than peaks of Chinese and Japanese immigration. The three playwrights I discuss were either the first in the family to be born in the United States or left Korea at a young age. Compared to other Asian American women playwrights, Korean American playwrights have only recently begun to address identity issues and to write about how they are different from their parents' generation. Their plays, therefore, present a more urgent and contemporary perspective on Asian American female identity.

The three playwrights approach identity using different dramaturgical styles and character types, but their plays are similar in how they address gender.[6] All three plays dramatize intergenerational relationships between women, with plot conflicts centering on mothers and grandmothers, daughters and babies. Male characters – real and imagined – occupy a significant part of the female characters' psyches and hauntingly shape how they deal with others. At the core of the plays, Asian American women characters deal with the difficulties of womanhood and with cultural expectations arising from both Korean and American gender politics. Each playwright is aware of the inseparability of gender and race and the legacy of stereotypes that have had a lasting impact on Asian American women. At the same time, they reject reductive trappings in representing gender and instead provide more complex and nuanced views of identity.

The complexities of staging identity in the work of contemporary Asian American women playwrights reflect the complexities of the field of Asian American studies, as well as the lived realities of those who identify themselves as Asian Americans. In the past twenty years, Asian American studies has grown from a small area of study focused on identity formation, history, and political representation to a major field that includes the meta-critical and decentered perspectives of poststructuralism and transnationalism.[7] In "Heterogeneity, Hybridity, Multiplicity: Asian American Differences," an often-cited chapter of her 1996 book *Immigrant Acts*, Lisa Lowe articulates the impossibility of making generalizations about Asian Americans,[8] and in literary and cultural studies, all assumptions about Asian Americans have been deconstructed, while concepts such as race, ethnicity, nationhood, and identity have been redefined as unstable and conditional. Despite these rapid changes and concerns, or perhaps because of them, scholars of Asian American culture have found productive ways to discuss racial and ethnic identities while acknowledging their fluidity and instability.

In *Imagine Otherwise: On Asian Americanist Critique*, Kandice Chuh argues for a definition of "Asian American" that "relies not on the empirical presence of Asian-raced bodies in the United States for its intelligibility, but...that instead emphasizes the fantasy links between body and subjectivity discursively forged within...literary and legal texts."[9] Chuh uses the term "fantasy links" to emphasize diegetic representations and to theorize the multiple forms of interconnected narratives, subjectivities, identities, and differences in Asian American literature. In particular, she develops Michel Foucault's theory of heterotopia to justify using an Asian Americanist critique to examine Korean American novels:

> [W]e might conceive "Asian America" as a heterotopic formation, one that enfigures the multiple and dissimilar spaces and places of discourse and history that collectively produce what seems at first glance, terminologically, to refer to a distinctly bounded site, "America." Foucault has theorized heterotopia as referencing both the real and unreal spaces that shape social relations.... As in the reflection of a mirror, where knowledge of self derives from seeing that self where she is not, where understanding of real places are determined by seeing through unreal spaces, these novels may be seen to articulate the imagined spaces and material locations variously referenced by "home" and "nation," by "Korean" and "Korean American."[10]

Chuh's interpretation of heterotopia applies to novels that are to be read, and the spaces and locations that she writes about are expressed literarily, but her interpretation of space and subjectivity also serves as a useful framework for analyzing the staging of identity in the plays of Cho, Son, and Lee.

In theatre, unlike literature, imagined spaces can materialize onstage, and the stage can function as a heterotopic site in which both real and unreal spaces can coexist. Foucault includes theatre as one of his examples of heterotopia because of its ability to bring onto the stage "a whole series of places that are foreign to one another."[11] He does not elaborate on theatre beyond a comparison to cinema and gardens in order to illustrate how heterotopia allows juxtaposition of several spaces in one location. In what follows, I take a cue from Chuh and Foucault and examine Cho's *99 Histories*, Son's *Satellites*, and Lee's *Songs of the Dragons Flying to Heaven* in terms of how the onstage spaces reflect the dilemma of the playwrights in representing identity.

"We remembered the wrong memories": *99 Histories* by Julia Cho

99 Histories was first produced by the Cherry Lane Theatre in New York City in 2002 and has been described by Cho as her identity play:

> I guess you could say *99 Histories* was my identity play. I think most writers start there. It wasn't autobiographical but I did write about issues I cared about, issues of home, immigration and family. Growing up, I had very little sense of what Korea was and I had no sense of family history. The play explored that sense of disconnection and loss. It reflects my belief that the past is slippery and often irretrievable. But our need for a sense of continuity and selfhood is so strong that we are able to invent and imagine what we cannot – or will not – remember.[12]

The play revolves around the relationship between Eunice Kim, a Korean American woman in her late twenties, and her mother, Sah-Jin, described by the playwright as an "American-Korean" in her fifties.[13] Eunice was a child prodigy, a virtuoso cello player and overachiever that everyone in town knew. Just before she turned twelve, she witnessed her father getting fatally shot at the convenience store her parents owned. For a while, she focused only on improving her cello-playing and becoming "great," but all of a sudden, she developed a mental illness. She ran away after piercing her hand with her cello bow. At the start of the play, Eunice returns to her childhood home after a long absence. She no longer suffers from mental illness, but she is pregnant and plans to give her baby up for adoption. Eunice is portrayed as someone without a goal, a vagabond whose only mission was, at the advisement of her mother, to not get pregnant and not get AIDS. She avoided the latter, but the pregnancy was an accident, the result of a brief relationship with a white boyfriend. As the plot develops, Eunice begins to speculate about her mother's past in Korea in order to answer fundamental questions about who she herself is. She looks to her mother for answers, but her frustration grows when her questions are met with secrets and silences. Sah-Jin prefers to remember Eunice as the genius cello player and tells her to choose to be happy by focusing on her talent and not looking back, but Eunice refuses to bury the past.

During her search for answers, Eunice finds an old photograph of a woman she initially thinks is her mother, but she is later told that it is her aunt, who had the same illness as her. The photograph functions as the key to Eunice finding answers to her questions. Sah-Jin, whose name means "photograph" in Korean, initially refuses to tell Eunice about the past and what happened in Korea. She wants Eunice to be the ideal American, the model minority who can overcome the curses of the past, but despite Sah-Jin's lifelong efforts to forget the past and give her daughter a new life in a new country, Eunice's inherited genetic illness has the upper hand. It is as if when the illness took over, all of the baggage left behind in Korea resurfaced, forcing mother and daughter both to remember. The play ends with Eunice accepting both the past and the present, picking up her cello again, and deciding to keep her baby. She also finally gets an answer to one of the questions she asked her mother: what is *chung*? Sah-Jin describes *chung* as "memory plus time" (82). Eunice does not say she understands this complex Korean concept, which defies translation, but she stops asking questions about the past.

During her search for answers, Eunice does not ask the familiar questions about ethnic identity, in the vein of "Am I Korean? Am I American?" or "Am I too assimilated?" Her questions are not either–or and are not solely based on culture, racial identity, experience, or other typical indicators of an identity play. Instead, she wants to know why her parents left Korea and sacrificed everything for her musical success, and whether she can genetically pass her mental illness on to her baby. She suspects everything, including love, memory, and even reality. The only constant in her life is the bond – *chung* – she has with her mother and the bond she is developing with her unborn baby. No matter what happens, even when reality collapses as it did for Eunice with her mental illness, she realizes that *chung* stays with and sustains her.

In her note on the play, Cho specifies how the play should be staged: "The scenes are fluid and run into each other, with only occasional brief beats. Keep in mind that scenes have different textures: some are memories, some are dreams, some are everyday realities. The shifts in texture should be reflected somehow, whether it's through a change in lighting, pacing or tone" (24). The stage described by Cho is a heterotopia where reality is reflected, distorted, and scattered. According to Foucault, "We are in the epoch of simultaneity: we are in the epoch of juxtaposition, the epoch of the near and far, of the side-by-side, of the dispersed."[14] The spaces occupied by Cho's characters are both real and unreal, but they are interwoven and connected as the scenes in the play shift between several versions of memory in Eunice's mind. The play begins with Eunice returning home, which is the present reality she has to deal with, but that reality is interrupted by a flashback to a conversation she had with Joe, the father of her baby. Cho indicates this temporal and spatial change with the simple stage direction, "The lights shift" (28). Eunice's reality alternates between present moments and memories of the past, and with each shift, her confusion about herself grows. In scene four, she asks her mother, "Ma, why'd you come here? You and dad?" to which Sah-Jin answers, "What kind of stupid question is that?" (44). When she does not get satisfying answers, Eunice begins to imagine her mother's past in Korea. In this fantasy Korea, a "woman," whom she decides is her mother, falls in love with a white American man who is different from her Korean dad in many ways, but this imagined "memory" overlaps with Eunice's memory of her boyfriend Joe. The layers of memory thicken with Eunice's remembrance of when she (she remembers herself as the "girl") had her mental breakdown.

Within each scene and between scenes, time and space change fluidly, and the boundaries between imagined memories and actual memories are never made clear. In the last scene, Eunice tells her unborn baby what she has come to realize:

We took pictures of the wrong things, and we recorded the wrong events. We told the wrong stories, and we remembered the wrong memories. What has lasted is sadness; it will outlast flesh. What has lasted is forgetfulness; it wins over memory every time. But sometimes, in the blue hour, between midnight and dawn, I'll wake up and my hands will be alive, moving over an imaginary cello all by themselves. (47)

Just as she feels the muscle memory of playing the cello, she feels the baby inside her, and with the help of Sah-Jin, she accepts the fact that neither her cello-playing nor the baby needs to be perfect. They are both beautiful to Eunice, and she can finally be at peace with herself. In the last moment of the play, Eunice, the "woman," and the "girl" from her imagined memories simultaneously repeat the words "goodness, good day, memory" while Bach's "First Cello Suite in G" is heard in the background (82–83). The three female characters exist in different times and spaces, yet they together make up Eunice's identity. The "woman" could be either her mother or the aunt who had the same illness as her, and the "girl" may or may not be her when she was younger. Thus, Cho's fluid and heterotopic use of onstage space dramatizes the various combinations of Eunice's imagined and real memories. In the absence of definitive history and answers about who she is, Eunice's identity needs to be constituted with what Cho describes as "99 histories," which connotes a sense of infinite variations of imagined moments and memories.

"We can make up the words": *Satellites* by Diana Son

In *Satellites*, which premiered at the Public Theater in New York City in 2006, Son's central character Nina is opposite of Cho's character Eunice in many respects. Although Son states that the play is not autobiographical, it was inspired by the Brooklyn neighborhood that she and husband moved to after they had children, and she envisions "Nina as having a similar upbringing" to hers.[15] A successful New York City-based architect in her mid-30s, Nina is driven, ambitious, and focused on success. She is also a new mother who moves to Brooklyn to start a family with her African American husband Miles, who was adopted by a white family and graduated from Columbia University with a degree in computer engineering. Throughout the play, Nina is overwhelmed by the demands of her baby, her work, and those around her. Sleep-deprived and barely able to deal with motherhood, a new house, and a new project at work, she hires a Korean woman as a nanny. Her primary reason for choosing a Korean nanny is to expose her baby to the Korean language because she herself cannot speak it. The nanny, Mrs. Chae, is described as a "Korean from Korea" in her mid-50s or early 60s.[16] Nina's own mother has passed away, so Mrs. Chae's role is in a sense that of surrogate mother to Nina. In their first meeting, Nina is deeply moved by the immediate connection Mrs. Chae makes with the baby, Hannah, and by her sympathy for Nina and her predicament. When Mrs. Chae tells the baby in Korean, "Oh, look at you, you're such a pretty girl," the stage direction reads: "This unexpectedly touches Nina." (269). In fact, everything Mrs. Chae does surprises and moves her, and when Mrs. Chae sings a song Nina's mother used to sing to her, she cannot help but compare Mrs. Chae to her deceased mother.

Nina quickly learns, however, that Mrs. Chae can never replace her mother, whom she sees as having been different from other Korean women in the way she taught her daughter about racial equality. As desperate as Nina is for help, she is adamant that Mrs. Chae must be let go when she makes a comment about the baby that Nina perceives as racist. Mrs. Chae tells Nina, "Hannah is not black. If you look at her, maybe you cannot tell. People cannot tell the daddy is black. She is just beautiful baby" (294). Mrs. Chae does not understand why she is being let go and pleads with Nina, but Nina shows no sympathy for the older woman. Instead, she angrily criticizes Koreans who feel superior to black people: "It makes me mad, it makes me ashamed of being Korean, fucking racists" (314). Nina's anger at Mrs. Chae's racism is compounded by the fact that the black neighborhood to which Nina and her family have moved does not seem to welcome them. Soon after they move to their new home, a rock is thrown by a neighbor and shatters one of the windows.

For Nina, the memory of her mother, whom Mrs. Chae can never replace, guides her in creating for her interracial child an ideal surrounding, a kind of utopia that neither she nor Miles could enjoy during their own childhoods. Both were denied history, culture, language, and a sense of belonging; Miles grew up as a black child in a white family, and Nina's childhood was spent in a predominantly white neighborhood. Both faced blatant racism while having to live as if they were white. As a single adult, Nina was a young Korean American woman with a successful career living the life of a "yuppie," as the characters put it in the play (286), but her interracial baby forces her to face her past and her ethnic background in order to make sense of how her family can belong in a neighborhood with a troubled past and in a home that was, as Miles observes, "a shooting gallery and a crack house before the city took it over" (299).

Throughout the play, Nina is mentally and emotionally pulled in multiple directions, each of which demands her full attention. She needs to hold and nurse her baby, work on an architecture project with a tight deadline, deal with a suspicious neighbor, and caution her husband against his manipulative brother, while at the same time trying to unpack moving boxes and renovate her new home. In her stage directions, Son specifies that "[t]he living room blends into the kitchen, a stairwell leads to the bedrooms above, another connects to the garden level office below" (406), while Ben Brantley of *The New York Times* provides a vivid description of the set that Mark Wendland designed for the original production at the Public Theater:

[R]ooms slide sideways, backward and forward in this study of big-city-identity crises.... A seemingly solid structure splits again and again into a house divided, as distinctions between outdoors and indoors, between public and private, melt and dissolve.[17]

Because of the constantly shifting space around her, Nina becomes overly sensitive about where things and people belong in the house, but she never actually gains control over them. The new house functions as a projection of Nina's vision of a utopic environment for her daughter but also as a symbol of her failures. As an architect, Nina is supposed to be an expert on living space, but she finds herself losing control over her own space and, by extension, her life. She thought that moving to a bigger place in a mostly black neighborhood and hiring a Korean nanny was the best decision for her family: she could have her office downstairs and work from home and the baby would be exposed to a diverse culture that she herself did not experience as a child. In the process of attempting to create a utopic ideal home, however, she has instead created a heterotopia of multiple, disjointed, and fluid spaces. The stage representation of the brownstone reflects Nina's overextended life, suggesting a heterotopia with multiple interconnected spaces, each of which represents a part of her identity.

In the last scene, Nina reaches the breaking point when some workers start making a lot of loud noise as they smash the old glass in order to replace the broken window. The stage directions describe her reaction:

Another smash. Nina releases a sound – something between a growl and a war cry. She picks up a pry bar and walks to the window and starts smashing the glass as Kit [Nina's friend and business partner] and Mrs. Chae watch. Reggie [the neighbor helping with the window], on the other side, backs up. Nina takes several whacks at it until there's little window left. The sound of Hannah crying. Nina takes a breath, her demeanor changes. (460)

As Nina heads upstairs to respond to the baby's crying, she sees Miles coming downstairs holding Hannah in his arms. When the two encounter each other, they seem to genuinely communicate for the first time in the play. In the last lines, Nina tells Miles that she thinks the rock that smashed the window was a meteorite that was "a chip off some billion-year-old comet that came crashing through here to let out all the ghosts, all the stories, all the history...To let us know...we can make up the words ourselves" (461).

The "words" that Nina refers to here are the lyrics of a lullaby that she and Miles had difficulty remembering earlier in the play, but they also signify the reality of their lives as they have been changed by the presence of the baby. Like a meteorite, she came into their lives and changed the way their relationship orbits, causing them to readjust everything, including who they are both alone and together. After smashing the window, Nina realizes that there is a bigger space, perhaps an infinite space, outside the house. Heterotopia, according to Foucault's definition, is a space that exists in relation to other spaces. Up to this point, Nina felt frustration in using the past as a point of reference, but at the end of the play, she decides to use other histories and the future's infinite potential to define her reality and spatial surroundings.

"I'm just a fucking white guy": *Songs of the Dragons Flying to Heaven* by Young Jean Lee

Songs of the Dragons Flying to Heaven was originally produced by Young Jean Lee's Theater Company and premiered in 2006 at New York City's HERE Arts Center, which also commissioned the play. It has since been produced in the United States and Europe at various avant-garde venues.[18] The play is about a character named "Korean-American" who is described as an "Asian-American female" and who encounters nightmarish yet outrageously comical situations with characters named "Korean 1," "Korean 2," and "Korean 3," all of whom are described as "Asian female[s]" in the version of the play published in *American Theatre*.[19] After the audio and video sequences described in the opening section of this essay, Korean-American enters the stage and talks directly to the audience about her experience as an Asian American of Korean ancestry. The monologue consists of her thoughts on Asian parents, racism in America, her grandmother, and white people. She jumps from one topic to another and positions herself in opposition to everyone she mentions. About Asian parents, she says, "It's like being raised by monkeys – these retarded monkeys who can barely speak English and are too evil to understand anything besides conformity and status," and then she adds, "I am so mad about all of the racist things against me in this country, which is America." She warns "white people," whom she seems to equate with the audience, "I can promise you one thing, which is that we will crush you. You may laugh now, but remember my words when you and your offspring are writhing under our yoke" (39–41). The entire passage is disjointed and without a central message. If anything, it sounds like a random patchwork of cynical comments that might be heard from a stand-up comedian.

After this monologue, Korean-American raises her fist and says "Let the Korean dancing begin! (40)," which prompts the Korean characters to come onstage in brightly colored traditional Korean dresses and begin their unpredictable and weird acts. They call each other by fake Asian names and speak Korean and Cantonese while slapping, kicking, and spitting on each other. What happens between the Korean characters and Korean-American in this scene has been described in reviews as "deconstructive," "Asian minstrelsy," "emotionally raw," "angry," "ridiculous," "ludicrous," and "bizarre."[20] Koreans 1 through 3 and Korean-American engage in a series of games and free play that is both funny and disturbing. They talk about prostitution, rape, dragons, and ancestral homes, but there is no logic or meaning to their words. Each character reacts to what the others say and do and each seems to have genuine emotional reactions, but they are far from coherent and consistent. As Lee states in an interview, each line and interaction is a cliché about Asian women:

> It's a destructive impulse – I want to destroy the show: make it so bad that it just eats itself, eating away at its own clichés until it becomes complicated and fraught enough to resemble truth. So, I started writing every horrible thing I

could possibly think of, like the story of the young Asian woman describing her brutal rape at the hand of some man that her father sold her to. Another was the intergenerational conflict scene between the grandmother and the granddaughter. Every cliché I could think of – I was just spewing them out.[21]

The incoherent yet bizarrely entertaining interaction between the characters continues until they are interrupted by the sudden appearance of White Person 1 and White Person 2, who are described as being female and male, respectively.

The white characters are dressed in gray, and when they appear, the fluorescent lights above turn on. In contrast to the fast pace of the previous scenes, the two white people talk only about their relationship, which is excruciatingly ordinary and uninteresting. Korean-American and Koreans 1 through 3 return, but the white characters gradually overtake the play, which eventually becomes entirely about them and their mundane lives. Lee has commented that she has heard many complaints about the white people taking over the play and she admits that the way the play ends has no obvious connection to the beginning or middle of the play, but she suggests that those who criticize this fact are missing the point. In fact, her intention with the white characters is evident in a passage spoken by Korean-American and the three Koreans in unison before the play is taken over by the white characters. After saying that they don't know "what the white people are doing in the show," they provide a possible explanation for why they take over:

I love the white patriarchy with all my heart because I'm ambitious and want power. My whole mentality is identical in structure to that of a sexist, racist, homosexual white male. People think of me as this empowered Asian female, but really I'm just a fucking white guy. (65)

After this passage, Korean-American and the Korean characters leave the stage, where the white characters remain until the end of the play.

Drawing on Sianne Ngai's notion of "ugly feelings," Karen Shimakawa has described the white characters as experiencing what Ngai calls "a concatenation of boredom and astonishment – a bringing together of what 'dulls' and what 'irritates' or agitates."[22] The white people do not know what is missing in their lives, and they are unbearably bored and unhappy. In the last scene, they have a realization that brings them closer to a sense of happiness. White Person 1 tells White Person 2 that she dreamed that they both "stopped drinking and smoking and using drugs and caffeine and began to eat healthy and exercise and get lots of sleep, and that suddenly the world opened up before us and many of our bad feelings went away" (73). Shimakawa sees this ending as the white characters' empty lives displacing what is supposed to be an Asian American identity play by "absorbing or ablating" earlier actions.[23] Expanding on Shimakawa's observation, I would argue that the white characters' spatial hijacking of the stage at the end of the play further illustrates Lee's pained effort to dramatize her identity.

When the Asian American characters say that they want to be white males, they confess, "My whole mentality is identical in structure to that of a sexist, racist, homosexual white male" (65). The wording here is significant because what the characters say is not that their mentality is the same as that of a white male, but that the "structure" of their mentality is identical. Lee's emphasis on structure is reflected in the way she constructs the set and the audience space. In the script, the theatre space and set are described in great detail:

> The audience enters the theater and finds itself stuck behind the set, which is a quasi-Korean-Buddhist temple with a large, multipaneled Korean dragon mural painted on the back. There are rafters extending above the walls, suggesting the elements of an Asian-looking roof. Colored paper lanterns hang from the ceiling to the rear and sides of the temple, and there is the sound of the Asian flute music and trickling water.... As soon as the house opens, the sound stops and the audience enters down narrow gravel paths on either side of the temple. The inside of the temple is a large, bare room made of sheets of unpainted light birch plywood. (34–35)

Lee goes on to describe four rows of fluorescent tubes that initially suggest the temple's ceiling and later turn on when the white characters appear. What the audience members experience as they walk into the performance space mirrors the plot of the play. While entering, they see the elaborate paintings of dragons and hear calming music that they may expect of a play with the title "*Songs of the Dragons Flying to Heaven*," yet when they are seated, they can see the back-side of the façade of the fake temple and witness how it is constructed with all of its exposed plywood. The house and stage are heterotopias consisting of both real and fake images of traditional Korean culture. At the same time, the fluorescent lights symbolize the mundane and unhappy contemporary life that can affect anyone anywhere. Paralleling this spatial structure, the plot begins as a clichéd identity play but ends with characters that literally and figuratively have no color. The white characters are like the unpainted plywood.

The play's façade, with the colorful stereotypes, and the internal view, with the boring white characters, are conjoined as two sides of the same structure, and this structure is a heterotopia that allows contradictions to coexist. For Lee, the best way – and perhaps the only way – to represent her identity is to let its contradictory sides mirror each other. This effect is similar to that of *mise en abyme*, a concept used in art to describe the visual illusion created when two mirrors reflect each other and copies are made infinitely.[24] Thus, the meaning of *Songs of the Dragons* should be found not simply in the façade or the white characters, but in how the two structurally mirror each other.

Lee has stated that she begins all of her plays by asking herself "what would be the last play in the world [she'd] ever want to write" and then forcing herself to write it.[25] An identity play was something she did not want to write. The face-slapping video at the beginning of the play can be interpreted as an expression of her pain and anxiety in having to write the play, but it is also a way of making her presence known in the production. The play is about her identity even though the characters do not seem to resemble her, and the virtual space of the video is yet another extension of the heterotopia she creates onstage. The playwright getting slapped is a Korean-American with minority issues, a Korean born in a Korean city, a woman who wants to be a man, and a white person with contemporary anxieties about happiness. She mirrors all of them, both real and imagined, and her identity can be represented only in the contradictory, inverted, yet linked spaces.

In this essay, I have analyzed three contemporary plays by Asian American women playwrights in order to understand how they have dealt with the dilemma of writing identity plays. They have resisted formulaic ways of dramatizing identity that are based on history, confession, and autobiography and have chosen instead to dramatize multi-dimensional and evolving identities. The stories told by Cho, Son, and Lee in what I call their identity plays may be semi-autobiographical, but this may also not be precisely the case. The reality they dramatize is not reliable, and what is reflected of them onstage may be misleading. Their characters do not seek cultural authenticity nor do they ask familiar questions about gender or race. Instead, the playwrights open up possibilities for more complex understandings of identity by using the space of the stage to blur, shatter, and invert their ontological subjectivity. Their stage spaces are heterotopias as defined by Foucault, and the key terms used by him to describe heterotopia – simultaneity, juxtaposition, dispersal, connection, and reflection – are visually shown onstage. In *99 Histories*, Cho uses lighting and minimal staging to show fluid changes in her character's memory and to let multiple versions of memory coexist. In Son's *Satellites*, the brownstone literally and figuratively shifts under the characters' feet, but the playwright's main character finds herself by shattering a window to connect to another space. In *Songs of the Dragons*, Lee uses the structure of the set to show contradictory yet mirroring facets of her identity. Like Lee getting her face slapped, all three playwrights may have found it personally painful to write identity plays, but the heterotopic worlds that they create represent the contradictions and complexities of identity as they themselves understand and experience it as Asian American women.

Notes

1 Jeffrey M. Jones, "Script Sabotage: An Interview with the Playwright," *American Theatre* (September 2007): 74–75.
2 Charles Isherwood, "Beneath Pink Parasols, Identity in Stark Form," *New York Times*, 16 January 2012, available at *http://theater.nytimes.com/2012/01/17/theater/reviews/young-jean-lees-untitled-feminist-show-review.html* (accessed 14 July 2012).

3   This first wave is represented in two important collections published in 1993: Roberta Uno, ed., *Unbroken Thread: An Anthology of Plays by Asian American Women* (Amherst: University of Massachusetts Press, 1993); and Velina Hasu Houston, ed., *The Politics of Life: Four Plays by Asian American Women* (Philadelphia: Temple University Press, 1993). Before 1993, only one anthology of Asian American plays, *Between Worlds: Contemporary Asian-American Plays*, ed. Misha Berson (New York: Theatre Communications Group, 1990), had been published, so the two new anthologies together made an unprecedented number of plays by Asian American women available for teaching and production. Also in 1993, Uno started what would become the "Roberta Uno Asian American Women Playwrights Scripts Collection, 1924–2002" at the University of Massachusetts, Amherst, while she was the Artistic Director of the New WORLD Theater. This archive is the only site in the world devoted to manuscripts of plays, interviews, and other research documents relating to Asian American women playwrights. For information on the collection, see *http://asteria. fivecolleges.edu/findaids/umass/mums345_main.html.*

4   For example, Velina Hasu Houston's *Tea* is about her mother and other Japanese women who married American G.I.s after World War II. Houston's characters are distilled versions of women she observed while growing up in a segregated military camp. The play sheds light on a group of women who have been rendered invisible as US citizens in the country's history. Based on interviews conducted by the playwright, the play is about four Japanese women who gather to have tea after the suicide of one of their friends. For the first time, they share their secrets and find consolation in each other. The play is historical, confessional, and autobiographical, all of which characteristics might be described as clichés by later Asian American women playwrights. Velina Hasu Houston, *Tea*, in *Unbroken Thread: An Anthology of Plays by Asian American Women*, ed. Roberta Uno (Amherst: University of Massachusetts Press, 1993), 155–200.

5   Esther Kim Lee, ed., *Seven Contemporary Plays from the Korean Diaspora from the Americas* (Durham, NC: Duke University Press, 2012).

6   For my discussion on gender in Korean diasporic plays, see *Seven Contemporary Plays*, xxii.

7   For examples of the field's development, see Lisa Lowe, *Immigrant Acts: On Asian American Cultural Politics* (Durham, NC: Duke University Press, 1996); Sau-ling Cynthia Wong, "Denationalization Reconsidered: Asian American Cultural Criticism at a Theoretical Crossroads," *Amerasia* 21, no. 1–2 (1995): 1–27; Kandice Chuh and Karen Shimakawa, eds., *Orientations: Mapping Studies in the Asian Diaspora* (Durham, NC: Duke University Press, 2001).

8   Lowe, *Immigrant Acts*, 60–83.

9   Kandice Chuh, *Imagine Otherwise: On Asian Americanist Critique* (Durham, NC: Duke University Press), x.

10 Ibid., 111.

11 Michel Foucault and Jay Miskowiec, "Of Other Spaces," *Diacritics* 16, no. 1 (Spring 1986): 25.

12 Julia Cho, e-mail interview with the author, 16 August 2010. Cho was responding to the question, "Why did you write the play?"

13 Julia Cho, *99 Histories*, in *Seven Contemporary Plays from the Korean Diaspora from the Americas*, ed. Esther Kim Lee (Durham, NC: Duke University Press, 2012), 22; subsequent references to the play will be given parenthetically in the text.

14 Foucault and Miskowiec, "Of Other Spaces," 22.

15 Diana Son, "Author's Statement," in *Version 3.0: Contemporary Asian American Plays*, ed. Chay Yew (New York: Theatre Communications Group, 2011), 396–7.

16 Diana Son, *Satellites*, in *Seven Contemporary Plays from the Korean Diaspora from the Americas*, ed. Esther Kim Lee (Durham, NC: Duke University Press, 2012), 247–320; subsequent references to the play will be given parenthetically in the text.

17 Ben Brantley, "Settling Down on Shaky Ground, in Diana Son's 'Satellites,'" *New York Times*, 19 June 2006, available at *http://theater.nytimes.com/2006/06/19/theater/reviews/19sate.html* (accessed 15 July 2012).

18 For details of the production history of the play, see "Songs of the Dragons Flying to Heaven," available at *http://www.youngjeanlee.org/songs* (accessed 14 July 2012).

19 Young Jean Lee, *Songs of the Dragons Flying to Heaven, American Theatre* (September 2007): 76. This character description does not appear in the version of the script included in the anthology *Songs of the Dragons Flying to Heaven and Other Plays* (New York: Theatre Communications Group, 2009), 31–74. Unless otherwise specified, subsequent references to the play will be to the anthology version and will be given parenthetically in the text.

20 According to reviewer David Cote of *TimeOut New York*

> The downtown playwright-director is building a jittery, jagged body of work that resists pat definition – except as emotionally raw dispatches from an angry mind that lacerates itself as much as it does the world. To date, Lee has penned profane lampoons of motivational bromides (*Pullman, WA*) and the Romantic poets (*The Appeal*). Now she piles her deconstructive scorn upon ethnic stereotypes in *Songs of the Dragons Flying to Heaven*, a sweet-and-sour parade of Asian minstrelsy and race-baiting that culminates in a perverse, soul-baring love scene between two Caucasians.

Peter Marks of *The Washington Post* provides an equally vivid description of the play:

> The events of "Songs of the Dragons" are not tied together dramatically in a classic sense: The play segues uncertainly from one vignette to another and ends in a most bizarrely anti-climactic fashion. The connectedness springs from the idea that any assigning we try to do of behavior by ethnic identity is patently ridiculous. And just as ludicrous, "Songs of the Dragons" tells us, is the "Kumbaya" notion that we could ever walk a mile in the other guy's shoes.

See David Cote, "*Songs of the Dragons Flying to Heaven* by Young Jean Lee," *TimeOut New York*, 28 September 2006, available at *http://www.timeout.com/newyork/theater/songs-of-the-dragons-flying-to-heaven* (accessed 14 July 2012); and Peter Marks, "Review: 'Songs of Dragons Flying to Heaven' at Studio Theatre," *Washington Post*, 8 October 2010, available at *http://www.washingtonpost.com/wp-dyn/content/article/2010/10/07/AR2010100706231.html* (accessed 6 October 2012).

21 Lee, in Jones, "Script Sabotage," 74.

22 Sianne Ngai, qtd. in Karen Shimakawa, "Young Jean Lee's Ugly Feelings About Race and Gender," *Women & Performance: a journal of feminist theory* 17, no. 1 (March 2007): 96. The quote is from Sianne Ngai, *Ugly Feelings* (Cambridge, MA: Harvard University Press, 2005), 271.

23 Shimakawa, "Young Jean Lee's Ugly Feelings," 100.

24 I thank Lesley Ferris for pointing out the similarity between the mirroring effect of heterotopia and *mise en abyme*.

25 Lee, in Jones, "Script Sabotage," 74.

16   Deb Margolin, Robbie McCauley, Peggy Shaw: Affect and Performance

Elin Diamond

A volume on contemporary women playwrights ought to include women who are still carrying on long and varied careers, working *in* the contemporary moment even if they are not, in conventional terms, *of* it. Over a decade ago, I wrote on the performances of Peggy Shaw's *You're Just Like My Father* (1994), Robbie McCauley's *Indian Blood* (1987), and Deb Margolin's *Carthieves! Joyrides* (1995) in the final chapter of my book *Unmaking Mimesis: Essays on Feminism and Performance*.[1] I'd noticed a convergence of ideas about fathers in these otherwise quite different pieces. Since Margolin, McCauley, and Shaw are political women who find edge and energy in feminist and racial struggles, since personal storytelling for political women is always a deep encounter with experience *in history*, they placed their personal fathers in the force field of American society of the 1940s and 1950s. The fathers beckoned seductively from a late-capitalist phantasmagoria of shiny new things – cars, stereos, TVs – things that were also wish images compressing both the dreams of an earlier era, when the fathers themselves were children, and of a future one – the present of the 1980s and 1990s when these women were performing. We look to performance to "imagine the present," as Barbara Johnson once put it.[2] When Shaw, McCauley, and Margolin put their words, images, and bodies before us – however mediated the distance between spectator and performer, however much the apparatus of performance intrudes – they give us news about the state of play in the here and now.

In other words, the confessional, autobiographical tendency of solo performance is, as McCauley puts it, part of a "personal bigger."[3] At its best, feminist performance art lights up dark corners of the social matrix by embodying its contradictions. It's what good political performance has always done, but the solo performer, close enough to her spectators to kiss or kick them, registers through her vulnerability the world we're too inured or distracted to feel. Since I wrote *Unmaking Mimesis*, the women of chapter five have aged and are now bringing us news of their aging bodies, particularly the most powerful encounter that most of us will ever have with forces beyond our control – the encounter with the biopolitics of medical science. Feminists have long critiqued the ways that women's bodies as objects of scientific inquiry have been pathologized, yet the surprise of injury or illness seems to wipe the historical slate clean. Thirty years of brilliant theorizing and agitation over medical politics in the feminist health movement of the 1970s and by the HIV/AIDS community in the 1980s and 1990s leave us informed, suspicious, cynical, and smart, and yet, in the moment, utterly shocked by a strange new body, with our name on its wristband, attached to machines, imaged, prodded, poked, drugged, and in some instances, radiated or chemically poisoned by way of cure. Horrible? Of course. Yet feminist performers in the habit of art-making *through* the body may find, as Eve Kosofsky Sedgwick did, that such frightening and debilitating experiences can also be "sheerly *interesting* with respect to exactly the issues of gender, sexuality and identity formation already on [our] docket[s]."[4] In other words, the body in medical distress summons up new capacities for performing and theorizing.

In this essay, I want to place new work by Margolin, McCauley, and Shaw in proximity to theoretical work – namely, affect theory – that was surfacing during their first performances in the late 1980s to mid-1990s. I was unaware of this work then, focused as I was on the gestic feminist theory I'd developed to explore how theatre and performance pose theoretical questions through the encounter of women's performing bodies and the discourses that gender and racialize them. Central to this method is the Brechtian *gestus*, an embodied or verbal gesture that, in the moment of the spectator's perception, produces a shock that opens the present moment to unseen historical contradictions, both personal and collective.[5] In McCauley's *Indian Blood*, for example, the family's fantasized and real traces of Native American heritage are juxtaposed to the proud tradition of McCauley men who felt dignified by their service in the military.[6] Slide projections during McCauley's show reveal her uniformed African American grandfather, who served in the Spanish-American war (a war that produced, to his granddaughter's disgust, US hegemony in Central and South America and furthered the expropriation of land from indigenous peoples). The grandfather fought in one of the Indian Wars, helping to ambush Native Americans returning from Canada. These are the conceptual and historical aspects of *Indian Blood*, but when, in performance, McCauley spreads her arms wide and says, "They used to tell me *I* had Indian blood...that I looked good in green," she produces a *gestus* that suddenly casts her body and identity into history's force field.[7] A Marxist by early inclination, McCauley in that moment liberates her personal/familial into the materialist historical, while pleasurably embodying the family legend of her Indian blood. And spectators, trying to *see* her blood and skin tones, are caught exercising the racist blood logic of the American legal system from slavery to Jim Crow. Gestic moments of similar power underpin the mid-1990s performances of Shaw and Margolin as well. Each performance about difficult yet alluring fathers – and the 1950s ideologies they imparted – contains a *gestus* (or several) that arrests the flow of performance and lets our minds feel the pressure of "dad" in all its permutations. In effect, these women are performing ideology critique, exposing through their skilled bodies and powerful images the unseen ideologies that shape our gendered lives, our ideas, our desires. Gestic feminist criticism follows their lead by demonstrating how ideology – particularly gender and racial ideologies – smoothes over intractable contradictions. It juxtaposes the sentient body of poststructuralist feminism with materialist Brechtian theatre theory and insists that performance is revelatory: there is activist potential in the bodies engaged in these public acts.

The gestic moment, because it surprises, even shocks, carries affect. A historical force field emerges suddenly, then instantly disappears – this is performance after all, not argument (even as I felt a powerful argument was being made). This point cannot be made too strongly. Bertolt Brecht hoped to awaken critical judgment in his spectators, but the inaugurating shock into judgment – and the aesthetic pleasure derived from it – is embedded in his theory and in the critical practice I am describing. And yet – if gestic feminist theory is unthinkable without affect, it is not affect theory. The "turn" to affect across the humanities, social sciences, and natural sciences in the early 1990s marks a turn away from interpretation based on language, discourse, ideology, and representation, and toward description of the body's powers to affect and be affected and the borderless relation of body to environment.[8] Affects are skin-level, autonomic (involuntary), nonconscious responses to stimuli in the environment – as in shivering with cold or gasping with excitement – and reveal a body's capacity to act, to engage, and to connect outside of conscious intention.[9] In the line of thought from Spinoza to Deleuze to Deleuze and Guattari's translator Brian Massumi, affect theory shifts the focus from the individual and personal, from discourse and constructivism, to "intensities" that pass *impersonally* "[from] body to body, human, non-human, part-human and otherwise."[10] That is, affects circulate; they act in the nervous systems of persons but also beyond persons. Rejecting the dualist subject–object matrix that has dominated western epistemology, affect theory depends on neuroscience to explain a "corporeal-affective system" *split off from* cognition, concepts, beliefs, intentions, and meanings.[11] For Massumi, this splitting off of affect from cognition is not about flipping the old Cartesian mind/body split, but about politics and transformation.[12] Affect is "a moment of unformed, unstructured potential" that sidesteps the habits of the intending subject.[13] Does this mean that ideology critique – presumably *not* split off from cognition, concepts, intentions – along with feminist analysis of gender systems and embodiment is swept off the table?

In her fine synoptic essay "An Affective Turn? Reimagining the subject of feminist theory," Anu Koivunen points out that, like feminist theory, affect theory covers a broad range of ideas and methods.[14] Feminists working with affect often distinguish, as does Massumi, between emotion and affect. Writes Elspeth Probyn: "Emotion refers to cultural and social expression, whereas affects are of biological and physiological nature."[15] Theresa Brennan and Sara Ahmed use affect and emotion interchangeably, or, like Rei Terada, see them as different responses to the same stimuli, emotion being "a psychological ... interpretive experience whose physiological aspect is affect."[16] Brennan is actually intriguingly close to Brecht: affect is "the physiological shift accompanying a judgment."[17] Erin Hurley, writing from the site of theatre specifically, notes that "affect happens *to* us ... and yet happens *through* us ... the body regulating itself...; emotion names our sensate bodily experience in a way that ... makes it legible to ourselves and consonant with others...."[18] Koivunen believes that while feminism's turn to phenomenology and to Darwin on the emotions is all quite real, the question of affect has always been central to feminist theory; a "reflexive link between ontology and epistemology were always already there in feminist self-consciousness." Indeed, "to talk about the affective turn is, to an extent, to ignore generations of feminist scholarship...."[19]

Those of us in performance theory may feel the same way. No less than affect theorists, though completely unrecognized by them, performance theorists have long been invested in the body's primacy, not only as a source and conductor of motor-physical affect and action but also as a source of intelligence, creativity, imagination, language itself. "Put those words in your knees," an acting teacher once shouted at me. In other words, let the intention build from the gesture, not the other way around. For actors, knowing, cognizing, and speaking about the world are profoundly corporeal. "The body knows," we now say casually, but acting regimes conceived by Vsevolod Meyerhold, Antonin Artaud, Bertolt Brecht, and Jerzy Grotowski, among others, enshrined this fact as first principle. From one's exercised, energized physical life, power emerges, a power transmissible in performance because it does an end-run around the actor's censoring intellect and the spectator's habits of reception. Affect theorists rely on neuroscientists like Joseph Le Doux, who proposes that the "basic emotions such as fear" are subserved by neural circuits in the brain, such as the subcortical group of neurons known as the amygdalae, which operate automatically and *more quickly* than the higher cognitive systems."[20] Meyerhold, attempting to bring theatre into the dynamism of post-revolutionary Soviet culture, was influenced by the science of reflexology. His famous biomechanics sought to expand the human sensorium in both performer and spectator, equipping both to send and receive impulses without mental decoding or interpretation. Artaud's "affective athlete," otherwise known as an actor, is one who "taps and radiates certain powers" and for whom "every emotion has organic bases."[21] As noted above, even Brecht, who brought spectators to the moment of judgment and critique with the rationally constructed *gestus* and his alienation-effect or *Verfremdungseffekt*, put in practice what Massumi calls "a shock to thought."[22] In his *Lehrstücke* (learning/teaching plays), Brecht taught dialectics through the body because he believed, with the reflexologists, that gesture and attitude were "prior or equal to thought."[23] All these theorist-practitioners understood performance as an affect machine, churning up and circulating feelings of delight, shock, fear, boredom, interest. All rejected the privatized, psychologized subject. In sum, for students of performance, affect theory's apotheosis of corporeality and its nonrational intensities beckons us back, through different terms, to where we have been for a very long time.

But what is certainly the case, or what became the case, is that ideology critique, of performance or any cultural object, seemed to repeat its moves, blotting out freshness and innovation. Thus Eve Kosofsky Sedgwick, among others, began to feel that purely poststructuralist (and feminist) arguments, while containing the seeds of social disruption, produced arguments that one could anticipate a mile away: always a deconstruction of essence, gender, identity, truth, power, hegemony no matter what the focus of discussion.[24] Poststructuralist feminism has always mistrusted biology as deterministic, trapped in culturalist, gendered, and racialist paradigms. Sedgwick turned toward biology, finding in psychologist Silvan Tomkins's work on affects corporeal understandings freed from cognitive habits. If affects are "hardwired in the human biological system," as Tomkins proposed, if our nervous system responds before our consciousness to a vast range of stimuli, we are freed, theoretically, from both "the presumption of a core self" (that would control our responses) and, more subtly, from "heterosexist teleologies." Like Massumi, then, but with a far more flexible view of "people's cognitive-affective lives," Sedgwick locates the relational and, potentially, the political, not in ideologies but in affects that attach to "things, people, ideas, sensations."[25]

Certainly there are elements in affect theory that speak to the recent performances of Margolin, McCauley, and Shaw. In *O Yes I Will*, *Sugar*, and *Must* (and even more so in Shaw's post-stroke performance piece *Ruff*), the historical-political-ideological, while palpable, is no longer pressing; instead, these performers bring their bodies close to us, wanting us to *feel* the sensation of corporeal forces split off from the mind's habits of regulation. They stand substantial before us, yet they invite us to see their bodies as porous, permeable, borderless. "As a playwright," Margolin has written, "I think I'd almost always prefer to have...you see inside me...absent that I give you [a] play."[26] And as Shaw says in *Must*: "There are different ways of seeing inside me. You could guess what's in here. You could x-ray me...."[27] McCauley and Shaw both project images of internal scans, cells, and organs. A biological, not a historical, force field is summoned, passionately, furiously, erotically, and with fascination ("sheerly interesting"). Audiences long familiar with these performers – and part of the pleasure and pain in seeing these performances is that long familiarity – awaken not only to the present but to the strangeness of the other standing before us. The vocal and physical gestures of these women – Deb's bulging eyes, cascading metaphors, and dark chortles; Robbie's rhythmic, authoritative alto; Peggy's butch bravado and James Brown flourish with a mic – feel familiar, but not the cell structure of what is making them ill. It's the frisson of that unknowable that belies familiarity; this is the bodily life (and death) that performance supposedly occludes. Yet these performers never secreted their embodied life, and what is called "ineptitude" in performance presentation has been happily embraced as participatory aesthetic in the poor-theatre downtown spaces where these performers began and mostly stayed. In such worlds, the performer is not the object of scrutiny but an active agent in the production of meaning. Looked at, she looks back – and more. In the heyday of feminist performance art, McCauley would feed her audience apples cut up in their presence; Shaw would come for a cuddle mid-show; and Margolin laughed at her own jokes along with her appreciative audience. These were canny performers' acknowledgements that spectators were fellow travelers seeking an experience of emotional expansion and sharing.[28]

In their recent work, however, the body's suffering, however satirized, poeticized, and expanded to a "personal bigger," is more palpable, altering the affective space of spectatorship. Simply put, the affect of "sheerly interesting" oscillates with a powerful negative affect made famous by Sedgwick (via Tomkins): the affect of shame. Among the nine affects hardwired into our nervous system (interest, surprise, joy, shame, anger, fear, distress, disgust, dissmell), Tomkins places shame in the "affect polarity *shame-interest*." Shame is "activated only after interest or enjoyment has been activated," suggesting that "the pulsations...around shame...are what either enable or disenable so basic a function as the ability to be interested in the world."[29] Shame is recognized quite early in infants when the circuit of mirroring expressions between the child's face and the caregiver's face are broken and the infant responds, setting a pattern for life, with eyes down, head averted. Writes Sedgwick: "Shame floods into being as a moment, a disruptive moment, in a circuit of identity-constituting identificatory communication. Indeed, like a stigma, shame is itself a form of communication. Blazons of shame, the 'fallen face' with eyes down and head averted...are semaphores of trouble *and at the same time of a desire to reconstitute the interpersonal bridge*." For Sedgwick, shame is isolating, yet also relational: "That's the double movement shame makes: toward painful individuation, toward uncontrollable relationality."[30]

As illness theorists from Susan Sontag to Arthur W. Frank have shown us, shame haunts the ill; a body diseased is a body stigmatized, unworthy.[31] At the same time, Sedgwick, Robin Bernstein, Nicholas Ridout, and many others show that shame, projected autonomically through face and gesture, is thoroughly theatrical.[32] Performers solicit our interest and it is a breach of theatre etiquette to look away. Yet when a prop is dropped, an actor freezes or forgets her lines, when someone in the audience snores or passes gas, the circuit is temporarily broken, the mutually constituting identities that performers and spectators have assumed at the outset of performance are recast into shamed isolation. And this shame spreads through the audience like contagion. Oh no, we think, what's going to happen? Yet there's the oscillation. As Tomkins puts it, "Once shame has been activated, the original [interest-]excitement...may be increased again and inhibit the shame...."[33] In fact, a precipitous reduction of shame, a heightening of interest-excitement, pushes us into laughter. Perhaps this explains performance art's "embrace of shame."[34] The hook of personal storytelling is often a shame-filled moment that performers relive, or make us believe they relive, so that we don't have to. The interest–shame oscillation creates pleasure, dramatic tension, explosions of delight, and mutual recognition.

My interest is in what can be learned from the ways these performers cross paths with affect theory when they risk, project, and exploit shame in order to bring bodily life into present awareness. The affective moments described below can feel gestic, yet the exposure of pernicious internalized ideologies is not the goal, or not the exclusive goal, in these performances. Rather, the performers dig deep into shame to deepen their audience's response to – their interest-enjoyment in – a shared bodily life. Sharing shame can, nonetheless, feel political. Margolin, McCauley, and Shaw are interested not only in the hardwiring of neural networks but also the hardwiring of disease in the toxic force fields of contemporary life.

Deb Margolin's *O Yes I Will (I will remember the spirit and texture of this conversation)*

> Performance is a kind of spiritual athletics. It's moment to moment and then it's over.
>
> –Deb Margolin[35]

Margolin found out that under the effects of sodium pentothal prior to surgery, she spoke to her anesthesiologist and physicians for twelve minutes until they finally put her under. She has no memory of what she said; the content was split off from consciousness and intentionality, yet her brain was alight and words came spilling out. In her play *O Yes I Will (I will remember the spirit and texture of this conversation)*, first performed in 2007 at Dixon Place in New York City, Margolin takes these absent twelve minutes as a provocation and fills them five times over with five utterly different versions of what she might have said when consciousness was suspended. Each is interrupted by the only words she remembers – "You know, we really should get started" and "You know, you won't remember any of this" – in response to which Margolin apparently replied in the words of the title: "O yes I will, I will remember the spirit and texture of this conversation."[36] Margolin's Actress knows from the doctors' anxious post-surgery questions that the words streaming from her were really juicy, maybe quite blue. No writer wants to lose track of great material, but *O Yes I Will* is not only about a writer emphatically taking back her twelve minutes; it is about a writer celebrating the power of her intensely stimulated brain, released from conscious prohibitions, to inhabit fully a scene of shameful abjection. Lying on the surgical table, utterly vulnerable and terrified, Margolin unwittingly derailed the hospital's timetable and the schedules of busy doctors who, with scalpels poised, were unable to get to work. *O Yes I Will* is a performance about that performance, an homage to a theatrical imagination that attaches itself to shame as a means of discovering the full comic and dramatic potential of a sick body's strangeness.

In the first moments of the piece, Margolin suddenly lends us her body. "I think we go to the theatre to imagine our lives in the bodies of others...theatre is in the flesh. So now: Look at this. Look at this body: this is your body" (175). Spectators may silently protest. Margolin's Actress is kitted out in a "bejeweled take-off on a hospital gown" (175), but a hospital gown nonetheless, and no one wants to see herself wearing that. Indeed the delightfully illicit looking that is theatre – "the only place where you have the unimpeachable right to stare at strangers"[37] – is tested by Margolin's insistence that we claim her sick body, that its chemo scars are our scars. Yet, disconcerted by performance, we're also protected by performance – not by its fictionality (we know Margolin has been diagnosed with Hodgkin's disease; we know these surgeries have happened), but by the "sheerly interesting" *affective* tension between invention and inevitability.

During her legendary years with Split Britches and in the last decade as a solo performer, Margolin has shown us a face torqued with feeling. Her audiences have come to love the moments when her eyes widen into a startled stare at the beauty or the ridiculousness conjured by her own eruptive imagery. As in all her pieces, words in *O Yes I Will* throb with affect ("You've caught love...from trees that are balling up to blossom the way babies go quiet and tight when they're about to shit" [185]), and her face reacts, eyes go large, seeming to see the image, then her face relaxes until the next wave of words. "The face may express both enjoyment and shame," writes Tomkins,[38] an understatement for the hilarity Margolin wrings from the self-alienation of disease. Supine on the table (constructed by three chairs), Actress realizes that she can't scratch her butt because, hospital gowns being what they are, she will, by scratching, "EXPOSE MY NIPPLES" (178). In the second monologue, bird images conjure a melancholy father who used to have flying dreams as well as her own helplessness: "I'm just some housewife you're about to cut open like a piece of chicken!" (180). The photo accompanying the published version of Margolin's text articulates the shame/comedy of such images. With her hands protectively covering her breasts and crotch, Actress cranes forward, eyes bulging in horror, marking in Margolinesque corporal style comedy's border with suffering. In a piece that announces its mimetic status, a performance about a performance, shame iterated and reiterated claims its lively connection to the "sheerly interesting."

The drama of oscillation in *O Yes I Will* is not in enactment but in image-building, a process that permits Actress a Houdini-like escape from the "small space" of her body. Only language can make her body grow, fly, dance. Margolin grants mental life its full range of bodily affect: "Is consciousness a body part?" "Is kindness a body part?" (176). If at first she shocked us by making her ill body our own, she now seduces us, with exactitude and metaphor, into celebrating biological being. "I think the heart knows how important it is.... I don't mean some metaphorical heart. I mean the beating thing, the muscle, with the chambers leading in and the odea leading out, the whole chorale of the blood being sung into and out of the chapel of the heart, the real beating heart" (180–181). The title of the piece, *O Yes I Will (I will remember the spirit and texture of this conversation)* introduces this "chapel of the heart." Ordinarily, "Oh" is a grunt of recognition, a weighty question, a meaningless particle or intensifier. "O," however, is the orthography of scripture, particularly the Psalms and Proverbs where impassioned personal voices cry out or instruct – an association Margolin relishes in a previous piece entitled *O Wholly Night and Other Jewish Solecisms*. "Spirit" presents a double entendre: a banal idiom for overall tone ("spirit of the age") or intended meaning ("spirit of the law") coupled with the soulful: spirit as the vast expanse of immaterial being. "Texture" insists that words are tongued, spat, drooled, whispered, yet joined to spirit like affects to bodies. "The brain is the place of knowing, so it can't know anything. It's the PLACE of knowing, but not the ACT" (181). The *act* of knowing is carried by affect, the human sensorium, attaching itself and responding to the world's stimuli.

With her metaphor-motor always running, Margolin surgically cuts into the new words illness has given her. In her penultimate fantasy version of the lost twelve minutes, when she's seducing her aged anesthesiologist, Actress contemplates the root meanings of anesthesia: "getting rid of beauty getting rid of feeling...bringing relief from feeling" (185). And from this zero-degree numbness, she starts another query: "What is language, anyway...? Does it just float, like smoke from fire, away from the speaker...?" (185). If this is so, she reasons, then the body is the source of fire (of purity, of energy), and so she asks in barely punctuated lines that the doctor "be gentle with this eternal flame as you extinguish it be mindful of its eternity, and bring it back dear...older gentleman" (185). In the piece's concluding moments, Actress and the old anesthesiologist perform a "tender," "oneiric" dance that adds spirit and texture to their conversation (185).[39] It also affirms, in another key, Actress's insistence on affect – on the life of the woman sharing her life by performing before our eyes. Writing herself back into twelve forgotten minutes, Margolin invites us all to imagine anew the present moment, one that we inhabit with her, and lose forever.

Robbie McCauley's *Sugar*

Sugar carries shame.

–Robbie McCauley, *Sugar*[40]

McCauley's recent performance piece, *Sugar* (2011–2013), travels across the performer's life to explore the shame and the racial politics of diabetes. In the southern United States, "sugar" is vernacular for diabetes – as when a family friend comments to the young McCauley, "Your sores take a long time to heal. You play hard and quit quick. You must have a l'il bit of sugar" (5). McCauley sets her stage with "*3 bound sheaves of raw sugar cane and two industrial sized bags of sugar, thigh-high, one white, one brown,*" and comes on stage eating candy: "You know I suppose to 'a been dead. Sugar is complicated, like love, full of pleasure and pain, gives you energy and can eat you up from the inside out" (1). In McCauley's "body memory," sugar drives recollections of delicious Southern cooking from the "pretty-skinned" women on her mother's side, all of it fresh, abundant, full of fat and tenderness: "Sometimes there was rice, and gravy that seemed to be stirred and spiced all afternoon. On Sundays [there were] cakes – Ma Willie, chocolate, Aunt Jessie coconut, and Aunt Nell a pound cake so good make you want to slap somebody" (2). Generations of strong women dating back to the era of slavery made cooking into community, insulating the family from the grim realities of Klan killings and segregation, which eventually pushed the family northward to Washington, D.C., in 1953. Life will open up for the young McCauley in this move north, and in a later move to New York in the 1960s. But first she opens up our senses and attaches affect to the sweet (and killing) pleasures of "flaky biscuits baked w/lard" and the sugarcane she sucked in the post-Depression years in the South, not to mention the sugary snacks she constantly craved (2). "Sugar carries shame," but it also carries, in the foods it sweetens, in the smells and tastes, in the rituals of serving and eating, a generation's social memory. "Food is everything, Mother said, that's all we do" (1).

McCauley's memories congeal around stage spaces created by chairs with a chalk-like substance at the bottom of each chair leg. They create and recreate the private and public zones of her life, from the family dinner table, to assorted workplaces, to husbands and lovers, friends and cityscapes. As McCauley moves the chairs (and their vanished inhabitants), they leave jagged white lines on the stage floor, a metaphor for the scarring of a full life and the scarring of the flesh produced by the ravages of diabetes. At one point, enraged by the memory of how decent medical care has been denied to black Americans, she throws the chairs, and her piano accompanist makes crashing chords. She shouts: "How do you continue to dance the contradictions with crashing doors?" (6). Not diagnosed until twenty, McCauley knows in her blood chemistry how race and class disparities ("crashing doors") prevent diagnosis and treatment, especially for women of color.

Both performance artist and public intellectual, McCauley has "danc[e]d the contradictions" – has built an aesthetic practice out of intractable social misery – for decades. Like *My Father and the Wars* (1985), *Indian Blood*, and *Sally's Rape* (1992), *Sugar* is a complex meditation on personal and family history and the "personal bigger" of race and class over the last half-century. It has the same beautifully jagged narratives, visuals, music, and interaction with the audience. Structured like jazz with verbal texts spoken rhythmically, McCauley's personal voice becomes over the course of the performance an orphic voice laden with time. Yet *Sugar* was composed to live in medical/social spaces, as well as aesthetic ones. For years leading up to the composition of the final script, McCauley revived the story-circle practice she learned from John O'Neal (Free Southern Theater, now Junebug Productions), in which a community comes together to tell stories related to painful issues. After storytelling comes "cross-talk" among participants, often the basis for stage dialogue. The story circle was necessary for McCauley's project because people have to be coaxed to speak from within the shame of diabetes. When she reported her diagnosis to her family, her father, already angry over the Marxist fliers McCauley had brought home, told her "you ain't got no diabetes" (19). Political about race from her earliest memories, McCauley allowed shame to stifle management of her disease until she recognized her own bad habits in "the three d's of diabetes, depression denial and drink" (7). The adult McCauley outlasted her father's dismissal and learned to see diabetes as a virulent social system she knew how to fight. When she went to a New York City clinic in the early 1960s with dangerously elevated blood sugar, she was denied a diabetes kit because clinic doctors were legally prohibited from giving needles to a black person. Eventually the law was reversed. Years of inequitable treatment were finally admitted to by *The New England Journal of Medicine*: "say the medical profession all those decades treated us different! Well, duh! But I'm glad it's on paper...." (21). It makes McCauley's survival all the more surprising. Shame, politicized and personalized in this way, becomes manageable, yet in her hands loses none of its affective power. As in *Indian Blood*, when she talked about politics to the audience while preparing and passing a tray of apples, in current performances of *Sugar*, McCauley recounts a humorous story about a friend and *"pulls out needles, prepares insulin, shoots up...Real time"* (20). This is an extraordinary moment. First she tests her blood with a glucometer, a computer that measures glucose in the blood, then because of the number it records that evening, she fills a syringe with insulin. She lifts her shirt and swabs with alcohol a spot on her belly, folds the skin, then injects herself. No one can witness this act, casually described in stage directions, without distress, without shame. We shouldn't be watching, yet we can't look away. The needle goes into the flesh, the insulin vial empties; the moment feels both intrusive and wholly impersonal. Wrongly dosed, the performer could, as Herbert Blau once warned, actually die in front of our eyes.[41] Yet, chatting away, McCauley puts before us a body that is both chronically ill and emphatically surviving. The political impact of McCauley's work intensifies not because she has triumphed over shame but because she invokes its affective power in her spectators. In performing the rituals of a diabetic's survival, she attaches affect to glucometer, syringe, cotton swab, and skin, offering her riff on shame's "double movement": the performer's toward painful individuation, the spectator's toward surprising yet uncontrollable relationality. Shame raises our interest and McCauley politicizes that interest, teaching us how diabetes is borne, endured, and managed in the flesh.

Peggy Shaw's *Must: The Inside Story*

I've been waiting for you and now you're here.

–Peggy Shaw, *Must: The Inside Story* (139)

With Shaw's *MUST: The Inside Story* (in collaboration with Suzy Willson and the Clod Ensemble, 2008), personal scars and the politics of global survival are poignantly and comically mapped across this familiar performer's body. Like McCauley and Margolin, Shaw's body presents itself as aging, multiply scarred, and heart-challenged. Like McCauley's *Sugar*, *Must* has a medical provenance, part of Clod Ensemble's Performing Medicine project, which "uses the arts to teach medical students and practicing health professionals."[42] I saw *MUST* at the Public Theater in New York in 2010 but wish I'd seen a 2009 performance in the lecture theatre of the University of Edinburgh Medical School – a more appropriate site. Standing before us in a somber suit, Shaw grants us fantastical MRI-eyes to see not only her internal organs but also her hurts, memories, desires, for these, too, are carried beneath the skin. Using a shadowy, insistent *film noir* voice, Shaw figures her body as a cityscape ripe for dangerous trespass: "When my skin cracks open ... [y]ou will see a magical landscape, like New York City in the seventies – [with] graffiti and layers of bone and blood and sex shops and garbage" (140). With powerful associative images and projections of x-ray slides of her heart and lungs, we're invited to see her body as our earth with its woeful stories of endangered species, loss of land mass, toxicity of water and food. Shaw is no earth mother – although we're treated to a hilarious tale of her giving birth to her daughter on the day she was to attend Woodstock. Instead, she asks us to join her digging "past the topsoil," even if this digging produces fear: "I'm afraid of finding something I didn't know about – like a bear shitting in my woods... or a huge, garbage swirling, plastic toxic mass in my pituitary gland that is close to the size of Texas" (140–141). Environmental shame, experienced as individual fear about the toxic horrors of present and future is, in Shaw's ingenious conception, uncontrollably relational. Like Margolin and McCauley, Shaw makes her body a switchpoint of affective attachment. Elspeth Probyn urges us to think affect by "pictur[ing] the body composed of thousands of bits all whizzing around."[43] Shaw gives us a body full of whizzing toxic garbage. Even the theatre we're sitting in has a dangerous biology: "The walls are made of red curtains, but they're not curtains at all; they are blood vessels carved to look like curtains" (139) – a theatre-body for affect to circulate.

A beloved cofounder, with Margolin and Lois Weaver, of Split Britches in 1982, Shaw turned to solo performance with *You're Just Like My Father*, a meditation on a father's military accoutrements as a secret goad to lesbian desire, while, with help from James Brown, Shaw's persona works to free herself and her beaten-down mother from the oppressive culture the father represents. *Must* follows the formal gambit of *You're Just Like My Father* and Shaw's other solo shows, *Menopausal Gentleman* (1997) and *To My Chagrin* (1999): image clusters gathered from childhood, current relationships, social violence, city life, lesbian desire, plus Shaw's own affect-brew of warmth and raw yearning, expressed in a raised eyebrow and Marlon Brando pose.

The trope of a rogue elephant in "must" (poised for seasonal mating) figures Shaw's butch lesbian's "rogue" behavior: "I spend too much time looking at beautiful ladies" (142). The Victorian elephant man, John (or Joseph) Merrick, creates another image cluster in this multi-layered piece. His bones are preserved in the Royal London Museum. Shaw's yowling "Rattlin' Bones" song speaks to the ghoulish nature of freak shows, but her full-throated rendering of the gorgeous Bill Withers tune "Ain't No Sunshine When She's Gone," accompanied throughout by gifted musicians, is more painful. "She" is the song's lover, "she" is Shaw's depressive mother, "she" is the earth we're poisoning.

Yet Shaw seems more concerned with "you" and the loss of a community of love and shared politics: she approaches a spectator and says, "It's funny talking to you this way now, as if, in a way you're a stranger. There was a time when I felt aligned with you, complicit in what we both knew. Now I'm not sure" (142). In the real time of performance, this moment felt both like a *gestus* and a provocation to shame. For Tomkins, shame arises "because one is looked at by one who is strange, or because one wishes to look at or commune with another person but suddenly cannot because he [sic] is strange... or suddenly appears unfamiliar."[44] Of course no performer personally knows the majority, or often any, of her spectators, but performance communities in commercial theatre's margins through the 1980s and 1990s, diverse and unstable as they always were, seemed to be building feminist alliances *through* performance. Sitting together in small ratty theatres in the presence of a performer whose erotic, comic, and political sensibilities extended our own, we recognized the performer and felt recognized by her. That scene has faded, replaced by others no doubt equally meaningful. In any case, the affect-expression of shame, eyes down, head averted, is recreated when Shaw, not actually feeling shame, mimes it for us: she lowers her eyes to speak to a seated spectator, and receiving no acknowledgement, looks away. If a connection has been broken, rousing a shared affect of shame, interest soon spikes; our affective commitment to the performance deepens. Near the end of *MUST*, Shaw describes her tears, like an elephant's in must, "crying for you," and her tears become a flood carrying away the earth's detritus and biological history ("ancient ships and ancient germs") (155). There is no redemption here, no positive project implied by ideology critique. Instead, in the last sections of *Must* that bring together elephant bones and blood full of "tiny objects floating in an alphabet soup of bottle caps and Tupperware and zip lock bags and thermoses and coffee cups and Mac books," Shaw leaves us with a Janus-faced image: "I thought that's what thoughts look like when they're finished. Dusty and in a pile. Now I know that molecules of dust are the future that exists by the side of the road that gets stirred up as I walk by" (157). Our planet is littered with the dust of dead thoughts, dead ideologies, yet her sentient presence, her body's power to affect and be affected, animates the dust, makes the future rise.

Coda: *Ruff*

Ruff, Shaw's most recent performance piece, co-written and directed by Lois Weaver, premiered at Dixon Place in New York City in January 2013 and is a perfect coda for the "sheerly interesting" of mortal illness. Like McCauley injecting herself with insulin in real time before an audience, Shaw displays her performance skills filtered through the effects of an ischemic infarction, the stroke she suffered, riffs on, mocks, and explores in *Ruff*. "In poetic terms," she says, "[I had a] stroke in my Pons, pronounced like 'The Fonz.'"[45] Shaw has lovingly covered soul and R&B ballads in all her shows; she gravitates here to bouncy rock 'n' roll that help with rhyme and name recall (Shirley Ellis's "The Name Game") or the child's tune "Hokey Pokey" hilariously set to an AC/DC backup: "you put your whole face in, you put your right arm out, you put your whole speech in and you shake shake it, shake it..." (11). *Ruff* is named for, and puns on, a drummer's "three stroke ruff" (da-da-DUM) that is both her lifeline ("I was hiding in the beat") and the expression of crashing noises associated with the assault on her brain (5). Shaw's set is dominated by a green screen where motion-capture technology is used to project her backup band of friends, synched to accompany her when she sings, or for the projection of digital video throughout the show. If the technology is new, the visual/virtual punning is classic Shaw. Motion capture lets the human subject be in two places at once; the subject is filmed in front of a green screen and in post-production another background is filled in. With "some of my brain missing now" (2), the green screen becomes Shaw's memory, allowing her access to images in her past, including a young Peggy in an old home video. (It also comically defies

Ellen Stewart, Shaw's old collaborator at La Mama, who hated green and who invaded Shaw's dreams after her death and "caused" her stroke.) Along with the green screen are four computer monitors with scrolling text for constant reference. The stage is full of delightful objects, actual and affective assists, like the colorful floating inflatable fish at the end that attempt to make a habitable world out of the terrible images that now haunt her – of being upside down, down at the bottom of a sea – and that mark her changed landscape.

Ruff is shot through with lively image clusters that echo Shaw's other performances, though on this brightly lit stage the associations feel darker: her dead sister Norma, who reminds Shaw of Amy Winehouse, took up residence in Shaw's body but disappeared after the stroke. Her depressive mother reappears from *You're Just Like My Father* with the same warning that black pepper might cause brain damage. The elephant's tears in *Must* – "Stuff...leaking out, dropping from my holes...emptying my brain" (155) – morph into Shaw's self-diagnosis for her stroke: "I started to leak ... I couldn't contain all this within my skull without touching the walls of my mind" (9). The intricate conceit from *Must* by which Shaw asks us to see the earth's amplitude and suffering through her own body and projected x-rays is gone. Instead she warns, "If you have a chance to see inside your body, don't do it. When I looked at the sonogram of my heart, for example, I saw two little flailing arms that wave back and forth pathetically. Best to think of a red, heart-shaped object like on a coffee mug or a t-shirt that looks like it will last forever" (15). Images of Earth's memory, elephant memory, human memory, produce an emotional collage in *Must*. In *Ruff*, Shaw admits: "I wonder what got erased from my memory. Of course I will never remember what it is...." Her next line, however, not heroic, or sentimental, or redemptive, or cathartic, is simply pragmatic: "But now I know I have more room in my brain for new thoughts" (22).

Those new thoughts flow into the audience. As she moves between her monitors, we see and feel that she is no longer quite in synch with herself. There is a pause as she waits for the word to come, to feel the next performance beat. In that pause, her damaged brain is speaking of its labor to synch up, and watching that effort feels shameful. Shaw has become a stranger. Yet the shame-interest polarity that hovers over all performance lands fully in our midst in *Ruff*. The otherness of the solo performer who solicits our look and fills us with feeling is not undermined but confirmed in this performance. If "we" have become unfamiliar to the performer in *Must*, we work harder to make ourselves present to her in *Ruff*. This becomes, without being articulated, our "new thought" about the activity of spectatorship: it is our ethical link to Shaw. At one point in the evening, she removes her jacket and asks a spectator to hold it; later she retrieves it with a stiff smile. This is the kind of shared intimacy with her audience Shaw has orchestrated sexily for years. In *Ruff*, that intimacy becomes contagious, spreading through the room. We always wanted to hold Shaw's coat. Now she needs us to.

***

[J]ust to feel it, just to feel it, just to feel the body....

–Deb Margolin, O Yes I Will (184)

You lose feeling down there.

–Robbie McCauley, Sugar (1)

You don't have to be under threat to feel fear.

–Peggy Shaw, Ruff (16)

In affect theory, feeling is a sensation that is personal and biographical, arising out of our pool of remembered feelings. Emotion is the social face of feeling: what we know is acceptable to show. Affect is the nonconscious experience of sensation: we blush, we jump with fear. As Eric Shouse puts it, "affect is the body's way of preparing itself for action...by adding intensity to the quality of experience."[46] Performance rarely demands fight or flight responses, yet we crave intensity, even the intensifier of shame. Eloquently, wittily, Margolin, McCauley, and Shaw beckon us into their states of emergency. Their backs are against the wall; we can feel their panic. Shame at their pain isolates us and yet queerly, beautifully, it also activates our interest, our uncontrollable relation to their bodily lives, not in spite of cancer, diabetes, and stroke, but because of them, and because of what we know of them in our own lives. "The body has a grammar all its own," Shouse writes, channeling, it would seem, these performance writers.[47] For years they have schooled themselves in that strange grammar, learned its politics, its nonsensical quirks, its capacities to affect and be affected. New body-worlds have altered the rules – maybe verbs don't agree so much, modifiers dangle, and someone forgets to close the quotations – but these artists transmit affect as powerfully and painfully as ever. On love, creation, disease, aging, rage, and time, their images are precise, funny, and disturbing. Deb Margolin, Robbie McCauley, and Peggy Shaw continue to bring us the news of how we live now. They are still lighting up the social matrix. Maybe, too, they're preparing us for action.

Notes

1. Elin Diamond, *Unmaking Mimesis: Essays on Feminism and Performance* (London: Routledge, 1997), 142–181.
2. The full line is "Cultural criticism at its best should offer a remedial course in imagining the present." It was part of Barbara Johnson's blurb for Patricia Williams's *The Rooster's Egg: On the Persistence of Prejudice* (Cambridge, MA: Harvard University Press, 1995). The line is one of the epigraphs used for chapter five of *Unmaking Mimesis*.
3. Robbie McCauley, telephone conversation with the author, 17 May 2010.
4. Eve Kosofsky Sedgwick, *Tendencies* (Durham, NC: Duke University Press, 1994), 12.
5. See "Brechtian Theory/Feminist Theory: Toward a Gestic Feminist Criticism" in Diamond, *Unmaking Mimesis*, 43–55.
6. *Indian Blood* exists only in typescript, and I thank Robbie McCauley for making it available to me.

7   McCauley, *Indian Blood*, 9.

8   See Brian Massumi, "Notes on the Translation," *A Thousand Plateaus: Capitalism and Schizophrenia*, by Gilles Deleuze and Félix Guattari (Minneapolis: University of Minnesota Press, 1987), xvi.

9   See Patricia T. Clough, introduction, *The Affective Turn: Theorizing the Social*, ed. Patricia T. Clough with Jean Halley (Durham, NC: Duke University Press, 2007), 1–33.

10 Gregory J. Seigworth and Melissa Gregg, "An Inventory of Shimmers," in *The Affect Theory Reader*, ed. Gregg and Seigworth (Durham, NC: Duke University Press, 2010), 1.

11 See Ruth Leys, "The Turn to Affect: A Critique," *Critical Inquiry* 37, no. 3 (2011): 438.

12 Brian Massumi, *Parables of the Virtual* (Durham, NC: Duke University Press, 2002), 1–109, especially 1–21 and 39–45.

13 Eric Shouse, "Feeling, Emotion, Affect," *M/C Journal* 8 (Dec. 2005): *journal.media-culture.org.au/0512/03-shouse.php*, 1.

14 Anu Koivunen, "An affective turn? Reimagining the subject of feminist theory," in *Working with Affect in Feminist Readings: Disturbing Differences*, ed. Marianne Liljeström and Susanna Paasonen (London: Routledge, 2010), 8–28.

15 Elspeth Probyn, *Blush: Faces of Shame* (Minneapolis: University of Minnesota Press, 2005), 11; cited in Koivunen, "An affective turn?," 9.

16 Rei Terada, *Feeling in Theory: Emotion after the 'Death of the Subject'* (Cambridge, MA: Harvard University Press, 2001), 4. Cited in Koivunen, "An affective turn?," 10. See also Sara Ahmed, *The Cultural Politics of Emotion* (Edinburgh: Edinburgh University Press, 2008).

17 Theresa Brennan, *The Transmission of Affect* (Ithaca, NY: Cornell University Press, 2004); cited in Koivunen, "An affective turn?," 10.

18 Erin Hurley, *Theatre & Feeling* (Basingstoke, UK: Palgrave Macmillan, 2010), 22–23.

19 Koivunen, "An affective turn?," 22.

20 Joseph Le Doux, cited in Leys, "The Turn to Affect: A Critique," 438.

21 Antonin Artaud, *The Theater and Its Double*, trans. Mary C. Richards (New York: Grove Press, 1958), 134, 140.

22 Walter Benjamin describes Brecht's method in terms of shock: "Like the pictures in a film, epic theater moves in spurts. Its basic form is that of the shock...." See "What is Epic Theater?" in *Illuminations: Essays and Reflections*, trans. Harry Zohn (New York: Schocken Books, 2007), 153.

23 Roswitha Muller, "Learning for a New Society: the *Lehrstück*," in *The Cambridge Companion to Brecht*, ed. P. Thomson and G. Sacks (Cambridge: Cambridge University Press, 1994), 92.

24 See Eve Kosofsky Sedgwick, with Adam Frank, "Shame in the Cybernetic Fold: Reading Silvan Tomkins," in Sedgwick, *Touching Feeling: Affect, Pedagogy, Performativity* (Durham, NC: Duke University Press, 2003), 93–121.

25 Ibid., 19, 94, 99, 133.

26 Deb Margolin, "'To Speak Is to Suffer' and Vice Versa," *TDR: The Drama Review* 52, no. 3 (T199) (Fall 2008): 96.

27 Peggy Shaw and Suzy Willson, *MUST: The Inside Story* in *A Menopausal Gentleman: The Solo Performances of Peggy Shaw*, ed. Jill Dolan (Ann Arbor: University of Michigan Press, 2011), 142; subsequent references will be given parenthetically in the text.

28 See Jill Dolan's *Utopia in Performance: Finding Hope at the Theater* (Ann Arbor: University of Michigan Press, 2005) for an extended meditation on precisely these moments of expansion and community experienced at the theatre. Her chapter "A Femme, a Butch, a Jew" looks at performances by Margolin and Shaw, as well as Holly Hughes (35–62).

29 Sedgwick, with Frank, "Shame in the Cybernetic Fold," 97.

30 Ibid., 36, 37; italics added.

31 Susan Sontag, *Illness As Metaphor* and *AIDS and Its Metaphors* (New York: Doubleday, 1990) and Arthur W. Frank, *At the Will of the Body: Reflections on Illness* (Boston: Houghton Mifflin, 1991). See especially Frank's chapter "Stigma," 91–98.

32 Robin Bernstein, "Toward the Integration of Theatre History and Affect Studies: Shame and the Rude Mechs's *The Method Gun*," *Theatre Journal* 64, no. 2 (May 2012): 213–230; Nicholas Ridout, *Stage Fright, Animals, and Other Theatrical Problems* (Cambridge: Cambridge University Press, 2006).

33 Silvan Tomkins, *Affect, Imagery, Consciousness* (New York: Springer, 1963), 123.

34 Bernstein, "Toward the Integration of Theatre History and Affect Studies," 216.

35 Deb Margolin, personal conversation with the author, 14 May 2013.

36 Deb Margolin, *O Yes I Will* (*I will remember the spirit and texture of this conversation*), *TDR: The Drama Review* 52, no. 3 (T 199) (Fall 2008): 177–178 ff; subsequent references to the text will be to this version unless otherwise specified and will be given parenthetically in the text.

37 Deb Margolin, "A Perfect Theatre for One: Teaching 'Performance Composition,'" *TDR: The Drama Review* 41, no. 2 (Summer 1997): 69.

38 Tomkins, *Affect, Imagery, Consciousness*, 146.

39 In a slightly later version of *O Yes I Will*, Margolin describes the final dance this way:
    a sensual movement piece, between PATIENT and an older GTLEMAN, as anesthesiologist. It is choreographed to a finger-snapping, articulate jazz piece that celebrates the eros of performance, and lends both patient and doctor a physical agency neither of them has under ordinary circumstances. (Typescript sent to the author by Deb Margolin)

40 Robbie McCauley, *Sugar* (Version 3/9/13), 16. This performance piece is still in typescript and I thank Robbie McCauley for making it available for the purpose of this article; subsequent references will be given parenthetically in the text.

41 Herbert Blau, *Take Up the Bodies: Theater at the Vanishing Point* (Champaign: University of Illinois Press, 1982), 82.

42 "Performing Medicine," available at *http://www.clodensemble.com/medicine.htm* (accessed 29 May 2013).

43 Elspeth Probyn, "Writing Shame," in *The Affect Theory Reader*, 77.

44 Tomkins, *Affect, Imagery, Consciousness*, 123.

45 Peggy Shaw, *Ruff*, unpublished typescript, 20; subsequent references will be given parenthetically in the text. I thank Lois Weaver for making this text available to me for the purpose of this article.

46 Shouse, "Feeling, Emotion, Affect," 1.

47 Ibid.

Bibliography

Adam, Julie. "The Implicated Audience: Judith Thompson's Anti-Naturalism in *The Crackwalker, White Biting Dog, I Am Yours,* and *Lion in the Streets*." Knowles 41–46.

Adams, Tim. "'I hate to be told somewhere is out of bounds for women.' Enter Enron....." *Observer.* Guardian News and Media, 5 July 2009. Web. 15 July 2010. <http://www.guardian.co.uk/stage/2009/jul/05/lucy-prebble-playwright-interview-enron>.

Aguirre, Carmen. *The Refugee Hotel.* Vancouver: Talonbooks, 2010. Print.

Ahmed, Sara. *The Cultural Politics of Emotion.* Edinburgh: Edinburgh University Press, 2004. Print.

——. *The Promise of Happiness.* Durham: Duke University Press, 2010. Print.

Alexander, Sally, and Marilyn Finlay. "Theatre Can Still Touch a Nerve." Letter. *Guardian.* Guardian News and Media, 30 Aug. 2008. Web. 26 Oct. 2010. <http://www.guardian.co.uk/culture/2008/aug/30/theatre>.

Almeida, Fabrizio O. Rev. of *Kita y Fernanda. New City Stage.* 6 Oct. 2008. Web. 23 Sept. 2012. <http://newcitystage.com/2008/10/06/recommended-kita-y-fernanda16th-street-theater/>.

Alter, Alexandra. "The Surge in Plays about Iraq." *Wall Street Journal.* Dow Jones & Company, Inc., 31 Oct. 2008. Web. 16 Oct. 2010. <http://online.wsj.com/article/SB122541854683986897.html>.

Anzaldúa, Gloria. *Borderlands/La Frontera: The New Mestiza.* 3rd ed. San Francisco: Aunt Lute Books, 2007. Print.

Arendt, Hannah. *Eichmann in Jerusalem – A Report on the Banality of Evil.* New York: Penguin Books, 1994. Print.

Arons, Wendy. "Queer Ecology/Contemporary Plays." *Theatre Journal* 64.4 (2012): 565–82. Print.

Arrizón, Alicia. *Queering Mestizaje: Transculturation and Performance.* Ann Arbor: University of Michigan Press, 2006. Print.

——. "Race-ing Performativity through Transculturation, Taste and the Mulata Body." *Theatre Research International* 27.2 (2002): 136–52. Print.

Artaud, Antonin. *The Theater and Its Double.* Trans. Mary C. Richards. New York: Grove Press, 1958. Print.

Aston, Elaine. *Feminist Views on the English Stage: Women Playwrights, 1990–2000.* Cambridge: Cambridge University Press, 2003. Cambridge Studies in Modern Theatre. Print.

——. Foreword. *Feminism and Theatre.* By Sue-Ellen Case. Reissued ed. Basingstoke: Palgrave Macmillan, 2008. ix–xxiii. Print.

——. "Reviewing the Fabric of *Blasted*." *Sarah Kane in Context.* Ed. Laurens De Vos and Graham Saunders. Manchester: Manchester University Press, 2010. 13–27. Print.

Aston, Elaine, and Sue-Ellen Case, eds. *Staging International Feminisms.* Basingstoke: Palgrave Macmillan, 2007. Print.

Aston, Elaine, and Geraldine Harris. "Feminist Futures and the Possibilities of 'We.'" Aston and Harris, *Feminist Futures?* 1–16.

——, eds. *Feminist Futures? Theatre, Performance, Theory.* Basingstoke: Palgrave Macmillan, 2008. Print.

——. *Performance Practice and Process: Contemporary [Women] Practitioners.* Basingstoke: Palgrave Macmillan, 2008. Print.

Aston, Elaine, Gerry Harris, and Lena Šimić. "'It Is Good to Look at One's Own Shadow': A Women's International Theatre Festival and Questions for International Feminism." Aston and Harris, *Feminist Futures?* 169–90.

Aston, Elaine, and Janelle Reinelt, eds. *The Cambridge Companion to Modern British Women Playwrights.* Cambridge: Cambridge University Press, 2000. Print.

Avery, Roberta. "Black Marchers Challenge Change in Name of Road: Negro Creek Rd. Called Tribute to Ancestors." *Toronto Star* 16 June 1996: A4. Print.

——. "Vandals Deface Collingwood Black Church with Profanity." *Toronto Star* 30 Aug. 1996: A18. Print.

Awad, Samir. "Qisat Awal Ma'had Li Fan Al-Tamtheel." *Al-Masrah* 39 (1992): 106. Print.

Bachelet, Michelle. "Closing Statement at the 57th Session of the Commission on the Status of Women." *UN Women.* N.p., 13 Mar. 2013. Web. 30 Apr. 2013. <http://www.unwomen.org/2013/03/closing-statement-michelle-bachelet-csw57/>.

——. "The 21st Century Will Be the Century of Girls and Women." *UN Women.* N.p., 23 Sept. 2011. Web. 30 Mar. 2013. <http://www.unwomen.org/2011/09/keynote-address-at-39th-commencement-of-laguardia-community-college/>.

Bahr, Iris. *Dai (Enough).* Evanston: Northwestern University Press, 2009. Print.

Baker, Tammy Haili'ōpua. *Kupua. He Leo Hou: A New Voice – Hawaiian Playwrights.* Ed. John H. Y. Wat and Meredith M. Desha. Honolulu: Bamboo Ridge Press, 2003. 111–40. Print.

Barbour, Ronald B. "Déline Dene Mining Tragedy." *First Nations Drum.* Firstnationsdrum.com, 22 Dec. 1998. Web. 15 Nov. 2012. <http://www.firstnationsdrum.com/1998/12/deline-dene-mining-tragedy/>.

Barfield, Tanya, Karen Hartman, Chiori Miyagawa, Lynn Nottage, and Caridad Svich. *The Antigone Project: A Play in Five Parts.* South Gate: NoPassport Press, 2009. Print.

Barton, Bruce. "Tributes of Another Order." Wilson and McIntyre 18–23.

Batuman, Elif. "Stage Mothers: A Women's Theatre in Rural Turkey." *New Yorker* 24 and 31 Dec. 2012: 72–85. Print.

Benedict, Helen. "The Lonely Soldier Monologues." *Plays from Actors Theatre of Louisville: Humana Festival 2005.* New York: Broadway Play Publishing, 2007. Print.

Benjamin, Walter. "Theses on the Philosophy of History." *Illuminations.* Ed. Hannah Arendt. Trans. Harry Zohn. New York: Schocken, 1969. Print.

——. "What is Epic Theater?" *Illuminations: Essays and Reflections.* Trans. Harry Zohn. New York: Schocken, 2007. 147–54. Print.

Bennett, Jane. *Vibrant Matter: A Political Ecology of Things.* Durham: Duke University Press, 2010. Print.

Berlant, Lauren. "Cruel Optimism." *The Affect Theory Reader.* Ed. Melissa Gregg and Gregory J. Seigworth. Durham: Duke University Press, 2010. 93–117. Print.

——. "Slow Death (Sovereignty, Obesity, Lateral Agency)." *Critical Inquiry* 33.4 (2007): 754–80. Print.

——. "Two Girls, Fat and Thin." *Regarding Sedgwick: Essays on Queer Culture and Critical Theory.* Ed. Stephen M. Barber and David L. Clark. New York: Routledge, 2002. 71–108. Print.

Berlant, Lauren, and Michael Warner. "Sex in Public." *Critical Inquiry* 24.2 (1998): 547–66. Print.

Berman, Sabina. "Backyard." *Gestos* 20.39 (2005): 107–81. Print.

Bernstein, Robin. "Toward the Integration of Theatre History and Affect Studies: Shame and the Rude Mechs's *The Method Gun.*" *Theatre Journal* 64.2 (2012): 213–30. Print.

Berson, Misha, ed. *Between Worlds: Contemporary Asian-American Plays*. New York: Theatre Communications Group, 1990. Print.

Bhabha, Homi K. *The Location of Culture*. London: Routledge, 1994. Print.

Billington, Michael. "Review: *Hamlet/Confidence:* Birmingham Rep." *Guardian* 26 Sept. 1998: 13. Print.

——. "Royal Court Theatre Gets Behind the Gaza Headlines." *Guardian*. Guardian News and Media, 11 Feb. 2009. Web. 16 Aug. 2010. <http://www.guardian.co.uk/stage/theatreblog/2009/feb/11/royal-court-theatre-gaza>.

Bilodeau, Chantal. *Sila*. 2011. MS.

Bitterman, Shem. *Harm's Way*. Woodstock: Dramatic Publishing, 2009. Print.

"Black Church Isn't Removing Racial Graffiti (Heritage Community Church in Collingwood)." *Canadian Press* [Toronto]. Proquest. 30 Aug. 1996. Web. 16 Jan. 2012. <http://ezproxy.lib.ucalgary.ca:2048/login?url=http://search.proquest.com/docview/359527795?accountid=9838>.

Blank, Jessica, and Erik Jensen. *Aftermath*. New York: Dramatists Play Service, 2010. Print.

Blau, Herbert. *Take Up the Bodies: Theater at the Vanishing Point*. Champaign: University of Illinois Press, 1982. Print.

Borland, Elizabeth, and Barbara Sutton. "Quotidian Disruption and Women's Activism in Times of Crisis, Argentina 2002–2003." *Gender & Society* 21.5 (2007): 700–22. Print.

Brantley, Ben. "April 3, 1968. Lorraine Motel. Evening." *New York Times* 13 Oct. 2011: C17. Print.

——. "Settling Down on Shaky Ground, in Diana Son's 'Satellites.'" *New York Times*. Nytimes.com, 19 June 2006. Web. 15 July 2012. <http://theater.nytimes.com/2006/06/19/theater/reviews/19sate.html>.

Brash, Nora Vagi. *Which Way, Big Man? and Five Other Plays*. Oxford: Oxford University Press, 1996. Print.

Brater, Enoch, ed. *Feminine Focus: The New Women Playwrights*. New York: Oxford University Press, 1989.

Brennan, Theresa. *The Transmission of Affect*. Ithaca: Cornell University Press, 2004. Print.

Brink, André. *Reinventing a Continent: Writing in South Africa*. London: Secker & Warburg, 1996. Print.

British Theatre Consortium. *Writ Large: New Writing on the English Stage 2003–2009*. London: Arts Council England, July 2009. Web. 12 May 2013. <www.artscouncil.org.uk/media/uploads/publications/writ_large_report.doc>.

Brittain, Victoria, and Gillian Slovo. *Guantanamo: 'Honor Bound to Defend Freedom'*. London: Oberon, 2004. Print.

Brown, Riwia. *Irirangi Bay. Ta Matou Mangai: Three Plays of the 1990s*. Ed. Hone Kouka. Wellington: Victoria University Press, 1999. 101–28. Print.

——. *Ngā Wahine*. 1992. TS. Playmarket, Wellington.

——. *Roimata. He Reo Hou: 5 Plays by Maori Playwrights*. Ed. Simon Garrett. Wellington: Playmarket, 1991. 163–218. Print.

——. *Te Hokina*. 1990. TS. Playmarket, Wellington.

Brown-Guillory, Elizabeth. "Place and Displacement in Djanet Sears's *Harlem Duet* and *The Adventures of a Black Girl in Search of God*." *Middle Passages and the Healing Places of History: Migration and Identity in Black Women's Literature*. Ed. Brown-Guillory. Columbus: Ohio State University, 2006. 155–70. Print.

Burke, Gregory. *Black Watch*. London: Faber & Faber, 2008. Print.

Burton, Rebecca. *Adding It Up: The Status of Women in Canadian Theatre; A Report of the Phase One Findings of Equity in Canadian Theatre: The Women's Initiative*. Ottawa: Canada Council for the Arts, 2 Oct. 2006. Web. 12 May 2013. <http://www.playwrightsguild.ca/sites/default/files/AddingItUp.pdf>.

——. "Dispelling the Myth of Equality: A Report on the Status of Women in Canadian Theatre." Wilson and McIntyre 3–8.

Cabrera, Eduardo. "Mujer e industria en 'Las máquinas de coser' de Estela Leñero." *Revista de Literatura Mexicana Contemporánea* 8.17 (2002): 25–33. Print.

Canning, Charlotte. "Feminist Performance as Feminist Historiography." *Theatre Survey* 45.2 (2004): 227–33. Print.

Carrillo Rowe, Aimee. *Power Lines: On the Subject of Feminist Alliances.* Durham: Duke University Press, 2008. Print.

Carl, Polly. 13P Company Overview. Web. 15 Jan. 2013. <https://www.facebook.com/13playwrights/info>.

Carlson, Marvin. *The Haunted Stage: The Theatre as Memory Machine.* Ann Arbor: University of Michigan Press, 2003. Print.

Caruth, Cathy. *Unclaimed Experience: Trauma, Narrative, and History.* Baltimore: Johns Hopkins University Press, 1996. Print.

Case, Sue-Ellen. *Feminism and Theatre.* London: Macmillan, 1988. Print.

——. *Feminism and Theatre.* 1988. Reissued ed. Foreword by Elaine Aston. Basingstoke: Palgrave Macmillan, 2008. Print.

——, ed. *Performing Feminisms: Feminist Critical Theory and Theatre.* Baltimore: Johns Hopkins University Press, 1990. Print.

Cataluna, Lee. *Aloha Friday.* 2000. TS. Kumu Kahua Theatre Archive, Honolulu.

——. *Da Mayah. He Leo Hou: A New Voice – Hawaiian Playwrights.* Ed. John H. Y. Wat and Meredith M. Desha. Honolulu: Bamboo Ridge Press, 2003. 147–202. Print.

——. *Super Secret Squad.* Honolulu: Kumu Kahua Theatre, 2002. Print.

Catanese, Brandi Wilkins. "Taking the Long View." Farfan and Ferris 547–51.

Cave, Damien. "Wave of Violence Swallows More Women in Juárez." *New York Times* 24 June 2012: A6. Print.

Charlebois, Gaetan L. "Burning Vision Mines a Sad Story." *The Gazette* [Montreal]. *Proquest*, D5. 4 June 2003. Web. 16 July 2012. <http://ezproxy.lib.ucalgary.ca:2048/login?url=http://search.proquest.com/docview/433950889?accountid=9838>.

Chaudhuri, Una. "Different Hats." *Theater* 33.3 (2003): 132–34. Print.

——. "The Ecocide Project's *Carla and Lewis.*" New York, 2011. Program Note.

——. "The Silence of the Polar Bears: Performing (Climate) Change in the Theater of Species." *Readings in Performance and Ecology.* Ed. Wendy Arons and Theresa J. May. New York: Palgrave Macmillan, 2012. 45–58. Print.

——. *Staging Place: The Geography of Modern Drama.* Ann Arbor: University of Michigan Press, 1995. Print.

Chaudhuri, Una, and Elinor Fuchs. "Land/Scape/Theater and the New Spatial Paradigm." Introduction. *Land/Scape/Theater.* Ed. Fuchs and Chaudhuri. Ann Arbor: University of Michigan Press, 2002. 1–7. Print.

"Chilean Immigration." *Encyclopedia of Immigration.* Immigration-online.org, 8 Feb. 2011. Web. 30 June 2012. <http://immigration-online.org/65-chilean-immigration.html>.

Cho, Julia. *99 Histories. Seven Contemporary Plays from the Korean Diaspora from the Americas.* Ed. Esther Kim Lee. Durham: Duke University Press, 2012. 21–84. Print.

Chuh, Kandice. *Imagine Otherwise: On Asian Americanist Critique.* Durham: Duke University Press, 2003. Print.

Chuh, Kandice, and Karen Shimakawa, eds. *Orientations: Mapping Studies in the Asian Diaspora.* Durham: Duke University Press, 2001. Print.

Churchill, Caryl. *Caryl Churchill Plays: 1.* London: Methuen Publishing, 1985. Print.

——. *Far Away.* New York: Theatre Communications Group, 2001. Print.

——. *Seven Jewish Children.* London: Nick Hern Books, 2009. Print.

——. *This Is a Chair.* London: Nick Hern Books, 1999. Print.

Cima, Gay Gibson. *Performing Women: Female Characters, Male Playwrights, and the Modern Stage.* Ithaca: Cornell University Press, 1993. Print.

Cixous, Hélène. "Enter the Theatre." Trans. Brian J. Mallett. *Selected Plays of Hélène Cixous.* Ed. Eric Prenowitz. London: Routledge, 2004. 25–34. Print.

Claycomb, Ryan. "Playing at Lives: Biography and Contemporary Feminist Drama." *Modern Drama* 47.3 (2004): 525–45. Print.

Clements, Marie. *Burning Vision.* Vancouver: Talonbooks, 2003. Print.

——. "Interview with Marie Clements." By Andrea Cochrane. *Playwrights' Workshop Montreal.* Playwrights.ca. 13 June 2002. Web. 7 Dec. 2012. <http://www.playwrights.ca/portfolios/burningvisioninterview1.html>.

Clod Ensemble. "Performing Medicine." *Clod Ensemble.* N.p., 2013. Web. 29 May 2013. <http://www.clodensemble.com/medicine.htm>.

Clough, Patricia T. "Introduction." *The Affective Turn: Theorizing the Social.* Ed. Patricia T. Clough with Jean Halley. Durham: Duke University Press, 2007. 1–33. Print.

Cohen, Patricia. "Charging Bias by Theaters, Female Playwrights to Hold Meeting." *New York Times.* Nytimes.com, 25 Oct. 2008. Web. 12 May 2013. <http://www.nytimes.com/2008/10/25/theater/25women.html?scp=1&sq=%E2%80%9CCharging%20Bias%20by%20Theaters,%20Female%20Playwrights%20to%20Hold%20Meeting,%E2%80%9D%20&st=cse>.

——. "Rethinking Gender Bias in Theater." *New York Times.* Nytimes.com, 24 June 2009. Web. 12 May 2013. <http://theater.nytimes.com/2009/06/24/theater/24play.html?_r=0>.

Colbert, Soyica Diggs. *The African American Theatrical Body: Reception, Performance and the Stage.* Cambridge: Cambridge University Press, 2011. Print.

Colleran, Jeanne. "Disposable Wars, Disappearing Acts: Theatrical Responses to the 1991 Gulf War." *Theatre Journal* 55.4 (2003): 613–32. Print.

Colleran, Jeanne, and Jenny S. Spencer, eds. *Staging Resistance: Essays on Political Theater.* Ann Arbor: University of Michigan Press, 1998. Print.

"Comisión Nacional Sobre Prisión Política y Tortura." 1 June 2005. Web. 30 June 2012. <http://www.bcn.cl/bibliodigital/dhisto/lfs/Informe.pdf>.

Cooke, Miriam. *Women and the War Story.* Berkeley: University of California Press, 1996. Print.

Corthron, Kia. *A Cool Dip in the Barren Saharan Crick.* New York: Samuel French, 2010. Print.

Cote, David. *"Songs of the Dragons Flying to Heaven by Young Jean Lee." TimeOut New York.* Timeout.com, 28 Sept. 2006. Web. 14 July 2012. <http://www.timeout.com/newyork/theater/songs-of-the-dragons-flying-to-heaven>.

Crawford, Elizabeth. "Naked Truths and the Suffragette Movement." Letter. *Guardian.* Guardian News and Media, 28 Aug. 2008. Web. 26 Oct. 2010. <http://www.theguardian.com/lifeandstyle/2008/aug/28/women1>.

Crean, Susan. "Africa Exhibit Added Insult to Original Injury." *Toronto Star* 6 Sept. 1990: A25. Print.

Croft, Susan. "Naked Truths and the Suffragette Movement." Letter. *Guardian.* Guardian News and Media, 28 Aug. 2008. Web. 26 Oct. 2010. <http://www.theguardian.com/lifeandstyle/2008/aug/28/women1>.

Cvetkovich, Ann. *An Archive of Feelings: Trauma, Sexuality, and Lesbian Public Cultures.* Durham: Duke University Press, 2003. Print.

——. *Depression: A Public Feeling.* Durham: Duke University Press, 2012. Print.

Dalby, Krista. *"Adding It Up* Takes More Than Just Numbers." Wilson and McIntyre 14–17.

D'Amico, Francine. "The Women of Abu Ghraib." McKelvey 45–50.

Dansey, Harry. *Te Raukura: The Feathers of the Albatross.* Auckland: Longman Paul, 1974. Print.

Davis, Angela Y. "Sexual Coercion, Prisons, and Female Responses." McKelvey 23–28.

Davis, Tracy C. *Actresses as Working Women: Their Social Identity in Victorian Culture.* London: Routledge, 1991. Print.

De Angelis, April. *Playhouse Creatures.* London: Samuel French, 1994. Print.

——. *Playhouse Creatures. April De Angelis: Plays.* London: Faber, 1999. 153–231. Print.

——. "Riddle of the Sphinx." *Guardian,* 9 Sept. 2005. Web. 30 Oct. 2012. <http://www.guardian.co.uk/stage/2005/sep/10/theatre>.

——. "Troubling Gender on Stage and with the Critics." *Theatre Journal* 62.4 (2010): 557–59.

De Angelis, April, and Michael Oakley. "Fly: Under *Playhouse Creatures.*" 27 July 2012. Web. 30 Oct. 2012. <http://www.youtube.com/watch?v=4_80zAV5H2A>.

Delgado, Maria M., and Caridad Svich, eds. *Theatre in Crisis? Performance Manifestos for a New Century.* Manchester: Manchester University Press, 2003. Print.

De Palma, Anthony. "The Quake That Shook Mexico Awake Is Recalled." *New York Times.* 19 Sept. 1995. Web. 15 Aug. 2012. <http://www.nytimes.com/1995/09/19/world/the-quake-that-shook-mexico-awake-is-recalled.html?pagewanted=all&src=pm>.

De Wagter, Caroline. "Land and Cultural Memory: Djanet Sears's *The Adventures of a Black Girl in Search of God* and Diane Glancy's *Jump Kiss: An Indian Legend.*" *Theatres in the Round: Multi-Ethnic, Indigenous and Intertextual Dialogues in Drama.* Ed. Dorothy Figueira and Marc Maufort, with the assistance of Sylvie Vranckzx. Brussels: Peter Lang, 2011. 55–70. Print.

Diamond, Elin. *Unmaking Mimesis: Essays on Feminism and Performance.* London: Routledge, 1997. Print.

D'Monté, Rebecca. "Thatcher's Children: Alienation and Anomie in the Plays of Judy Upton." *Cool Britannia? British Political Drama in the 1990s.* Ed. Rebecca D'Monté and Graham Saunders. Basingstoke: Palgrave Macmillan, 2008. 79–95. Print.

Dolan, Jill. *The Feminist Spectator as Critic.* 2nd ed. Ann Arbor: University of Michigan Press, 2012. Print.

——. *The Feminist Spectator: Reviews and Ruminations on How Theatre, Film, and Television Shape and Reflect Our Lives.* Feministspectator.com, 2005. Web. <http://www.thefeministspectator.com/>.

——. *Presence and Desire: Essays on Gender, Sexuality, Performance.* Ann Arbor: University of Michigan Press, 1993. Print.

——. "Ruined, by Lynn Nottage." *The Feminist Spectator.* Thefeministspectator.com, 16 Mar. 2009. Web. 16 Oct. 2010. <http://www.thefeministspectator.com/2009/03/16/ruined-by-lynn-nottage/>.

——. *Utopia in Performance: Finding Hope at the Theater.* Ann Arbor: University of Michigan Press, 2005. Print.

Drainie, Bronwyn. "Black Groups Protest African Show at 'Racist Ontario Museum.'" *Globe and Mail* 24 Mar. 1990: C1. Print.

"Earth Matters on Stage Festival." *Earth Matters on Stage Ecodrama Festival.* Wordpress.com. Web. 26 Feb. 2013. <http://emosfestival.wordpress.com/>.

Elam, Harry J., Jr. *The Past as Present in the Drama of August Wilson.* Ann Arbor: University of Michigan Press, 2006. Print.

El-Assal, Fathiya. *Al-Kharsaa.* Cairo: Al-Thaqafa Al-Gadida Publishing House, 1981. Print.

——. *Nisaa' Bila Aqni'a.* Cairo: General Egyptian Book Organization, 2002. Print.

El-Banhawi, Nadia. *Al-Wahag wa Masrahiyat Ukhra.* Cairo: General Egyptian Book Organization, 1996. Print.

El-Sa'dawi, Nawal. *Al-Ilah Yuqadim Istiqalatahu fi Igtimaa' Al-Qimmah.* 1996. Cairo: Madbouli, 2007. Print.

——. *Isis.* Cairo: Dar Al-Mustaqbal Al-Arabi, 1986. Print.

El-Zayyat, Latifa. *Bee' wi Shira*. Cairo: General Egyptian Book Organization, 1994. Print.

Enelow, Shonni. *Carla and Lewis*. Jan. 2013. MS.

Enloe, Cynthia. *Maneuvers: The International Politics of Militarizing Women's Lives.* Berkeley: University of California Press, 2000. Print.

Ensler, Eve. *The Vagina Monologues*. New York: Random House, 1998. Print.

Evans, Christine. *Trojan Barbie*. Tasmania: Australian Script Centre, 2007. Print.

Faludi, Susan. *Backlash: The Undeclared War against Women*. New York: Crown, 1991. Print.

Farber, Yael. *Molora*. London: Oberon Books, 2008. Print.

——. *Theatre as Witness: A Woman in Waiting, Amajuba, He Left Quietly*. London: Oberon Books, 2008. Print.

Farfan, Penny. "Monstrous History: Judith Thompson's *Sled*." *Canadian Theatre Review* 120 (2004): 46–9; reprinted in *Judith Thompson*, ed. Knowles 99–104.

——. *Women, Modernism, and Performance*. Cambridge: Cambridge University Press, 2004. Print.

Farfan, Penny, and Lesley Ferris, eds. *Contemporary Women Playwrights*. Spec. issue of *Theatre Journal* 62.4 (2010). Print.

Feinman, Ilene. "Shock and Awe: Abu Ghraib, Women Soldiers, and Racially Gendered Torture." McKelvey 57–80.

Feitz, Lindsey, and Joane Nagel. "The Militarization of Gender and Sexuality in the Iraq War." *Women in the Military and in Armed Conflict*. Ed. Helena Carreiras and Gerhard Kümmel. Wiesbaden: VS Verlag, 2008. 201–25. Print.

Ferris, Lesley. "The Female Self and Performance: The Case of *The First Actress*." *Theatre and Feminist Aesthetics*. Ed. Karen Laughlin and Catherine Schuler. Madison: Fairleigh Dickinson University Press, 1995. 242–57. Print.

"50/50 in 2020: About." *50/50 in 2020*. Wordpress.com, 2010. Web. 14 May 2013. <http://5050in2020.org/about/>.

Filewod, Alan. *Performing Canada: The Nation Enacted in the Imagined Theatre*. Kamloops: University College of the Cariboo, 2002. Print. Textual Studies in Canada. Vol. 15.

Firehall Arts Centre. N.p., 2012. Web. 10 Dec. 2012. <http://firehallartscentre.ca/>.

Flanders, Laura. "Eve Ensler Rising." *The Nation* 26 Nov. 2012: 11–17.

Flockemann, Miki. "On Not Giving Up – An Interview with Fatima Dike." *Contemporary Theatre Review* 9.1 (1999): 17–26. Print.

Foot-Newton, Lara. *Karoo Moose*. London: Oberon Books, 2009. Print.

——. "Reach!." *At this Stage*. Ed. Greg Homann. Johannesberg: Witwatersrand University Press, 2009. 31–68. Print.

——. *Tshepang*. Johannesberg: Witwatersrand University Press, 2005. Print.

Fornes, Maria Irene. "Maria Irene Fornes Discusses Forty Years in Theatre with Maria M. Delgado." *Conducting a Life: Reflections on the Theatre of Maria Irene Fornes*. Ed. Maria M. Delgado and Caridad Svich. Lyme: Smith and Kraus, 1999. 248–77. Print.

——. *The Summer in Gossensass*. *What of the Night? Selected Plays*. New York: PAJ, 2008. 47–95. Print.

Foucault, Michel. *Discipline and Punish: The Birth of the Prison*. Trans. Alan Sheridan. New York: Vintage, 1977. Print.

——. "Friendship as a Way of Life." *Foucault Live: Collected Interviews 1961–1984*. Ed. Sylvère Lotringer. New York: Semiotext(e), 1996. 308–12. Print.

Foucault, Michel, and Jay Miskowiec. "Of Other Spaces." *Diacritics* 16.1 (1986): 22–27. Print.

Frank, Arthur W. *At the Will of the Body: Reflections on Illness*. Boston: Houghton Mifflin, 1991. Print.

Fraticelli, Rina "The Invisibility Factor: The Status of Women in Canadian Theatre." *Fuse* 6.3 (1982): 112–24. Print.

Freeman, Elizabeth. "Chronic Thinking." Strategic Ruptures Lecture Series. Cornell University, Ithaca, NY. 23 Feb. 2012. Public Lecture.

——. *Time Binds: Queer Temporalities, Queer Histories*. Durham: Duke University Press, 2010. Print.

Friedman, Sharon, ed. *Feminist Theatrical Revisions of Classic Works: Critical Essays*. Jefferson: McFarland, 2009. Print.

Fuchs, Elinor. "Reading for Landscape: The Case of American Drama." *Land/Scape/ Theater*. Ed. Elinor Fuchs and Una Chaudhuri. Ann Arbor: University of Michigan Press, 2002. 30–50. Print.

Fuemana, Dianna. *Falemalama*. Two Plays. Wellington: Playmarket, 2008. 53–75. Print.

——. *Mapaki*. *Mapaki/Frangipani Perfume*. By Dianna Fuemana and Makerita Urale. Wellington: The Play Press, 2004. 37–66. Print.

Gann, Myra S. "Masculine Space in the Plays of Estela Leñero." *Latin American Women Dramatists: Theater, Texts, and Theories*. Ed. Catherine Larson and Margarita Vargas. Bloomington: Indiana University Press, 1999. 234–42. Print.

García-Romero, Anne. *Transculturation and Twenty-First Century Latina Playwrights*. Diss., University of California Santa Barbara, 2009. Print.

Gassman, Ben. "The Imminent Implosion of 13P." *The Brooklyn Rail*. N.p., 1 Aug. 2012. Web. 28 Sept. 2013. <http://www.brooklynrail.org/2012/08/theater/ the-imminent-implosion-of-13p>.

Gates, Joanne E. *Elizabeth Robins, 1862–1952: Actress, Novelist, Feminist*. Tuscaloosa: University of Alabama Press, 1994. Print.

Gaylord, Chris. "Conflict Minerals: Genocide in Your Gadgets?" *Christian Science Monitor*, 24 Feb. 2011. Web. 15 Apr. 2013. <http://www.csmonitor.com/Innovation/ Responsible-Tech/2011/0224/Conflict-minerals-Genocide-in-your-gadgets>.

Genzlinger, Neil. "The Feminine, Touched: War as Women's Work." *New York Times*. The New York Times Company, 10 Mar. 2009. Web. 16 Oct. 2010. <http://theater. nytimes.com/2009/03/10/theater/reviews/10lone.html?_r=0>.

George, Madeleine. *Seven Wooly Mammoths Wander New England*. 2011. TS.

George, Miria. *and what remains*. Wellington: Tawata Press, 2007. Print.

——. *Sunset Road*. 2012. TS. Playmarket, Wellington.

——. *Urban Hymns*. Three Plays: Young and Hungry. Wellington: Playmarket, 2010. 127–77. Print.

Giddings, Paula. *When and Where I Enter: The Impact of Black Women on Race and Sex in America*. New York: William Morrow, 1984. Print.

Glaude, Eddie. *Exodus!: Religion, Race, and Nation in Early Nineteenth-Century Black America*. Chicago: University of Chicago Press, 2000. Print.

Gobrait, Valérie. *Matari'i*. Tahiti: Ouvrage édité à compte d'auteur, 2008. Print.

——. *Le partage de la terre*. *Théâtre Océanien: Anthologie*. Ed. Sonia Lacabanne. Papeete: Au Vent Des Iles, 2011. 87–145. Print.

——. "Valérie Gobrait." *Les Nouvelles de Tahiti*. lesnouvelles.pf, 22 May 2009. Web. 2 Mar. 2013. <http://www.lesnouvelles.pf/article/a-laffiche/valerie-gobrait>.

Goddard, Lynette. *Staging Black Feminisms: Identity, Politics, Performance*. Basingstoke: Palgrave Macmillan, 2007. Print.

Goethe, Johann Wolfgang von. "Goethe's 'Women's Parts Played by Men in the Roman Theater.'" Trans. Isa Ragusa. *Crossing the Stage: Controversies on Cross-Dressing*. Ed. Lesley Ferris. London: Routledge, 1993. 47–51. Print.

Goodman, Lizbeth. *Contemporary Feminist Theatres: To Each Her Own*. New York: Routledge, 1993. Print.

Gottlieb, Richard. *Forcing the Spring: The Transformation of the American Environmental Movement*. Washington: Island Press, 1993. Print.

Gouws, Amanda, ed. *(Un)thinking Citizenship: Feminist Debates in Contemporary South Africa*. Aldershot: Ashgate, 2005. Print.

Goyanes, Maria. "The Finite Animal: 13P's End Days." *HowlRound*. GAIAhost, 7 Oct. 2012. Web. <http://www.howlround.com/the-finite-animal-13ps-end-days-by-maria-goyanes/?utm_source=feedburner&utm_medium=email&utm_campaign=Feed%3A+HowlRound+%28HowlRound.com%27s+Journal%2C+Blog%2C+%26+Podcasts%29>.

Grace-Smith, Briar. *Flat Out Brown*. 1996. TS. Playmarket, Wellington.

——. *Haruru Mai*. *Haruru Mai/Strange Resting Places*. By Briar Grace-Smith, and Paolo Rotondo and Rob Mokaraka. Wellington: Playmarket, 2012. 23–98. Print.

——. *Ngā Pou Wahine*. Wellington: Huia, 1997. Print.

——. *Potiki's Memory of Stone*. 2003. TS. Playmarket, Wellington.

——. *Purapurawhetū*. Wellington: Huia, 1999. Print.

Green, Maureen, and David Butler. "Theatrical Spectacle and the Suffragettes' Real Achievements." Letter. *Guardian*. Guardian News and Media, 1 Sept. 2008. Web. 26 Oct. 2010. <http://www.guardian.co.uk/politics/2008/sep/01/women.theatre>.

Greenberg, Joel. Rev. of *The Adventures of a Black Girl in Search of God*. *Aisle Say (Toronto)*. TheatreNet Enterprises, 2002. Web. 19 June 2012. <http://www.aislesay.com/ONT-ADVENTURES.html>.

Greenburg, Linda Margarita. "Learning from the Dead: Wounds, Women, and Activism in Cherríe Moraga's *Heroes and Saints*." *MELUS* 34.1 (2009): 163–84. Print.

Greene, Alexis. "Women and War: The Plays of Emily Mann, Lavonne Mueller, Shirley Lauro, Naomi Wallace, Shirley Gee, and Anne Devlin." *Women Writing Plays: Three Decades of the Susan Smith Blackburn Prize*. Ed. Greene. Austin: University of Texas Press, 2006. 82–92. Print.

Griffin, Gabrielle. *Contemporary Black and Asian Women Playwrights in Britain*. Cambridge: Cambridge University Press, 2003. Print.

Griffiths, Linda. *Age of Arousal*. Toronto: Coach House Books, 2007. Print.

Groskop, Viv. "Sex and the Suffragette." *Guardian*. Guardian News and Media, 26 Aug. 2008. Web. 26 Oct. 2010. <http://www.guardian.co.uk/stage/2008/aug/26/theatre.women>.

The Guerilla Girls. "Parody and Parity." Interview by Alisa Solomon. *Theater* 29.2 (1999): 45–55. Print.

Gurira, Danai. *Eclipsed*. New York: Dramatists Play Service, 2010. Print.

Habib, Samia. *Masrah al-Mar'a fi Misr*. Cairo: General Egyptian Book Organization, 2003. Print.

Halberstam, Judith. *The Queer Art of Failure*. Durham: Duke University Press, 2011. Print.

Hall, Jacquelyn Dowd. "The Long Civil Rights Movement and the Political Uses of the Past." *The Journal of American History* 91.4 (2005): 1233–63. Print.

Hall, Katori. Introduction. *Katori Hall Plays: 1*. London: Methuen Drama, 2011. ix–xiv. Print.

——. *The Mountaintop*. *Katori Hall Plays: 1*. London: Methuen Drama, 2011. 187–249. Print.

Hamburger, Tony. "*Tshepang*: A Morality Play?" Introduction. *Tshepang: The Third Testament*. By Lara Foot-Newton. Johannesburg: Witwatersrand University Press, 2005. 8. Print.

Hamilton, Cicely. *A Pageant of Great Women*. London: The Suffrage Shop, 1910.

Hammond, Brean S. "Is Everything History?: Churchill, Barker, and the Modern History Play." *Comparative Drama* 41.1 (2007): 1–23. Print.

Hargreaves, Allison. "'A Precise Instrument for Seeing': Remembrance in *Burning Vision* and the Activist Classroom." *Canadian Theatre Review* 147 (2011): 49–54. Print.

Hart, Lynda, ed. *Making a Spectacle: Feminist Essays on Contemporary Women's Theatre*. Ann Arbor: University of Michigan Press, 1989. Print.

Hart, Lynda, and Peggy Phelan, eds. *Acting Out: Feminist Performances*. Ann Arbor: University of Michigan Press, 1993. Print.

Hartman, Saidiya. *Lose Your Mother: A Journey Along the Atlantic Slave Route*. New York: Farrar, Strauss, and Giroux, 2007. Print.

Harvie, Jen. "Constructing Fictions of an Essential Reality, or 'This Pickshur is Niiiice': Judith Thompson's *Lion in the Streets*." Knowles 47–58.

Hau'ofa, Epeli. "Our Sea of Islands." *A New Oceania: Rediscovering Our Sea of Islands*. Ed. Eric Waddell, Vijay Naidu, and Epeli Hau'ofa. Suva: University of the South Pacific, 1993. 2–16. Print.

Hauptfleisch, Temple. "The Background: Reza de Wet and the South African Literary Establishment." *Contemporary Theatre Review* 9.1 (1999): 53–7. Print.

Hayes, Peter. "Brief Encounter With ... *Ncamisa! Kiss the Women*." By Jo Caird. *What's on Stage*. Whatsonstage.com, 8 Oct. 2010. Web. 14 May 2012. <http://www.whatsonstage.com/interviews/theatre/off-west+end/E8831285243428/Brief+Encounter+With+...+Ncamisa!+Kiss+the+Women+.htm>.

Hereaka, Whiti. *Collective Agreement*. 2005. TS. Playmarket, Wellington.

——. *Rona and Rabbit on the Moon*. 2011. TS. Playmarket, Wellington.

——. *Te Kaupoi*. 2010. TS. Playmarket, Wellington.

Hereaka, Whiti, and Open Book Productions. *I Ain't Nothing But / A Glimmer in the Dark, She Said*. Shed 11, Wellington, 17–26 Oct. 2006. Performance.

Hesford, Wendy S. "Rhetorical Memory, Political Theater, and the Traumatic Present." *Transformations* 16.2 (2005): 104–17. Print.

Hesse, Monica. "'Jewish Children' Comes to D.C. Already Upstaged by Controversy." *Washington Post*. The Washington Post Online, 17 Mar. 2009. Web. 23 Aug. 2010. <http://articles.washingtonpost.com/2009-03-17/news/36854605_1_british-playwright-caryl-churchill-theaters-jewish-community>.

Hill, Christopher. *The World Turned Upside Down: Radical Ideas during the English Revolution*. New York: Penguin, 1984. Print.

Hine, Darlene Clark, and Kathleen Thompson. *A Shining Thread of Hope: The History of Black Women in America*. New York: Broadway, 1998. Print.

Hoffman, Tyler. *American Poetry in Performance: From Walt Whitman to Hip Hop*. Ann Arbor: University of Michigan Press, 2011. Print.

Holdsworth, Nadine. *Theatre & Nation*. Basingstoke: Palgrave Macmillan, 2010. Print.

Holland, Sharon. *The Erotic Life of Racism*. Durham: Duke University Press, 2012. Print.

Holledge, Julie, and Joanne Tompkins. *Women's Intercultural Performance*. London: Routledge, 2000. Print.

Horovitz, Israel. *What Good Fences Make. The Theater J Blog*. Theater J, 19 Apr. 2009. Web. 22 Sept. 2010. <http://theaterjblogs.wordpress.com/2009/04/19/a-new-response-play-to-7jc-by-israel-horovitz-what-good-fences-make/>.

Houston, Velina Hasu, ed. *The Politics of Life: Four Plays by Asian American Women*. Philadelphia: Temple University Press, 1993. Print.

——. *Tea. Unbroken Thread: An Anthology of Plays by Asian American Women*. Ed. Roberta Uno. Amherst: University of Massachusetts Press, 1993. 155–200. Print.

Howe, Elizabeth. *The First English Actresses: Women and Drama, 1660–1700*. Cambridge: Cambridge University Press, 1992. Print.

Hudes, Quiara Alegría. *Elliot, A Soldier's Fugue*. New York: Dramatists Play Service, 2007. Print.

Huggan, Graham, and Helen Tiffin. *Postcolonial Ecocriticism: Literature, Animals, Environment*. London: Routledge, 2010.

Hunt, Krista, and Kim Rygiel, eds. *(En)Gendering the War on Terror: War Stories and Camouflaged politics.* Aldershot: Ashgate, 2006. Print.

Huria, John. Introduction. *Purapurawhetū.* By Briar Grace-Smith. Wellington: Huia, 1999. 8–19. Print.

Hurley, Erin. *Theatre & Feeling.* Basingstoke: Palgrave Macmillan, 2010. Print.

Hutchison, Yvette. "Post-1990s Verbatim Theatre in South Africa: Exploring an African Concept of 'Truth.'" *Dramaturgy of the Real on the World Stage.* Ed. Carol Martin. Basingstoke: Palgrave Macmillan, 2010. 61–71. Print.

——. "Verbatim Theatre in South Africa: 'Living Theatre in a Person's Performance.'" *Get Real: Documentary Theatre Past and Present.* Ed. Alison Forsyth and Chris Megson. Basingstoke: Palgrave Macmillan, 2009. 209–23. Print.

Iqbal, Nosheen. "'I've had two hours sleep!' Katori Hall Was the Surprise Winner at This Year's Olivier Awards." *Guardian* 24 Mar. 2010: 19. Print.

Isherwood, Charles. "'Amajuba: Like Doves We Rise': Apartheid's Private Pain Becomes Group Art." *Theater Review.* nytimes.com, 26 July 2006. Web. 4 Oct. 2012.

——. "Beneath Pink Parasols, Identity in Stark Form." *New York Times.* 16 Jan. 2012. Web. 14 July 2012. <http://theater.nytimes.com/2012/01/17/theater/reviews/young-jean-lees-untitled-feminist-show-review.html>.

Jacobson, Howard. "Let's See the 'Criticism' of Israel for What It Is." *Independent.* independent.co.uk, 18 Feb. 2009. Web. 16 Aug. 2010. <http://www.independent.co.uk/voices/commentators/howard-jacobson/howard-jacobson-letrsquos-see-the-criticism-of-israel-for-what-it-really-is-1624827.html>.

Jajeh, Jennifer. *I ♥ Hamas and Other Things I'm Afraid to Tell You.* Dir. W. Kamau Bell. Perf. Jennifer Jajeh. Bedlam Theatre, Minneapolis. 19 Feb. 2010. Performance.

Jay, Gregory S. "Other People's Holocausts: Trauma, Empathy, and Justice in Anna Deavere Smith's *Fires in the Mirror.*" *Contemporary Literature* 48.1 (2007): 119–50. Print.

John, Angela V. *Elizabeth Robins: Staging a Life 1862–1952.* London: Routledge, 1995. Print.

Jonas, Susan, and Suzanne Bennett. "Report on the Status of Women: A Limited Engagement." *New York State Council on the Arts Theatre Program.* Women Arts, Jan. 2002. Web. 26 May 2013. <http://www.womenarts.org/nysca-report-2002/>.

Jones, Jeffrey M. "Songs of the Dragons Flying to Heaven; Script Sabotage." *American Theatre* 24.7 (2007): 74–75. Print.

Kane, Sarah. *Blasted. Complete Plays.* London: Methuen, 2001. 1–62. Print.

Kaplan, Sara Clarke. "Souls at the Crossroads, Africans on the Water: The Politics of Diasporic Melancholia." *Callaloo* 30.2 (2007): 511–26. Print.

Kaufman-Osborn, Timothy. "Gender Trouble at Abu Ghraib?" McKelvey 145–66.

Kelly, Joan. "Did Women Have a Renaissance?" *Becoming Visible: Women in European History.* Ed. Renate Bridenthal, Claudia Koonz, and Susan Stuard. Boston: Houghton Mifflin, 1987. 137–64. Print.

Kelly-Gadol, Joan. "The Social Relations of the Sexes: Methodological Implications of Women's History." *Signs: Journal of Women in Culture and Society* 1.4 (1976): 809–23. Print.

King, Martin Luther, Jr. "The American Dream." *A Testament of Hope: The Essential Writings and Speeches of Martin Luther King, Jr.* Ed. James M. Washington. New York: Harper Collins, 1991. 208–16. Print.

Kneubuhl, Victoria Nalani. *Emmalehua. Hawai'i Nei: Island Plays.* Honolulu: University of Hawai'i Press, 2002. 81–141. Print.

——. *Fanny and Belle: The Story of Mrs. Robert Louis Stevenson and Her Daughter Belle Osbourne.* 2004. TS. Kumu Kahua Theatre Archive, Honolulu.

——. *The Holiday of Rain.* 2011. TS. Kumu Kahua Theatre Archive, Honolulu.

——. *Ola Na Iwi. Hawai'i Nei: Island Plays.* Honolulu: University of Hawai'i Press, 2002. 143–227. Print.

——. *The Story of Susanna*. *Seventh Generation: An Anthology of Native American Plays*. Ed. Mimi Gisolfi D'Aponte. New York: Theatre Communications Group, 1999. 291–370. Print.

Knowles, Ric, ed. *Judith Thompson*. Toronto: Playwrights Canada Press, 2005. Print.

Knudsen, Jan Sverre. "Dancing *cueca* 'with your coat on': The Role of Traditional Chilean Dance in an Immigrant Community." *British Journal of Ethnomusicology* 10.2 (2001): 61–83. Print.

Koivunen, Anu. "An Affective Turn? Reimagining the Subject of Feminist Theory." *Working with Affect in Feminist Readings: Disturbing Differences*. Ed. Marianne Liljeström and Susanna Paasonen. London: Routledge, 2010. 8–28. Print.

Kolin, Philip C., ed. *Contemporary African American Women Playwrights: A Casebook*. London: Routledge, 2007. Print.

Kouka, Hone. Introduction. *Ta Matou Mangai: Three Plays of the 1990s*. Ed. Kouka. Wellington: Victoria University Press, 1999. 9–28. Print.

Kron, Lisa. *Well*. New York: Theatre Communications Group, 2006. Print.

Kruger, Loren. "Democratic Actors and Post-apartheid Drama: Contesting Performance in Contemporary South Africa." *Contesting Performance: Global Sites of Research*. Ed. Jon McKenzie, Heike Roms, and C. J. W.-L. Wee. Basingstoke: Palgrave Macmillan, 2010. 236–54. Print.

Kushner, Tony, and Alisa Solomon. "Tell Her the Truth." *The Nation*. thenation. com, 26 Mar. 2009. Web. 17 Sept. 2010. <http://www.thenation.com/article/tell-her-truth#>.

Lahr, John. "Good Vibrations." *New Yorker*. Condé Nast, 30 Nov. 2009. Web. 30 June 2010. <http://www.newyorker.com/arts/critics/theatre/2009/11/30/091130crth_theatre_lahr>.

——. "Surreal Life: The Plays of Sarah Ruhl." *New Yorker*. Condé Nast, 17 Mar. 2008. Web. 29 Oct. 2010. <http://www.newyorker.com/arts/critics/atlarge/2008/03/17/080317crat_atlarge_lahr>.

Lally, Elaine, in consultation with Sarah Miller. "Women in Theatre: A Research Report and Action Plan for the Australia Council for the Arts." Sydney: Australia Council for the Arts, Apr. 2012. Web. 12 May 2013. <http://www.australi-acouncil.gov.au/_data/assets/pdf_file/0008/127196/Women-in-Theatre-April-2012.pdf>.

Latorre, Sobeira, and Joanna L. Mitchell. "Performing the 'Generic Latina': A Conversation with Teatro Luna." *Meridians: Feminism, Race, Transnationalism* 7.1 (2006): 19–37. Print.

Lee, Esther Kim, ed. *Seven Contemporary Plays from the Korean Diaspora from the Americas*. Durham: Duke University Press, 2012. Print.

Lee, Young Jean. "Songs of the Dragons Flying to Heaven." *American Theatre* 24.7 (2007): 76–85. Print.

——. *Songs of the Dragons Flying to Heaven*. *Songs of the Dragons Flying to Heaven and Other Plays*. New York: Theatre Communications Group, 2009. 31–74. Print.

Leñero, Estela. *El huso y el sexo: La mujer obrera en dos industrias de Tlaxcala*. Mexico, DF: CIESAS, 1984. Print.

——. *Las máquinas de coser*. Mexico City: Universidad Autónoma Metropolitana, 1989. Print.

Lenkiewicz, Rebecca. *Her Naked Skin*. London: Faber & Faber, 2008. Print.

——. "Rebecca Lenkiewicz on *Her Naked Skin*." *National Theatre Bookshop Talk*. National Theatre, 1 Sept. 2008. Web. 26 Oct. 2010. <http://www.nationaltheatre.org.uk/?lid=37491>.

Lerner, Gerda. *Why History Matters: Life and Thought*. New York: Oxford University Press, 1997. Print.

Lewis, E. M. *Song of Extinction*. New York: Samuel French, 2010. Print.

Leys, Ruth. "The Turn to Affect: A Critique." *Critical Inquiry* 37.3 (2011): 434–72. Print.

"The Lilly Awards: About." *The Lilly Awards*. N.p., 2013. Web. 14 May 2013. <http://www.thelillyawards.org/about/>.

Lin, Brian. "Tuning Into Humanity with Burning Vision." *Raven's Eye* 5.12 (2002): 8. Web. 15 Dec. 2012. <http://www.ammsa.com/publications/ravens-eye/tuning-humanity-burning-vision>.

Lowe, Lisa. *Immigrant Acts: On Asian American Cultural Politics*. Durham: Duke University Press, 1996. Print.

Ludmer, Josefina. "Mujeres que matan." *Revista Iberoamericana* 62.176–177 (1996): 781–97. Print.

Mahran, Fawziya. *Capuche wa al-Tamathil Aydan Tantahir*. Cairo: General Egyptian Book Organization, 1995. Print.

Margolin, Deb. *O Yes I Will (I will remember the spirit and texture of this conversation)*. N.d. TS.

——."O Yes I Will (I will remember the spirit and texture of this conversation)." *TDR* 52.3 (2008): 174–86. Print.

——. "A Perfect Theatre for One: Teaching 'Performance Composition.'" *TDR* 41.2 (1997): 68–81. Print.

——. "Seven Palestinian Children." *Reb Barry's Blog*. The Neshamah Centre, n.d. Web. 17 Sept. 2010. <http://www.neshamah.net/seven-palestinian-children>.

——. "'To Speak Is to Suffer' and Vice Versa." *TDR* 52.3 (2008): 95–97. Print.

Marks, Peter. "Review: 'Songs of the Dragons Flying to Heaven' at Studio Theatre." *Washington Post*. washingtonpost.com, 8 Oct. 2010. Web. 6 Oct. 2012. <http://www.washingtonpost.com/wp-dyn/content/article/2010/10/07/AR2010100706231.html>.

Marlowe, Sam. Rev. of "*The Mountaintop*." By Katori Hall. *Times* [London] 24 Mar. 2011, sec. T2: 16. Print.

Martin, Carol, ed. *Dramaturgy of the Real on the World Stage*. Basingstoke: Palgrave Macmillan, 2010. Print.

Marx, Gerhard. Designer's Note. *Tshepang: The Third Testament*. By Lara Foot-Newton. Johannesburg: Witwatersrand University Press, 2005. x–xi.

Massumi, Brian. "Notes on the Translation." *A Thousand Plateaus: Capitalism and Schizophrenia*. By Gilles Deleuze and Félix Guattari. Minneapolis: University of Minnesota Press, 1987. xvii–xx. Print.

——. *Parables of the Virtual*. Durham: Duke University Press, 2002. Print.

Maugham, W. Somerset. "Rain." *The Trembling of a Leaf*. Melbourne: Heinemann, 1935. 234–95. Print.

Maxwell, Justin. "Cartography Lessons with Caridad Svich: The Ancient and Contemporary Combine in the Dreamscapes of Her Plays." *American Theatre* 26.6 (2009): 32–35. Print.

May, Theresa J. "Beyond Bambi: Toward a Dangerous Ecocriticism." *Theatre Topics* 17.2 (2007): 95–110. Print.

——. "Greening the Theatre: Taking Ecocriticism from Page to Stage." *Journal of Interdisciplinary Studies* 7.1 (2005): 84–103. Print.

——. "Kneading Marie Clements' *Burning Vision*." *Canadian Theatre Review* 144 (2010): 5–12. Print.

McCauley, Robbie. *Indian Blood*. N.d. TS.

——. *Sugar*. 9 Mar. 2013. TS.

McFerran, Ann. "The Theatre's (Somewhat) Angry Young Women." *Time Out* 26 Oct.–3 Nov. 1977: 13–15. Print.

McGuire, Danielle L. *At the Dark End of the Street: Black Women, Rape, and Resistance – a New History of the Civil Rights Movement from Rosa Parks to the Rise of Black Power*. New York: Vintage, 2011. Print.

McKelvey, Tara, ed. *One of the Guys*. Emeryville: Seal Press, 2007. Print.

McRobbie, Angela. *The Aftermath of Feminism: Gender, Culture and Social Change*. London: Sage, 2009. Print.

Mead, Margaret. *Coming of Age in Samoa: A Psychological Study of Primitive Youth for Western Civilisation*. New York: William Morrow, 1928. Print.

Meersman, Brent. "*Karoo Moose* (Baxter Theatre)." The Real Review. therealreview. co.za, 14 Oct. 2007. Web. 6 Oct. 2012. <http://realreview.co.za/tag/lara-foot-newton/>.

Meredith, Courtney Sina. *Rushing Dolls*. Urbanesia: Four Pasifika Plays. Ed. David O'Donnell. Wellington: Playmarket, 2012. 259–312. Print.

Meštrović, Stjepan G. *Postemotional Society*. London: Sage Publications, 1997. Print.

Meyer, Michael. *Ibsen: A Biography*. New York: Doubleday, 1971. Print.

——. *Three Plays About Ibsen and Strindberg*. London: Oberon Books, 2000. 89–135. Print.

Moffett, Helen. "'These Women, They Force Us to Rape Them': Rape as Narrative of Social Control in Post-Apartheid South Africa." *Journal of Southern African Studies* 32.1. (2006): 129–44. JSTOR. Web. 9 Sept. 2012. <http://www.jstor.org/stable/25065070>.

Mogobe, Ramose B. *African Philosophy through Ubuntu*. Harare: Mond Books, 1999. Print.

——. "The Ethics of *Ubuntu*." *Philosophy from Africa*. Ed. P. H. Coetzee and A. P. J. Roux. Oxford: Oxford University Press, 2002. 324–30. Print.

——. "The Philosophy of *Ubuntu* and *Ubuntu* as Philosophy." *Philosophy from Africa*. Ed. P. H. Coetzee and A. P. J. Roux. Oxford: Oxford University Press, 2002. 230–38. Print.

Moïse, Lenelle. *Expatriate*. TS.

Moraga, Cherríe. *Heroes and Saints*. Contemporary Plays by Women of Color: An Anthology. Ed. Kathy A. Perkins and Roberta Uno. New York: Routledge, 1996. 331–75. Print.

Morrow, Martin. "From Hell: Judith Thompson's New Play Finds Scapegoats and Heroes in Iraq." *CBC News*. CBCNews.ca, 16 Jan. 2008. Web. 26 Oct. 2010.

Morton, Timothy. *The Ecological Thought*. Cambridge: Harvard University Press, 2010. Press.

——. "Ecologocentrism: Unworking Animals." *SubStance* 37.3 (2008): 73–95. Print.

——. "Guest Column: Queer Ecology." *PMLA* 125.2 (2010): 273–82. Print.

Muller, Roswitha. "Learning for a New Society: The *Lehrstück*." *The Cambridge Companion to Brecht*. Ed. Peter. Thomson and Glendyr Sacks. Cambridge: Cambridge University Press, 1994. 101–17. Print.

Murphy, Brenda, ed. *The Cambridge Companion to American Women Playwrights*. Cambridge: Cambridge University Press, 1999. Print.

Murray, Maureen. "Chanting Group Pickets ROM but Respects Court Injunction." *Toronto Star* 13 May 1990: A3. Print.

Myatt, Julie Marie. *Welcome Home, Jenny Sutter*. Ashland: Oregon Shakespeare Festival Scripts, 2008. Print.

Naguib, Nahid-Na'ila. *Ahl Al-Markeb, wa Masrahiyyat 'Ukhrah*. Cairo: Anglo-Egyptian Bookshop, 1984. Print.

——. *Kalila wa Dimna wa Ba'd*. Cairo: Anglo-Egyptian Bookshop, 1988. Print.

——. *Yawmiyat Mukhbir wa Masrahiyat Ukhra*. Cairo: Anglo-Egyptian Bookshop, 1998. Print.

Neal, Mark Anthony. *Soul Babies: Black Popular Culture and the Post-Soul Aesthetic*. London: Routledge, 2002. Print.

Neill, Rosemary. "The Sound and Fury of Australia's Women Playwrights and Theatre Directors." *The Australian*. Newsspace.com, 3 Nov. 2012. Web. 12 May 2013. <http://www.theaustralian.com.au/arts/review/the-sound-and-the-fury-of-australias-women-playwrights/story-fn9n8gph-1226508371732>.

Nickerson, Colin. "Cancer, Remorse Haunt Tiny Village." *Boston Globe* 6 Aug. 1998: A2. Print.

"Nightwood Theatre." N.p., 2013. Web. <http://www.nightwoodtheatre.net/>.

Nikiforuk, Andrew. "Echoes of the Atomic Age: Uranium Haunts a Northern Village." *Calgary Herald* 14 Mar. 1998: A4. Print.

Norman, Marsha. "Not There Yet." *American Theatre* 26.9 (2009): 28–30, 79. Print.

Nottage, Lynn. *Intimate Apparel. Intimate Apparel and Fabulation.* New York: Theatre Communications Group, 2003. Print.

——. *Ruined.* New York: Theatre Communications Group, 2009. Print.

O'Donnell, David. Introduction. *Frangipani Perfume/Mapaki.* By Dianna Fuemana and Makerita Urale. Wellington: The Play Press, 2004. i–x. Print.

"One Billion Rising." N.p., 2013. Web. 19 May 2013. <http://onebillionrising. org/>.

Onedera, Peter R. "Theater in a Chamoru Sense." Unpublished paper. Prepared for Art and Culture in Micronesia. Micronesian Studies Graduate Program, University of Guam, 1999.

Ortiz, Fernando. *Contrapunteo Cubano del tabaco y el azucar.* Caracas: Biblioteca Ayacucho, 1978. Print.

O'Toole, Fintan. "*He Left Quietly* – Reviews." *Irish Times.* Farber Foundry, 29 Nov. 2002. Web. 4 Oct. 2012. <http://www.farberfoundry.com/he-left-quietly-press. html>.

Owen, Rena. *Te Awa i Tahuti. He Reo Hou: 5 Plays by Maori Playwrights.* Ed. Simon Garrett. Wellington: Playmarket, 1991. 125–61. Print.

Ozieblo, Barbara, and Noelia Hernando-Real, eds. *Performing Gender Violence: Plays by Contemporary American Women Dramatists.* Basingstoke: Palgrave Macmillan, 2012. Print.

Packer, George. *Betrayed.* New York: Faber and Faber, 2008. Print.

Parks, Suzan-Lori. *The America Play and Other Works.* New York: Theatre Communications Group, 1995. Print.

"Performing Medicine." Clod Ensemble, n.d. Web. 29 May 2013. <http://www. clodensemble.com/medicine.htm>.

Perkins, Kathy A., and Sandra L. Richards. "Black Women Playwrights in American Theatre." Farfan and Ferris 541–45.

Persino, María Silvina. "Espacio y opresión en el teatro de Patricia Zangaro." *Latin American Theatre Review* 40.1 (2006): 61–78. Print.

Petropoulos, Jacqueline. "'The Ground on Which I Stand': Rewriting History, African Canadian Style." *Signatures of the Past: Cultural Memory in Contemporary Anglophone North American Drama.* Ed. Marc Maufort and Caroline de Wagter. Brussels: Peter Lang, 2008. 73–81. Print.

Podalsky, Laura. *The Politics of Affect and Emotion in Contemporary Latin American Cinema: Argentina, Brazil, Cuba, and Mexico.* New York: Palgrave Macmillan, 2011. Print.

Potiki, Roma, and He Ara Hou. *Whatungarongaro. Ta Matou Mangai: Three Plays of the 1990s.* Ed. Hone Kouka. Wellington: Victoria University Press, 1999. 29–72. Print.

Powell, Lucy. "Shakespeare's Sisters." *Times* [London]: 40–1, 1 Aug. 2009. *Newspaper Source.* Web. 23 May 2013.

Pratt, Mary Louise. *Imperial Eyes: Travel Writing and Transculturation.* London: Routledge, 1992. Print.

Prichard, Rebecca. *Yard Gal.* London: Faber & Faber, 1998. Print.

Probyn, Elspeth. *Blush: Faces of Shame.* Minneapolis: University of Minnesota Press, 2005. Print.

——. "Writing Shame." Gregg and Seigworth 71–90.

Pullen, Kristen. *Actresses and Whores: On Stage and in Society.* Cambridge, Cambridge University Press, 2005. Print.

Raffo, Heather. *Nine Parts of Desire.* New York: Dramatists Play Service, 2006. Print.

Rama, Angel. "Processes of Transculturation in Latin American Narrative." *Journal of Latin American Cultural Studies* 6.2 (1997): 155–71. Print.

——. *Transculturación narrativa en América Latina.* Mexico City: Siglo XXI, 1982. Print.

Reddy, Sudeep. "New Facts on the Gender Gap from the World Bank." *Wall Street Journal Blogs.* Wsj.com, 18 Sept. 2011. Web. 10 May 2013. <http://blogs.wsj.com/economics/2011/09/18/new-facts-on-the-gender-gap-from-the-world-bank/?mod=WSJBlog>.

Reid, Kerry. "Tanya Saracho Catching the Wheel: A Mexican-Born Playwright Steps Boldly from Teatro Luna into Chicago's Larger Scene." *American Theatre* 28.4 (2011): 38–40. Print.

Reinelt, Janelle. "Creative Ambivalence and Precarious Futures." Farfan and Ferris 553–56.

——. "Navigating Postfeminism: Writing Out of the Box." Aston and Harris, *Feminist Futures?* 17–33.

Renée. *Te Pouaka Karaehe.* 1992. TS. Playmarket, Wellington.

Rich, Adrienne. "When We Dead Awaken: Writing as Re-Vision." *College English* 34.1 (1972): 18–30. Print.

Ridout, Nicholas. *Stage Fright, Animals, and Other Theatrical Problems.* Cambridge: Cambridge University Press, 2006. Print.

Riesman, David. Foreword. *Postemotional Society.* By Stjepan G. Meštrović. London: Sage Publications, 1997. ix–x. Print.

Roach, Joseph. *Cities of the Dead: Circum-Atlantic Performance.* New York: Columbia University Press, 1996. Print.

Robins, Elizabeth. *Both Sides of the Curtain.* London: Heinemann, 1940. Print.

——. *Theatre and Friendship: Some Henry James Letters.* London: Jonathan Cape, 1932. Print.

Robins, Steven. "At the Limits of Spatial Governmentality: A Message from the Tip of Africa." *Third World Quarterly* 23.4 (2002): 665–89. *JSTOR.* Web. 28 June 2012. <http://www.jstor.org/stable/3993482>.

Robinson, Marc. *"The Summer in Gossenass*: Fornes and Criticism." *The Theater of Maria Irene Fornes.* Ed. Robinson. Baltimore: Johns Hopkins University Press, 1999. 109–29. Print.

Robnett, Belinda. *How Long? How Long?: African-American Women in the Struggle for Civil Rights.* New York: Oxford University Press, 1997. Print.

Rodríguez, Ileana. "Femicidio, or the Serial Killings of Women: Labor Shifts and Disempowered Subjects at the Border." *Liberalism at its Limits: Crime and Terror in the Latin American Cultural Text.* Pittsburgh: University of Pittsburgh Press, 2009. 153–74. Print.

Roiphe, Katie. *The Morning After: Sex, Fear, and Feminism.* London: Hamish Hamilton, 1994. Print.

Rose, Jacqueline. "Why Howard Jacobson Is Wrong." *Guardian.* Guardian News and Media, 24 Feb. 2009. Web. 23 July 2010. <http://www.guardian.co.uk/commentisfree/2009/feb/23/howard-jacobson-antisemitism-caryl-churchill>.

Ross, Fiona C. *Bearing Witness: Women and the Truth and Reconciliation Commission in South Africa.* London: Pluto Press, 2003. Print.

Roth, Maya E. "Revealing and Renewing Feminist Theatrical Engagement: The Jane Chambers Contest for Women Playwrights." *Theatre Topics* 20.2 (2010): 157–69. Print.

Ruhl, Sarah. *In the Next Room or the Vibrator Play.* New York: Samuel French, 2010. Print.

Sakhleh, Mirna. "Seven Palestinian Children." *Palestine Telegraph.* PT News, 11 May 2009. Web. 17 Sept. 2010. <http://www.paltelegraph.com/opinions/diaries/799-seven-palestinian-children.html>.

Sanders, Leslie. "History at Negro Creek; Djanet Sears' *The Adventures of a Black Girl in Search of God." Testifyin': Contemporary African Canadian Drama.* Ed. Djanet Sears. Vol. 2. Toronto: Playwrights Canada Press, 2003. 487–89. Print.

Sanders, Mark. *Ambiguities of Witnessing – Law and Literature in the Time of the Truth Commission.* Johannesburg: Witwatersrand University Press, 2007. Print.

Sandoval, Chela. *Methodology of the Oppressed.* Minneapolis: University of Minnesota Press, 2000. Print.

Sandoval-Sánchez, Alberto. *José, Can You See?: Latinos On and Off Broadway.* Madison: University of Wisconsin Press, 1999. Print.

Sandoval-Sánchez, Alberto, and Nancy Saporta Sternbach. *Stages of Life: Transcultural Performance & Identity in U.S. Latina Theater.* Tucson: University of Arizona Press, 2001. Print.

Saracho, Tanya. "El Nogalar." *American Theatre* 28.6 (2011): 69–87. Print.

Schneider, Rebecca. *Performing Remains: Art and War in Times of Theatrical Reenactment.* New York: Routledge, 2011. Print.

Scott, Shelley. "Nightwood Theatre: A Woman's Work Is Always Done." Wilson and McIntyre 24–29.

Sears, Djanet. *The Adventures of a Black Girl in Search of God.* Toronto: Playwrights Canada Press, 2003. Print.

——. "An Interview with Djanet Sears." By Mat Buntin. *Canadian Adaptations of Shakespeare Project.* University of Guelph, Mar. 2004. Web. 14 Nov. 2012. <http://www.canadianshakespeares.ca/i_dsears.cfm>.

——. "Interview with Djanet Sears: A Black Girl in Search of God." By Robin Breon, *Aisle Say (Toronto).* TheatreNet Enterprises, 2002. Web. 27 June 2012. <http://www.aislesay.com/ONT-SEARS.html>.

Sedgwick, Eve Kosofsky. *Tendencies.* Durham: Duke University Press, 1994. Print.

——. *Touching Feeling.* Durham: Duke University Press, 2003. Print.

Sedgwick, Eve Kosofsky, with Adam Frank. "Shame in the Cybernetic Fold: Reading Silvan Tomkins." *Touching Feeling: Affect, Pedagogy, Performativity.* By Sedgwick. Durham: Duke University Press, 2003. 93–122. Print.

Seigworth, Gregory J., and Melissa Gregg, eds. *The Affect Theory Reader.* Durham: Duke University Press, 2010. Print.

——. "An Inventory of Shimmers." Gregg and Seigworth 1–28.

Selaiha, Nehad. "Blood Wedding." *Al Ahram Weekly.* Al Ahram, 12–18 Aug. 2004. Web. 17 Sept. 2010. <http://weekly.ahram.org.eg/2004/703/cu1.htm>.

——. "A Dip into the Dark." *Al-Ahram Weekly.* Al-Ahram, 22–28 Mar. 2007. Web. 17 Sept. 2010. <http://weekly.ahram.org.eg/2007/837/cu1.htm>.

——. *The Egyptian Theatre: Perspectives.* Cairo: General Egyptian Book Organization, 2004. Print.

——. "Of Silence and Violence." *Al-Ahram Weekly.* Al-Ahram, 25–31 Aug. 2005. Web. 17 Sept. 2010. <http://weekly.ahram.org.eg/2005/757/cu1.htm>.

——. "Politics Centre-Stage." *Al-Ahram Weekly.* Al-Ahram, 20–26 Mar. 2008. Web. 17 Sept. 2010. <http://weekly.ahram.org.eg/2008/889/cu2.htm>.

Shamieh, Betty. "The Art of Countering Despair: Naomi Wallace." *The Brooklyn Rail.* Brooklyn Rail, May 2008. Web. 23 Aug. 2010. <http://www.brooklynrail.org/2008/05/theater/the-art-of-countering-despair-naomi-wallace>.

——. *Tamam. Talk to Me: Monologue Plays.* Ed. Eric Lane and Nina Shengold. New York: Vintage Books, 2004. 471–82. Print.

Shannon, Sandra. *The Dramatic Vision of August Wilson.* Washington: Howard University Press, 1995. Print.

——. "An Intimate Look at the Plays of Lynn Nottage." *Contemporary African American Women Playwrights: A Casebook.* Ed. Philip C. Kolin. New York: Routledge, 2011. 185–93. Print.

Shatz, Adam. "Mubarak's Last Breath." *London Review of Books* 32.10 (2010): 6–10. Web. 25 Sept. 2010. <http://www.lrb.co.uk/v32/n10/adam-shatz/mubaraks-last-breath>.

Shaw, Peggy. *Ruff.* N.d. TS.

Shaw, Peggy, and Suzy Willson. *MUST: The Inside Story. A Menopausal Gentleman: The Solo Performances of Peggy Shaw.* Ed. Jill Dolan. Ann Arbor: University of Michigan Press, 2011. 139–58. Print.

Shimakawa, Karen. "Young Jean Lee's Ugly Feelings About Race and Gender." *Women & Performance: a journal of feminist theory* 17.1 (2007): 89–102. Print.

Shiva, Vandana. *Water Wars: Privatization, Pollution, and Profit.* Cambridge: South End Press, 2002. Press.

Shouse, Eric. "Feeling, Emotion, Affect." *M/C Journal* 8.6 (2005): n.p. Web. <journal. media-culture.org.au/0512/03-shouse.php>.

Sichel, Adrienne, "Remembering and Healing." *Star* [Johannesberg]. Faber Foundry. 3 July 2001: 9. Web. 4 Oct. 2012. <http://www.farberfoundry.com/amajuba-press. html>.

Sierz, Aleks. *In-Yer-Face Theatre: British Drama Today.* London: Faber & Faber, 2000. Print.

——. "'We All Need Stories': The Politics of In-Yer-Face Theatre." D'Monté and Saunders 23–37.

Sihra, Melissa, ed. *Women in Irish Drama: A Century of Authorship and Representations.* Basingstoke: Palgrave Macmillan, 2007.

Silverstein, Melissa. "The Lilly Awards Honor Women in Theatre." *Women's Media Center.* N.p., 3 June 2010. Web. 14 May 2013. <http://www.womensmediacenter. com/feature/entry/the-lilly-awards-honor-women-in-theatre>.

Simmons, Deborah. "Sahtú and the Atomic Bomb." *Deline: Where the Water Flows.* Deline Land Corporation, 2012. Web. 15 Nov. 2012. <http://www.deline.ca/ culture-and-community/deline-stories/uranium/>.

Singh, Nikhil Pal. *Black Is a Country: Race and the Unfinished Struggle for Democracy.* Cambridge: Harvard University Press, 2004. Print.

Smith, Anna Deavere. *Fires in the Mirror: Crown Heights, Brooklyn and Other Identities.* New York: Anchor Books, 1993. Print.

Solga, Kim. "*Blasted*'s Hysteria: Rape, Realism, and the Thresholds of the Visible." *Modern Drama* 50.3 (2007): 346–74. Print.

Somers-Willett, Susan B. A. *The Cultural Politics of Slam Poetry: Race, Identity, and Verse in America.* Ann Arbor: University of Michigan Press, 2009. Print.

Son, Diana. Author's Statement. *Version 3.0: Contemporary Asian American Plays.* Ed. Chay Yew. New York: Theatre Communications Group, 2011. 396–97. Print.

——. *Satellites. Seven Contemporary Plays from the Korean Diaspora from the Americas.* Ed. Esther Kim Lee. Durham: Duke University Press, 2012. 247–320. Print.

Sontag, Susan. *Illness as Metaphor* and *AIDS and Its Metaphors.* New York: Doubleday, 1990. Print.

Spelman, Elizabeth V. *Inessential Woman: Problems of Exclusion in Feminist Thought.* Boston: Beacon Press, 1988. Print.

Spillers, Hortense. *Black, White, and in Color: Essays on American Literature and Culture.* Chicago: University of Chicago Press, 2003. Print.

Spitta, Silvia. *Between Two Waters: Narratives of Transculturation in Latin America.* Houston: Rice University Press, 1995. Print.

Spretnak, Charlene. "Radical Nonduality in Ecofeminist Philosophy." Warren, *Ecofeminism: Women, Culture, Nature* 425–36.

Stephenson, Heidi, and Natasha Langridge. *Rage and Reason: Women Playwrights on Playwriting*. London: Methuen, 1997. Print.

Stewart, Kathleen. *Ordinary Affects*. Durham: Duke University Press, 2007. Print.

St. John, Christopher. *The First Actress*. 1911. MS. Lord Chancellor's Play Manuscripts 14. British Lib., London.

Suárez, Patricia. *El tapadito*. *Dramática Latinoamericana* 162 (2005): 1–36. *CELCIT*. Web. 2 Sept. 2012. <http://www.celcit.org.ar/publicaciones/dla.php>.

——. *El tapadito*. *La Germania*. Buenos Aires: Losada, 2006. 159–94. Print.

Subramani. "The Oceanic Imaginary." *The Contemporary Pacific* 13.1 (2001): 149–62. Print.

Svich, Caridad. Interview by Adam Szymkowicz. *Adam Szymkowicz*. Blogspot.com, 27 Sept. 2009. Web. 23 Sept. 2012. <http://aszym.blogspot.ie/2009/09/i-interview-playwrights-part-61-caridad.htm>.

——. Introduction to *Prodigal Kiss*. *Prodigal Kiss and Perdita Gracia: Two Plays*. By Svich. South Gate: Lizard Run Press, 2009. 12. Print.

——. *Prodigal Kiss: a play with songs*. *Prodigal Kiss and Perdita Gracia: Two Plays*. South Gate: Lizard Run Press, 2009. 11–138. Print.

Svich, Caridad, and María Teresa Marrero, eds. *Out of the Fringe: Contemporary Latina/Latino Theatre and Performance*. New York: Theatre Communications Group, 2000. Print.

Taylor, Diana. *The Archive and the Repertoire: Performing Cultural Memory in the Americas*. Durham: Duke University Press, 2003. Print.

——. "Transculturating Transculturation." *Performing Arts Journal* 13.2 (1991): 90–104. Print.

Taylor, Jane. "Reform, Perform: Sincerity and the Ethnic Subject of History." *South African Theatre Journal* 22 (2008): 9–24. Print.

——. *Ubu and the Truth Commission*. Cape Town: University of Cape Town Press, 1998. Print.

Terada, Rei. *Feeling in Theory: Emotion after the 'Death of the Subject.'* Cambridge: Harvard University Press, 2001. Print.

The Theater J Blog. Theater J, Mar. 2007. Web. 17 Sept. 2010. <http://theaterjblogs.wordpress.com/>.

13P. "A People's History of 13P." *13P*. 13 Playwrights, n.d. Web. 28 Sept. 2013. <http://13p.org/>.

Thomas, Sue, ed. *The Feminist History Reader*. New York: Routledge, 2006. Print.

Thompson, Judith. "A Conversation with Judith Thompson." Interview with Cynthia Zimmerman. *Canadian Drama/L'Art dramatique canadien* 16.2 (1990): 184–94. Print.

——. *Palace of the End*. Toronto: Playwrights Canada Press, 2007. Print.

——. *Sled*. Toronto: Playwrights Canada Press, 1997. Print.

Thurman, Judith. "The Playwright Who Makes You Laugh about Orgasm, Racism, Class Struggle, Homophobia, Woman-Hating, the British Empire, and the Irrepressible Strangeness of the Human Heart." *Ms.* May 1982: 51–57. Print.

Todd, Paula. "African Exhibits Inspire Awe and Anger." *Toronto Star* 7 May 1990: A6. Print.

Tomkins, Silvan. *Affect, Imagery, Consciousness*. New York: Springer, 1963. Print.

Tompkins, Joanne. *Unsettling Space: Contestations in Contemporary Australian Theatre*. Basingstoke: Palgrave Macmillan, 2006. Print. Studies in International Performance.

"Top Ten Things To Do: 50/50 in 2020 Action List." *50/50 in 2020*. Wordpress.com, 13 Dec. 2010. Web. 14 May 2013. <http://5050in2020.org/2010/12/13/top-ten-things-to-do/>.

Truth and Reconciliation Commission of South Africa. *Final Report*. Vol. 2. London: Macmillan, 1998. Print.

tucker green, debbie. *Stoning Mary.* London: Nick Hern Books, 2005. Print.

Turpin, Jennifer. "Many Faces." *The Women and War Reader.* Ed. Lois Ann Lorentzen and Jennifer Turpin. New York: New York University Press, 1998. 3–18. Print.

Tutu, Desmond. *No Future Without Forgiveness.* New York: Image, 1999. Print.

Tycer, Alicia. "'Victim. Perpetrator. Bystander': Melancholic Witnessing of Sarah Kane's *4.48 Psychosis.*" *Theatre Journal* 60.1 (2008): 23–36. Print.

"UN Creates New Structure for Empowerment of Women." Press Release from *UN Women.* N.p., 2 July 2010. Web. 1 May 2013. <http://www.unwomen.org/2010/07/un-creates-new-structure-for-empowerment-of-women/>.

"UN Women Welcomes Agreed Conclusions at the Commission on the Status of Women." *UN Women.* N.p., 15 Mar. 2013. Web. 24 May 2013. <http://www.unwomen.org/2013/03/un-women-welcomes-agreed-conclusions-at-the-commission-on-status-of-women/>.

Uno, Roberta, ed. *Unbroken Thread: An Anthology of Plays by Asian American Women.* Amherst: University of Massachusetts Press, 1993. Print.

Urale, Makerita. *Frangipani Perfume. Mapaki/Frangipani Perfume.* By Dianna Fuemana and Makerita Urale. Wellington: The Play Press, 2004. 1–35. Print.

Urban, Ken. "Cruel Britannia." D'Monté and Saunders 38–55.

Vega, Marta Moreno. "The Candomblé and Eshu-Eleggua in Brazilian and Cuban Yoruba-Based Ritual." *Black Theatre: Ritual Performance in the African Diaspora.* Ed. Paul Carter Harrison, Victor Leo Walker II, and Gus Edwards. Philadelphia: Temple University Press, 2002. 153–66. Print.

Vire, Kris. "Playwright Tanya Saracho." *TimeOut Chicago.* Timeout.com, 6 June 2010. Web. 22 June 2012. <http://timeoutchicago.com/arts-culture/theater/82931/playwright-tanya-saracho>.

Wagdi, Wafaa. *Al-Shagarah, Aw Al-Su'ood Ila Al-Shams.* Cairo: General Egyptian Book Organization, 1993. Print.

——. *Nisaan wa Al-Abwab Al-Sab'ah.* Cairo: General Egyptian Book Organization, 1984. Print.

Walcott, Rinaldo. "Dramatic Instabilities: Diasporic Aesthetics as a Question for and about Nation." *Canadian Theatre Review* 118 (2004): 99–106. Print.

Wall, Cheryl. *Worrying the Line: Black Women Writers, Lineage, and the Literary Tradition.* Chapel Hill: University of North Carolina Press, 2005. Print.

Wallace, Naomi. *The Fever Chart: Three Visions of the Middle East.* New York: Theatre Communications Group, 2009. Print.

——. *In the Heart of America.* New York: Theatre Communications Group, 2001. Print.

Warner, Sara. *Acts of Gaiety: LGBT Performance and the Politics of Pleasure.* Ann Arbor: University of Michigan Press, 2012. Print.

Warren, Karen J., ed. *Ecofeminism: Women, Culture, Nature.* Bloomington: Indiana University Press, 1997. Print.

——. "Taking Empirical Data Seriously." Warren, *Ecofeminism: Women, Culture, Nature* 3–20.

Watts, Richard. "Breaking Down the Boy's Club." *ArtsHub.* N.p., 7 Oct. 2009. Web. 23 May 2013. <http://www.artshub.com.au/au/newsPrint.asp?sId=179399>.

Weinert-Kendt, Rob. "Mexican? American? Call Her a Writer." *New York Times.* Nytimes. com 22 Mar. 2011. Web. 22 June 2012. <http://www.nytimes.com/2011/03/27/theater/tanya-sarachos-nogalar-mexican-take-on-chekhov.html?_r=1>.

Weller, Michael. *Beast.* New York: Dramatist Play Service, 2009. Print.

White, Deborah Gray. *Too Heavy a Load: Black Women in Defense of Themselves 1894–1994.* New York: W. W. Norton, 1999. Print.

Whittaker, Robin C. "Fusing the Nuclear Community: Intercultural Memory, Hiroshima 1945 and the Chronotopic Dramaturgy of Marie Clements's *Burning Vision.*" *Theatre Research in Canada* 30.1–2 (2009): 129–51. Print.

Whoriskey, Kate. Introduction. *Ruined*. By Lynn Nottage. New York: Theatre Communications Group, 2009. ix–xiii. Print.

Wiegman, Robyn. *Object Lessons*. Durham: Duke University Press, 2012. Print.

Wilson, Anne, and Hope McIntyre, eds. *Canadian Women Playwrights: Triumphs and Tribulations*. Spec. issue of *Canadian Theatre Review* 132 (2007). Print.

withers, debi. Rev. of *Her Naked Skin*. *The F Word: Contemporary UK Feminism*. The F-Word, 7 Sept. 2008. Web. 26 Oct. 2010. <http://www.thefword.org.uk/reviews/2008/09/her_naked_skin>.

"Women, Power and Politics: Now." *Tricycle Theatre*. Arts Council England, n.d. Web. 21 May 2013. <http://www.tricycle.co.uk/about-the-tricycle-pages/about-us-tab-menu/archive/archived-theatre-production/women-power-politics-now/>.

"Women, Power and Politics: Then." *Tricycle Theatre*. Arts Council England, n.d. Web. 21 May 2013. <http://www.tricycle.co.uk/about-the-tricycle-pages/about-us-tab-menu/archive/archived-theatre-production/women-power-politics-then/>.

Wong, Rita. "Decolonizasian: Reading Asian and First Nations Relations in Literature." *Canadian Literature* 199 (Winter 2008), *Literature Online*. Web. 14 Nov. 2012. <http://gateway.proquest.com/openurl?ctx_ver=Z39.88-2003-&xri:pqil:res_ver=0.2&res_id=xri:lion-us&rft_id=xri:lion:ft:abell:R04149198:0>.

Wong, Sau-ling Cynthia. "Denationalization Reconsidered: Asian American Cultural Criticism at a Theoretical Crossroads." *Amerasia* 21.1–2 (1995): 1–27. Print.

Woolf, Virginia. *A Room of One's Own*. 1929. San Diego: Harvest, 1989.

Wright, Melissa W. "Urban Geography Plenary Lecture – Femicide, Mother-Activism, and the Geography of Protest in Northern Mexico." *Urban Geography* 28.5 (2007): 401–25. Print.

Zangaro, Patricia. *A propósito de la duda. Teatro x La Indentidad*. Teatrox la indentidad. net, 2012. Web. 1 Sept. 2012. <http://www.teatroxlaindentidad.net>.

——. *Tiempo de aguas. Por un reino y otras obras*. Buenos Aires: Losada, 2008. 133–59. Print.

Zinsstag, Estelle. "Sexual Violence against Women in Armed Conflicts: Standard Responses and New Ideas." *Social Policy and Society* 5.1 (2006): 137–48. Print.

Index